THE OXFORD HISTORY C

COMPANIO

The British Empire gave rise to various new forms of British identity in the colonial world outside the Dominions. In cities and colonies, and in sovereign states subject to more informal pressures such as Argentina or China, communities of Britons developed identities inflected by local ambitions and pressures. As a result they often found themselves at loggerheads with their diplomatic or colonial office minders, especially in the era of decolonisation. The impact of empire on metropolitan British identity is increasingly well documented; the evolution of dominions' nationalisms is likewise well known; but the new species of Britishness which attained their fullest form in the mid-twentieth century have received significantly less attention.

Settlers and Expatriates revisits the communities formed by these hundreds of thousands of Britons, as well as the passages home taken by some, and assesses their development, character, and legacy today. Scholars with established expertise in the history of each region explore the communalities that can be found across British communities in South, East and Southeast Asia, Egypt, and East and Southern Africa, and highlight the particularities that were also distinctive features of each British experience. These overseas Britons were sojourners and settlers; some survived in post-independent states, others were swept out quickly and moved on or back to an often uninterested metropolitan Britain. They have often been caricatured and demonized, but understanding them is important for an understanding of the states in which they lived, whose politics were at times a crucial part of British history and the history of migration and settlement.

Robert Bickers joined the University of Bristol in 1997 after receiving a Ph.D. at the School of Oriental and African Studies, and holding post-doctoral fellowships at Nuffield College, Oxford and the University of Cambridge. He is the author of *Empire Made Me: An Englishman Adrift in Shanghai* (2003), which won the American Historical Association's Morris D. Forkosch prize, and *The Scramble for China: Foreign Devils in the Qing Empire, 1832–1914* (2011).

'Bickers should be commended for the coherence and uniformly high quality of this collection. The essays all provide political and economic frameworks in which to understand the presence of these communities overseas, as well as perspectives on each community's composition, beliefs, and experiences'

Kevin Grant, *Victorian Studies*

'Few edited collections display a topic in such a comprehensive and fascinating manner, or open up an area for teaching and research as this book does'

Simon J. Potter, *Twentieth Century British History*

'This authoritative collection deftly puts...colonial caricatures in their proper place, revealing instead a much more complex and contested range of British identities. By emphasising the diverse experience of Britons overseas, it not only expands the current limits of 'British world' scholarship but offers a conceptual substitute—"a world of Britains"'

Felicity Barnes, *English Historical Review*

'convincingly re-exposes the lives of the imperial British as a deserving field of academic research, drawing interesting parallels without submerging the diverse or particular'

Anna Sanderson, *History Today*

'a first-rate addition to the *Oxford History of the British Empire Companion Series*'

Christopher Prior, *Immigrants and Minorities*

'this collection constitutes a crucial contribution to the study of imperial mobility and to the consolidating field of settler colonial studies'

Lorenzo Veracini, *The Journal of Imperial and Commonwealth History*

'As a thought-provoking discussion of migration, colonialism and identity... and as a collection to inspire future research, this is a rich volume with much to offer'

Laura Ishiguro, *Journal of Colonialism and Colonial History*

THE OXFORD HISTORY OF THE BRITISH EMPIRE

COMPANION SERIES

Wm. Roger Louis, CBE, D. Litt., FBA

*Kerr Professor of English History and Culture, University of Texas, Austin
and Honorary Fellow of St Antony's College, Oxford*

EDITOR-IN-CHIEF

Settlers and Expatriates: Britons over the Seas

EDITED BY

Robert Bickers

OXFORD

UNIVERSITY PRESS

OXFORD
UNIVERSITY PRESS

Great Clarendon Street, Oxford OX2 6DP

Oxford University Press is a department of the University of Oxford.
It furthers the University's objective of excellence in research, scholarship,
and education by publishing worldwide.

Oxford New York

First published 2010
First published in paperback 2014

Published in the Unites States of America by Oxford University Press
198 Madison Avenue, New York, NY 10016, United States of America

British Library Cataloguing in Publication Data
Data available

Library of Congress Cataloging in Publication Data
Data available

ISBN 978–0–19–929767–2 (Hbk)
ISBN 978–0–19–870337–2 (Pbk)

CONTENTS

CONTRIBUTORS

ROBERT BICKERS is Professor of History, University of Bristol, and the author of *Britain in China: Community, Culture and Colonialism* (1999), *Empire Made Me: An Englishman Adrift in Shanghai* (2003), and *The Scramble for China* (2011).

ELIZABETH BUETTNER is Professor of Modern History at the University of Amsterdam. Her publications include *Empire Families: Britons and Late Imperial India* (2004) in addition to articles in the *Journal of Modern History, Ab Imperio, History and Memory*, the *Scottish Historical Review*, and elsewhere. She is completing a comparative study entitled *Europe After Empire: Decolonization, Society, and Culture*.

JOHN DARWIN teaches Imperial and Global History at Oxford where he is a Fellow of Nuffield College. His most recent books are *After Tamerlane: The Global History of Empire since 1405* (2007) and *The Empire Project: The Rise and Fall of the British World System 1830–1970* (2009).

TIM HARPER is Reader in Southeast Asian and Imperial History, University of Cambridge, and a Fellow of Magdalene College. He is the author of *The End of Empire and the Making of Malaya* (1999) and, with Christopher Bayly, *Forgotten Armies: The Fall of Britain's Asian Empire, 1941–45* (2004) and *Forgotten Wars: The End of Britain's Asian Empire* (2007).

MARGARET JONES is a Research Fellow and Deputy Director, Centre of Global Health Histories at the University of York. She is the author of *Health Policy in Britain's Model Colony: Ceylon, 1900–1948* (2004) and *The Hospital System and Health Care: Sri Lanka, 1815–1960* (2009). She has also published articles on the medical and social history of Hong Kong and Jamaica.

JOHN LAMBERT is a Professor Emeritus and Research Fellow in the Department of History at the University of South Africa in Pretoria. He has published widely in the field of Natal studies and on the history both of African society in colonial Natal and of white English-speaking identity in Natal and in South Africa generally. His monograph, *Betrayed Trust: Africans and the State in Colonial Natal* (1995) examines the emergence and decline of an African peasantry in colonial Natal and the relationship between Africans and British settlers in the colony.

JOHN LONSDALE is a Fellow of Trinity College, Cambridge, and Emeritus Professor of Modern African History. He is co-author, with Bruce Berman, of *Unhappy Valley: Conflict in Kenya in Africa* (1992), and was President of the African Studies Association of the United Kingdom, 2000.

DONAL LOWRY is Reader in Imperial History and Head of the Department of History at Oxford Brookes University. He is a Fellow of the Royal Historical Society and is book review editor of the *Journal of Southern African Studies*. He has published articles and essays on imperial, dominion, southern African, and Irish topics and is currently completing a history of Ireland's imperial connections for Cambridge University Press.

DAVID ROCK, a Professor of History at the University of California, Santa Barbara, is the author of numerous books and articles on the history of Argentina. His books include *Argentina 1516–1987* (1987) and *State Formation and Political Movements in Argentina 1860–1916* (2002). He is completing a book on the British community in Argentina 1806 to the present.

DAVID WASHBROOK is a Senior Research Fellow at Trinity College, Cambridge. Previously, he taught at Warwick, Oxford, and Harvard Universities and at the University of Pennsylvania. His principal interests lie in the history of southern India between the seventeenth and twenty-first centuries on which he has published extensively.

JAMES WHIDDEN is currently an associate professor at Acadia University. His Ph.D. was completed at the School of Oriental and African Studies, University of London, where he studied Egypt and North Africa. He has published articles in the *Journal of North African Studies*, *Encyclopedia of African History*, and the collection, *Re-envisioning Egypt 1919–1952* (2005).

1

Introduction: Britains and Britons over the Seas

Robert Bickers

The British empire was never static; neither were its peoples. They moved by choice, or were moved by compulsion. Individual circumstance or state policy often blurred the difference. Other volumes in this series highlight the movements of the enslaved, the indentured, the punished, and the colonized. They discuss the major movements of British nationals into the dominions—as well as return and onward migration, and the Irish experience of empire. Settlement and the resulting development of new nationalisms and identities has been a clear and dominating theme. But Britons were also of course service sojourners too. They went 'out', they served their careers, and they returned 'home'.[1] Chapters in volumes iii and iv of the *Oxford History of the British Empire* explored the various colonial administrative services through which the imperial state governed its multifaceted empire, and also the experience of those in military service.[2] But the overseas Britons outside the dominions, and outside the colonial or military services, generally fall outside the major categories of research. The non-officials and unofficials, traders, planters, men and women in the professions, and in service trades, state functionaries at all levels—police, public works and health, customs, merchant marine, railways—and the entrepreneurs who

Funding for the workshop and conference at which these chapters were first proposed and discussed was provided by the 'Oxford History of the British Empire', the British Academy's Conference Fund, and the Bristol Institute for Research in the Humanities and Arts, to all of which I would like to express my own thanks, and those of the contributors. I am also grateful for the encouragement and support of Professor Wm Roger Louis, our referees, Kent Fedorowich, participants at the 2005 conference, particularly Alan Lester and Stephen Howe, and especially our succession of editors at Oxford University Press.

[1] Elizabeth Buettner, *Empire Families: Britons and Late Imperial India* (Oxford, 2004).

[2] John W. Cell, 'Colonial Rule', in Judith M. Brown and Wm Roger Louis (eds.), *The Oxford History of the British Empire (OHBE)*, iv. *The Twentieth Century* (Oxford, 1999), 232–54.

filled the remaining gaps—journalists and hoteliers, for example—all of
these together formed significant populations of their own. This volume
explores a cross-section of such communities in the world of formal empire
and informal influence—the latter encompassing wide degrees of power
relations between the British and other states and indigenous populations—and while it places them within their discrete geographical contexts,
it explores commonalities, and demonstrates how strongly these overseas
Britons were interwoven into the fabric of the imperial experience that is
more readily recognized by patterns of scholarship.

The numbers are striking enough overall. Between 1900 and 1909, for
example, almost 1,700,000 Britons migrated overseas. In the 1920s the total
was over 1,800,000. Forty-five per cent of them went to non-empire destinations (mostly the United States, but also to many of the regions covered in
this volume), and increasingly they moved in the twentieth century to the
empire, and overwhelmingly to the settler dominions.[3] These net emigration figures hide the scale of remigration—40 per cent of English and Welsh
migrants returned between 1870 and 1914—and patterns of chain and serial
migration are also hard to follow.[4] Migrants returned, and they also kept in
touch. They wrote, they summoned out their brides and siblings, they
revisited, and they remitted. Migration often sundered ties, but mostly it
knitted people together in new ways. The complex webs of obligation and
financial responsibility which continued to link migrants with their families
at home are being uncovered.[5] As the 'Neo-Britains'—the white settler
societies—garnered the largest share of empire migration, they have also
received the largest share of scholarly attention, but the mini-Britains, built
from the same blocks, are thereby overshadowed. These are the British
communities in Ceylon, Egypt, and India, in British Malaya, Argentina,
and beyond. They too developed new identities, or new inflections of
familiar identities, as much as did the British-Australians, and the British-
Canadians. They sometimes had an impact on their adopted or adapted
home out of all proportion to the gross numbers. Ten thousand Britons in

---

[3] Figures from Stephen Constantine, 'Migrants and Settlers', *OHBE* iv 166–7.
[4] Marjory Harper, 'Introduction', in Marjory Harper (ed.), *Emigrant Homecomings: The Return Movement of Emigrants, 1600–2000* (Manchester, 2005), 2; Dudley Baines, *Migration in a Mature Economy: Emigration and Internal Migration in England and Wales, 1861–1900* (Cambridge, 1985), 279.
[5] Gary B. Magee and Andrew S. Thompson, '"Lines of Credit, Debts of Obligation": Migrant Remittances to Britain, c.1875–1913', *Economic History Review*, 59/3 (2006), 539–77.

Shanghai did inadvertent wonders for nascent Chinese nationalism in the mid-1920s.

Some of the communities covered here were and are better known in some ways. There are studies and surveys of the white Kenyans, Rhodesians, and Natalians. Others were obscured by their official brethren, in India for example, or obscured, paradoxically, by reputation—their sins diverting attention from their more mundane characteristics and impact, in Singapore perhaps. Others were seen as oddities, slightly exotic, and outside the mainstream. Post-colonial legacies have also heightened or diminished prominence—'white farmers' in Zimbabwe faced a belated expropriation of property in the late Mugabe state. Land ownership remains an issue in South Africa and in Kenya, and bloody white mischief there too. Argentinians of British descent, who still perform a British identity in many prominent ways, negotiated a difficult passage during the 1982 Falklands/Malvinas conflict.[6] British nationals had mostly left the People's Republic of China by 1954, but a large British community quietly and quiescently remains in post-handover Hong Kong, subsuming its British settler origins and habits within an internationalized expatriate community that also includes many more recent British migrants or sojourners.[7] The history of these communities, which operated within a wide range of political environments, offers insights into the ways in which, mostly outside formal settlement schemes, and what scholars would identify as 'settler projects', Britons took advantage of the often interstitial opportunities provided by imperial power and British ascendancy to migrate overseas, entrench themselves, and thereafter negotiate the passages they faced.

Individual choice underpinned these developments, and three biographical sketches highlight some of the questions this movement and these new communities prompt. Basil Hare Duke (1908–1982), an empire servant, at home there—wherever 'there' was—Arnold Wright (c.1857–1941), a professional journalist and empire publicist, and Ronald Campbell (1836–1897), a soldier and sometime journalist, can hardly represent the full range of individual experience (not least as all were men), but they bear presentation

---

[6] Andrew Graham-Yooll, *The Forgotten Colony: A History of the English-Speaking Communities in Argentina*, rev. edn. (Buenos Aires, 1999), 269–306.

[7] Although numbers of British nationals resident grew from 15,000 in 1987 to 33,000 in 2001, this was actually a fall from 8.7 to 6.26% of the total foreign population. Figures adapted from table 6, in W. Breitung and M. Günter, 'Local and Social Change in a Global City: The Case of Hong Kong', in Fulong Wu (ed.), *Globalisation and the Chinese City* (London, 2006), 85–107.

here. Duke, released from the Sudan Political Service to serve in the Indian army, wrote to his mother from Kohima in May 1942: 'I cannot but realise that I am more of a citizen of the Empire than of England and it is really the duty of such to settle in the empire if we want to keep it.'[8] Home, insofar as it had a meaning for him, lay with family, wherever they were. In the world opened up by British empire—the 'British world' of recent scholarship—and beyond, that family could be widely dispersed, and Duke himself was a highly mobile Briton. Aged 34 when he wrote, he had already worked for British Petroleum in London, as a farmer in New Zealand, in the Samoan Police, as a clerk in Bombay, and as a policeman in Shanghai for six years before joining the elite Sudan service. He had been born in Cawnpore (Kanpur), the son of an Indian Civil Service officer. It is with some justifi-cation that Duke described himself as a citizen of the empire—although he ultimately failed to fulfil that duty to settle. In his 1942 letter he went on to state that 'this business of always retiring AT HOME, understandable and attractive though it is, has to some extent been one of the factors responsible for bringing us to our pretty pass'. Duke returned to Sudan after the war, before retirement—'AT HOME'—beckoned in the shape of a sub post office in Suffolk. But with sisters married into empire, and his children eventually part of a new British diaspora at the close of the century—working in the Middle East—this family's journeys encapsulate the dislocating but wholly ordinary impact of the imperial experience and the opportunities of empire settlement and sojourn on the British.

Duke had travelled through a representative slice of the variegated world of British imperial service and settlement, from non-domiciled India, through—amongst other ports of call—Antipodean settler dominion, the informal world of private British power in Shanghai, and the condominium administration in Sudan. His nationality and his comfortable sense of a broader imperial identity had eased his careering, in Alan Lester and David Lambert's term, through the various options open to him as a white, adult British male in the difficult 1930s.[9] Class, too, gave Duke connections and a distance, and some situations proved a better fit than others: Shanghai he found vulgar beyond measure. This trajectory offers an introduction to one

---

[8] All citations from copies of Duke's letters in my possession, additional information from his Shanghai Municipal Police personnel file and from communications with his family.

[9] David Lambert and Alan Lester (eds.), *Colonial Lives across the British Empire: Imperial Careering in the Long Nineteenth Century* (Cambridge, 2006).

key strand in this volume, the strong correspondences that can be identified through a comparative survey of the communities of Britons that developed overseas within and beyond the margins of British empire. The sheer variety of local particularities remains important. No two British communities were entirely alike, although all offered opportunities for transformation, if not advancement, and all offered too, the routine dangers of over-reach, failure, or quiet mediocrity—life, in other words, was lived there as it was lived anywhere. Beyond the settler dominions, British settlement patterns, and identities, depended on the local structures of British authority, changing patterns of power, the politics and policies of the host state (and its degree of autonomous action), and on factors like war, cold war, economics, and resistance. This strand of the volume explores the local British in their international, and usually internationalized, settings. While Duke and others saw one world of empire settlement stretching from New Zealand via Shanghai, India, to Sudan and beyond, a world in which they encountered and re-encountered members of the same social circles, outside observers will see a world of multifaceted difference and particularity. Both strands have much to offer an understanding of the inter-related world of Britain and its colonies, dominions, and other settlements, as well as their interconnectedness on their own non-metropolitan terms, the difficulties of decolonization, and British domestic history's long imperial shadow.

Arnold Wright spent eight years on the *Times of India* from 1879, and then worked for a while as private secretary to the traveller and author Lady Anna Brassey.[10] He travelled with her and her husband (the recently created Baron Brassey, who had served in the Admiralty in Gladstone's second administration, and who would be appointed Governor of Victoria 1895–1900) on the 1886–7 voyage of their yacht the *Sunbeam*. They journeyed from India to Borneo and then on to Australia, from where—after a sojourn—they sailed towards Port Elizabeth.[11] This was a singular introduction to the wider world of empire and of domestic and imperial politics for Wright, who then worked for the *Yorkshire Post* as its London editor until 1900. Amongst other work thereafter, he was a leading figure in the Lloyd's Greater Britain Publishing Company series of volumes, published between 1901 and 1914,

---

[10] 'Mr. Arnold Wright, A Varied Journalistic Career', *The Times* (17 Feb. 1941), 7.
[11] *The Times* (13 Oct. 1887), 11. Anna Brassey died at sea on this voyage. See also James R. Ryan, '"Our Home on the Ocean": Lady Brassey and the Voyages of the Sunbeam, 1874–1887', *Journal of Historical Geography*, 32/3 (2006), 579–604.

which under the shared title *Twentieth Century Impressions of . . .* were 'designed to give in an attractive form full and reliable information with reference to the outlying parts of the Empire'.[12] These books covered Natal (1906), Ceylon (1907), British Malaya (1908), Siam (1908), Hong Kong, China, and other treaty ports (1908), Egypt (1909), Burma (1910), as well as *Netherlands India* (1909), and, in a second wave, Argentina (1911), Uruguay (1912), Brazil (1913), Cuba (1913), the West Indies (1914), and Chile (1915).[13] Wright was editor in chief or editor of most of the volumes published between 1907 and 1909, and evidently travelled to Ceylon during the development of that volume.[14]

These lavishly illustrated books were certainly a paying enterprise, as subventions were sought from businesses in return for having photographs of their plant or managers inserted—and 'in this appeal to human vanity will be found the best financial prospects of so expensive a book' remarked one review[15]—but this was also clearly an ideological project, motivated by a professed desire to disseminate a 'fuller knowledge of the "Britains beyond the Sea" and the great dependencies of the Crown'.[16] What is noticeable is that it mapped out a world of 'Britains' which overlapped but mostly stood outside the formal boundaries of empire. The volumes solicited articles from public officials in the various locales, and added copy generated from the visiting staff writers. Wright in particular supplied the historical introductions, a line of writing he developed further in *Early English Adventurers in the East* (1914), and *The Romance of Colonisation* (1923). The Lloyd's volumes portray a world of individual and investment opportunity and,

[12] Introduction to e.g. Arnold Wright (ed.), *Twentieth Century Impressions of Hong Kong, Shanghai, and Other Treaty Ports of China: Their History, People, Commerce, Industries and Resources* (London, 1908).

[13] The Argentina, Brazil, and Uruguay volumes appeared in Spanish as well, and the title and format were also used by (if not cribbed from in the first instance) *Twentieth Century Impressions of Western Australia* (Perth, WA, 1901) and H. J. Boam (ed.), *Twentieth Century Impressions of Canada* (Montreal, 1914).

[14] Working later with the Foreign & Colonial Compiling & Publishing Co., Wright also edited Somerset Playne, assisted by J. W. Bond (comp.), *Southern India: Its History, People, Commerce, and Industrial Resources* (1914) and *Bengal and Assam, Behar and Orissa: Their History, People, Commerce, and Industrial Resources* (1917), *The Bombay Presidency, the United Provinces, the Punjab, etc.: Their History, People, Commerce, and Natural Resources* (1920).

[15] By F. L. Petre, of *Twentieth Century Impressions of Ceylon*, in *The Times Literary Supplement* (12 July 1907), 219.

[16] Quotation from the preface of, *inter alia*, *Twentieth Century Impressions of British Malaya* and *Twentieth Century Impressions of Hong Kong*.

in their encyclopedic vision they regularize the wide world of the Britons overseas. What a reviewer described as 'local advocates' were the main sources of the material, and their own eagerness to incorporate themselves into the normal world of empire comes through very strongly. Their worlds were normal, and comfortably equipped, healthy and ready to welcome newcomers. There were guides to the local cost of living (the price of a half-pint of Lea & Perrins sauce, Australian jam, Crosse & Blackwell sausages, champagne, Guinness), and of starting up in business (the cost of ploughs in Natal, for example). In this series, local advocacy and ambition melded well with the metropolitan visions (and economic hopes) of men like Arnold Wright. The volumes also highlight the internationalized character of these communities. Asian and other European businessmen are fully incorporated into the China and British Malaya volumes. These were not monoglot zones, and in most cases the British, while in different ways often advantaged, were not in authority. When in 1913 Lloyd's advertised for a sub-editor for a paper in Argentina, they specified that applicants must be 'free of racial prejudices'.[17] Working for a key Anglophone institution within such a community required a clear understanding and acceptance of local realities. The advertisement also specified 'Scotsman, Irishman or Colonial'.[18] A 'Colonial' was suitable for Argentina, and Scots and Irish disproportionately staffed empire, and so might better fit. The transposition of British Isles identities into the new worlds, and their interaction there is a recurrent theme in this volume.

Ronald Campbell, Baron Craignish, was born in New South Wales to a Cape Town-born father, and a mother of Scottish descent in 1836. His father, Pieter Laurentz Campbell, was schooled for the Army in England, served as Private Secretary to Acting Cape Colony Governor Richard Bourke in 1826–8, and followed Bourke to Australia, taking up various colonial administrative positions in New South Wales in 1832–41.[19] Campbell *père* then returned to Britain, living and working mostly in London until his death in 1848. Ronald Campbell was educated in Germany until 1853, secured a military cadetship with the East India Company, and served in different

---

[17] *The Times* (27 Nov. 1913), 22.

[18] And no members of the National Union of Journalists either.

[19] Information in this paragraph comes from *The Times* (14 Nov. 1891), 7, (13 January 1892), 3, (22 Mar. 1892), 3, (24 Dec. 1897), 4; Hazel King, 'Campbell, Pieter Laurentz (1809–1848)', *Australian Dictionary of Biography*, i (Melbourne, 1966), 201–2.

military units in India until 1869. He worked thereafter mostly in Europe, generally based from London, as a war correspondent, and in the service of Turkish and then German armies. His title was awarded him by the Duke of Saxe-Coburg-Gotha, in 1882. Campbell/Craignish comes to our attention as a result of his attempt to claim a Scottish domicile in 1891, and thereby a half-share of his deceased wife's large estate (which he would have been entitled to under Scottish law, instead of the annuity he was allotted in her will). Divorced from his first wife in 1879, a marriage contracted in India, Campbell married the wealthy Charlotte Meeking in Paris in March 1883. He listed his residence as Sydney, New South Wales. His grandfather had clearly been Scottish, and his father had spent some time in the country after 1841. This, and his claim to have discussed with his wife the purchase of Craignish itself, combined with his desire to live in Scotland, underpinned his argument. The case hinged on domicile, and explored Craignish's use of the word 'home' in his letters, and wider popular usage (his actual evidence in court was only accepted 'with a very considerable reserve'). In his judgment dismissing the claim the presiding judge, Sir Joseph Chitty, remarked that:

The term 'home' may be, and is, often used in different senses. An Englishman permanently settled in one of the English colonies may without impropriety speak of going home when he is paying a visit to England. When asked to explain himself, he would probably say that he used the term in reference to the mother country from which he and his brother colonists had emigrated or originally sprung, and that his own true home was in the colony.[20]

Chitty found that Craignish's domicile was India, until 1869, and England thereafter. 'That a man with Scottish blood in his veins should have dreams of Scotland and an ancestral estate there is natural enough', Chitty noted, but 'this was but a waking dream'. The appeal court upheld the judgment. Craignish was a child of empire, from a family eventually dislocated by colonial service across three continents, who had been trained up to serve in it, and whose rootless existence had continued thereafter. The question prompted by the Craignish case is about aftermaths, and about home: how it is to be defined, narrowly in law as formal domicile (and the judgment is still referred to in law[21]), emotionally perhaps in terms of those 'waking dreams'—dreams of individual return, but also dreams of future statehood—and practically, in

---

[20] *The Times* (13 Jan. 1892), 3.
[21] Re Craignish [1892] 3 Ch. 180.

terms of employment, property, residence, home-making, comfort. Campbell/ Craignish, like many others, experienced as a child and as an adult the opportunities (and their limitations) offered to Britons by the colonial world and beyond.[22] The resulting derangement of the world of the British (in this case a Scottish-Afrikaner-Australian-born Briton) was a feature of British life, still too often standing outside domestic history. The overseas Briton was a Rhodesian, or a Shanghailander, but she was also a colonial, a 'citizen of the empire', as Duke put it, set aside from the British mainstream by self-perception and the perception of home Britons.[23]

All three of these men lived and worked overseas, and remigrated. All three seem restless. The communities they passed through and served were often characterized by steady and systematic population turnover, but were equally concerned to normalize themselves and to root themselves. Population turnover aside, impermanence and contingency are recurring features of the histories of the communities analysed here. In most cases these Britons lacked power, struggled for it, or had to surrender it. There were limits to any self-government that they achieved. Their position was generally oblique to, at times contradicted, sometimes opposed, that of the British state and its local agents. They were colonial subjects in most places, albeit highly privileged ones, able often to subvert legal structures and practices on account of their nationality, status, and colour. Their positions were buttressed by multi-tiered legal systems, or colour-sensitive legal or policing practices. Outside the world of formal empire they had—with varying degrees of official British support—to negotiate their own way through the laws and politics of local states and nationalist challenges to their positions. They also faced pressure from the imperial centre, or the viceroy 'over the sea', and increasingly from the late nineteenth century from a web of supra-national agreements and institutions (the Office International d'Hygiène Publique, the League of Nations), which pried into their local governments, their policies and practices. International conflict, principally the Second World War, heralded a critical emergency for them. War itself did not remove their communities (although it left some on the wrong side

---

[22] The German connection is additionally worth noting, for it was not unusual: his brother served with German forces in 1870, and was also ennobled by Saxe-Coburg-Gotha, as Baron Campbell von Laurentz: *Freiherrliches Taschenbuch 1891* (Gotha, 1891), 111; Baron Campbell von Laurentz, 'A Scotchman at Mars-la-Tour', *Cornhill Magazine*, 94 (Sept. 1906); 'The German Manoeuvres', *The Times* (22 Sept. 1883), 7.

[23] Buettner, *Empire Families*, 2.

of the front line), but it did lead to some practical assessment by British strategic planners of where exactly the bounds of empire lay. And the mobilization of British empire for survival and total war set in motion new modes of nationalism which signalled the end of the colonial phase of their presence.[24]

We know that empire families and individuals often came home, but many did not, physically or emotionally. British historians have perhaps been too coy overall in exploring the history and character of the post-colonial British diaspora. The persistence of communities is one theme of the contributors here, but the persistence of migration and of other Britons, the expats, the retired, younger mobile workers of all classes (British builders in Hong Kong, senior managers in the Gulf), is a key feature of twenty-first-century British society.[25] Human geographers have explored the phenomenon as a basically contemporary development relating to late-twentieth-century globalization of expatriate and other labour markets. From the mid-late 1990s onwards out-migration from the United Kingdom, especially of 25–44 year olds, certainly accelerated sharply, but the story from these chapters, and from individual families—like Duke's—suggests strong continuities between the world of the empire citizen and that of the Britons seemingly 'missing' from the 2001 census, presumed overseas.[26] A rump post-colonial infrastructure might be one factor here, a familiar language and a critical mass of compatriots and their bars and clubs making moves and networking easier, in Cyprus, or Hong Kong for example, but the bigger factor may be the longer term predisposition to migration that characterizes British society. That was based in turn on British power,

[24] C. A. Bayly, '"The Nation Within": British India at War 1939–1947', *Proceedings of the British Academy*, 125 (2004), 265–85.

[25] Dhananjayan Sriskandarajah and Catherine Drew, *Brits Abroad: Mapping the Scale and Nature of British Emigration* (London, 2006); Russell King, Tony Warnes, and Allan Williams, *Sunset Lives: British Retirement Migration to the Mediterranean* (London, 2004); Jonathan V. Beaverstock, 'Transnational Elites in Global Cities: British Expatriates in Singapore's Financial District', *Geoforum*, 33/4 (2002), 525–38.

[26] 'We've Lost a Million People? Don't Count on it', *The Times* (1 Oct. 2002), 3; on the migration picture generally from 1975–2004 see Giles Horsfield, 'International Migration', in Roma Chappel (ed.), *Focus on People and Migration* (Basingstoke, 2005), 115–29; Office of National Statistics, 'Implications of the 2001 Census Results: Why Census Shows Fewer Men', URL: <http://www.statistics.gov.uk/census2001/implications.asp>, accessed July 2009, although see e.g. Philp Redfern, 'An Alternative View of the 2001 Census and Future Census Taking', *Journal of the Royal Statistical Society Series A*, 167/2 (2004), 209–28.

which for all its collaborations with indigenous elites and indigenous personnel, needed to deploy Britons in colonial service. It provided incentives and opportunities overseas, employment and relocation schemes, and normalized expatriate life and emigration. As British power travelled, so did Britons.

The overseas British experience was navigated, then, by men and women like Basil Hare Duke, Ronald Campbell, and Arnold Wright, articulated and publicized by men like Wright in public projects, and by the likes of Duke in their private thoughts on duty and service and it raised questions for legal judgment. It has received less than adequate attention from scholars. The story of the British presence in this colony or that protectorate has reliably formed the subject of popular history, memoir or celebration, and some monographs.[27] But the British remain mostly unfashionable, and, as the communities which form the subject of this volume mostly lost out to the challenge of nationalism, it does not help that they were losers. Their advocates, journalists and amateur scholars, had usually developed a body of historical work feting their development and achievements—as they saw them—and this fed into their discrete senses of local identity and self-assurance. They liked to hear about themselves and to read about themselves. Their political opposition to reform was often grounded in understandings of their particular histories and birthrights which they articulated with some force, seamlessly integrating them into wider notions and claims for self-evident rights. But in the new nations that superseded them nationalist histories were uncovered or recovered, and created and celebrated after decolonization. The colonial era became in part a prehistory of the new state in which the colonist was not to figure because scholarship served nation building, tracing only narrow paths through that pre-time, the path of conquest and resistance, and then the path of contestation and liberation. Colonizers lost favour as subjects, if they did not in fact become entirely suspect. In metropolitan society they found themselves mostly mocked, and their history reduced to a 'carry on'. As a subject of research they lacked credibility

---

[27] Some monographs: John G. Butcher, *The British in Malaya, 1880–1941: The Social History of a European Community in Colonial South-East Asia* (Kuala Lumpur, 1979); Helen Callaway, *Gender, Culture and Empire: European Women in Colonial Nigeria* (Basingstoke, 1987); Dane Kennedy, *Islands of White: Settler Society and Culture in Kenya and Southern Rhodesia, 1890–1939* (Durham, NC, 1987), and *The Magic Mountains: Hill Stations and the British Raj* (Berkeley, Calif., 1996).

in the eyes of many academic area studies disciplines. They often appeared, if at all, as what can only be described as a caricatured and demonized Occidental other. Indeed, as was revealed as this volume was developed, they are often still regarded as lying beyond the pale of scholarship. The absence of the Caribbean from our collection stems from this situation, as did the difficulty experienced initially in securing interest in studying a Middle East and a South American case study. There were certainly other voices and histories, long suppressed by colonist and colonial discourse, which needed rescuing—but this pointed neglect of the colonizer is no longer tenable.

Change is taking place at a different pace in different subdisciplines. The key developments which have placed the British (and the Germans, French, Japanese as well as United States' citizens) back in the colonial and post-colonial picture overlap, although they do not always precisely engage. What might be termed the Manchester school of British imperial history, through the 'Studies in Imperialism' series, recasts the domestic history of modern Britain as one infused with empire experience. At the same time it has inspired and provided a forum for new work on the socio-cultural history of the British imperial experience, much of it comparative in scope. Some of the work on the domestic impact of empire has not been without its critics, but understandings of colonial practices and ideologies have been greatly enriched nonetheless.[28] At the same time came the Saidian turn in literary studies, and then wholesale development of cultural studies, which has seen much attention paid to colonial, anti-colonial, and post-colonial literatures, and—by extension—to colonists and colonizer communities. The latter has mostly come from explorations of literary discourses, of the local fictional worlds of the new communities, of the familiar terrain of Rudyard Kipling or Joseph Conrad, and through more archaeological approaches to the mainstream canon. Travel writing has been the focus of much attention, but this work has also moved to explore the more formal documentation generated by the business and life of colonialism. The colonial turn is in full swing.[29]

---

[28] The noisiest critic is Bernard Porter, *The Absent-Minded Imperialists: Empire, Society and Culture in Britain* (Oxford, 2004). For nuance and balance see Andrew S. Thompson, *The Empire Strikes Back?: The Impact of Imperialism on Britain from the Mid-Nineteenth Century* (Harlow, 2005).

[29] Antoinette Burton (ed.), *After the Imperial Turn: Thinking with and through the Nation* (Durham, NC, 2003); Frederick Cooper, *Colonialism in Question: Theory, Knowledge, History* (Berkeley, Calif., 2005).

More recently, and coming notably out of social anthropology in the United States, there has been a rapid growth in work on European colonialism and colonial actors. Dominant issues here have been race, sexuality—and the intersection of the two—violence, power, and failure. A key underlying premise has been the assertion that 'Europe was made by its imperial projects, as much as colonial encounters were shaped by conflicts within Europe itself'.[30] This agenda has been extended to US history, and to Japanese colonialism.[31] The obvious key voice has been that of Ann Stoler, while the work of Nicholas Thomas has also offered much in its exploration of settler failure, for example.[32] The trend has seen the development of new journals (*Journal of Colonialism and Colonial History*) and book series (University of California Press's 'Colonialisms' series), and a growth in university courses and course modules in the subject at all levels.[33] It has altered hiring patterns in university departments, where British imperial history has edged out British domestic history, especially in the US job market. Frederick Cooper and Ann Stoler's *Tensions of Empire* (1997), and most recently Cooper's *Colonialism in Question* (2005) have mapped out the state of the changing field and its controversies.[34] The settler has also been put back in, not with any ambition to privilege, but as a belated scholarly recognition of the seemingly obvious fact that colonizer and colonized were both constitutive, on different and differing terms, of the colonial experience. An ideologically driven reassessment of the impact, character, and legacy of British empire in particular is certainly also under way,

[30] Ann Laura Stoler and Frederick Cooper, 'Between Metropole and Colony: Rethinking a Research Agenda', in Frederick Cooper and Ann Laura Stoler (eds.), *Tensions of Empire: Colonial Cultures in a Bourgeois World* (Berkeley, Calif., 1997), 1.

[31] Ann Laura Stoler (ed.), *Haunted by Empire: Geographies of Intimacy in North American History* (Durham, NC, 2006); Louise Young, *Japan's Total Empire: Manchuria and the Culture of Wartime Imperialism* (Berkeley, Calif., 1998).

[32] Ann Laura Stoler, *Race and the Education of Desire: Foucault's History of Sexuality and the Colonial Order of Things* (Durham, NC, 1995); Nicholas Thomas, *Colonialism's Culture: Anthropology, Travel and Government* (Cambridge, 1994) and Nicholas Thomas and Louis Becke, *Bad Colonists: The South Seas Letters of Vernon Lee Walker and Louis Becke* (Durham, NC, 1999).

[33] North American Conference on British Studies, *Report on the State and Future of British Studies in North America* (1999). URL: <http://www.nacbs.org/documents/reportonfield1999.html>, accessed Dec. 2009. See also Lynn Hunt, 'Is European History Passé?', *Perspectives*, 40/8 (Nov. 2002), 5–7.

[34] Cooper and Stoler (eds.) *Tensions of Empire*; Cooper, *Colonialism in Question*.

but tangentially to the main currents in scholarship, and without much credibility.[35]

The work of the 'British world' network has aimed to bring back the imperial experience into the history of the former British dominions. The initiative was in part a reaction against nationalist historiographies that have excised the empire epoch (and the British empire activities of the now independent states) almost as comprehensively as did the new histories of former Asian or African colonies.[36] By reintegrating imperial, national, and British metropolitan histories—whether social history, the history of the press, of imperial policy-making and governance—work in this field has come closer to an understanding of how the world worked for Britons— Britons by passport, protected status or by empire's shadow—in the years before the 1960s.[37] Although this work deals with the British 'diaspora', or less controversially as a term, 'dispersal', the focus on the 'expansion of Britain and the peopling and building of the trans-oceanic British world' has tended to exclude the other overseas Britons, those in the world of informal empire in Asia or South America, or in the United States, and in the variegated colonies, protectorates, and condominiums painted red on empire maps. Here, too, were participants in that 'consensual association' of scattered Britons that made up a British world.[38] The British world initiative has also under-recognized other worlds of movement and identification with British empire, such as the world of (in one category of analysis) colonial 'auxiliaries'—Lebanese, Sephardic Jews from India, Macanese, for example—communities and groups in a territory who were neither the colonized (strictly, and locally), nor the colonizer, but who often performed

[35] See e.g. Niall Ferguson, *Empire: How Britain Made the Modern World* (London, 2003).

[36] Phillip Buckner, 'Whatever Happened to the British Empire', *Journal of the Canadian Historical Association*, 4 (1994), 3–32.

[37] The objectives and their rationale are clearly laid out in Carl Bridge and Kent Fedorowich, 'Mapping the British World', *Journal of Imperial and Commonwealth History*, 31/2 (2003), 1–15. The work generated by the project includes Phillip Buckner and R. Douglas Francis, *Rediscovering the British World* (Calgary, 2005), and Stuart Macintyre, Kate Darian-Smith, and Patricia Grimshaw (eds.), *Britishness Abroad: Transnational Movements and Imperial Cultures* (Melbourne, 2007). See also other volumes in the companion series: Philip Buckner (ed.), *Canada and the British Empire* (Oxford, 2008), and Deryck M. Schreuder and Stuart Ward (eds.), *Australia's Empire* (Oxford, 2008).

[38] Bridge and Fedorowich, 'Mapping the British World', 8, 11. A suggestive survey of ties between the formal world of empire and Canada can also be found in J. F. Bosher, 'Vancouver Island in the Empire', *Journal of Imperial and Commonwealth History*, 33/3 (2005), 349–68.

critical functions, and who often identified very strongly with the colonial state and colonizer community. Such lacunae are now starting to be addressed, most significantly in James Belich's recent exploration of what he terms the 'Anglo-world' of English-speaking settler societies.[39]

This rich, contextualizing literature underpins the return to the unfashionable figures of the colonist, migrant, settler, and sojourner, whose communities form the subjects of this volume. Explored here is a great part of the world mapped out by Arnold Wright and Reginald Lloyd in their series. The chapters survey British communities in a wide range of contexts in which Britons were subject to different types of colonial authority, or were present as a result of the exercise of British power—by treaty or privilege extracted and maintained by force. A geographically organized volume like this has two drawbacks. First, as discussed, it lacks comprehensiveness, and second its focus in the main on locality serves to compartmentalize experience at the same time as the authors have striven to explore connections, networks, and parallels. Clearly a volume exploring different professional groups within the wide world of British empire would also add much to our understandings of the opportunities opened to Britons, and British subjects. Groups barely touched on here would repay close attention, such as medical professionals, scientists, engineers, agriculturalists, policemen, development workers, missionaries, journalists, the military, and the administrative services.[40] Mindful of these dangers, the volume presents surveys of communities that are close or direct neighbours (Kenya, Rhodesia, Natal in southern Africa, India and Ceylon in south Asia), that are based on cognate models of power imbalance between Britain and independent states (Argentina, China), or that otherwise provide strong parallels (the port cities in China and the Straits Settlements). To aid understandings of the convergence of experience we also present a study of the return 'home', and discussion in the various chapters of the patterns of retirement and remigration—or persistence after independence—of the various Britons.

[39] James Belich, *Replenishing the Earth: The Settler Revolution and the Rise of the Anglo-World, 1783–1939* (Oxford, 2009).

[40] On the latter see in particular the body of work by Anthony Kirk-Greene: *Symbol of Authority: The British District Officer in Africa* (London, 2006); *Britain's Imperial Administrators, 1858–1966* (Basingstoke, 2000); *On Crown Service: A History of HM Colonial and Overseas Civil Services, 1837–1997* (London, 1999). On policemen we now have Georgina Sinclair, *Colonial Policing and the Imperial Endgame 1945–80: 'At the End of the Line'* (Manchester, 2007).

The chapters focus on the late nineteenth and the twentieth centuries, and contributors were asked to consider in particular the decades after 1919 and transitions to independence. Nothing perhaps better prompts the articulation of identity, or the mobilization of organized discontent, than the threat—or perceived threat—of dissolution. Here we also see identity in flux, growing stronger in the face of perceived betrayal by the imperial state, or evolving as political reality changed (and as economic reality often did not, at least not immediately). What emerges from the following essays is a strong sense of particular interests, and in most cases, particular identities. These have been too easily dismissed as quaint, transitory, or irrelevant. But particular identities fed or were fed by particular interests, and as the chapters reveal, also by plurality within many of those broad interests.

This volume fails to offer a conclusion to a long-running debate on nomenclature. Do we need a name for the overseas Britons, if that alone will not suffice? This is not a new question, and it is not one that recent scholarship has resolved. 'Name these children' wrote Owen Seaman, editor of *Punch* magazine, in 1931. Reflecting on the origins of the members of the Oxford University cricket team he lamented the inadequacy of the available terms to distinguish between players from Britain and the dominions. The terms which came to mind were either imprecise ('British, as opposed to English, Scottish etc.'), or they had been disowned ('colonial'). But the 'transmarine' members of the team needed distinguishing—not least because they outplayed their 'home' fellow-players. P. S. Cassidy responded from Hong Kong. It was indeed a problem which 'defied solution': 'You and I want to coin a word which will cover any Briton from Overseas,' he wrote, 'be he from the Dominions, India, the Crown Colonies, Protectorates, Mandated Territories or the Scilly Isles', the 'genus British in the sub-species Overseas', distinct from the 'home-reared'.[41] The Hong Kong-er settled finally for 'British', but the light-hearted exchange touched in its languid way on the recognition of difference, and of the difficult necessity of disentangling the different identities which had developed as Britons (and their conjoined others) moved within and beyond the world of empire, building new communities and loyalties, which overlapped with those which still continued themselves to evolve and shift back in the British Isles. Perhaps we should rest content with 'British', and work to stress that its

[41] O.S., 'Name These Children', *Punch* (22 July 1931), 58; 'Constant Reader', 'Help from Hong Kong', *Punch* (16 Sept. 1931), 301.

accepted early twenty-first-century connotations—plural identities and cultures—should be stretched back in time to include the 'transmarine' British across and beyond the British world, and so thereby perhaps help to lay to rest the notion of an insular island story.

Select Bibliography

JAMES BELICH, *Replenishing the Earth: The Settler Revolution and the Rise of the Anglo-World, 1783–1939* (Oxford, 2009).

CARL BRIDGE and KENT FEDOROWICH, 'Mapping the British World', *Journal of Imperial and Commonwealth History*, 31/2 (2003), 1–15.

PHILLIP BUCKNER and R. DOUGLAS FRANCIS, *Rediscovering the British World* (Calgary, 2005).

ELIZABETH BUETTNER, *Empire Families: Britons and Late Imperial India* (Oxford, 2004).

JOHN G. BUTCHER, *The British in Malaya, 1880–1941: The Social History of a European Community in Colonial South-East Asia* (Kuala Lumpur, 1979).

HELEN CALLAWAY, *Gender, Culture and Empire: European Women in Colonial Nigeria* (Basingstoke, 1987).

FREDERICK COOPER and ANN LAURA STOLER (eds.) *Tensions of Empire: Colonial Cultures in a Bourgeois World* (Berkeley, Calif., 1997).

DANE KENNEDY, *Islands of White: Settler Society and Culture in Kenya and Southern Rhodesia, 1890–1939* (Durham, NC, 1987).

—— *The Magic Mountains: Hill Stations and the British Raj* (Berkeley, Calif., 1996).

ANTHONY KIRKE-GREENE, *On Crown Service: A History of HM Colonial and Overseas Civil Services, 1837–1997* (London, 1999).

DAVID LAMBERT and ALAN LESTER (eds.), *Colonial Lives across the British Empire: Imperial Careering in the Long Nineteenth Century* (Cambridge, 2006).

DHANANJAYAN SRISKANDARAJAH and CATHERINE DREW, *Brits Abroad: Mapping the Scale and Nature of British Emigration* (London, 2006).

NICHOLAS THOMAS, *Colonialism's Culture: Anthropology, Travel and Government* (Cambridge, 1994).

—— and LOUIS BECKE, *Bad Colonists: The South Seas Letters of Vernon Lee Walker and Louis Becke* (Durham, NC, 1999).

2

The British of Argentina

David Rock

The British population of Argentina climbed to a maximum of around 60,000 in the 1930s.[1] At that time the community became the largest group of British expatriates outside the empire or dominions in any foreign country except the United States. Its size far surpassed similar British groups elsewhere in Latin America, including the British settlements of Brazil, Chile, and Uruguay. Within Argentina, by contrast, the British ranked among the smaller Western European diasporas that had formed over the previous hundred years. The Italians, Spaniards, and French attained far greater numbers than the British, while the Germans for a time became approximately equal.

The community formed in the early nineteenth century during a period of expanding British trade. Decades of export-led expansion in the late nineteenth century and supportive local liberal institutions consolidated its development.[2] Late nineteenth-century British immigration coincided with large British investment mainly in railways.[3] Economic ties evolved to an extent that many historians and ideologues depicted Argentina as the prototype of informal imperialism. The claim was based on the alleged oligopoly power of British

[1] The figure of 60,000, an acknowledged guess and a likely overstatement, appears in Enclosure in Despatch No. 2, 9 Feb. 1932, National Archives (Kew) (TNA), FO 369/2232. The term 'British Community' raises issues of definition, components, and boundaries. To mention a basic problem: Argentine census data counted the children and descendants of British settlers (the 'Anglo-Argentines') as local citizens, thus understating the community's aggregate number. Since all white English speakers including Americans could join the community, the term 'Anglophone' is a more accurate designation, although it too, with its exclusively linguistic connotation, does not quite fit a group that defined itself primarily as a cultural entity.

[2] For an introductory history, see David Rock, *Argentina 1516–1987: From Spanish Colonization to Alfonsín* (Berkeley, Calif., 1987).

[3] H. S. Ferns, *Britain and Argentina in the Nineteenth Century* (Oxford, 1960) remains a classic study.

merchants and investors and often included the proposition that the resident British community exercised quasi-colonial influence.[4] The British commanded high status among the European *colectividades europeas* throughout the Rio de la Plata region, although most Britons were situated in intermediate social strata. In earlier years the community became closely linked with foreign trade and shipping but after 1870 its fortunes grew dependent on British companies formed by private foreign investment.

The development of the community comprised three overlapping stages. From 1807 to 1880, British merchants engaged primarily in foreign trade remained dominant in an ethnic community in Buenos Aires including many families of shopkeepers and artisans; from 1825 rural settlers immediately outside the city formed a subgroup of the community. Secondly, in 1860–1914, the community mostly comprised a suburban middle class tied to British businesses, principally railways, banks, and import firms. Lastly, the community stagnated after the First World War when investment almost ceased and Anglo-Argentine commerce dwindled. Secular decline, first noticeable around the mid-1940s, reflected trends in Argentina such as the decline of the farm economy and the effects of the nationalist era of Juan Perón in 1943–55. Changing conditions in Britain further sapped the community. In the 1950s, the expansion of European and Commonwealth agriculture reduced demand for Argentine meat and grains; the post-war reorganization of British industry weakened the staples that previously supported the Anglo-Argentine connection. The decline of the community became an exceptionally prolonged process and its remnants, eventually just a few hundred people living mostly in Greater Buenos Aires, survived into the twenty-first century.[5]

About half the earlier nineteenth-century emigrants to Argentina originated in the Celtic nations of the United Kingdom. In the mid-1820s, Scottish families founded one of the first European farming settlements near Buenos Aires; Scots settlers later spread to other parts of the country, notably in southern Patagonia. In the mid-nineteenth-century rural Buenos

[4] For my recent discussion, see David Rock, 'The British in Argentina: From Informal Empire to Postcolonialism', in Matthew Brown (ed.), *Informal Empire in Latin America: Culture, Commerce and Capital* (Oxford, 2008), 49–77.

[5] Florencia Cortés Conde, *Los angloargentinos en Buenos Aires: Lengua, identidad y nación antes y después de Malvinas* (Buenos Aires, 2007), a work emphasizing the impact of the war of 1982 between Britain and Argentina over possession of the Falkland/Malvinas Islands.

Aires attracted numerous Irish shepherds and labourers.[6] In 1865 settlers established Welsh-speaking agricultural colonies on the Rio Chubut in Patagonia.[7] From around 1870 many English clerks, engineers, and managers immigrated under contract to British firms, outnumbering the Celtic groups. Until the late 1940s, they were found 'wherever there are banks to be managed, railways to be maintained, and machinery to be sold'.[8] The earlier Celtic migrants thus became tied primarily to agriculture, cattle and sheep farming, and the later predominantly English settlers to railways, commerce, and banks.

1806–1870: Invasion, the Commercial Community, and Rural Settlement

The formation of the community followed two military engagements known to the Argentines as *las invasiones inglesas*. In June 1806 1,600 British troops captured Buenos Aires, at that time a city of around 40,000 people, although Sir William Carr Beresford retained control of the city for only six weeks until a creole militia forced him to surrender.[9] In July 1807 the British sought to recapture the city with a much larger force, but met disaster. Sir John Whitelocke divided his army into numerous detachments at the approaches to the city's narrow streets, ordering them to advance on strategic positions. Riddled by grapeshot and musketry, and showered with 'hand-grenades, stink-pots, brick-bats, and all sorts of combustibles', the British suffered total defeat. Whitelocke capitulated and returned home in disgrace with the survivors of his shattered forces.[10]

---

[6] Edmundo Murray, *Devenir irlandés: Narrativas íntimas de la emigración irlandesa a la Argentina. 1844–1912* (Buenos Aires, 2004).

[7] Glyn Williams, *The Welsh in Patagonia: The State and the Ethnic Community* (Cardiff, 1991), 95.

[8] J. A. Hammerton, *The Real Argentine: Notes and Impressions of a Year in the Argentine and Uruguay* (New York, 1915), 261.

[9] The best contemporary account of the first British expedition, which crossed to South America following the capture of the Cape of Good Hope, is Alexander Gillespie, *Gleanings and Remarks; Collected during Many Months of Residence at Buenos Ayres, and Within the Upper Country* (Leeds, 1818).

[10] See Carlos Roberts, *Las invasiones inglesas del Rio de la Plata (1806–1807) y la influencia inglesa en la independencia y organización de las provincias del Rio de la Plata* (Buenos Aires, 1938). In English, Klaus Gallo, *Great Britain and Argentina: From Invasion to Recognition* (London, 2001).

Led by Viscount Castlereagh, British governments abandoned conquest and pursued trade; subsequent conflicts between Britain and Buenos Aires remained few. Violence flared on a single occasion in 1845 when an Anglo-French expedition landed on the shores of the Rio Paraná in an attempt to force the river open to foreign trade. British merchants in Montevideo led by Samuel Lafone, currently in competition with those in Buenos Aires and in combination with steamboat pioneers in Liverpool, became the chief instigators of this brief, unsuccessful imperialist adventure. The strong opposition to intervention among resident British merchants and land-owners in Buenos Aires became a notable feature of the conflict.[11]

From 1807 on, the British employed Buenos Aires as the point of access to Spanish South America and to exchange manufactures for silver mined in Upper Peru (Bolivia).[12] As the governments of Buenos Aires grew dependent on revenue from duties on British imports (and utilized some revenues to finance the wars of independence), they began to welcome British merchants. Following the 1810 overthrow of Spanish rule, the merchants ensconced themselves in the city and began transporting manufactures upriver along the Paraná. British merchant houses grew from 12 in 1811 to 56 by 1822 and to more than 100 by the mid-1820s.[13] Several hundred Britons settled as shop-keepers, artisans, river-boat sailors, and hotelkeepers. The Latin American mining boom of the mid-1820s attracted British adventurers and mining engineers to the Rio de la Plata, of whom some published accounts of

[11] A modern study is David McLean, *War, Diplomacy and Informal Empire: Britain and the Republics of the River Plate 1836–1853* (London, 1995). On the relatively unexplored Liverpool angle see Thomas Baines, *Observations on the Present State of the Affairs of the River Plate* (Liverpool, 1845).

[12] British policy is examined by many authorities. See John Lynch, 'British Policy and Spanish America, 1783–1808', *Journal of Latin American Studies*, 1/1 (1969), 1–30; John Street, *Gran Bretaña y la independencia del Rio de la Plata* (Buenos Aires, 1967). For the late 18th-cent. background to policy, see Adrian J. Pearce, *British Trade with Spanish America, 1763–1808* (Liverpool, 2007). On the subsequent period, more informative on the post-1870s, see D. C. M. Platt, *Latin America and British Trade 1806–1914* (London, 1972).

[13] Vera Blinn Reber, *British Mercantile Houses in Buenos Aires, 1810–1880* (Cambridge, Mass., 1979). The best known contemporary source on the British community during the 1820s is a work by Thomas George Love, editor of *The British Packet and Argentine News*, an English-language newspaper that survived into the 1850s: *A five years' residence in Buenos Ayres, during the years 1820 to 1825* (London: G. Herbert, 1825). An underutilized primary source on British merchants is the Hodgson and Robinson Archive (John Rylands University Library, University of Manchester).

journeys through the pampas and across the Andes into Chile and Bolivia.[14] Among the British explorers of this period, Charles Darwin of course left the most memorable mark. He visited Buenos Aires in 1833 and voyaged along the Patagonian coast on the *Beagle* en route to the Pacific.[15]

At the instigation of Foreign Minister George Canning, in the mid-1820s Great Britain recognized the independence of the United Provinces of the River Plate. In 1825 Consul Woodbine Parish negotiated a Treaty of Amity, Commerce and Navigation with the fledgling state. The treaty commanded strong support from the dominant liberal faction in Buenos Aires under Bernardino Rivadavia and shaped Anglo-Argentine contact for more than a century. It conferred religious freedom, including the right to consecrate cemeteries, and exemption from military service and forced loans. In 1830 the British population in Buenos Aires climbed to around 4,000, of whom a fifth were merchants and clerks and more than half artisans and shopkeepers.[16] In the 1810s, young British merchants took wives from well-connected local families, some of them metropolitan Spanish in origin, agreeing to raise their children as Catholics. When the immigration of British females increased in the 1820s, marriages with Argentine women grew less frequent. Endogamy took precedence and became one of the community's principal features.[17] The nascent ethnic community remained predominantly urban; artisans and shopkeepers were its principal components until the rise of private foreign investment in the 1860s.

The war of 1825–8 between the United Provinces and the Empire of Brazil brought the collapse of early nineteenth-century British trade. A steep fall in commercial profits prompted some British merchants to shift to investment in land. Glasgow-born John Gibson, for example, started out as a city merchant in 1818 but then set up a great *estancia* south-east of the city on

---

[14] Of the classic British travel writings, see Sir Francis Head, Bt., *Rough Notes Taken during some Rapid Journeys across the Pampas and among the Andes*, 4th edn. (London, 1846); J. P. and W. P. Robertson. *Letters on South America, in three volumes* (London, 1843); on travellers, see S. Samuel Trifilo, 'A Bibliography of British Travel Books on Argentina, 1810–1860', *The Americas*, 16/21 (1959), 133–43.

[15] A more recent edn. by Richard Darwin Keynes is *Charles Darwin's Beagle Diary* (Cambridge, 1988).

[16] Deborah Lynn Jakubs, 'A Community of Interests: A Social History of the British in Buenos Aires, 1860–1914', Ph.D. thesis (Stanford, Calif., 1986), 115.

[17] Marriage data are based on Maxine Hanon, *Diccionario de británicos en Buenos Aires (Primera época)* (Buenos Aires, 2005).

the Rio de la Plata estuary.[18] In the late 1840s the author William MacCann rode across rural Buenos Aires from one British or Irish *estancia* to another.[19] Local lore credited the British landowners with efforts to modernize cattle and sheep breeding. They imported pedigree livestock, including the celebrated 'Tarquin', said to have been the first Shorthorn bull brought to Buenos Aires in the 1820s. Richard Black Newton, a merchant *estanciero* born in Lambeth in 1801, introduced barbed wire. In the late 1860s, the Anglo-Argentine landowners helped found the Sociedad Rural Argentina, the powerful guild of cattlemen.[20]

At mid-century Irish sheep farmers became the largest component of the population of United Kingdom origin.[21] Commonly of rural middle-class background, the settlers mainly originated in the Irish midland counties of Westmeath and Wexford and congregated in *partidos* (counties) mostly west of the city. Newly arrived young Irish women worked in domestic service alongside the daughters of existing Irish families.[22] Like many other ethnic groups, the Irish established their own churches under priests who provided secular as well as spiritual leadership. From 1843 to 1871, Father Anthony Fahy, a celebrated Irish cleric, ministered to several thousand people in the 'camp' of rural Buenos Aires and served as an adviser, banker, and business partner of many aspirant Irish landowners. Loans from Fahy assisted a few Irish immigrants to progress from ditchers to *estancieros*. From around mid-century, personages like Michael and Matthew Duggan, Edward Casey, and Patrick Ham stood out among a select group of Irish landed magnates. Despite his Protestant background, Thomas Armstrong, another notable Irishman, provided Fahy with the funds he lent out to Irish farmers. The *Standard* founded in 1861 by the Dublin-born brothers, Edward and Michael

---

[18] Herbert Gibson, *The History and Present State of the Sheep-Breeding Industry in the Argentine Republic* (Buenos Aires, 1893).

[19] William MacCann, *Two Thousand Miles Ride through the Argentine Provinces*, i (London, 1853), 18–70.

[20] Roy Hora, *The Landowners of the Argentine Pampas: A Social and Political History, 1860–1945* (Oxford, 2001), 46–83.

[21] Reports in the 1870s specified an Irish population of 15,000–20,000 in the province of Buenos Aires: Thomas Murray, *The Story of the Irish in Argentina* (New York, 1919), 375. For some key figures, see Eduardo A. Coghlan, *Apuntes para la historia y la genealogía de las familias irlandesas en la República Argentina en el siglo XIX* (Buenos Aires, 1970).

[22] The Irish adopted a practice noted in the Danish-Argentine community of lending out daughters as domestic servants to neighbouring households. See María Bjerg, *Entre Sofie y Tovelille: Una historia de los inmigrantes daneses* (Buenos Aires, 2001).

Mulhall, grew into an Anglophone propaganda organ and the leading source of intelligence on the Argentine Republic for British businessmen and investors. It survived for almost a century as the oldest newspaper in the country.[23] The advantage of the Irish against other ethnic groups lay in having arrived during the 1840s before the enormous rise of land prices of the second half of the century. The Irish landed classes diminished or acculturated in the early twentieth century but Irish ethnic strands survived in the Argentine middle class.

In 1824, John Parish Robertson and William Parish Robertson, two noted merchant entrepreneurs, set up an agrarian settlement at Monte Grande near Buenos Aires City, bringing around 220 immigrants, mostly artisans, small farmers, and servants from lowland Scotland.[24] The colony collapsed in 1829 when civil war led to the settlement being pillaged and abandoned. Most of the failed colonists migrated into the city where they established St Andrews 'Scotch' Church, later one of the leading British institutions in Argentina.[25] Subsequently, Scottish immigrants became prominent in Chascomús sixty miles south-east of Buenos Aires and in smaller numbers much further south near Bahía Blanca.[26]

In an era of booming wool exports in the 1860s, a small English farm community developed at Fraile Muerto ('Dead Monk'). These dispersed homesteads lay several hundred miles north-west of Buenos Aires along the projected route of the Central Argentine Railway from Córdoba to Rosario.[27] In one of the compelling nineteenth-century narratives of farming in the pampas, Richard Seymour of Warwickshire described his journey across the plains to set up a sheep *estancia* where he adopted the widely employed share system of 'halves' (*medianería*). Seymour endured hard labour for meagre rewards and witnessed Indian attacks that killed fellow Britons. Like many English frontier pioneers of the 1860s, within two years

[23] The *Buenos Aires Herald*, founded in 1876, and ultimately much longer lived than the *Standard*, became the other notable English-language newspaper.

[24] See Iain A. D. Stewart, *From Caledonia to the Pampa: Two Accounts of the Early Scots Emigrants to the Argentine* (East Linton, 2000); names and occupations of the *Symmetry* settlers are listed in James Dodds, *Records of the Scottish Settlers in the River Plate and their Churches* (Buenos Aires, 1897), 18–20, and reproduced in Arnold Morrison, 'The Scots in Argentina', URL: <http://myweb.tiscali.co.uk/scotsinargpat>, accessed 1 Dec. 2009.

[25] J. Monteith Drysdale, *A Hundred Years in Buenos Aires: Being a Brief Account of St. Andrew's Scots Church and its Work during the First Century of its Existence* (Buenos Aires, 1929).

[26] The settlements at Monte Grande and Chascomús are treated in Dodds, *Scottish Settlers*.

[27] Arthur E. Shaw, *Forty Years in the Argentine Republic* (London, 1907), 28.

he abandoned the enterprise to return home. En route Seymour bypassed Rosario, a city in the throes of both an insurrection and a cholera epidemic.[28] A few young Englishmen succeeded in establishing *estancias* in distant parts of the pampas. For example, Walter Larden visited his brother in 1888 and once more in 1908 on farmland in Santa Fe Province, where the latter had first worked as a sharecropper. In the 1880s, 'things were in the rough. We had no milk or butter... there was hard biscuit instead of bread. Vegetables were a delicacy unknown.' Twenty years later, conditions had greatly improved. Larden's brother now held title to the land, which had become a vast grain farm worked by Italian tenants and seasonal labourers.[29]

In 1865 Welsh immigrants established the remote settlements of Puerto Madryn, Rawson, Trelew, and Gaimán on the Río Chubut. The settlers numbered less than 300 but grew tenfold during the next thirty years. Michael Daniel Jones, a nationalist ideologue, planned the colony as a retreat from industrialism and a bastion of Welsh identity. In struggling to survive, the colonists abandoned Welsh practices they had sought to resurrect and adopted irrigation. As their annals emphasized, they partly attributed their survival to their exceptionally good relations with the indigenous peoples. In their own versions of their history, democracy including female suffrage tempered excessive authority. By the 1880s exports of wheat and a newly constructed railway enabled them to achieve stability and modest prosperity.

For more than a generation, the Welsh existed in near-isolation. Eventually, fearing their inhabitants would seek even greater autonomy or try to establish a British protectorate, the Argentine government asserted authority. Late-century growth encouraging the influx of an ethnically mixed population further undermined Welsh exclusiveness. The twentieth century brought relative decline. Agriculture stagnated during the inter-war period; the co-operative and irrigation societies founded by the settlers collapsed during the Great Depression.[30] Despite ethnic and cultural differentiation, the Chubut region retained a residual Welsh identity visible in chapels, schools, and in the survival of unique forms of the Welsh language.

---

[28] Richard Arthur Seymour, *Pioneering the Pampas: Or, the First Four Years of a Settler's Experience in the La Plata Camps* (London, 1869).

[29] Walter Larden, *Argentine Plains and Andean Glaciers: Life on an Estancia, and an Expedition into the Andes* (London, 1911), 43.

[30] Williams, *Welsh in Patagonia*, 95; also *The Desert and the Dream: A Study of Welsh Colonization in Chubut, 1865–1915* (Cardiff, 1975).

Nineteenth-century British rural settlement became a story of harsh wilderness pioneering and of friction with rebarbative Indians and gauchos. The British resisted pressures to integrate but outside Chubut had insufficient numbers to create or defend a clearly defined cultural zone.[31] The tactics for cultural survival included protecting their churches, clinging to the English (or Welsh) language, and endogamy. In the 1840s an observer described the principal features of the Celtic rural communities then developing in the Province of Buenos Aires:

[The people] maintain their distinctive British habits and institutions... Scattered widely apart though they are over an extensive surface, they maintain by intercourse with one another the feelings and habits of a home community. They educate their children to the extent they are able in the home principles and manners, and they come together at stated times from a circuit twenty or thirty miles in diameter for the purpose of divine service.[32]

Unknown but substantial numbers of nineteenth-century Anglo-Argentines abandoned the ethnic community. Acculturation grew particularly pronounced under Governor Juan Manuel de Rosas in 1829–52, a period of rural political predominance and relative isolation. The bi-cultural Anglo-Argentines included some noted figures. William Henry Hudson (1841–1923), a famed author of tales of the Argentine gauchos, exemplified a fascinating form of cultural hybridity. As a second example, Cecilia Grierson (1859–1935), who grew up on a remote homestead before moving into the city, gained celebrity as the first female physician in Argentina. She had an Irish mother, Scots paternal ancestors, and an Anglophone upbringing, but scored her achievements in an exclusively Argentine milieu.[33]

1860–1930: Residential and Institutional Features

The railway booms of 1862–1913 transformed the British community. The early 1860s marked the founding of the Buenos Aires Great Southern

---

[31] On conflict between British settlers and the Argentine gauchos, see John Lynch, *Massacre in the Pampas, 1872: Britain and Argentina in the Age of Migration* (Norman, Okla., 1998).

[32] Ouseley to FO, 30 May 1845, TNA, FO 6-123.

[33] More recent works on Hudson include Ruth Tomalin, *W. H. Hudson: A Biography* (London, 1982); David Miller, *W. H. Hudson and the Elusive Paradise* (New York, 1990); Felipe Arocena, *William Henry Hudson: Life, Literature, and Science*, tr. Richard Manning (Jefferson, NC, 2003). Grierson is treated in works in Spanish. See Asunción Taboada, *Vida y obra de Cecilia Grierson: Primera médica argentina* (Buenos Aires, 1983).

Railway, the largest network in the country. The Central Argentine Railway, another British company, was founded in 1862 to tie Córdoba, the gateway to the interior provinces, to the port of Rosario and the Rio de la Plata. The Buenos Aires Western Railway, originally an Argentine railway part-financed by leading Anglo-Argentine merchants, linked the metropolis with the Irish sheep farms.[34] Numerous smaller British-owned rail, tramway, and water companies followed.

A census in 1914 totalled the British population at 28,300: 19,500 men and 8,700 women, an understated enumeration that excluded an unknown number of the children and descendants of British and Irish settlers.[35] In this period members of the community in and near the capital city far outgrew those outside. The settlers diversified on the arrival of railway entrepreneurs, financiers, accountants, engineers, and technicians. Their lower ranks extended to include skilled railway workmen, and managers and employees of British firms in importing and shipping. Railwaymen and tramway men—drivers, engineers, repair specialists, workshop managers, and stationmasters—comprised a growing proportion of the community. The residents included the employees of banks headed by the London and River Plate Bank (later the Bank of London and South America) founded in 1862.[36] British assistants staffed great stores in downtown Buenos Aires selling imported agricultural and industrial equipment. A branch of Harrods founded in 1904 epitomized the opulence of the Argentine capital. British employees worked in telegraph companies that kept the city abreast of London and other financial centres. The English-language press expanded to include quality periodicals headed by *The Review of the River Plate*. A floating British population of so-called beachcombers hung around the taverns and the port area of the city.

Many British immigrants were young men who, to judge from high return rates of migration, were sojourners rather than settlers. The turnover of personnel reflected the prevalence of fixed-term contracts and the relative

---

[34] Colin M. Lewis, *British Railways in Argentina, 1857–1914: A Case Study of Foreign Investment* (London, 1983).

[35] República Argentina, *Tercer Censo Nacional: Levantado el 10 de junio de 1914* (Buenos Aires, 1916). A previous census in 1895 enumerated a total British population of 21,758, of whom 7,633 (35%) were women. República Argentina, *Segundo Censo de la República Argentina: Mayo 10 de 1895*, ii. *Población* (Buenos Aires, 1898), p. clxiii.

[36] David Joslin, *A Century of Banking in Latin America, to Commemorate the Centenary in 1962 of the London and South America Bank Limited* (London, 1963), 39.

scarcity of British women. Between 1880 and 1940, the typical British female immigrant found employment as a governess at the home of one of the great Argentine landed families, as a nurse in the British Hospital, or as a teacher in an English-speaking school. British and Anglo-Argentine men had difficulties in finding endogamous partners. Those who married faced a disincentive to remain in the country because as Argentine citizens their sons became liable to military service, an experience considered degrading.[37] The development of Argentine liberal jurisprudence in the late nineteenth century homogenized the legal status of the resident foreign communities, leaving the British community in a slightly paradoxical position. Its informal social and economic standing increased with the expansion of investment and British enterprise, but the legally acknowledged superior status it enjoyed under the treaty of 1825 diminished.

British working men and women remained tied to their churches, their social and sports clubs, and their employers.[38] They never developed the strong sense of autonomy or solidarity of the activist German immigrant workers in Buenos Aires of the 1880s or that of British emigrants to such countries as Canada and Australia. British workmen played no visible role in the development of the Argentine trade union movement, which in the 1940s became the largest in Latin America. Even La Fraternidad, the aristocratic union binding railway drivers and firemen founded in 1887, was modelled on labour organizations in the United States.

Most British people lived in Greater Buenos Aires, comprising the federal capital instituted in 1880 and its outlying suburbs in the Province of Buenos Aires. In the capital, the British residents included some of the denizens of Barracas, a south-side neighbourhood where for many years railway yards, a workingmen's institute, and a church school functioned. Middle-class Britons lived in north-side neighbourhoods and for a time in Flores, an outlying village to the west. Better-off community members relocated to new suburbs to the south outside the capital, several established by the

[37] The Argentine Nationality Law of 1862 instituted the *ius solis* determining citizenship by place of birth; this principle contrasted with British and common European practice, which applied the *ius sanguinis* or national affiliation by descent. Children and later descendants of British settlers remained British subjects under British law but were never acknowledged as such under Argentine law. Disputes over the military service of the sons of British settlers occurred perennially.

[38] Alistair Hennessy and John King (eds.), *The Land that England Lost: Argentina and Britain, a Special Relationship* (London, 1993), 23.

Great Southern Railway. To the west lies Hurlingham, the site of a highly prestigious sporting club founded by the British in 1889. Other Britons moved further north. An upper crust lived in Belgrano, a village annexed to the capital in 1880; still more moved to northern suburbs along the shoreline of the Rio de la Plata. The annual cricket match 'North versus South' founded in the early 1890s denoted the principal residential locations of the British community on the metropolitan extremes.

Smaller British concentrations emerged in nearby La Plata, the capital of the Province of Buenos Aires, Montevideo, the capital of Uruguay, and Rosario and Bahía Blanca, two major ports of the pampas that developed in 1870–1910. Further west and north, British clusters connected with banks, railways, and farming developed in Córdoba, Mendoza, and Tucumán. British holidaymakers popularized hotels developed by the railway companies in the Sierras de Córdoba. A few eccentrics, fugitives, and tramps disappeared into the peasant societies of the north-west. In Jujuy, a province bordering Bolivia, the firm of Leach's Argentine Estates Ltd employed British personnel to manage sugar haciendas and refineries. The Forestal Land, Timber and Railway Co. Ltd., a British company of dubious reputation, established huge camps in northern Santa Fe and the Chaco region to exploit (and destroy) the hardwood forests. Liebig's Extract of Meat Co. Ltd located in the Uruguayan border town of Fray Bentos became the largest cattle breeding company in the world whose dividends averaged 27 per cent in 1897–1914. Rio Gallegos in the extreme south became a region of vast sheep *estancias* part-developed by Scottish remigrants from the Falkland Islands.[39]

The British community in Argentina evolved in an exceptionally permissive environment. Its members acquired little attachment to a country that one visitor defined as 'a vast space scantily occupied by various nationalities'.[40] The British influenced politics through pressure groups tied to the Argentine upper class but never through elections or parties.[41] Outside the realm of sports, they made little cultural impact by comparison with the French, Italians, or Spaniards and as far back as the 1820s acquired a reputation for insularity. MacCann noted how community members upheld

---

[39] For detailed descriptions of the provincial communities, see Reginald Lloyd (ed.), *Twentieth Century Impressions of Argentina* (London, 1911). The 'Forestal' grew notorious in the 1920s for abusive labour practices.

[40] Larden, *Life on an Estancia*, 115.

[41] As a case study, see David Rock, *Politics in Argentina 1890–1930: The Rise and Fall of Radicalism* (Cambridge, 1975).

'the most unbending adherence to their own habits, and most carefully avoid whatever would alter their manners and customs'.[42] Hudson, the renowned locally born writer, had little liking for British immigrants he knew in his youth. His rural neighbours were 'typical of the lower middle class, who read no books and conversed with considerable misuse of the aspirate, about nothing but their own and their neighbours' affairs'.[43] Decades later an observer stressed the community's inbred traits. He noted the 'endless visiting lists, friends in every suburb, churches, polo, cricket, football and tennis fields, boating on the [River] Tigre, concerts, dramatics, lectures etc in the [city] centre, and the host of private entertainments, calls and other social duties'.[44] Sir Reginald Leeper, a British ambassador of the late 1940s, defended the community against insinuations of disloyalty. He emphasized that the British were 'extraordinarily retentive of their language, their institutions, their sports and even their drinks. They are not easily absorbed by a foreign community.'[45]

Ethnic defensiveness had some roots in religion. Anglicanism and Presbyterianism took root in the 1820s; for almost fifty years both established churches received British government subsidies under the Consular Chaplaincy Act of 1826. Twenty years later Irish Catholic churches headed by Fahy were flourishing among the sheep farmers; from the 1860s Nonconformist denominations led by Congregationalists proliferated in Welsh Chubut. The ties between religion and ethnicity found a typical expression in a late nineteenth-century Scots minister's promotional view of Sunday Schools. In his view, schools protected against 'the influence of the language of this country, and the prevailing form of religion, [namely Argentine Catholicism, which] tend to the absorption of the Anglo-Argentine, to his disuse of the English language, and to his being lost to Protestantism'.[46]

The British denominations imported clerics who grew prominent in the founding fictions of the denominational communities. The history of the Irish centred on the deeds of Father Fahy and that of the Scots on those of Revd William Brown and his successor James 'Padre' Smith, who led St Andrew's Scots Church. The Scots and Welsh developed community

[42] MacCann, *Two Thousand Miles Ride*, ii. 92.
[43] W. H. Hudson, *Far Away and Long Ago: A History of my Early Life* (New York, 1918), 211.
[44] *Review of the River Plate (RRP)* (10 Mar. 1894).
[45] Quoted in *Standard* (31 Mar. 1948).
[46] Monteith Drysdale, *St Andrew's Scots Church*, 25.

myths typical of American emigrant communities. The voyage of the Scots on the *Symmetry* in 1825 and that of the Welsh on the *Mimosa* in 1865 drew upon North American precedents. The Anglicans evinced a strong missionary orientation. Their heroes included Allen Gardiner, a former naval officer who perished in Tierra del Fuego in the 1850s in a hopeless enterprise among the Indians.[47]

The cult of sport, reflecting the presence of numerous young British bachelors, produced numerous exclusive clubs; attachment to 'clubs' became one of the most distinctive traits of the British. Recorded cricket stretched back to the amusements of the British prisoners of war following the expedition of 1806. The Buenos Aires Cricket and Rugby Club was founded in 1864. Rowing regattas organized by the Buenos Aires Rowing Club grew popular in the 1870s with the opening of suburban railway services to the nearby river delta. Rugby and football proliferated. Polo was first played at Flores and then at the Hurlingham Club. The *Standard* recorded one football match in 1869 between Conservatives and Liberals, an echo of the duels of the day between Disraeli and Gladstone.[48] In the 1880s Alexander Watson Hutton, the Scots founder of the Buenos Aires English High School, set up schoolboy (and old boy) football leagues. Legend held that Hutton kindled the popular enthusiasm for football in Argentina. Except cricket, which remained a ritual display of ethnic insularity, all the British sports spread into local society. Polo and racing formed bridges between the British and the Argentine upper class; golf and tennis, which grew well established during the 1920s, further enhanced the status of the British community.[49]

The British resembled other resident Western European communities by building an enormous number of ethnic associations. The British Hospital founded in 1844 became the most venerable of their institutions, the only hospital outside imperial territory to receive a British subsidy under the Act of Parliament of 1826. In early days, the hospital served as a refuge for sailors and a hospice for alcoholics. In 1848, its director lamented the 'depravity

---

[47] On Anglicanism, I am indebted to David George for a manuscript titled 'Historia de la iglesia anglicana de la Argentina, 1825–1900'. A remarkable biographical and anthropological work stemming from life in a missionary family in Tierra del Fuego is E. Lucas Bridges, *Uttermost Parts of the Earth* (London, 1948).

[48] *Standard* (5 Dec. 1869).

[49] Sports are researched in Victor Raffo, *El origen británico del deporte argentino: Atletismo, cricket, polo, remo, rugby durante las presidencias de Mitre, Sarmiento y Avellaneda* (Buenos Aires, 2004).

and drunkenness in the very depth of which a large part of the labouring class of the British population in this city is sunk'.[50] In the early 1880s the hospital began engaging nurses in Britain and eventually developed into the proudest emblem of the British community.[51]

Numerous British cultural associations included the English Literary Society of the late Victorian era, which enforced male-only membership because 'the presence of ladies would intimidate nervous speakers'.[52] Two other institutions stood out. The British and American Benevolent Society (BABS) founded in June 1880 at the height of revolutionary turmoil survives today to support the aged. The Asociación Argentina de Cultura Inglesa disseminated British literature, language, and arts. Founded by Ambassador Sir Malcolm Robertson in 1927 the 'Cultura' evolved into an influential centre of learning.[53]

The British associations included a chamber of commerce founded in 1912, orphanages, philanthropic associations, and asylums.[54] The Institute of Engineers of the River Plate founded in 1898 on the premises of the 'Scotch' Church illustrated that many railway engineers possessed a Scottish background.[55] Most institutions retained their vitality for around a generation before slowly crumbling as their memberships aged. By 1956, for example, the British Society founded in 1912 possessed 500 members, but only because 'most of them have not energy enough to resign'.[56]

The elite merchants and *estancieros* in Argentina sent their children to Britain for education: 'Winchester, Sandhurst, Cambridge' became an exceptional but not unknown trajectory. As elsewhere, a home education

[50] Hugh Fraser Warneford-Thomson, *The British Hospital of Buenos Aires: A History* (Buenos Aires, 2000), 18.

[51] A British ambassador of the mid-1930s noted the enthusiasm with which the community supported the Hospital. In his view, 'There is no more patriotic and generous community to be found anywhere than the British in Argentina.' Sir Nevile Henderson, *Water under the Bridge* (London, 1945), 199.

[52] *Standard* (27 Aug. 1880).

[53] For the creation of 'BABS' by Chargé d'Affaires Egerton, see *Standard* (26 June 1880). On the 'Cultura', see *RRP* (20 Apr. 1956).

[54] A listing in 1922 included: British and American Benevolent Society, British Society, English Literary Club (founded in 1880), English Club, Navy League, Royal Colonial Institute, St Andrews Society, St David's Society, British Social Club, British Aged and Infirm Fund, St John's Anglican Church, St Andrew's Scotch Church, British Ex-Servicemen's Club: *RRP* (3 Mar. 1922).

[55] An outline history appears in *RRP* (28 Feb. 1919).

[56] *Standard* (10 May 1956).

provided foundations for successful careers and marriages.[57] Community residents unable to afford a British education for their children supported local English schools.[58] They were battling to avoid 'Argentinization'— cultural hybridity and linguistic pollution. From early days the spoken English of many Anglo-Argentines evolved into a distinctive mélange of vocabulary and syntax.[59] As once noted by an American commentator: 'They spoke Spanish with an English accent, and English with a Spanish accent, and their English broke down, and became odd, deformed.'[60]

In the nineteenth century English language schools remained underdeveloped. Initially, doubtful characters known as camp schoolmasters scraped a living from touring the *estancias* of the Anglophone populace.[61] In town, a few financially struggling private schools provided limited, low-quality instruction for boys and girls. In the 1820s, the Buenos Airean School Society founded by an Anglican cleric supported by British merchants lasted less than one decade. Thereafter the 'Scotch School' (later St Andrew's 'Scotch' School) began in 1839 under the Presbyterians but suffered bouts of stagnation and near-extinction. The Irish too established schools under clerical control.[62]

A transition occurred as the community became replenished from the metropolis. The most notable British schools after 1880 included the rejuvenated St Andrew's Scotch School, St George's College for Boys founded in 1897 (modelled on an English public school), and the Buenos Aires English High School (initially tied to the Great Southern Railway) established by Hutton in 1880. By the 1920s, at least sixty English schools, including

---

[57] Lloyd, *Argentina*, 339, 510.

[58] 'Various English residents [stated] that they had only been able to make their children grow up with the English language by thrashing them when they spoke Spanish': Hammerton, *Real Argentine*, 240.

[59] Larden remarked: 'An Englishman resident in France does not say "I aimer'd her very much", "I manger'd a tasty lunch" or "I blesser'd my arm". But in Argentina, the English residents use, in the case of verbs without number, such forms as "That pivot is gastar'd (worn)", "He golpear'd his foot (knocked)", or "They revocar'd the wall (plastered)".' Larden, *Life on an Estancia*, 113.

[60] Ysabel Rennie, *The Argentine Republic* (New York, 1945), 65.

[61] Hudson, who had a smattering of education from camp schoolmasters, wrote that an education in Buenos Aires was not popular among Britons in the country on the grounds of city diseases and poor teaching (Hudson, *Far Away and Long Ago*, 250). Dodds, *Scottish Settlers*, provides the best published source on early schools.

[62] Murray, *Devenir irlandés*, cites letters home from Irish settlers in which education appeared as a leading theme.

numerous girls' schools, functioned in Greater Buenos Aires and many others elsewhere.[63] Catering to expatriates and upper middle-class Anglo-Argentines, the schools propagated cultural imperialism more directed at strengthening the ethnic community than proselytizing among the Argentines.[64] The mission of English boarding schools headed by St George's College was to 'save to the British Empire and British traditions the numerous families in the Camp who though of British lineage are in danger of growing up in total ignorance of the language and ideals of their fathers'.[65] 'Every child we are unable to educate', declared a Scottish association in the 1920s, 'is a child lost to the British community in this Republic.'[66] For many years English-language education ended at the age of 14 but provided Anglo-Argentines with access to white-collar positions in British firms.

As education, employment, ethnicity, and class became closely interlinked, Anglo-Argentine society grew progressively status conscious. An observer in 1915 referred to 'the pettiness of [the community's] interest, the little corroding jealousies, its snobbishness'. He thought that Anglo-Argentine women were becoming picky about British marriage partners, less likely than before to take the first man off the boat.[67] Anglo-Argentine families discovered or invented lineages. Cecilia Grierson, for example, proudly enunciated her descent from minor Scottish nobility, despite her minimal contact with the British community.[68]

The First World War demonstrated the power of ethnic loyalty. Almost 5,000 young men, possibly half the men of military age, volunteered for service. In late 1914, many left on the spur of the moment and paid their own shipping fares. The recruits included 1,000 railway employees, who received promises of reinstatement on their return. Many rural Argentine volunteers joined cavalry regiments. The official history of the community during the Great War reiterated the jingo discourse of the era. On the boat train carrying the first contingent of volunteers in August 1914, the shouts rang out: '"God save the King," full of cheerful hope... "Back in a Year" said

---

[63] For additional commentary, see Rock, *British in Argentina*, 68–72.

[64] See J. T. Stevenson, *The History of St. George's College Quilmes, Argentina 1898–1935* (London, 1936).

[65] Revd James William Fleming quoted in Monteith Drysdale, *St Andrew's Scots Church*, 25.

[66] *RRP* (7 Apr. 1922).

[67] Hammerton, *Real Argentine*, 274.

[68] Preface to Cecilia Grierson, *Colonia de Monte Grande, Provincia de Buenos Aires: Primera y única colonia formada por escoceses en la Argentina* (Buenos Aires, 1925).

some. "See you there soon," shouted others [followed by] a final rendering of "It's a long way to Tipperary".[69]

At home women raised funds for the British Red Cross and enlisted with the British Women's Patriotic Association or the Queen Mary Needlework Guilds. Under Sir Reginald Tower, the British Legation directed the mobilization, tagged men for commissions, and exhorted the fund-raisers; under Sir John O'Conor, the British Hospital screened thousands of potential recruits. In May 1918, when married men were being urged to enlist, community leaders set up the Anglo-Argentine War Fund to assist invalids, war widows, and returnees seeking re-employment.[70]

Post-War Challenges

The conditions that drew Britons to Argentina were ending even before the war. Railway construction largely terminated in 1913. In the 1920s British exporters struggled against an overvalued currency, obsolescent goods, and, as some argued, the incompetence of British salesmen to regain their position in the Argentine market.[71] The standing of the British deteriorated as they came to be seen as manipulative, money-grubbing, and reactionary. During the war, the railway companies could no longer import Welsh coal and their costs sharply increased. They opposed wage increases and raised freight and passenger rates, incurring the wrath of workers, commuters, and ranchers. British companies supported the National Labour Association, a strike-breaking body founded in 1918, which in 1921 endorsed military action against the unions.[72] In 1921–2, British *estancieros* in Patagonia assisted Colonel Héctor Varela whose men killed shepherds and rural workers stirred up by the post-war collapse of wool prices.[73]

The standing of the British revived superficially in 1925 on the centenary of the treaty, when the Prince of Wales visited as the guest of President Marcelo T. de Alvear. The later 1920s again proved discouraging, as British trade faced competition from the United States. American transportation

---

[69] Arthur L. Holder, *Activities of the British Community in Argentina during the Great War, 1914–1919* (Buenos Aires, 1920), 26, 117, 207.

[70] Ibid.

[71] Roger Gravil, *The Anglo-Argentine Connection* (Boulder, Colo., 1985); Rory Miller, *Britain and Latin America in the Nineteenth and Twentieth Centuries* (London, 1993).

[72] Details in Rock, *Politics in Argentina*, 209–17.

[73] Osvaldo Bayer, *La Patagonia rebelde*, 2 vols. (Buenos Aires, 1980).

and consumer durable goods (epitomized by the Model T Ford) captured large swathes of the market. Ambassador Robertson warned the Foreign Office: 'The United States under [President Herbert] Hoover means to dominate this country by hook or by crook. It is British interests that chiefly stand in their way. These are to be bought out or kicked out.'[74] Robertson urged bilateral trade: 'Buy from those who buy from us'. In 1929 the British Board of Trade sent a trade mission headed by Lord D'Abernon. Its apparent success dissipated in September 1930 when the military overthrew the government and prevented ratification of the agreement by the Senate.

The British grew more forceful. A 1930 report underlined the extent of British economic interests and potential bargaining power. Current investments in Argentina at £500–600 millions exceeded the sums invested respectively in Canada, the United States, or Brazil; investment in Argentina totalled 60 per cent of combined investment throughout North America and Brazil.[75] The bargaining power the British claimed derived from the dependence of the Argentine landed class and meat exporters on the British market. In 1933 the British government pressured a visiting delegation into the Roca-Runciman Treaty, which protected the access of Argentine exporters to the British market in return for concessions to British firms and British trade. In 1936 another round of pressure led to an urban transport monopoly that attempted to force commuters back onto antiquated British trains and trams. Despite the strong tactics, Anglo-Argentine trade stagnated. As a symptom of British weakness, numerous import firms and some smaller banks were liquidated. The profits of the railway companies plunged definitively. By the late 1930s British companies including the railways appeared ready to sell out.[76] Insecurity gradually enveloped the British community. As the *Standard* noted in 1944, 'Every schoolboy knows that the British community is dwindling away due to lack of imports. ... In a number of years, there will be no British-born people in the country at all.'

In the late 1930s, 500 British firms and 500 British-owned *estancias* still operated in the country. The wartime fund-raisers of 1939–45 registered 8,000 heads of household as contributors, a figure that suggested a possible

[74] On US trade competition, see Gravil, *Anglo-Argentine Connection*.
[75] UK, *Department of Overseas Trade, Report of the British Economic Mission to Argentina, Brazil and Uruguay* (London, 1930).
[76] The British instigated the nationalization of the Córdoba Central, the least solvent railway. See *Standard* (29 Dec. 1938).

total of 30,000–40,000 members of the community (using a multiple of 4–5 to include family members). In 1951, the British Consul General stated that 18,000 British-born persons lived in Argentina and the people of British ancestry totalled an additional 30,000.[77] Other data depicted accelerating decline. In 1914–60, the censuses registered a fall in the number of British-born residents from 28,000 to 6,000.[78] As another illustration of regression, the wartime volunteers of 1914–18, at 4,852, exceeded by more than two to one those of 1939–45, who totalled 2,076 including 534 women.[79]

The 1930s marked a brief *belle époque* for some Anglo-Argentines, who found easier access to British firms as recruitment from Britain ceased. 'The golden age of importation of staffs', wrote the *Standard* in 1943: 'Vanished a decade or two ago. [Before 1914] not a liner arrived but carried young recruits for the banks, the railways and other branches of commercial activity... [Today] the Anglo-Argentine and not the native-born [Briton] tends to dominate the British community.'[80] In 1927 Ambassador Robertson failed to bring the British schools under metropolitan supervision.[81] Unchecked, the schools expanded to a point that by the 1940s the supply of places far exceeded the demand. By now, the British schools survived only by permitting the enrolment of non-Anglophone pupils. In 1944, for example, half the children at St Andrew's School were neither British nor 'Anglo'.[82] The commitment to ethnic education nevertheless remained. In the late 1930s, the British Society in Buenos Aires continued to fund the education of Anglo-Argentine children.[83] In 1945 community leaders described the ethnic schools as:

---

[77] Based on *Standard* (4 Jan. 1942; 28 Apr. 1944; 4 Dec. 1951; 8 July 1952). For the community in the 1950s, see Donald Boyd Easum, 'The British–Argentine–U. S. Triangle. A Case Study in International Relations', Ph.D. thesis (Princeton, 1953).

[78] Census figures showed the British community at 27,692 in 1914, 11,425 in 1946, and 6,628 in 1960. See *Revista de Dirección Nacional de Migraciones*, 1/3 (July–Sept. 1960), 165.

[79] *Standard* (8 July 1952) reproduced a commemorative report on Second World War activities.

[80] *Standard* (24 Sept. 1943).

[81] Sources on this issue remain unpublished. My data on schools are based on F. R. G. Duckworth, 'The British Schools in Argentina. Report on a Visit of Inspection May 2nd–July 13th, 1927', enclosed in TNA, FO 118/595.

[82] *Standard* (21 Nov. 1944). I discovered from interviews that in the 1940s St George's College also began to admit non-Anglophones.

[83] In 1937, the Nazi regime was subsidizing 1,500 German schools in Brazil.

[T]he keystone of any community survival policy. It will give our children a training which keeps them within our fold and equips them well for life in this country so that the economic status of the community is maintained, and its sons and daughters can reach the highest positions in commerce, the professions and public life.

At this point ethnic education united and divided the Anglo-Argentine population simultaneously. The community was separating into a majority of Anglophones educated in British schools and a minority lacking such education and subject to acculturation. A commentator of 1942 called the Anglophones 'insufferable young pups', whose arrogance he blamed on the type of education they were receiving: they had never learnt correct Spanish and could never find local employment except in British firms. The second subgroup he identified had excellent Spanish and much poorer English but inferior employment. Driven onto the national labour market, its members felt little kinship with Britain and commonly refused to volunteer for military service. They would not 'fight for the English and have the same thing happen to them as happened to many others in the last war—to be on the seat of their pants in a foreign country'.[84] The Anglophones still thrived but appeared unaware of their vulnerable dependence on weakening British firms and declining British trade. The Spanish-speaking segment, acquiring a local identity and indifferent to the fate of Britain, appeared to be growing. Education in English schools, with the opportunity it conferred for employment in British firms, marked the crucial difference between the two groups.

Second World War and After

Although volunteers for the British forces halved in 1939–45, community organization became even more extensive than in 1914–18. Reflecting the greater weight and influence of the Anglo-Argentines, during the Second World War the community preferred to support its own volunteers rather than funnel resources to the British. It funded the transportation of volunteers and some of their equipment; it brought them home after the war and provided the needy with war pensions. As a second priority, the community shipped millions of eggs to England and tons of food and clothing to British prisoners of war. By September 1944, the community had raised the large

---

[84] *Standard* (9 Apr. 1942; 13 May 1944; 2 Feb. 1945; 3 Mar. 1948).

sum of £2.8 million.[85] If not all supported the British, Anglo-Argentines figured prominently among the volunteers. Miguel Angel Cárcano, a wartime Argentine ambassador, claimed he had encountered British soldiers in the streets of London singing the Argentine national anthem. German U-boats caused several mishaps to the volunteers crossing the Atlantic. In 1943, for instance, one woman narrated her escape from a sinking ship with only her knitting. Nearly all the surviving volunteers, including the women, returned after the war, suggesting once more that they were mainly Anglo-Argentines with few metropolitan ties.

Ambassador Sir Esmond Ovey formed the British Community Council (BCC) in 1939 to organize wartime fund-raising. The council operated dually as a federation of British charitable and sporting associations and as a set of geographical units illustrating the current distribution and concentrations of the community. The affluent neighbourhoods of the capital headed by Belgrano provided the largest flow of contributions, followed by the northern and southern suburbs. Smaller donations came from the provinces and the distant territories of the far south. Cliques of senior railwaymen, shipping leaders, and importers ran the BCC. Sporadic opposition to their leadership highlighted social divisions between the top-level native-born Britons and the middle-class Anglo-Argentines. One critic attacked the council's 'self-elected social-climbing leaders'. He urged the BCC to fund Anglo-Argentine volunteers rather than send money to Britain. The council needed the efforts of 'little men . . . with no prospective OBEs in mind'. The wrong people to run the BCC were the parents of 'little Archibald who was probably sent home for a subsidised English education'.[86]

In 1942 Sir David Kelly succeeded Ovey as ambassador, serving during the Nationalist Revolution of June 1943 that overthrew the liberal regime. The juntas of 1943–6 adopted rhetoric reminiscent of Vichy France yet posed little direct threat to the British community. They allowed meat shipments to Britain on the system of indefinitely deferred payment (the so-called blocked sterling balances) instituted in 1939. Kelly objected to the juntas but tempered his criticisms until after the war. His more difficult task stemmed from the growing presence of the United States. During the 1930s, Argentina rebuffed the Good Neighbor policy and the Pan-American

---

[85] A figure reported by Ambassador David Kelly in *Standard* (6 Mar. 1945).

[86] Preceding segments based on *Standard* (16 Oct. 1939; 5 Apr. and 7 Oct. 1942; 9 May 1943; 5 May 1947).

alliance sponsored by the Roosevelt administration, but in the Second World War a new situation emerged as US influence expanded throughout Latin America. Caught between the US State Department and the military juntas, Kelly struggled with only short-term success to protect British interests.[87]

When war ended, leaders of the BCC sought to turn the council into a miniature welfare state controlling community education, health, and care for invalids and the aged. Their efforts failed as the flow of contributions fell as the volunteers, the *raison d'être* of wartime fund-raising, returned. The BCC found itself having to choose between education of the young on one hand or charity and support for the British hospital for the old and the sick on the other. In 1949 it abandoned education in order to fund the hospital and the BABS.

A debate on sponsored education in 1948–9 illustrated that the community had entered a critical era. Opponents of scholarships noted that the community was growing poorer and older; its institutions were becoming too large and diverse for its narrowing base. Education in the English schools prepared children for white-collar jobs that no longer existed. Why, then, asked the *Standard*, bring up children as 'little gentlemen' when British firms were pulling out of the country? The English language began losing status and that of Spanish grew: '"We speak Spanish to our baby," a young Anglo-Argentine mother announced defiantly at a family gathering. "He is Argentine-born and only fourth generation British."' An air of defeat pervaded the community. 'Ten years is not a long time,' remarked a 1949 commentator, but 'In that space we won the war, lost all or most of our assets. . . . Our winnings consist of a legacy of charities belonging to better days and a mounting claim on a dwindling purse to meet the cost.'

Underlying the crisis stood the nationalization of the railways in 1948, a measure conceded by the post-war British Labour government in return for a year's supply of Argentine meat. 'This year we eat the railways,' remarked a detractor in the House of Commons. 'What next year?'[88] British

---

[87] See Sir David Kelly, *The Ruling Few, or The Human Background to Diplomacy*, 3rd edn. (London, 1953); David Rock, 'Argentina 1930–1946: Economy and Politics in Depression and War', in Leslie Bethell (ed.), *Cambridge History of Latin America*, viii (Cambridge, 1991), 3–72. On other important wartime events, see Sir Eugen Millington-Drake, *The Drama of Graf Spee and the Battle of the River Plate: A Documentary Anthology 1914–1964* (London, 1964). Millington-Drake, ambassador to Uruguay in 1939, played a conspicuous part in publicity as head of the British Council in Buenos Aires.

[88] Data based on *Standard* (2 May 1946; 10 Feb. 1948; 2 Aug. 1949; 30 Oct. 1950).

investment fell from £356 million in 1946 to only £69 million in 1950. Nationalization damaged the Anglo-Argentine community by decoupling the linkages between investment and trade. As the *Standard* noted: 'The end of British ownership of the railways would mean the displacement of a large segment of the British community, which, in turn, buys British goods, British insurance and upholds British institutions. The sale of the railways would go a long way towards getting the British out of Latin America.' In the early post-war, the British failed to regenerate manufacturing industry fast enough to meet Argentine demand for capital goods to develop local industry. The British ceded this market to US exporters, although the Americans won a hollow victory since the Argentine market collapsed in 1948 as foreign reserves became exhausted. Henceforward, the Argentine economy grew weak, unbalanced, and stagnated. The anti-agrarian policies of the Perón government disrupted agrarian exports, including beef shipments.[89] Falling beef exports contributed to a 50 per cent decline in Anglo-Argentine trade between 1947 and 1950. By the early 1950s trade had lapsed into bartering meat for petroleum from British-controlled oil reserves in the Middle East. A few large British companies such as the Bank of London and South America and Liebig's Meat remained strong, but innumerable other firms faced bankruptcy. In 1951 Harrods, for example, reported that 'the company has never been beset with so many problems'. Profits had fallen by 50 per cent in the past two years; the Argentine Central Bank refused the company permission to repatriate profits; affected by concessions to the unions, company costs rose steeply.[90]

Other changes wrought by the Perón regime hastened the decline of the British community. The government nationalized welfare and instilled a narrow national allegiance threatening all forms of ethnic pluralism. Its pressures included attempts to force the ethnic schools to adopt exclusively Spanish curricula. The *peronista* discourse of social welfare and state interventionism provided ammunition to Anglo-Argentine opponents of subsidized scholarships to the English schools. 'Why pay for other people's children?' asked a commentator in the *Standard*, endorsing the regime's

---

[89] For a discussion of post-war economic policy, see Rock, *Argentina 1516–1987*, ch. 7. Effects on bilateral ties are explored in Noel Fursman, 'The Decline of the Anglo/Argentine Economic Connection in the Years Immediately after the Second World War: A British Perspective', D.Phil. thesis (Oxford, 1988).

[90] *RRP* (6 Mar. 1951).

view that all education should be state-controlled. Ethnic charities also appeared moot during the expansion of welfare services promoted by the Eva Perón Foundation, the rich and powerful body established by the president's wife.[91]

Within the British community, the British-born segment was plainly moribund and the Anglo-Argentines increasingly disconnected from metropolitan ties. British institutions appeared museum pieces. In 1949, Sir John Balfour, the British ambassador, recalled visiting 'the dignified but mustily Victorian country clubs' of the old British *estancias*, where 'time stood still'.[92] The income of the British churches collapsed; churches closed and then tumbled down. Members of the community retrenched in Olivos, one of the northern suburbs, which in the early 1950s became the new site of St Andrew's Church and School. Beyond Olivos and Belgrano, many of the BCC's fund-raisers elsewhere became extinct. In 1954, St Andrew's School instituted a curriculum to prepare students for admission to American and British universities, a change that became a signal to the youth to emigrate.[93]

The fall of Perón in 1955 encouraged hopes of resurgent Anglo-Argentine ties. They faded as the British developed closer European or Commonwealth ties while the Argentines suffered prolonged political and economic instability. In 1950–80 empathy between most Britons and many Argentines evaporated. The British grew aggrieved at ostensible cases of mistreatment such as that meted out to several hundred former British railwaymen who were forcibly retired in 1948. They received pensions that inflation and foreign exchange restrictions soon rendered valueless.[94] In Argentina, the British faced an onslaught of nationalist attacks that grew into a vilification of the entire Anglo-Argentine connection since independence.[95]

Community institutions either died or became radically modified. By 1970 the need to appoint local teachers provoked a collapse of standards

[91] *Standard* (7 Jan. 1949).

[92] John Balfour, *Not Too Correct an Aureole: The Recollections of a Diplomat* (London, 1983), 148.

[93] Data from *Standard* (3 Apr. 1944; 27 Apr. 1949; 30 Nov. 1953; 1 Sept. 1954).

[94] The dispute about the railway pensions continued into the 1960s. See TNA, FO 371/167882 (1963) and 271/173746 (1964).

[95] The critique of the British connection began under Argentine 'Historical Revisionism' founded in the 1930s. A recent study is Thomas Michael Goebel, 'Argentina's Partisan Past: Nationalism, Peronism and Historiography, 1955–1976', Ph.D. thesis (London, 2007).

as defined by British examination boards. The former ethnic schools possessed only nominal British affiliations and adopted curricula oriented to local university admission. The community diminished sharply through emigration and the abandonment of endogamy. Sharp intergenerational rifts appeared between Anglo-Argentines born before and after 1950. The former group retained some of the community's self-image, such as its claim of superior integrity (the so-called *palabra inglés*) and the belief in fair play inculcated by the Victorian sports. Younger Anglo-Argentines increasingly identified with the local environment. Among the young, the English language continued to lose prestige, although demand for English language skills was growing in advanced sectors of the economy.[96]

The civil strife of the early 1970s produced kidnappings and ransom demands targeting the Anglophone executives of multinational corporations. At this point some members of the Argentine militant left possessed Irish ancestral connections, while leaders of military governments (or more frequently their wives) displayed part-British genealogies. In 1966–73, leading British businessmen commonly endorsed the 'Roundhead' military governments who declared war on internal 'subversion'.[97]

The war of 1982 over the Falkland/Malvinas Islands highlighted the near-extinction of the Anglo-Argentine tie and the collapse of common interests or understanding between the two nations. The episode provoked an agonized response in the British community, with its members caught between irreconcilable forces. People of British background grew fearful of losing their property, or suffering internment or expulsion. In ways reminiscent of the responses of British landowners and merchants to the Anglo-French landing of 1845, many Anglo-Argentines opted for the Argentine side.

In increasingly diminished form, the community survived the erosion of its membership and the blighting of its cultural autonomy. British Council and British Embassy subsidies preserved a few annual community events such as Remembrance Day. Its salient institutions—the Hospital, the BABS, the 'Cultura' and the BCC—remained alive at the end of the twentieth century but most, except the Hospital Británico, which became entirely Argentine in

---

[96] See Florencia Cortés Conde, 'The Anglo-Argentine Bilingual Experience'. Ph.D. thesis (University of Texas, Austin, 1993). The responses of several hundred Anglo-Argentines to a lengthy questionnaire conducted by Cortés Conde in 1991 are held by the library of the Universidad San Andrés.

[97] See *Buenos Herald* (11 Mar. 1970) for endorsements of 'Roundhead' military governments by British business leaders under General Roberto M. Levingston.

staffing and clientele, grew smaller and less conspicuous. The leading schools reinvented themselves as businesses in which the British connection survived only for advertising purposes or as a dimly recalled 'tradition'.

Select Bibliography

FLORENCIA CORTÉS CONDE, *Los angloargentinos en Buenos Aires. Lengua, identidad y nación antes y después de Malvinas* (Buenos Aires, 2007).

H. S. FERNS, *Britain and Argentina in the Nineteenth Century* (Oxford, 1960).

KLAUS GALLO, *Great Britain and Argentina: From Invasion to Recognition* (London, 2001).

ALEXANDER GILLESPIE, *Gleanings and Remarks; Collected during Many Months of Residence at Buenos Ayres, and Within the Upper Country...* (Leeds, 1818).

ROGER GRAVIL, *The Anglo-Argentine Connection* (Boulder, Colo., 1985).

MAXINE HANON, *Diccionario de británicos en Buenos Aires: Primera época* (Buenos Aires, 2005).

SIR FRANCIS HEAD, Bt., *Rough Notes Taken during some Rapid Journeys across the Pampas and among the Andes* (4th edn. London, 1846).

ALISTAIR HENNESSY and JOHN KING (eds.), *The Land that England Lost: Argentina and Britain, a Special Relationship* (London, 1993).

ARTHUR L. HOLDER, *Activities of the British Community in Argentina during the Great War, 1914–1919* (Buenos Aires, 1920).

W. H. HUDSON, *Far Away and Long Ago: A History of my Early Life* (New York, 1918).

REGINALD LLOYD (ed.), *Twentieth Century Impressions of Argentina* (London, 1911).

GEORGE THOMAS LOVE, *A Five Years' Residence in Buenos Ayres during the Years 1820–1825: containing remarks on the country and inhabitants, and a visit to Colonia del Sacramento* (London, 1825).

WILLIAM MACCANN, *Two Thousand Miles Ride through the Argentine Provinces* (London, 1853).

RORY MILLER, *Britain and Latin America in the Nineteenth and Twentieth Centuries* (London, 1993).

VERA BLINN REBER, *British Mercantile Houses in Buenos Aires, 1810–1880* (Cambridge, Mass., 1979).

J. P. and W. P. ROBERTSON. *Letters on South America. In three volumes* (London, 1843).

DAVID ROCK, *Argentina 1516–1987: From Spanish Colonization to Alfonsín* (Berkeley, Calif., 1987).

GLYN WILLIAMS, *The Welsh in Patagonia: The State and the Ethnic Community* (Cardiff, 1991).

3

Expatriates in Cosmopolitan Egypt: 1864–1956

James Whidden

Introduction

'Social apartheid' was the term applied by Peter Mansfield to describe colonial society in Egypt.[1] And although Mansfield observed that the attitudes of some of the British might have been exceptions to the rule, these only highlighted an underlying system of social exclusivity that divided the 'two nations': Egyptian and British.[2] Mansfield's description of social relations could be compared to Edward Said's theory that imperialism was a cultural, as well as political, system that projected power by negating non-European peoples.[3] For sure, imperial agents like Evelyn Baring (later Lord Cromer) and Alfred Milner published works on Egypt to influence public opinion in Britain, as well as the British community in Egypt.[4] Their purpose was to prolong the British occupation indefinitely by arguing that the Egyptians were incapable of self-government. To draw out the analogy between Mansfield and Said, it might be argued that 'Orientalism' manifested itself in a colonial society that constructed impermeable boundaries between a British 'ruling caste' and the Egyptian 'subject race'.[5] However, recent studies of Britons in Egypt during the Second World War

---

[1] Peter Mansfield, *The British in Egypt* (New York, 1971), 315. See also Anthony Sattin, *Lifting the Veil: British Society in Egypt 1768–1956* (London, 1988), 173–214, 268–80.

[2] Mansfield, *British in Egypt*, 311.

[3] Edward W. Said, *Orientalism* (London, 1978).

[4] H. S. Deighton, 'The Impact of Egypt on Britain: A Study of Public Opinion', in P. M. Holt (ed.), *Political and Social Change in Modern Egypt* (London, 1968), 247–8, and Roger Owen, *Lord Cromer: Victorian Imperialist, Edwardian Proconsul* (Oxford, 2004), 247–9.

[5] On Cromer's use of the term see Said, *Orientalism*, 36–9.

suggest that some were hardly champions of imperialism.[6] Rather, British identities were shaped by what Nicholas Thomas has referred to as their 'diasporic location'.[7] From this perspective the British in Egypt were not always servants of imperial power. Rather, some were concerned to invent new identities that fitted an imperial diaspora inclusive of diverse cultural communities. Thus, just as Mansfield and Said emphasized the supremacist attitudes of Britons in Egypt, it is equally important to investigate points of cultural or social intersection.

The cosmopolitan character of colonial society is one way to pursue this process of interaction. Sami Zubaida has written on the subject of cosmo-politanism in the Middle East, noting that belonging to a cosmopolitan society does not necessarily result in a cosmopolitan attitude. In the words of Zubaida, 'the co-existence of a multiplicity of cultures in one place is not what is meant by cosmopolitan'.[8] Rather, Zubaida associates cosmopolitan-ism with Mannheim's theory of 'deracination' whereby individuals emerged from the tightly bounded communal or caste-like social structures of medieval Europe. Liberated from the old boundaries of religion or caste, individuals entertained alternative perspectives and ideas, which were more easily available in a world marked by new systems of commerce and media.[9] These changes were characteristic of Egypt in the nineteenth and twentieth centuries, largely as a result of its incorporation into British economic and strategic networks.

The point of such reflections is that cosmopolitanism was a conflicted process of change. Lord Cromer reacted against cosmopolitanism. Ruling like an imperial viceroy from 1883, Cromer attempted to limit or even suppress the emergence of a cosmopolitan society that threatened to dis-solve the clear-cut boundaries that delineated the 'ruling and subject races'.[10] While many Britons endorsed this imperial narrative, British iden-

---

[6] Roger Bowen, *'Many Histories Deep': The Personal Landscape Poets in Egypt 1940–45* (London, 1995) and Jonathan Bolton, *Personal Landscapes: British Poets in Egypt during the Second World War* (New York, 1997).

[7] Nicholas Thomas, *Colonialism's Culture: Anthropology, Travel and Government* (Cambridge, 1994), 168.

[8] Sami Zubaida, 'Cosmopolitanism in the Middle East', *Amsterdam Middle East Papers*, 12 (1997), 1–21.

[9] Ibid. 5.

[10] Lord Cromer, *Modern Egypt*, ii (London, 1908), 171–98. Indeed, it has been argued that the British 'civilizing mission' was articulated specifically with Egypt in mind, beginning with the

tities were not fixed. The British in Egypt might just as easily censure imperial policies if they too blatantly disregarded Egyptian sensibilities and thus threatened the close partnership that underpinned British relations with Egyptians. More than a show of power or a system of social exclusions, British imperialism involved social relationships and a delicate—and often deadly— political game. In their relations with Egyptians, Britons vacillated between overbearing assertiveness and subtle manipulation. This is reflected in the political history of the era, wherein the mastery of Lord Cromer was suc- ceeded by the liberal self-effacement of Sir Eldon Gorst, followed by the authoritarian bearing of Lord Kitchener that preceded the overwhelming British military presence of the war years. However, these years gave way to the remarkably liberal concessions of Milner and Edmund Allenby. Liberal experiments afterwards provoked imperial retrenchment, as represented by Lord George Lloyd and Sir Miles Lampson (later Lord Killearn). The shifts of political history are reflected in the social history of the British community. Much more than a narrow ruling caste, social relations in Egypt involved British and Egyptians, as well as other communities, in what Roger Owen has referred to as a 'process of related experience'.[11] To fully understand the British experience in Egypt it is necessary to move beyond the imperial narrative and turn instead to the intermingling cultural milieus of Alexandria and Cairo.

Cosmopolitan Egypt

According to Michael Reimer the European communities in Alexandria acted as a bridgehead of European commercial and political power in Egypt, well before the British occupation of 1882.[12] The dynamic growth of the export and import economy in the latter half of the nineteenth century brought to Alexandria and Cairo European banks, insurance, and shipping companies, so that on the eve of the British occupation Alexan- dria's total population of 200,000 included 20,830 Greek, 8,993 Italian, 8,417 French, and 2,191 British residents. At the same time, Cairo's population of

claim that the British had a duty to protect the Egyptian people (*fellahin*) from the injustices of the khedival rulers and the 'rapacious' Europeans, Deighton, 'Impact of Egypt on Britain', 242–3.

[11] Owen, *Lord Cromer*, p. xii.

[12] Michael J. Reimer, *Colonial Bridgehead: Government and Society in Alexandria 1807–1882* (Boulder, Colo., 1997).

350,000 included over 20,000 Europeans. The cosmopolitan character of Alexandria, and to a lesser extent Cairo, meant that by the 1870s Egypt was one of the more colonial societies in Africa and Asia without ever having been formally colonized by a European power. The British commercial families ('Peels, Aldersons, Carvers and Barkers') of Alexandria were a minority in colonial society and had little cause to view themselves as representatives of the British empire until 1882.[13] It is noteworthy that in 1864 a British Institute was formed, representing twenty merchant companies, including Henry Bulkeley, Barker & Co., and the Carver Brothers.[14] Yet, the interests of these companies were realized only with the formation of the municipality of Alexandria in 1869. Egyptian, Greek, and Jewish merchants dominated the municipal council, not the British. After the military occupation of 1882, the British community tended to cluster around the summer residence of the British consul on the hill above Stanley Bay. New suburbs were constructed in Ramleh, Bulkeley, and Mustapha Bey where typically British institutions were formed, such as the Alexandria Sporting Club founded by a British resident in 1890. There were few explicitly imperial monuments in Egypt, but the Alexandria municipality erected the Khartoum column commemorating Kitchener's victory. It was situated in a roundabout at the northwestern corner of the Shallalat Gardens. The column, the gardens, and the museum represented some of the cultural works supported by the predominately business-oriented municipality in the era of occupied Egypt.[15]

Although always a minority within the overall European colony, the British community rapidly increased its size after 1882. By 1897 the foreign population of Egypt had nearly doubled to 112,000, out of a total Egyptian population of 9,734,000. In the same period the number of Britons increased to 19,557.[16] The British community in Egypt was multinational, with large numbers of Maltese, as well as Indians and Cypriots, counted as British subjects. The population of Cairo in 1917 was divided nearly equally between the so-called 'in-land' (those born in Britain) and 'out-land'

---

[13] Laurence Grafftey-Smith, *Bright Levant* (London, 1966), 34.

[14] Middle East Centre Archives (MECA), St Antony's College, Oxford, GB 165-0246 35, Frederick Terry Rowlatt papers.

[15] E. M. Forster, *Alexandria: A History and Guide and Pharos and Pharillon* (London, 2004), 81, 129.

[16] *Egypt*, no. 1 (1898): *Reports on the finances, administration, and condition of Egypt, and the progress of reforms* (London, 1898), 651. The number of Britons given here included the army of occupation (4,909), the Maltese (6,463), and Indians (614).

British. The out-landers increased proportionally so that by the Second World War it was estimated that 60,000 Britons resided in Egypt, of whom 10,000 were 'in-land' Britons.[17] By 1917 most Britons lived in Cairo and Alexandria, with approximately a fifth residing in Ismailiyya, Suez, and Port Said. The British Army of Occupation was a significant percentage of the British resident population. It numbered around 5,000 in the years before 1914 and 10,000 strong between the two world wars.[18] Until the end of the Second World War most of the military installations were in Cairo, with the result that the city had the air of an armed camp even during peacetime. In wartime, the British presence was immense. A quarter of a million servicemen were based in Egypt during the First World War and approximately half a million British troops saw service in Egypt during the course of the Second World War. In 1941 there were 140,000 troops stationed in the vicinity of Cairo.[19] Moreover, Egypt was the frontline in both wars, with the construction of massive defences in the Eastern and Western Deserts respectively. The requisite infrastructure made the military presence a behemoth, with personnel drawn from all corners of the empire. Wars and military occupation altered the geography of Cairo. As one of the most important seats of British imperial power, a royal palace known as Qasr al-Nil (The Nile Palace) was converted into a British barracks at the time of the occupation. In addition, a substantial residence was completed for the British agent and consul general in 1893 and, near the residence and barracks, the Anglican All Saints Cathedral was completed in 1938. According to Edward Said, a resident of Cairo during the first half of the twentieth century, this complex of buildings—barracks, diplomatic residence, and cathedral—communicated 'a sense of monumental power and absolute confidence, which was so much the hallmark of the British presence in Egypt'.[20]

Before the First World War, most British lived on the east bank of the Nile in residential quarters such as Ezbekiyya, Abdin, Khalifa, and Matariyya.

[17] Bowen, *Many Histories Deep*, 207.

[18] Over 50,000 Australian, Indian, and New Zealander troops were stationed in Egypt, alongside the 42nd East Lancashire division upon the outbreak of the war in 1914. The figures for the interwar period are given in the National Archives (Kew) (TNA), FO 371/20125, 'Strength of the British Garrison in Egypt', Lampson, 14 Aug. 1936.

[19] Penelope Lively, *Oleander, Jacaranda: A Childhood Perceived* (London, 1994), 53, and Muhammad Hasanayn Haykal, *Sunday Times* (10 Sept. 1967), as cited by Mansfield, *British in Egypt*, 323.

[20] Edward W. Said, *Out of Place: A Memoir* (New York, 1999), 143.

A new suburb was developed on the island of Zamalek (known as Gezira) after the founding of the Gezira Sporting Club in 1886. The club included polo grounds, a race track, tennis courts, pool, and a golf course; and although in effect a quasi-British institution, the club was not exclusive. It was however elitist. Britons socialized with Egyptians of their own class. Polo and horse racing were familiar to the Egyptian elites; tennis was readily adopted. Elitism and class, rather than ethnicity and race, also defined the society of new suburbs like Zamalek and Garden City, the latter nearby the Residency, as well as Heliopolis, Helwan, and Ma'adi, which appeared on the periphery of Cairo in the early twentieth century. All of these districts were designed to reproduce the comforts and conveniences of 'home', although large numbers of the residents were Levantine and Egyptian, as well as European. In Cairo the Gezira Palace Hotel, the Continental, and the Savoy Hotel were constructed by the 1890s. These venues accommodated the balls, parties, and dinners of Cairo's cosmopolitan elite, which included British military officers, government officials, their families, as well as the throngs of tourists that came to Cairo during the 'season' from November to April. The oldest European hotel, Shepheard's, was rebuilt after the occupation and the old British residency was converted into the Turf Club. This club was founded on the British model of a gentleman's club for members only, with the rules restricting membership to British. There were also internationally renowned resorts: Mena House near the pyramids of Giza and the Grand Hotel in Helwan, favourite haunts of expatriate Britons. As one British official recalled of the years before the First World War, 'We lived in Cairo in an atmosphere of stability and security.'[21]

The Dominance of the Official Briton: 1882–1922

The consolidation of the British occupation occurred around the turn of the century. The idea of the exclusive British ruling caste was a legacy of this period. Cromer's financial reforms balanced Egypt's budgets and brought in new investors. By 1904 negotiations with the French resolved the bitter political controversy between those two countries—although it did not end their rivalry for commercial, bureaucratic, and cultural influence in Egypt. The number of Britons working as officers in the Egyptian government increased. Cromer's Egypt began to recruit personnel at Oxford and

---

[21] Derek Hopwood, *Tales of Empire: The British in the Middle East 1880–1952* (London, 1989), 9.

Cambridge, with successful candidates completing two terms of Arabic at Cambridge before coming to Egypt. At the same time, restrictions were placed upon admissions of Egyptians into the higher government schools in Egypt, limiting the pool of Egyptians qualified for positions in the administration. There were 455 Britons employed in the Egyptian civil service by 1898, most of them monopolizing the highest positions in the Egyptian administration.[22] In 1919 official Britons numbered 1,671.[23] According to Ronald Storrs, Cromer's policies brought about an unfortunate change in social relations between Britons and Egyptians. Whereas in the 1880s and 1890s Britons and Egyptians socialized on an equal footing, Cromer's expansion of the official British community meant that the officials grew increasingly aloof by the turn of the century. The larger number of officials, the extension of the club and sport system, and the 'mass production' of tourism resulted in 'less mixing with and understanding of Egyptians'.[24] Scion of a very prominent political family, Edward Cecil drew an infamous portrait of this exclusive community in *The Leisure of an Egyptian Official*. Cecil came to Egypt in 1890 because he seemed ill-prepared for a career in Britain. Living in an exile imposed by his family, estranged from his wife and children, who refused to bear the burdens imposed by imperial service, Cecil's recollections exposed the pomposity of British official circles without ever trumpeting the imperial mission.

We are very particular socially in Cairo. There is the swagger military set. There is the Egyptian army set; there is the smart official set; there is the smug official set. There is the smart professional set; there is the smug professional set, and so on. One may move in two or even several of these sets, but you belong to one.[25]

The growth of the official community, according to John Marlowe, made it 'unwieldy and inflexible, governed by prejudice rather than reason'.[26] Proving the point, Edward Cecil reviled and avoided social contact with Egyptians and as financial adviser avoided collaborating with Egyptian ministers. His book is thus a portrait of the prejudices of the British ruling caste. But to what

---

[22] *Egypt*, no. 3 (1899): *Report by Her Majesty's agent and Consul-General on the finances, administration, and condition of Egypt and the Soudan in 1898* (London, 1899), 1011.

[23] Barry Carman and John McPherson (eds.), *The Man Who Loved Egypt: Bimbashi McPherson* (London, 1983), 74.

[24] Ronald Storrs, *Orientations* (London, 1937), 91–4.

[25] Lord Edward Cecil, *The Leisure of an Egyptian Official* (London, 1921), 89.

[26] John Marlowe, *Anglo-Egyptian Relations 1800–1953* (London, 1954), 204.

degree is Cecil's attitude typical? One of Cromer's new recruits, Humphrey Bowman, arrived in Egypt in 1903 and moved into a flat in Cairo with four other Oxford men, attended by three servants, a cook, and two waiting men. Employed in the department of public instruction, Bowman's energies were engaged in gentlemanly pursuits at the club, the races, and shooting parties, while he desperately tried to find a higher position in the Egyptian administration. His leisure activities reflected the customs and habits of home. Christmas included champagne, singing by the piano, dancing, followed by punch, all of which 'reminded us more of Oxford than anything'.[27] Indeed, certain passages of Bowman's memoirs leave the impression that Britons in Egypt were largely men for whom empire had provided the opportunity to be, or at least aspire to be, 'English' gentlemen.

Without contradicting the general impression of British social exclusivity, Bowman's memoirs certainly suggest that this view is an over-simplification. Bowman learnt Arabic and took an interest in ancient Egyptian history—the craze of all the 'callous' tourists—but also in Islamic history and Egyptian popular culture. In his private journals he complained that this could hardly be said of 'one in a hundred' of his fellow Britons in Cairo where 'splendid specimens of Arabic and Saracenic art surrounds one literally'.[28] Showing an almost ethnographic interest in Egyptian popular culture, Bowman was a keen observer of the modern multicultural character of Egypt. His encounter with a British youth participating in a football match at the Abbasiyya School illuminated the diversity of the British community in Egypt. The boy's widowed mother worked in a Christian seminary. But she placed her son in an Egyptian state school so that, the boy said, he could be educated in Arabic and English. Bowman remarked that it was 'funny seeing him don his tarboosh' and watch him 'go off in company with about 800 Egyptians—to all appearances one of them'.[29] Bowman observed that the boy's 'Englishness' persisted through his prowess on the football pitch. Yet, indicating the hybridity of the cultural milieu, this 'English' sport was avidly pursued by Egyptians. Certainly, Bowman's commentary suggests that social and cultural boundaries were blurred and that the British community was much more complex than a portrait of the Oxbridge men of officialdom might suggest.

---

[27] MECA, GB 165-0034, Humphrey Bowman papers, box 3, letter, 1 Jan. 1905.

[28] Bowman papers, box 3, letter, 8 Jan. 1905.

[29] Bowman papers, box 3, letter, 1 Jan. 1905.

Another representative of the new cadre of officials, Thomas Russell, followed his cousin Percy Machell into the Egyptian service in 1902. Russell was impressed by his cousin's 'high sense of duty', both to the empire and the Egyptian government. Unlike Cecil's wife, Dorothea Russell joined her husband in Cairo. Their two children were born in England but brought up in a Cairo household that included an English nanny, an English maid, a cook, and three Egyptian servants. Thomas Russell's leisure hours were spent riding, hunting, and gardening, while his wife pursued her interest in Cairo's mosques and great houses (she wrote a book on the subject).[30] His view of imperial service was significant because he was clearly inspired by the mission to 'civilize'. Yet, for Russell this did not mean an unwavering loyalty to British authorities in Egypt, because he saw himself as a public servant of a reformist Egyptian government. This is a central theme in Ronald Seth's treatment of Russell's career in *Russell Pasha*. Seth asserts that Egyptian politicians of all parties regarded him as 'an impartial friend and adviser who put the general good of Egypt before anything else'.[31] One can gauge the distance between Russell and British agents at the residency during the nationalist demonstrations of 1906. Russell (then an inspector in the Ministry of Interior) noted that nationalism created 'some excitement in the House [the Residency] with the Boyles [a reference to Cromer's Oriental Secretary, Harry Boyle] & Co it's a nasty eye opener for everyone. We in the districts have always disbelieved in the theory of the "dear native".'[32] With this observation Russell kicked the feet out from under a central prop of Cromer's theory of imperial rule, which was that the Egyptian *fellahin* were securely wrapped in a hermetic agricultural world and content as long as British technical expertise ensured the steady flow of Nile waters and not too excessive taxes.

Russell was hardly more impressed with Cromer's successor, Sir Eldon Gorst, of whose policy Russell remarked, 'It's pretty certain to be "Egypt for the Egyptians". The interesting thing will be to see if possible from his face whether he really believes it himself. No one does but we must do as we are told.'[33] His observations suggest that, far from being a caste, the official community did not simply follow the lead of the British agent and consul

---

[30] Ronald Seth, *Russell Pasha* (London, 1966), 20–1, and Thomas Russell, *Egyptian Service* (London, 1949).

[31] Russell, *Egyptian Service*, 171.

[32] MECA, GB 165-0247, Thomas Russell papers, letter, 7 July 1906.

[33] Russell papers, letter, 30 Oct. 1907.

general but acted as a constituency with its own power and influence. Many official Britons considered Gorst's policy 'weak'.[34] The community particularly resented Gorst's custom of inviting Egyptians to the residency for social occasions, not because this was a novelty, but as it was practised almost to the exclusion of Britons. There was a concern that a policy of appeasing the nationalists would undermine the interests of the British colony. Initially these criticisms were voiced at the Turf Club, yet they were repeated by tourists and found an echo in London. Rumours of discontent were at least partly responsible for a loss of confidence in Gorst's policy.[35] Similarly, members of the official community blamed Sir Reginald Wingate, High Commissioner 1917–19, for 'encouraging Native nationalist aspirations' during the First World War. Wingate complained to the Foreign Office of the 'growing unrest on the part of the British Officials'.[36] Again in 1920, the official community responded with dismay after Milner's recommendations for Egyptian self-government were leaked. Bowman reported that 'there's no doubt that the reforms are far more sweeping than the majority of people of either country anticipated'.[37]

Social relations between Britons and Egyptians were about to change; nevertheless, in September 1920 we find Bowman lunching at Shepheard's with Muhammad Mahmud, who was a prominent member of the nationalist delegation (Wafd) engaged in negotiations with Milner. Mahmud confided to Bowman that the talks in London had been conducted in a 'friendly spirit', but that Egyptian nationalist opinion had triumphed with Milner's admission that a 'radical change' had to be made in the imperial system in Egypt. Bowman probably expressed the opinion of most official Britons when he wrote in his diary, 'What is to happen to us?'[38]

Relations with Egyptians

Memoirs indicate that British attitudes underwent a profound change after the First World War. John Young remarked that the 'stability and the security' of pre-war Cairo had been shattered by the national revolt of

---

[34] Storrs, *Orientations*, 77.
[35] Ibid. 82.
[36] Both complaints cited in C. W. R. Long, *British Pro-Consuls in Egypt, 1914–1929* (London, 2005), 69.
[37] Bowman papers, box 3B, diaries, 16 Sept. 1920.
[38] Ibid.

1919. Young, like others, was unsettled by the Egyptian nationalist assaults upon Britons (forty Britons died in 1919) and the British reaction (as many as 1,000 Egyptians died). To restore order General Edmund Allenby was appointed high commissioner. But the Milner Mission set the stage for reform, which Allenby ultimately supported. The unilateral declaration of Egyptian independence in 1922 and the election of a government led by the Wafd in 1924 undermined the privileged position of the British in the Egyptian government service. The number of British in the Egyptian government declined and, thus, British officials ceased to dominate government as had been the case before the war. Young's memoirs indicate that the advance of the nationalists marked an important turning point in the life of the British community in Egypt. 'I elected to go in 1924 and wisely for I saw that Zaghloul [the leader of the Wafd] was anxious that the first Department to be cleared of British control should be the Inspectorate of the Interior.'[39]

Herbert Addison was representative of an unofficial British community, composed of business people, cotton brokers, bankers, teachers, clerical workers, as well as engineers and laborers employed in the maritime and railway transport industry. British women not occupied as wives and mothers were largely engaged as teachers, as nannies, or in domestic service. Addison, who was recruited to teach in Egypt by an Egyptian studying in Manchester, arrived in Cairo in 1921 in the midst of the treaty negotiations between Lord Curzon and 'Adli Yakan Pasha. After these talks failed late in that year the more radical nationalists renewed a campaign of assassinating British residents in Egypt. Addison recalled that 'Club circles' in Cairo blamed Allenby's 'weakness' for these attacks. On 2 January 1923 1,500 official and unofficial Britons assembled at Shepheard's Hotel in what was intended as a formal protest against Allenby's policies. However, opinion at the meeting was mixed. For his part, Addison did not censure Allenby. He concluded that Allenby's unilateral declaration of 1922 succeeded in diverting Egyptians towards more 'orthodox political action' and ultimately restored good relations between British and Egyptians.[40] For Addison, the more radical nationalists were but one voice in a 'multi-racial society'. Addison identified cosmopolitan Egypt with the internationalism of the

[39] MECA, GB 165-0310, John Young, 'A Little to the East: Experiences of an Anglo-Egyptian Official 1899–1925', unpublished manuscript, fo. 15.

[40] MECA, GB 165-0002, Herbert Addison papers, 'Engineers Sustain Egypt', in 'The Pleasures of Anglo-Egyptian Co-operation', unpublished manuscript, fos. 7–8.

post-war era. He remarked that 'the conditions that idealists dream about today—though with less and less conviction—were visible for all of us to see in Cairo'. As for social relations, Addison remarked upon the 'tolerance' of the Egyptians, noting that foreigners were allowed social and commercial freedom—the largest shops (mostly Jewish owned) were open on the Muslim holy day. Addison remarked, 'Anyone could go into Shepheard's if he seemed to be appropriately dressed, in a summer suit, in a dark suit, in white tie and tails, in the uniform of an Egyptian or a British army officer, or what was then beginning to be described as National dress—cloak and turban, agal and kuffieh.' Unlike southern Africa, class, rather than race, was the important social indicator in Egypt.[41]

Addison highlighted the inclusive, rather than exclusive, character of colonial Egypt. Although his arguments might be viewed as an apology for empire, Addison's recollections certainly suggest that a high degree of interaction between the 'nations' fitted the colonial milieu and the neo-colonial status quo of the interwar period. Moreover, the war bred a sense of disillusion or even scepticism towards imperialism and extreme forms of nationalism. E. M. Forster volunteered for Red Cross work in Egypt during the First World War, principally so that he could avoid conscription. In exile from Britain, his observations of Alexandria suggest that he identified neither with empire nor Egypt. Forster observed that Alexandria's society had become less cosmopolitan since 1882 and that after 1922 Egyptian national governments erased vestiges of the European presence, such as place names.[42] Although he did not overtly support the nationalists, he felt no particular regret for such changes. For him, nationalism and imperialism were equally lamentable manifestations of modern change. Instead, he identified with the classical city buried beneath the European and 'Arab' quarters.[43] Identification with the classical past was, for him, a badge of his self-imposed exile from Britain. Forster envisaged the ancient city of Alexandria as a symbol of a classical society 'destroyed' by the Arabs. 'Though they had no intention of destroying her, they destroyed her, as a child might a watch. She never functioned again properly for over a 1,000 years.'[44] This observation reproduces the imperial motif of the civilizing

---

[41] Herbert Addison, 'Egypt and its Universities', in 'The Pleasures of Anglo-Egyptian Co-operation', fos. 4–5.

[42] Forster, *Alexandria*, 82.

[43] Ibid. 103.

[44] As cited by Lawrence Durrell, *Justine* (London, 1961), 253.

mission, since, according to Forster's logic, the arrival of European modernity reactivated the city. Certainly, Forster sometimes expressed chauvinist attitudes.[45] His image of classical Alexandria was typical of Orientalist thought, which imagined an Orient, rather than engaging with the peoples and cultures. Yet he took an Egyptian lover. Egypt was a refuge, in a political and emotional sense. Thus when his lover was beaten by British soldiers and subsequently fell ill, Forster engaged in a press campaign against the political injustices of the wartime British regime.[46]

Although an altogether different type of personality, the wartime memoirs of John de Vere Loder illuminate the impact the Egyptian setting had upon British identities. A young officer in the British army, Loder served in Gallipoli and afterwards convalesced in Alexandria. Like Forster he initially found Alexandria a disappointment, 'It is not really an Egyptian city. The greatest peculiarity is the extraordinary mixture of races. Most people speak English of a sort.'[47] He contrasted Alexandria to Cairo. The latter, he said, was an 'Arab city and the best sights are Arabic'.[48] These attitudes changed as he established social relationships with Egyptians. He was soon enraptured with Alexandria's grand avenues, villas, and gardens. A villa nearby his quarters was occupied by a wealthy cotton-growing family from the southern province of Asyut. The family spent their summer evenings playing tennis and sitting on the verandah. Invited into their garden by the men, Loder noticed the relative seclusion imposed upon the daughters, yet their governess was British. Their customs, habits, manners, and sports were British. Indeed they had, he wrote, acquired 'a very tolerable English imitation considering the fact that most of them have never been to England'.[49]

Loder was later appointed to the wartime intelligence bureau at the residency in Cairo, where his social life involved a constant round of dinners, dances, balls, and theatre. At the Continental Hotel Lady Allenby held a weekly 'dansant' for off-duty soldiers. Loder wryly observed that invitations to these events were restricted to 'unattractive English womanhood' to ensure that the officers were not enticed by Levantine 'beauties'.[50]

---

[45] Mary Lago and P. N. Furbank (eds.), *Selected Letters of E. M. Forster*, i. *1879–1920* (Cambridge, Mass., 1983), and E. M. Forster, *Pharos and Pharillon* (London, 1967), 73–8.

[46] Forster, *Alexandria*, pp. lviii–lix.

[47] MECA, GB 165-0184, John de Vere Loder papers, memoirs, 28 July 1915.

[48] Ibid., 29 Feb. 1916.

[49] Ibid., 24 July 1916.

[50] Ibid., 17 Jan. 1918.

In letters home, Loder teased his mother that he would surely succumb to the temptations of the Levant. In reply his mother sent stern warnings not to do so.[51] Yet Loder noticed a subtle change in his cultural habits and attitudes: 'My only amusement is to know all sorts and kinds of people and to go out to tea and have drinks with them. It doesn't sound a very high ideal but then I am getting to be quite a passable Levantine now.'[52] In a most cosmopolitan way, Loder absorbed new cultural sensibilities and habits—a process of deracination that dissolved some of the certainties of his 'British' identity. For sure, it was a constant concern among the leaders of the British community that the Egyptian setting would sap the patriotic resolve of Britons during wartime.[53] Thomas Russell noted that most people took little interest in the war because Egypt was 'such a mixed nationality place'.[54] Stern measures were required to maintain morale. The wartime high commissioners, Sir Henry Macmahon and Sir Reginald Wingate, banned the drinking of alcohol at the residency.[55]

Loder's example suggest that Britons in Egypt were drawn towards other cultures, whether 'native' or 'Levantine'. He found amusing—and perhaps pathetic—attempts of those like Lady Allenby to preserve intact British identity and social propriety. She was not unique. Committees formed by British women in Cairo, and elsewhere, typically vetted invitations to social events.[56] The tension between cultural immersion and cultural purity was recurring. Issues relating to women were particularly sensitive. It was a feature of British society in Egypt that young British women came to Egypt during the season seeking husbands among the relatively well-off British officials. Egyptian men lingering on the terraces of fashionable hotels in Cairo and Alexandria courted these women also. Encounters on the terraces did not usually result in marriage.[57] Indicating the significance of class, rather than racial boundaries, marriages between upper-class Egyptian

---

[51] MECA, GB 165-0184, John de Vere Loder papers, memoirs, 20 Aug. 1917.
[52] Ibid., 1 July 1917.
[53] Mansfield, *British in Egypt*, 212.
[54] Seth, *Russell Pasha*, 130.
[55] 'Residence', edited version of Janet Boyce's booklet, *Bayt al-Lurd*, July 2001, on 'UK in Egypt', URL: <http://ukinegypt.fco.gov.uk/en/our-offices-in-egypt/our-ambassador/residence>, accessed 2 Dec. 2009.
[56] MECA, GB 165-0233, Thomas Rapp papers, 'Memoirs of Sir Thomas Rapp', unpublished manuscript, fo. 14, and Grafftey-Smith, *Bright Levant*, 112, notes that 'our matriarchs' guarded the 'enclosed social garden' of British society.
[57] Mansfield, *British in Egypt*, 318.

men and British women were acceptable, if hardly normal. Indeed, for some Egyptians marrying a Briton marked entry into British social circles on an equal footing. Marriages between British men and Egyptian women were not common, although British soldiers and workers in Egypt often married Levantine women. For some consular officials, this was viewed as an inevitable, if unfortunate, consequence of empire.

According to Thomas Rapp, who served as a consul in Suez and Cairo between 1921 and 1953, British men usually abandoned their local wives, whether Levantine or Egyptian, and, bereft of social support, such women, who of course carried British passports, fell upon the care of British charitable institutions. British women frequently enquired at the consulate about marrying Egyptian men and sometimes these marriages turned out happily, especially, as Rapp said, when the couples had similar educational and cultural backgrounds. There is no sense in Rapp's commentary that social or cultural 'equivalence' was in any way precluded by the colonial milieu.[58] In a somewhat different commentary, John Young regarded such marriages as a social ill to be cured rather than tolerated, particularly if these marriages involved lower class people. When it was reported to him that a British woman was living in a provincial village he concluded, with little evidence, that life with her Egyptian husband must be one of poverty, regular beatings, and drudgery, in short, as a kind of imprisonment in an Arab-speaking Muslim society. It is hardly surprising therefore that Young reported the case to the consulate and the woman was deported back to Britain, 'saving' her from her chosen fate.[59] Rapp also commented on cases where 'British girls' had married Egyptians, usually when they were students in England, and had found the conditions of life to which they were now exposed 'intolerable'.[60] As for those women who acquired a British passport through marriage, Rapp said that many fell on 'evil times' after being abandoned by their husbands. An Anglican nun, Sister Margaret Clare, was especially devoted to such cases. Evidently, Rapp and Young had somewhat different attitudes towards cross-cultural social relations. Rapp was indifferent, whereas Young's commentary reflected a quasi-official view that marriages between British and Egyptian posed a threat to the British community's sense of cultural supremacy and civilizing mission. This divergence in attitudes might be generational: Young quit the Egyptian service in 1925,

---

[58] Rapp, 'Memoirs of Sir Thomas Rapp', 37.
[59] Young, *A Little to the East*, 'Early Days of the War in Egypt', 1–3.
[60] Rapp, 'Memoirs of Sir Thomas Rapp', 37.

whereas Rapp joined the British consular service after the First World War and remained in Egypt until 1953.

The recollections of Young and Rapp reveal a side of colonial life far removed from the ruling caste. According to Rapp the indiscipline of the era was partly the result of the war, although he noted that social unrest was a characteristic of the expatriate abroad well into the post-war period. Sex trades, drug trafficking, and addiction were endemic. Government regulations ensured the legal operation of safe brothels near the Ezbekiyya quarter of Cairo and the Ramleh district in Alexandria, where most European shops and hotels were located. Sometimes viewed as an example of the way Egyptians were forced to serve European masters, the sex trade in Cairo was carried out by both Egyptians and Europeans (British women were prohibited). In Cairo the Wasa'a district was under government medical authority and largely operated by Egyptian gangs, whereas European prostitutes worked in the Wigh al-Birka district, as well as in the vicinity of Ezbekiyya. The sex trade during wartime was notorious. It was estimated that during the two world wars sexually transmitted diseases caused as many casualties among British troops as did armed conflict.[61] Drugs represented another threat to the prestige of the British colony.[62] According to Rapp, the British soldier was an easy prey for shady drug dealers. Some of these turned to drug trafficking and were subsequently prosecuted and deported by the British authorities. In the 1920s cocaine and heroin replaced the 'less harmful hashish, hitherto the traditional dope, whose import from Lebanon was now being rigorously suppressed'. Rapp recalled that many of his 'weaker brethren'—the 'tragic casualties of the East'—succumbed to 'Cairo's temptations'. In any case, Cairo was a likely sink pot for Britons involved in drugs. As Rapp said, the sordid lifestyles of drug 'casualties' contrasted strikingly with the imperial sporting life at the clubs.[63]

As commandant of Cairo's police force, Russell was familiar with the drug business and its victims. His chief concern was however the impact of drugs upon the Egyptian population. Russell's views reflect the prevalent culture of 'civilization', wherein drug addiction was regarded as a peculiarly Eastern vice. Yet he lamented that it was exploited by European drug traffickers who

[61] Rapp, 'Memoirs of Sir Thomas Rapp', 14, and Mansfield, *British in Egypt*, 214, where he notes that 12% of the Egyptian Expeditionary Force had venereal disease in 1916.

[62] Bolton, *Personal Landscapes*, 57–8.

[63] Rapp, 'Memoirs of Sir Thomas Rapp', 20–1, 30–7.

were shielded from Egyptian law enforcers (like Russell) by the consular courts. This was also true of the European prostitution rings.[64] Forster on the other hand highlighted an altogether different attitude, which was equally typical of the British overseas. In his article 'The Den' he described his quest to uncover a hash den, which he considered a necessary element of the Oriental tour.[65] The only den he found was one run by a British expatriate from Malta. Forster's disappointment was increased when shortly afterwards the establishment was shut down, doubtless as a result of Russell's war on the 'drug barons'.[66] Forster resented this as yet another sign of the encroachment of a crass modernity. Russell's attitudes represent the imperial mission to 'civilize' the Egyptians, while Forster indulged in dangerous exoticism. Forster reminds us that drink, drugs, and loose sexual mores were the legendary attributes of the 'bar-propped cosmopolitan' and perhaps just as typical of the imperial diaspora as were the duty-bound servants of empire. Thus, alongside the figures of Russell there was the world-weary and indifferent servant of empire, who, in the poetry of G. S. Fraser, 'likes to hear the news from home in letters / But readily returns to his wastes'.[67]

This kind of cosmopolitan disconnectedness from 'home' contrasts with the equally legendary exclusivity of British expatriate society, with all its emphasis upon maintaining a distinctly British identity. Mansfield's portrayal of social segregation suggests that the community was deeply racial and paternalistic in its relations with Egyptians, as reflected in offensive terms such as 'wog' and *walad* (boy).[68] According to this theory, relations between Britons and Egyptians followed the pattern of master and servant. In the official world Egyptians were obliged to carry out the orders of British superiors. Outside government, social relations often took a similar form. In private homes, on railways, restaurants, hotels, clubs, and tourist sites, Egyptians served Europeans. Memoirs suggest that relations between British and Egyptians were somewhat more complicated, combining elements of intimacy and servitude. While acting as an inspector in Egypt before the First World War, Alexander Keown-Boyd engaged an Egyptian corporal

---

[64] Seth, *Russell Pasha*, 169–95.

[65] Forster, *Pharos and Pharillon*, 79–81.

[66] Ibid. 81, and Seth, *Russell Pasha*, 169.

[67] G. S. Fraser, 'Letter from Asmara, May 1943', cited by Bolton, *Personal Landscapes*, 112.

[68] John Marlowe, *Cromer in Egypt* (London, 1970), 228, and Humphrey Bowman, *Middle East Window* (London, 1942), 40.

(*ombashi*) as his official orderly and as his domestic man-servant (*suffragi*).
Known only as 'Ahmed', he remained in the employ of the Keown-Boyd
household for a half century. Ahmed exerted considerable influence over
the domestic household. Keown-Boyd's son Henry recalled, 'Ahmed was
certainly one of my earliest memories'. His father and Ahmed had a 'curious
relationship as I do not think I ever heard them address a word to each
other... When my father died Ahmed wept... Was he mourning a beloved
master and friend or a meal-ticket? Who knows—perhaps both.' Afterwards, Ahmed transferred his loyalty to Henry. And although he served
the family through two generations, 'when things looked bad for the British
during the 1956 Suez crisis he disappeared and I never saw or heard of him
again'.[69] From the same generation of post-war Britons growing up in
Egypt, Penelope Lively recalled that her parents' household contained a
British governess, an Egyptian *suffragi*, cook, gardeners, and a youth. She
compared social relations in the colonial household to those of Edwardian
England.[70] Servants and children inhabited a social sphere far removed
from masters or parents, which meant that Lively's most intimate relations
were with the Egyptian servants gathering in the kitchen or back steps. She
was relatively secluded from social contact with other British children.
Perhaps because of this, her parents employed a governess to instruct her
on British history and customs. Yet, Lively recorded that she never felt
comfortable or secure in her 'Englishness'.[71] Expatriate life involved a
persistent effort to sustain a British identity against alienation and exile.
Lively's and Keown-Boyd's recollections suggest that relations between
British and Egyptians combined elements of intimacy and mastery/servi-
tude. For these expatriates, Egypt was more than a station in the imperial
system where British and Egyptians were harnessed to the yoke of empire.
Each experienced a richly layered social and cultural milieu, wherein exclusivity was reaction, not an unchanging norm. In public Britons had to guard
against any innuendo of having 'gone native', just as Egyptians hid their
close associations with Britons to avoid the stigma of collaboration.[72] But it

---

[69] MECA, GB 165-0167, Alexander Keown-Boyd papers, box 1, file 3, 'TS Memoir by Henry
Keown-Boyd of his father's orderly Ahmed'.
[70] Lively, *Oleander, Jacaranda*, 37.
[71] Ibid. 18–25.
[72] Grafftey-Smith, *Bright Levant*, 92–5, 113.

is debatable to what degree racial attitudes predominated. Henry Keown-Boyd argued that racialism was typical of some, notably British soldiers. The infamous racial insult endured by Muhammad Mahmud at the Gezira Sporting Club was made by a subaltern in the British army.[73] Penelope Lively also recalled that soldiers displayed extreme xenophobia during the Second World War, but this differed from the attitudes of British professional classes. They had learnt that such sentiments should never be openly expressed.[74]

The world wars accentuated racial and cultural tensions, whereas social interaction increased in the interwar years as more Egyptians, men and women, were educated in foreign schools.[75] As a result, British and middle- or upper-class Egyptians often shared a common set of values, forged at the schools, clubs, and other cultural institutions that actively encouraged cultural exchange. The British Council was created in the interwar years to ensure British 'cultural expansion'.[76] Another venue for British culture was at the new Egyptian university in Cairo, where Robert Graves took the first post as professor of English, followed by the likes of Malcolm Muggeridge, Robin Fedden, Bernard Spencer, Denys Johnson-Davies, and Martin Lings. The milieu was cosmopolitan. The German linguist J. Schacht taught Arabic and Islamic subjects in the university, as did the renowned Egyptian scholar, 'Ali 'Abd al-Raziq, and the French scholar of Islamic mysticism, Louis Massignon. Schools and other cultural institutions were regarded as a way to cement friendly relations with a new generation of Egyptians.

Edward Said's memoirs connect the educational system with cultural supremacy, reminiscent of his analysis in *Orientalism*. He attended Victoria College, which was founded in 1901 by the British residents of Alexandria. The purpose of the college was to inculcate British values in the British and non-British students. The 'English School' was more exclusive, founded in 1914 under the patronage of Edward Cecil specifically for the education of

[73] MECA, GB 165-0295, Gordon Waterfield papers, box 5, letter, Delany to Waterfield, 27 Jan. 1974. Delany recalled the incident in the Gezira Sporting Club when a young army officer in the dressing room turned to a fellow subaltern, and within the hearing of Mahmud asked, 'Who is the bloody nigger?' Mahmud ceased to use the club for many years, not returning in fact until he became prime minister.

[74] Lively, *Oleander, Jacaranda*, 54.

[75] Young, *A Little to the East*, 'Introduction', 3–4.

[76] MECA, GB 165-0115, Sir Robert Allason Furness papers, box 3, folder 2, letter from British Council to Furness, 22 Sept. 1937.

children of 'British in-land or Dominion parentage'. Candidates of non-British parentage were accepted, but limited to 20 per cent of the student body. Lord Lloyd led the campaign to enlarge and fund new buildings for this school, laying the foundation stone of a new building in March 1938.[77] Said recalled of the English school system that British staff taught English history and literature to instill within the children identification with 'home' and pride in the empire, although the students were composed of diverse national groups, including Egyptians.[78] At Victoria College the first rule was a ban on the speaking of Arabic. And although most of the students were not British, Britons staffed the administrative and teaching posts, except for the instructors of Arabic and French. The curriculum was similar to preparatory schools in Britain. In his memoirs Said showed that by defining 'home' in terms of a faraway island that few in the classroom had ever visited the schools imparted more a sense of dislocation than belonging. Said clearly enjoyed the irony of Omar Sharif lording it over the other schoolboys at Victoria College, his ridicule and insults delivered in the best of British accents.[79] Of Egyptian parentage, Omar Sharif of course played the archetypal 'Arab' in *Lawrence of Arabia*. Although inverted, the sense of cultural dislocation experienced by Said and Sharif was experienced by many Britons.

During the Second World War the British became increasingly anxious about their imperial roles. In her *Levant Trilogy* Olivia Manning gives a fictional account of her exile in Egypt during the war when her husband taught at the British Council. It is interesting to contrast her impression of British attitudes to the imperial mind-set portrayed by Said. Her husband's fictional counterpart, Guy Pringle, felt that by teaching English literature and language he 'had been peddling the idea of empire to a country that only wanted one thing, to be rid of the British for good and all. And to add to the absurdity of the situation, he had himself no belief in the empire.'[80] The juxtaposition of Said's account of frustrated, silenced students and Manning's perturbed English instructor suggests a dialogue, albeit muted, wherein Egyptians and Britons confronted very similar doubts and uncertainties.

---

[77] 'The English School', *The Egyptian Gazette* (12 Mar. 1938), 2.

[78] Said, *Out of Place*, 36–45.

[79] Ibid. 200–1.

[80] Olivia Manning, *The Levant Trilogy* (London, 2003), 513–14, and Phyllis Lassner, *Colonial Strangers: Women Writing the End of the British Empire* (London, 2004), 37.

Lawrence Durrell was a product of the imperial diaspora. Born in India he went to school in England, but reviled contemporary British culture and sought refuge in Greece before the Second World War. After the Nazi invasion, he escaped to Egypt. Durrell met other poets in the garden of the Anglo-Egyptian Union, a cultural organization in Zamalek created by the British Council to promote dialogue between British and Egyptians. Egyptians were marginal at the Union. Nevertheless Durrell and other wartime poets, such as Bernard Spencer, Robin Fedden, Robert Liddell, and Terence Tiller, explicitly rejected the propaganda and extreme nationalism of wartime Britain.[81] The most well-known of the wartime poets, Keith Douglas and G. S. Fraser, were poets of exile. Douglas saw Egypt as decadent, a wasteland of profiteers and prostitutes, which replicated typical Orientalist representations. Yet in his 'Cairo Jag' and Fraser's 'Monologue for a Cairo Evening' the outrage of the tourist is mixed with, if not entirely replaced by, the bemusement of the seasoned expatriate.[82] Likewise, Durrell's portrait of cosmopolitan society in the *Alexandria Quartet* captured the anxiety of a colonial city in an African setting, its sense of impermanence, which was symbolically represented by Alexandria's classical heritage. But Durrell's writings also dealt with the problem of cosmopolitanism and nationalism, for instance contrasting the richness of cosmopolitan society in Alexandria to the austerity of Zionism in Palestine, with its commitment to duty and community service, as well as its immersion of the individual in the folk life or communalism of the nation.[83] In Durrell's narrative twentieth-century nationalism destroyed the archetypal cosmopolitan city, as represented by the hero of the first novel in his quartet, *Justine*. Like Forster and the wartime poets, Durrell's poetry and fiction expressed a sense of disappointed exoticism wherein Egypt—'ash heap of four cultures'— represented the terminal point of the British empire.[84]

Imperial Power and the British Community: 1922–1956

While the official British community dwindled in size after 1922, the establishment of the British Council, the Anglo-Egyptian Union, and the con-

---

[81] Bowen, *Many Histories Deep*, 40–1.
[82] Ibid. 33, 78.
[83] Forster, as cited by Durrell, *Justine*, 241–3.
[84] Bowen, *Many Histories Deep*, 148, 159, 164.

struction of the Anglican cathedral and the new English school suggest that
the British community was far from declining. It was changing. The official
Briton no longer dominated. The leaders of the community included
business, religious, scientific, educational, as well as military and diplomatic
persons. A new generation of Britons shaped by the First World War often
seemed indifferent to the empire's fate. Robert Graves's *Goodbye to All That*
expressed that disillusion; aptly, he sums up his account of wartime Britain
with an unblinking appraisal of Britain's cultural and political mission in
Egypt.[85] Of the same generation, Thomas Rapp remarked that after the war
Britons lacked the determination to maintain imperial rule.[86]

These tendencies were however resisted by an imperial old guard. In 1919
a 'British Union' was formed to represent the British community in Egypt.
Its report to the Milner Mission in 1920 demanded that the residency stem
'terrorism and disorder', assure 'security of life and property', and restore
British 'prestige'. In a critical assessment of the residency's policies, members
of the non-official British community called for a restoration of the type of
control characteristic of Cromer and Kitchener.[87] A critic of the British
Union's politics, Gerald Delany, argued that, as 'an old Egyptian official',
Milner had never thought of Egypt as an 'integral part of the British
Empire'.[88] Milner's proposals were not a radical departure from imperial
traditions, according to Delany, but restored British and Egyptian relations
to one of equal partners, which, he said, had always been the basis of
Britain's power and influence in Egypt.[89] These positions—imperial mastery versus equitable partnership—sum up the political dynamics of the
interwar period.

According to Delany, British ministers in post-war governments and a
large section of public opinion were astonished that Milner, whose imperialism was thought to be unimpeachable, should have proposed the surrender of Egyptian territory. When it fell to high commissioner Edmund
Allenby to implement Milner's policy he had, Delany claimed, to contend

---

[85] Robert Graves, *Goodbye to All That* (London, 2000), 264–378.

[86] Rapp, 'Memoirs of Sir Thomas Rapp', 41.

[87] TNA, FO 141/581, 'British Union in Egypt: Cairo Non-Official British Community: Views
on Egyptian Political Situation'; letter, Allenby to Curzon, 19 Apr. 1919, with Deputation and
Resolutions; 'Report of the Council of Cairo Non-Official British Community to the British
Mission of Enquiry'.

[88] Waterfield papers, box 5, 'Spender and Egypt by Gerald Delany'.

[89] Waterfield papers, box 5, letter, Delany to Waterfield, 28 Jan. 1964.

with the 'hostile attitude' of the 'British community at large'.[90] In particular Delany pointed to 'business people' in Egypt who 'disliked Allenby's policy of concessions to the Egyptians' and were connected to influential political circles in Britain.[91] Led by K. C. Beasley, an investor controlling 24,000 feddans of land in Egypt, the British Union protested against Allenby's proposal that criminal jurisdiction over Britons be handed over to the Egyptian government after independence. The British Union demanded that the 'rights of British subjects now existing under consular jurisdiction' be maintained.[92] In 1922 the British Union openly attacked Allenby and his closest advisers, claiming that they had failed to win the confidence of the British community: 'It is obvious there is a lack of the deeper knowledge of the problem, ability to see through the manoeuvers of Orientals, and above all strength of purpose.'[93] This memo was forwarded to Winston Churchill, who circulated it to members of the cabinet. Another meeting of the British community was planned in March 1923, when the British Union called for the creation of a committee to advise the residency, which was to be composed of members of the non-official community.[94] The Union's campaign against Allenby continued until he resigned in 1925.[95]

The unofficial community thus had a political voice and some influence to counter the reforms envisaged by Milner and Allenby. The appointment of Lord Lloyd in 1925 was regarded as a victory for the British Union and a restoration of the authoritarian style of imperial control characteristic of Cromer and Kitchener. Lloyd's retrenchment of British power was comprehensive. He resisted French and later German attempts to infiltrate the government services, as well as putting a brake on the nationalist campaign to reduce British numbers in government services. At the same time the Foreign Office reorganized its staff in Cairo.[96] Lloyd frustrated treaty negotiations by alienating Egyptian nationalist politicians, beginning with Sa'd Zaghlul, while mobilizing the British business community against any more

---

[90] Waterfield papers, box 5, letter, Delany to Waterfield, 11 Oct. 1973.

[91] Waterfield papers, box 5, 'Addendum' to the Lloyd Manuscript by Gerald Delany.

[92] TNA, FO 141/581, Kingsford to Allenby, 8 Dec. 1921.

[93] TNA, FO 141/581, 'Copy of Memorandum sent on 2 February by British Union in Egypt'.

[94] TNA, FO 141/581, 'Minutes of First Meeting of the British Union Advisory Committee held at the Residency on Weds the 7th March, 1923'.

[95] TNA, FO 141/581, 'The Egyptian Question', signed by Kingsford, Cairo, July 1924.

[96] Maurice Amos resigned and returned to Britain. Reginald Furness eventually resigned and took up a post at the university in Cairo.

concessions. When Percy Lorraine replaced Lloyd, after the victory of the Labour Party in 1929, the business community gave him a 'sullen reception'.[97]

The uncompromising imperialists scored with the appointment of Lord Killearn as high commissioner in January 1934. He remarked that the 'best form of permanent relationship with Egypt lay in her incorporation in some form in the British Empire'.[98] While political circumstances forced him to negotiate rather than dictate terms to the Egyptians in 1936, Killearn's interventionist style resulted in poor relations with the Egyptian royal family. He challenged King Faruq's decision to dismiss the leader of the Wafd Party, Nahas, in 1937 and forced the resignation of the king's favourite, 'Ali Mahir, in 1939. In 1942 he threatened the throne itself. Not only was Killearn intolerant of Egyptian political opinion, but he cared little about the opinion of the British community. As he observed in 1935, 'The plain fact is that nothing can ever be done quite right here in the eyes of the [British] community—not that it matters a hoot.'[99] His primary concern was Egypt as a strategic asset to the British empire. Relations with Egyptians and the British community were secondary. Killearn had the support of British businesspeople in Egypt and, by consulting regularly with its leading figures he was able to pose as the guardian of the British community and the guarantor of Britain's commercial future in the Middle East.[100]

Soured relations between Egypt and Britain cannot be credited solely to the attitudes of high commissioners and the British business community. The Second World War was catastrophic for the neo-colonial order of things. The movement of half a million troops through Egypt during the war transformed Cairo and Alexandria. Norman Mayers, a diplomatic official, observed that Cairo's city centre resembled something like Brighton or Blackpool on a bank holiday weekend.[101] Cairo was the intelligence and operational headquarters of British forces in the eastern Mediterranean and the scene of British wartime cultural and intellectual activity—literary, musical, and theatrical, as well as feverish activity at restaurants, bars,

---

[97] TNA, FO 141/626/6, 'File: British Union in Egypt', letter from British Union in Egypt, Cairo, to Ramsay MacDonald, 7 June 1930, protesting the appointment of Percy Lorraine.

[98] Artemis Cooper, *Cairo in the War 1939–1945* (London, 1989), 296.

[99] M. E. Yapp (ed.), *Politics and Diplomacy in Egypt: The Diaries of Sir Miles Lampson 1935–1937* (Oxford, 1997), 192.

[100] Waterfield papers, box 5, Gerald Delany, 'Lord Killearn, An addendum following the publication towards the end of 1972 of the "Killearn Diaries"'.

[101] MECA, GB 165-0201, Norman Mayers papers, letter, 26 May 1943.

clubs, and shops. The war exposed large numbers of Britons to the pleasures
and discomforts of expatriate life. According to Alec Strahan, an officer in
the Royal Artillery, after several years of desert warfare, the British soldier in
Egypt 'felt more and more detached from home'.[102] Strahan's diaries evoke
images of the 'faded magnificence' of Cairo's Continental Hotel, the 'mon-
strous citadel of sporting imperialism' at Gezira, and the crumbling
'nineteenth century splendour' of Qasr al-Nil barracks. 'The whole place
has an air of imminent decay.'[103] At the Gezira Sporting Club Strahan was
awestruck by the 'daughters of the rich Greeks and Egyptians, performing
gracefully on the diving boards... We never tried to speak to them; they
seemed quite out of our world.' Levantine luxury jarred middle-class sensibilities. So did first-hand contact with the 'British working man'. Add to
this mix the cultural diversity of the imperial diaspora and one gets some
sense of the disorientation experienced by the average Briton. 'The first
surprise was the presence of Indian soldiers everywhere, all very smartly
turned out.' British regular troops spoke a 'mixture of dialects from Tyne-
side to Devon, sprinkled with anglicized Urdu and Arabic'.[104] On leave in
Cairo, Strahan's social life involved 'an increasing circle of friends to gladden
my ample leisure hours'. He attended the Anglo-Egyptian Union where he
met the renowned British Arabist, Freya Stark, who helped convert the
Anglo-Egyptian Union to the work of British propaganda or 'counter-
intelligence'. Her targets were Axis collaborators in Egypt and Iraq.[105] The
war turned cultural institutions like the Anglo-Egyptian Union into vehicles
for British war aims, which, like Killearn's policy of intervention, undermined the 1936 treaty and the politics of collaboration.

Ultimately political persuasion gave way to the strong-arm tactics of
imperial power. Strahan's artillery unit took part in Killearn's 4th February
coup d'état in 1942 that toppled a pro-Axis Egyptian government and
installed a now-compliant Wafd. Killearn's ultimatum to Faruq required
the king to either dismiss his government or forsake his throne. As Strahan
noted in his diaries, 'Doubtless we shall now be at even greater pains to
emphasize that our gallant ally is a sovereign state and His Majesty's

---

[102] MECA, GB 165-0273, Alec Strahan, 'Memoirs' (unpublished manuscript), ch. 12, p. 2.
[103] Ibid., ch. 12, p. 1.
[104] Ibid., ch. 9, pp. 2–6.
[105] Ibid., ch. 12, pp. 1–7.

Government has no wish to interfere in her internal affairs.'[106] With cynicism so easily entertained by a subaltern officer, clearly British–Egyptian relations had reached their nadir. The commentary speaks of the everyday disillusion of ordinary British—not to mention Egyptians—with empire. The episode, it has been argued, dealt a fatal blow to British–Egyptian political collaboration. This was the view of Alexander Keown-Boyd, although his wife thought Killearn 'too soft'.[107] Other long-time residents voiced their protests, including Thomas Russell and Gerald Delany. Russell believed that Killearn had undermined the trust that British like himself had established with Egyptians over the previous half century. Given that Russell and Keown-Boyd were pillars of the British community in the interwar period, the 4th February *coup* clearly opened deep rifts between the community and the policies of the British government.[108]

The war and its aftermath were troubling for long-term British residents in Egypt. One observer was 'lost in wonderment' at the spectacle of British troops flocking to the races and the boulevards. Never had British society been so "vast".'[109] Delany reported that the majority of the British community greeted Killearn's departure in 1946 'with a sigh of relief', but troop numbers remained high in the two years immediately following the war.[110] Delany, Rapp, Addison, and Lord Wavell (commander-in-chief of the Middle Eastern theatre of war 1939–41) supported the view that the post-war crisis was at least partly the result of the failure to withdraw troops in strict accordance with the 1936 treaty. Transferred from Egypt to India in 1941, Wavell wrote to Delany in 1946 that he had never agreed with Killearn's 'policy of the Big Stick and the High Hand . . . I cannot believe there was any necessity for keeping fighting troops in the middle of Cairo.'[111]

Ronald Campbell succeeded Killearn, but inherited a legacy of political mistrust. Tensions resulted in the dissolution of the Anglo-Egyptian Union in April 1946. And although British troops were withdrawn from Cairo in 1947, nationalist attitudes had hardened. British troops remained in the Canal Zone even as Egyptians watched the withdrawal of British forces from

---

[106] MECA, GB 165-0273, Alec Strahan, 'Memoirs' (unpublished manuscript), ch. 12, p. 10.
[107] Henry Keown-Boyd, *The Lion and the Sphinx: The Rise and Fall of the British in Egypt 1882–1956* (Spennymoor, 2002), 139.
[108] Seth, *Russell Pasha*, 13.
[109] Mayers papers, box 1, folder 3, letter, 16 Mar. 1941.
[110] Waterfield papers, box 5, letter, Delany to Waterfield, 27 Jan. 1974.
[111] MECA, GB 165-0083, Gerald Delany, file 1, Wavel to Delaney, 19 Mar. 1946.

India and Palestine. Egyptian governments attempted to control and lead the popular dissatisfaction with legislation that imposed restrictions on the foreign communities and ultimately abrogated the 1936 treaty, setting the stage for Black Saturday on 26 January 1952, when twelve Britons (and one Canadian) were killed during rioting in Cairo. Legislation limiting the numbers of non-Egyptians employed in government schools and private businesses resulted in a rapid decline of the British community. The Egyptian government dismissed all British officials in Egypt after violent confrontations in the Canal Zone in November 1951. Consequently, about 500 British residents departed from Cairo. At the same time, the families of more than 1,000 British servicemen were hastily evacuated from the Canal Zone. The deteriorating situation meant that the number of 'Anglo-Saxon' British in Cairo declined from 6,615 in 1938 to 1,909 in 1953. Maltese and Cypriot British communities declined less rapidly, however they were impoverished by the flight of the metropolitan British. As relations between Egypt and Britain worsened, most of these British Egyptians either returned to their Mediterranean homelands or emigrated to Australia, Canada, or South Africa.[112]

Conclusion

Imperialism was alive and well in the interwar period. The construction of the cathedral completed the triumvirate of British institutions described by Edward Said. But only the residency (embassy after 1936) survived the twentieth century. The cathedral and barracks were reduced to rubble as Cairo was rebuilt after 1952. Hastening to this conclusion, the British community deteriorated rapidly after the Second World War. Intelligence at the embassy failed to alert or protect Britons from the assaults of Black Saturday, and the British army in the Canal Zone was also to blame for this tragedy, launching an ill-advised attack on an Egyptian police contingent in Isma'iliyya, which cost the lives of forty-seven Egyptians. Rapp, who was a high-ranking official in the Canal Zone at the time, remarked that the British government failed to perceive that the political costs of defending the Suez Canal far outweighed its military and strategic importance.[113] This

---

[112] TNA, FO 369/5024, 'Extract from Inspector's Report on the British Community in Cairo, 30 January 1954'.

[113] Rapp papers, 'Middle East Office: 1950–3', pp. 376–413.

observation could also be applied to Eden's miscalculation in 1956, which signalled the end of British influence in the Middle East, as well as compromising the remnants of the British community in Egypt. Lingering Britons were arrested and deported, their properties sequestered and ultimately confiscated by the Egyptian government.

It is worth asking to what degree this outcome was inevitable. Said's analysis of imperial power suggests that it was. But did the British community necessarily wither before the historically irresistible forces of nationalism? In 1940 the British community was part of a vibrant cosmopolitan society. Indeed, Said's memoirs indicate that cosmopolitan society only unravelled after the Second World War when Egyptian and Levantine elites began to withdraw from the English schools and other integrative social relations with the British community. As a result, the British were increasingly isolated as symbols of imperial power.[114] The alienation of Egyptian elites indicates that the British position in Egypt was founded on interdependent social relations with Egyptians, questioning the assumption that 'monumental power and absolute confidence' were the hallmarks of the British in Egypt.[115] Once social relations were ruptured, the monuments of British power came crashing down.

Select Bibliography

JONATHAN BOLTON, *Personal Landscapes: British Poets in Egypt during the Second World War* (New York, 1997).

ROGER BOWEN, *'Many Histories Deep': The Personal Landscape Poets in Egypt 1940–45* (London, 1995).

HUMPHREY BOWMAN, *Middle East Window* (London, 1942).

EDWARD CECIL, *The Leisure of an Egyptian Official* (London, 1921).

H. S. DEIGHTON, 'The Impact of Egypt on Britain: A Study of Public Opinion', in P. M. Holt (ed.), *Political and Social Change in Modern Egypt* (London, 1968), 247–8.

LAWRENCE DURRELL, *Spirit of Place: Letters and Essays on Travel* (New York, 1971).

E. M. FORSTER, *Alexandria: A History and Guide* and *Pharos and Pharillon*, ed. Miriam Allot (London, 2004).

LAURENCE GRAFFTEY-SMITH, *Bright Levant* (London, 1966).

DEREK HOPWOOD, *Tales of Empire: The British in the Middle East 1880–1952* (London, 1989).

---

[114] Said, *Out of Place*, 198.
[115] Ibid. 143.

PHYLLIS LASSNER, *Colonial Strangers: Women Writing the End of the British Empire* (London, 2004).

PENELOPE LIVELY, *Oleander, Jacaranda: A Childhood Perceived* (London, 1994).

PETER MANSFIELD, *The British in Egypt* (New York, 1971).

ROGER OWEN, *Lord Cromer: Victorian Imperialist, Edwardian Proconsul* (Oxford, 2004).

ANDRÉ RAYMOND, *Cairo* (London, 2000).

THOMAS RUSSELL, *Egyptian Service, 1902–1946* (London, 1949).

ANTHONY SATTIN, *Lifting the Veil: British Society in Egypt 1768–1956* (London, 1988).

RONALD STORRS, *Orientations* (London, 1937).

SAMI ZUBAIDA, 'Cosmopolitanism in the Middle East', *Amsterdam Middle East Papers*, 12 (1997), 1–21.

4

Kenya
Home County and African Frontier

John Lonsdale

Which Man's Country?

In 1922 Robert Coryndon, secretary to Cecil Rhodes in his youth and allegedly able to bend a coin between thumb and forefinger, was promoted from the Uganda Protectorate to Kenya Colony. He cabled a friend, 'Have accepted governorship of Kenya: no more peace.'[1] His predecessor in Nairobi, the one-eyed General Northey, had been sacked for being too close to Kenya's 10,000 white settlers. Britain had to consider the two million or more Africans and 25,000 Indians as well. Of seven previous governors four had now left under a cloud of racial conflict, being considered too partial to the tiny white minority, or too perplexed.[2] Coryndon knew that history. His fears were soon fulfilled. Some ex-officers, survivors of the Great War, conspired to intern him by a stream stocked with Scottish trout. They refused to obey London's wish that they vote on a single electoral roll shared with British Indians, fellow immigrants. While the proposed franchise was hedged with qualifications, it looked like political suicide. Even educated native subjects might, unthinkably, one day be citizens. The plotters cited

For advice I am grateful to colleagues—David Anderson, Susanne Mueller, Michael Redley, Atieno Odhiambo, and Richard Waller—and to those who were there, Roger Dracup, David Lovatt Smith, Michael McWilliam, Isabel Nanton, Ali Rattansi, and Jennifer Riggs, but all errors of fact and judgement are mine.

[1] Elspeth Huxley, *White Man's Country: Lord Delamere and the Making of Kenya*, ii (London, 1935), 132.

[2] Eliot, Commissioner 1901–4, and Girouard, Governor 1909–12, resigned. Indecisive Sadler, 1905–9, was moved: G. H. Mungeam, *British Rule in Kenya 1895–1912* (Oxford, 1966), 114, 204–7, 261–70. For Northey (1919–22) who lost an eye at polo: Robert M. Maxon, *Struggle for Kenya: The Loss and Reassertion of Imperial Initiative, 1912–1923* (London, 1993), 243–6.

Ulster as precedent for loyal revolt, 'for King and Kenya'. Kenya too could show the stuff of which overseas Britons were made.[3]

Kenya was Britain's most troublesome African colony. It was neither a 'West Coast' trading colony, ruled in the name of native trusteeship, nor a 'South African' colony of settlement, fit for minority rule. London vacillated accordingly, muddling through the local crises its indecision provoked. British banks thought Kenya a bad bet; Indian credit was cheaper. Before 1942, when war brought solvency, Kenya was always hard up. Britain had to write off the £5 million (£430 million) it had spent in the 1890s on building the 'Uganda railway'; settler exports had failed to pay for the line that made white settlement thinkable. In white Kenya's first decade, before 1914, its 5,500 pioneers represented only one-sixth of 1 per cent of all British emigrants and after the war Kenya was thought so risky that the soldier-settlement scheme that nearly doubled white numbers required its applicants to have £5,000 (£171,000) in capital. Only the top 3 per cent of Britons qualified. Around half of all 'settlers' were always transients, staying five years or less. Between the wars the reason was clear. Of the £32 million invested before 1930, probably up to £20 million (£1,034 million) was lost by 1935. In the same period the colony bought one quarter of 1 per cent of Britain's exports and supplied even fewer imports. Kenya caused more imperial trouble than it was worth and, before 1942, unmade more settler fortunes than it made.[4]

To rescue Coryndon, tame the settlers, mollify India, and save the African future for the future to decide, the Colonial Office famously stated in its 'Devonshire Declaration' of 1923 that Kenya was 'primarily' African. African interests were 'paramount'. Britain was their trustee, a role it could share with no other immigrant group. But there were weasel words too. 'Primarily' suggested negotiable priorities. And immigrant interests were safeguarded unless they hurt African needs, when the latter would 'prevail'.

---

[3] C. J. Duder, 'The Settler Response to the Indian Crisis of 1923 in Kenya: Brigadier-General Philip Wheatley and "Direct Action"', *Journal of Imperial and Commonwealth History*, 17/3 (1989), 349–73; Christopher Youé, *Robert Thorne Coryndon: Proconsular Imperialism in Southern and Eastern Africa, 1897–1925* (Gerrards Cross, 1986), 164–74.

[4] Robert A. Remole, 'White Settlers', Ph.D. thesis (Harvard, 1959), 368; Max Salvadori, *La Colonisation européenne au Kenya* (Paris, 1938), 186–223; C. J. Duder, '"Men of the Officer Class": Participants in the 1919 Soldier Settlement Scheme in Kenya', *African Affairs*, 92/366 (1993), 72. Where converted, monetary values are given at 2008 prices, calculated on MeasuringWorth URL: <http://www.measuringworth.com> (Retail Price Index conversion tool).

But who would be the judge of that? For Britain aspired to 'advance' as well as defend the 'native races' and no European thought Africans could advance on their own. The declaration or, better, 'Devonshire fudge' rebutted the settlers' case for self-rule but conceded their sole right to 'highland' land and a segregated electoral roll, so denying equal citizenship to Indians.[5] Wait-and-see remained British policy until the 1950s. An independent Kenya, hard to imagine anyway, would have to be shared between the 'races'—and how that mutual understanding could be achieved was an enigma best resolved by the gradualist balm of 'advance', later called 'development', not by invasive imperial surgery in unripe time. Which man's country Kenya would be was in question until late 1957, and even then officials would deny that they had at last decided.

A 'white man's country' in Kenya was always 'an exotic fantasy'. The numbers did not add up nor were likely to, since Britain preferred settlers 'of independent means' who would be no burden on the state—another vain hope. By 1940 whites had more than doubled again, to 23,000, but were still barely one-third of the number of Kenya's Indians, at 66,000, and not half of 1 per cent of the African total of over four million. Comparison with Southern Rhodesia was discouraging. White Rhodesians were a 'sergeants mess' to Kenya's 'officers mess' but made up in arithmetic what they lacked in class. Their 64,000 were then more than 3 per cent of Rhodesia's two million total, almost all Africans. Whites had won internal self-rule in 1923 on a fancy franchise that made them an electoral majority. Only in 1960 did London publicly deny a similar future for Kenya's whites whose numbers, ironically, had in the previous twelve years grown at their fastest rate ever, from 30,000 in 1948 to nearly 60,000. But Africans had also increased, from over 5 to 8.6 million. No longer primarily an African territory, in 1963, forty years after the Devonshire Declaration, Kenya became not a 'multi-racial' fudge but a fully African state.[6]

The geopolitics of empire reinforced the local mathematics of race. Before 1952 Kenya's Indians were the main obstacle to white minority rule. They filled the openings in trade and jobs that might have supported a white

[5] Great Britain, *Indians in Kenya*, Cmd 1922 (London, 1923), 10–11; Maxon, *Struggle*, 247–79. The Duke of Devonshire was then Colonial Secretary.

[6] Ronald Hyam, *Britain's Declining Empire: The Road to Decolonisation 1918–1968* (Cambridge, 2006), 13; D. A. Low and Alison Smith (eds.), *History of East Africa*, iii (Oxford, 1976), 576.

lower class, as in Rhodesia. Their allies were weightier than the settlers' old-boy network at home, for India's own nationalists took up their grievances with the viceroy, senior to any colonial governor. 'British East' had been acquired in the 1890s mainly to plug the equatorial gap in India's African defences, based on Cairo and the Cape.[7] Kenya could not be permitted to become an offshore base for India's subversion. Militant white supremacy endangered from without the empire's greatest asset, already challenged within. In 1947 Nehru, harbinger of the empire's hoped-for successor, a multi-racial commonwealth, replaced the viceroy. His continued concern for overseas Indians was a guarantee, scarcely needed at this late date, that Britain would not hand Kenya to settler rule.

Settler Image and Reality

As the only settler colony under direct British rule after South Africa's unification, and gadfly to Indian nationalism, Kenya became an imperial issue. As the settlers' herald Elspeth Huxley put it, 'Once the Kenya fox is out of the bag, away go all the speakers and writers and lecturers in full cry.' 'Sentimentalist pro-natives', including such establishment figures as Lord Lugard and the Archbishop of Canterbury, relied on two retired officials, the doctor Norman Leys and engineer William McGregor Ross, to analyse why settlers should not have more power. Settlers themselves felt unfairly pilloried for being born too late to enjoy the moral certainties of earlier colonists. They believed, as their critics did not, that their often profitless pioneer farming was good for primitive natives who should in natural justice be forced to repay in land, labour, loyalty, and tax, the costs of a compulsory education in progress. In the 1950s many whites felt 'blind rage' against the injustice of history as the world rejected European imperialism and, in Kenya, ungrateful Africans joined a terrorist movement, Mau Mau.[8]

---

[7] Robert G. Gregory, *India and East Africa: A History of Race Relations within the British Empire 1890–1930* (Oxford, 1971); Ronald Robinson and John Gallagher, with Alice Denny, *Africa and the Victorians: The Official Mind of Imperialism* (London, 1961), 283–378.

[8] M. G. Redley, 'The Politics of a Predicament: The White Community in Kenya 1918–32', Ph.D. thesis (Cambridge, 1976); Elspeth Huxley and Margery Perham, *Race and Politics in Kenya* (London, [1944] 1956), 23; Margery Perham, *East African Journey: Kenya and Tanganyika 1929–30* (London, 1976), 138; Norman Leys, *Kenya* (London, 1924); W. McGregor Ross, *Kenya from Within* (London, 1927); Kathryn Tidrick, *Empire and the English Character* (London, 1990), 160.

Meanwhile settlers—women especially, who numbered only four to every five men as late as 1931—were moved to write.

They wrote in self-defence. Their memoirs, and Mrs Huxley's biography of the puckish, prickly, Lord Delamere, must be read with care, their silences especially. They tell, truly, of the hardship and setbacks of frontier farming—'penal servitude' one of them called it. They celebrate, frankly, the fun, freedom, and fascination of a self-reliant working life in open country with an exhilarating climate, often on horseback, in command. A gallop at sunrise was a cure for homesickness. Horses carried settler culture, at polo, race weeks, or riding to hounds, after days on tented safari to meet one's friends. Hospitality to unexpected guests was an unwritten law. All accounts also reveal white dependence on black labour at the tolling of the farm bell, a discipline replacing sun and seasons. A few even admit to cross-racial friendship, to theological debate, a cook's courage against a trigger-happy white drunk, and kitchen gossip about white adulteries—all breaches in the wall of racial prestige. Only two authors confessed defeat and, released from solidarity by 'coming home', felt free to accuse fellow farmers of betraying gentlemanly standards of probity or hospitality. Even these were silent on the costs of white supremacy to Africans—apart from a few floggings stoically borne—and on settlers' political differences. This literature evokes nostalgia for high-spirited gallantry, once misunderstood and now departed. It needs to be questioned, like any roseate view of the past.[9]

Between the wars settlers certainly seemed at one. If at a farm baptism they had no hymnbooks, all knew the carol 'Hark the herald angels sing'. When politically agitated they waved Union flags and sang 'God save the King'. On Armistice Day they honoured their fallen in silence, decently different from 'Indians talking and gesticulating' and Africans who turned ritual into farce with 'incessant noise and chatter'. They hailed royal events with hilltop bonfires, fireworks, tree-planting, and 'Indian bun and treacle' teas. While their aristocrats were often Scots, settlers were largely English by birth. Even the 18 per cent of their number who in 1930 were South African-born were more Briton than Boer. British and Afrikaner schoolboys traded

---

[9] Perham: *Journey*, 190; Pamela Scott, *A Nice Place to Live* (Wilton, 1991), 65; Erroll Whittall, *Dimbilil: The Story of a Kenya Farm* (London, 1956), 15, 25; Joan Considine and John Rawlins (eds.), *Childhood Memories of Colonial East Africa 1920–1963* (Lancaster, 2004), *passim*; V. M. Carnegie, *A Kenyan Farm Diary* (Edinburgh, 1930), for foreman Omar; Alyse Simpson, *The Land that Never Was* (London, 1937), 83, 79, 96–106, 109, 120, 158; Karen Blixen, *Out of Africa* (London, 1937), 214, 277–9.

insults but both were Kenyans when dismissing newcomers fresh from 'home' as poms, pongoes, or rednecks, *rooineks.*[10]

Importing a diverse Britishness, settlers created an Englishness 'of the public school type'. This distinguished them from the often illiterate Afrikaner patriarchs of the Uasin Gishu plateau far upcountry, the first district with as many white women as men. In 1931 7 per cent of whites were continental Europeans—mostly missionaries, not settlers at all. 'Catholic sisters do not set the social tone!' as one scandalized English wife remonstrated with another who in 1917 helped the nuns nurse naked black casualties of the Great War. Some continentals did, however, set the tone. Of these the best known, Karen Blixen, returned from the foot of the Ngong hills to Denmark in 1931, broken by dysentery, drought, locusts, slump, and the deaths of both her workers' patron, chief Kinyanjui, and her Etonian lover Denys Finch Hatton, crack-shot second son of a cash-strapped earl. Her failure as a farmer while extolling the nobility of patronage epitomized the fragility of settler ambition.[11]

Settlers, moreover, were never united. One first senses this from the many anonymous letters to the local press. Few were the independent family heads—dairy or cereal farmers, or small coffee-growers—of white Kenya's self-image. Large plantation companies grew most of Kenya's main exports, coffee, sisal, and, from the 1930s, tea. Moreover, there were, at best, only 3,300 white farms, ranches, or plantations, in thirty farm districts, each with different worries over water and markets, crop and animal disease. While one-third of whites were on the land in the 1920s, thereafter only one-quarter farmed, barely more than British officials. Growth brought in ever more professionals and businessmen but of these only one wrote a memoir, and then another, which said more about his rural youth than his commercial career. Farmers hated bankers, export agents, and officials, all townsmen

[10] Carnegie, *Diary*, 241; Michael Blundell, *So Rough a Wind* (London, 1966), 79; Evelyn Brodhurst-Hill, *So This is Kenya!* (London, 1936), 120; Elspeth Huxley (ed.), *Nellie: Letters from Africa* (London, 1980), 108; slang at Old Cambrian Society, URL: <http://www.old-cambrians.com/KenyaSchoolSpeak.html>, accessed Sept. 2009; personal experience.

[11] Dane Kennedy, *Islands of White: Settler Society and Culture in Kenya and Southern Rhodesia, 1890–1930* (Durham, NC, 1987); Elizabeth Watkins, *Olga in Kenya* (London, 2005), 116; Finch Hatton's plane crash also killed his servant Kamau or Hamisi: compare Errol Trzebinski, *Silence will Speak: A Study of the Life of Denys Finch Hatton and his Relationship with Karen Blixen* (London, 1977), 308–10, with Sarah Wheeler, *Too Close to the Sun: The Life and Times of Denys Finch Hatton* (London, 2006), 235.

with a security unknown to producers plagued by treacherous tropical nature and fickle markets, while townsmen resented the protected prices they paid for settler produce. The Second World War brought a healing prosperity but hostility lingered. After 1945 Nairobi housed half white Kenya in suburbs like 'the better part of Woking'. Upcountry youths despised urban schoolmates, poor at bushcraft and probably rotten shots. In 1950 settlers advertised Kenya's attractions. They dismissed Nairobi in two of their booklet's one hundred pages. City life was all too familiar with traffic jams, office hours, supermarkets, ice-cream parlours, and bistros. While white-owned hotels and restaurants could still by custom, not in law, refuse entry to Indians and Africans, Indian drive-in cinemas observed no colour-bar, whites and blacks stood together in the same queues at post offices or bus stops, and black policemen could arrest white suspects.[12]

Upcountry life remained different. Power and water utilities were confined to townships; long-drop latrines enjoyed the best view from the garden; oxen had not all made way for tractors. Farmers bathed before supper, dined in pyjamas, and put out the paraffin lamp or turned off the generator after the 9 p.m. BBC overseas news, ready to be up at dawn with their workers' bell. Town and country was not the only divide. Farmers and planters were often at odds. Farmers came to imagine Kenya as a British home county of a passing era. Many planters, salaried managers, continued to gamble, more realistically, on the opportunities of the African frontier.[13]

Home County and African Frontier

Whatever their differences all whites knew they were of superior race, encircled by natives of doubtful temper and undoubted backwardness. Their intuition was neither socially reactionary, since Europe and white America then thought the same, nor scientifically racist. Settlers paid little heed to the eugenics peddled by the crankier of their doctors in the 1930s.

---

[12] Blundell, Wind; Michael Blundell, A Love Affair with the Sun: A Memoir of Seventy Years in Kenya (Nairobi, 1994); Redley, 'Predicament', 176–82, 199–202; Peter Hewitt, Kenya Cowboy (Johannesburg, 2001), 68; Peter Evans, Law and Disorder, or Scenes of Life in Kenya (London, 1956), 7; Leonard Gill, Military Musings (Victoria, BC, 2003), 14, 27; Kenya Association (1932), Kenya, Britain's Most Attractive Colony (Nairobi, 1950).

[13] Cherry Lander, My Kenya Acres (London, 1957), 67–8; Whittall, Dimbilil, 45–6. The Kenya Settlement Handbook 1949 (London, 1949), 114; James Foster, 'The Settlement of Timau 1910–1940' (unpublished, Nairobi, 1979), 20; Negley Farson, Last Chance in Africa (London, 1949), 193.

Their own folk eugenics focused on the 'prestige' with which manly white authority protected white female honour. They had no need of science. Each race or nation, they knew, was distinct, by nurture or nature. Public-school types of the officer class, they were themselves the best trained, highest born members of humanity's most stoic, gentle race. While the habit of command lent restraint to their power, their civilized status gave them the right, and their tiny number the will, to dominate their native majority—if necessary by force. All that was understood. But settlers differed when thinking of the future. Most excluded Indians from account—with an impenetrably alien civilization of their own—but Africans had everything still to learn, if they could. Some whites imagined, and practised, an inter-racial partnership, even 'blood-brotherhood', on a shared frontier of opportunity and risk. Most, increasingly, sought safety in segregation, fenced within a home county on the roof of Africa.

The contrary racial premises behind these divergent views, often held equally firmly in the same mind, were epitomized by two local satirists, Davis and Robertson, in their *Chronicles of Kenya*. In their home view 'the African' was 'of similar fibre to the Englishman, only black, with the misfortune of centuries of savagery behind him', but longing for civilization. Settlers should therefore help Africans as friends. The alternative, colonial, view was that the African had, by nature, 'qualities and faults and vices of his own'. Black and white were parallel lines; a donkey could not learn to be a horse; a poodle was no bloodhound. It was hypocrisy to claim to be the African's trustee. As Britons, settlers called a spade a spade, 'not a crozier or a shepherd's crook'. Self-interest was in any case enough. What was good for settlers was good for Africans, in ending their supposed idleness and vice.

The first premise, that Africans might one day be equal, was tested by the personal trust required on the frontier. The other, that Africans were inferior, untrustworthy, persuaded settlers that highland Kenya must become a British home county to which they were native and their black workers immigrant. These correlations were neither exact nor unchanging. The frontier view internalized the pioneer vulnerability that continued upcountry until 1942. Before then the home county was an impossible dream and thereafter a fatal attraction. Such inconsistency was a settler condition. It had little to do with the altitude, actinic solar rays, alcohol, and adultery of popular belief. It simply reflected the settlers' predicament, supposedly of superior race yet subjects of a multi-racial empire; clients of a state unreliably and often ineffectively helpful to them; self-disciplining but not self-governing; materially privileged but only arguably self-supporting; racially private and yet, as a class, always on public display.[14]

Before they learnt how to use the land, before the branch railways of the 1920s allowed them to farm in outlying areas, whites had to negotiate racially reciprocal frontier bargains, later redefined as cultural treachery. Some shot and smuggled ivory, reliant on indigenous guides and porters, or traded livestock with Somali dealers who then converted trans-racial commercial trust into personal service. Others were transport riders or labour contractors for government, or safari guides for rich or royal tourists, even Indian princes. All shot for the pot and defended their cattle against predators, helped by African hunters. Fictional children hoped to redeem daddy's debts by trading their treasures to the houseboys. On the frontier Africans were partners in risk, not servants on a wage but, without access to official protection, were junior partners, investing in their relationships still more trust than whites.[15]

Even when settlers took up farming they did so as brokers of peasant tenures, recruiting workers by offering them shares in the new frontier: 'squatter' rights to cultivate and graze on 'white' land in return for labour. The forced labour common to African colonies but for which 1920s Kenya was notorious worked mainly for the state on public works. Settlers bene-fited to some extent, but most of their labour was supplied according to cross-border recruiting agreements with known partners, official African chiefs, mainly in Gikuyuland. Squatters valued production rights more than any paltry wage. Early settlers were often landlords, 'kaffir farmers' living off African rents, not farm sales. The 'white highlands', taken mainly from the Maasai, were really 'black highlands' colonized by more African clients than white patrons. In the early 1930s squatters controlled three-quarters of all white land in active use. Settler fiction praised squatter loyalty and the health-giving butterfat from their cows, but in these frontier origins lay the settlers' end. In the 1940s they began to close the gate of patronage. Wartime profit and fear for the political future drove many to repudiate rights that squatters believed were theirs by colonial custom and Gikuyu

---

[14] For these three paragraphs: Chloe Campbell, *Race and Empire: Eugenics in Colonial Kenya* (Manchester, 2007); A. Davis and H. G. Robertson, *Chronicles of Kenya* (London, 1928), 241–5; M. G. Redley, 'White Settler Racial Interaction and Boundary-Maintenance' (Cambridge University, Department of Anthropology seminar paper, 19 Oct. 1977).

[15] Wheeler, *Too Close*, 70–4; Edward I. Steinhardt, *Black Poachers White Hunters* (Oxford, 2006); May Baldwin, *Kenya Kiddies: A Story of Settlers' Children in East Africa* (Philadelphia, [1926]), 223–7; Gerald Hanley, *Warriors and Strangers* (London, 1971), 141, 176.

law, but which had no formal legal standing. White sponsorship of a peasant frontier gave way to the private property of a home county. Mau Mau was in part the squatter response, a desperate attempt to reopen the gate.[16]

To shut out the frontier seemed feasible only after official veterinary and crop scientists, backed by on-farm private experiment, had learnt to manage tropical plagues and pests. Some settlers also applied African knowledge. Memoirs are divided between respect and disdain for native expertise. In the 1920s Violet Carnegie, a Scottish aristocrat with a war-disabled husband, relied on the frontier lore of Okiek (Dorobo) hunters and Maasai herders in running her farm. Her Somali headman Omar took Maasai advice on moving sheep between seasonal pastures, *osopuko* and *olpurkel*. Her Kipsigis herdsmen knew her cows better than her herd-book. She valued the martial virtues of some Africans not because they kept other Africans in order but because they stood by you in a corner, facing a lion. Okiek society remained welcome into the 1940s but not their game traps, frontier tools that ensnared inside the farm fence the expensive dairy cows, cross-bred between imported and local stock, that by now earned a regular milk cheque from the co-operative creamery.[17]

Boundaries of Community

Over time, settlers tried to define their boundaries more closely. An open frontier bristled increasingly with more traps than Okiek knew, as other Africans learnt skills that they tried to convert into political capital within the frontier called 'civilization'. African utility became a danger, heightened by fears for the converse, white degeneration from too much veranda'd ease and idle minds. Determination to resist any levelling of racial status stemmed from the often nervous paternalist contempt which many, unlike Mrs Carnegie, felt for their workers. One wife, a notorious snob, plagued by debt and a useless husband, projected all her troubles on to these spiteful

---

[16] Baldwin, *Kiddies*, 62, 136, 167; Anthony Clayton and Donald C. Savage, *Government and Labour in Kenya 1895–1963* (London, 1974), 44, 95–6, 113–15, 134–9; R. M. A. van Zwanenberg, *Colonial Capitalism and Labour in Kenya 1919–1939* (Nairobi, 1975), ch. 8; Tabitha Kanogo, *Squatters and the Roots of Mau Mau 1905–1963* (London, 1987); Frank Furedi, *The Mau Mau War in Perspective* (London, 1989); Blundell, *Love Affair*, 90.

[17] Richard Waller, '"Clean" and "Dirty": Cattle Disease and Control Policy in Colonial Kenya, 1900–40', *Journal of African History*, 45/1 (2004), 45–80; Carnegie, *Diary*, 16–17, 140–9; Whittall, *Dimbilil*, 26–30, 44, 58.

children, lecherous 'little apes', feckless loafers—so trying to the British
fortitude that normally overcame native stupidity or superstition. Africans,
she admitted, were not personally to blame since they had not 'been "put
through it"'—a course of instruction that...humbled, strengthened and
steadied' the British character. Early settlers, and official doctrine as late as
1927, thought farm labour was the best way to put Africans through it.[18]

How far one or another type of farming taught esteem or disdain for
African knowledge is hard to say. Before the growth of liberal opinion
among urban professionals in the 1940s, those who showed most respect
were among the best born—like Baroness Blixen, for whom Kenya had two
aristocracies, her white peers and the Maasai; or Violet Carnegie, wife to the
third son of a ninth earl; or Elspeth Huxley's mother Nellie Grant, born a
Grosvenor and married into The Royal Scots; Pam Scott, granddaughter of a
duke on her father's side and a viceroy on her mother's; or the third baron
Delamere himself, settler Kenya's founder, who allegedly preferred Maasai
company to that of many whites. That patrician animal, the horse, not only
created settler society but could also transform blacks and even Indians,
temporarily, into whites. Well-born Englishmen partnered Somali horse-
breeders; the Molo hunt's African whips called its English hounds with
English cries; Indian owners raced horses in Nairobi under Calcutta rules;
in the 1940s Pam Scott, whose Grenadier father was for years the settlers'
leader, wore 'the sweat-soaked colours that an African jockey had just worn'
when she rode for the same owner in the next race and 'no one thought it
odd'.

Labouring aristocrats, however, set limits to their cultural relativism.
Committed to Kenya, they loathed the 'unsavoury notables' of the season-
ally migrant 'Happy Valley' set who made Kenya infamous for addiction and
adultery. As to their Africans, even the devotedly Kenyan Delamere got
bored with the Maasai and admitted to 'liking his own people best'.
Mrs Carnegie thought her headman 'the best type of old family retainer'
because he was 'perfectly frank but never familiar'. Finch Hatton took his
servant, the Somali Billea Issa, not only to war in 1914 but also on visits

---

[18] Blundell: *Wind*, 76–7, 90; Eve Bache, *The Youngest Lion: Early Farming Days in Kenya*
(London, 1934); Brodhurst-Hill, *So This is Kenya!* (her manager, Michael Blundell, was wiser;
Bache was possibly her *nom de plume*). For Blundell's view see his *Love Affair*, 4–8, 14; D. A. Low,
'British East Africa: The Establishment of British Rule 1895–1912', in V. Harlow and E. M. Chilver
(eds.), *History of East Africa*, ii (Oxford, 1965), 50–6; Clayton and Savage, *Government and
Labour*, 125–6.

home, perhaps because Billea too, 'like a medieval retainer', kept five paces behind his master, undemanding of intimacy.[19]

Kenya has been said to illustrate how well racial inequality serves the impersonal class interests of capitalism.[20] It appears, rather, that white ideas of race and class varied and changed. Many arrived with aristocratic, pre-capitalist instincts of personal obligation between persons of unequal status that transgressed but did not dissolve hierarchies of class and race. Face-to-face relations also reflected the weakness of the early colonial state. Self-help by means of cross-racial alliance or vendetta was essential where contracts were verbal and, until the 1940s, the police several hours away. A collective defensiveness, made thinkable by advances in the state's disciplinary capacity, later forbade the impersonal, capitalist, trans-racial negotiation of labour relations, as if between classes, especially in the case of squatters. By contrast, colonial officials and larger urban employers, transient managers not settled pioneers, accepted that an organized black working class could be a means to blunt racial antagonism.

Similar contradictions penetrated white culture to its core—in gardening, eating, holidays, class discipline, and sex—as settlers tried both to possess Kenya as it was with all its insecurities, and turn it into what it was not, an equatorial England deferential to the officer class.

Gardening was a settler passion, abetted by 'shamba boys' and the tropical extravagance that festooned verandas in colour. Gardens enclosed reassuringly domestic space but opened on untamed horizons. Memoirs glory in the splendour of the view but pacify the frontier by likening Kenya's hills to English downs, combining 'the charm of dairy pasture with the vastness of space'. Two growing seasons a year brought both joy and distress, with torrential rain, burning wind and sun, antelope that devoured flowers, and locusts that, until brought under control in the 1940s, reduced garden to desert in minutes. Exotic—that is, English—flowers bloomed so often that they aged before their time but the indigenous figtree provided the best fencing material, unlikely to rot or be stolen. There was also much to be said for 'our native orchids'. 'Our native' said it all. A colonizing instinct lent to

---

[19] For these two paragraphs: Blixen, *Out of Africa*, 237; Huxley, *White Man's Country*, i. 151; Carnegie, *Diary*, 25, 186; Scott, *Nice Place*, 143, 157; David Cannadine, *The Decline and Fall of the British Aristocracy* (London, 1996), 439–43; Perham, *Journey*, 138–9; Wheeler, *Too Close*, 68; Kennedy, *Islands*, 148–66; Wilfred Thesiger, *My Kenya Days* (London, 1994), 208.

[20] Robert Miles, *Racism* (London, 1989), 9–10, 100–10.

unfamiliar native trees a 'natural appearance', lending a comforting 'permanence and homeliness'. Nellie Grant used squatter manure. Her home-county
kitchen garden owed its fertility to the alien peasants' frontier.[21]

Until electric refrigerators replaced charcoal or paraffin models and a
food industry grew, after 1945, settler meals offered a similar contrast
between the family china shipped out from home and the plain fare served
upon it, often game or goat accompanied by the maize, 'mealies', for which
the *Settlers Cookery Book* offered two dozen recipes. Delamere had gazelle
chops, blancmange, and tinned peaches for tea. In 1932 a family due for
leave longed for English cuisine, notoriously stodgy yet a relief from the
stringy chicken bought, squawking, from African traders on bicycles, the
'smoke-flavoured milk, unripe pawpaw pretending to be apple sauce and
the ubiquitous banana', with most other food out of tins, including sardines
and baked beans, staples of the 1930s. Another family even remembers the
luxury of tomato ketchup in that pinched decade. But, again, settlers made
the strange their own. Curries, adopted from the unknowable, in-between,
Indians, became Sunday roasts. They were easy for the cook to simmer on
his wood-fired Dover stove into the afternoon, until 'people finished their
pink gins'. For children nothing could compare with Okiek hunters' honey
'with the tang of smoke and a few dead bees caught in the comb'.[22]

If meals varied from deadly dull to boldly oriental, conflict with cooks was
unending—or so the language primer, *Up-Country Swahili*, warned. The
servant problem grew more difficult in step with each new linguistic exercise:

This cook is very lazy... The cook is drunk, send him away, I shall get another...
Stop talking (leave words), it is just your fault... Who are you? I'm just a man! Yes,
but what is your name?... What is your illness? Do you sleep at night? Show me
your tongue. I don't know, what do you think it is? Witchcraft? No, that's just
nonsense.

Resorts whose names evoked both equatorial England and a domesticated
Africa offered escape from the kitchen. If seeking respite from the alleged

[21] Susan Wood, *A Fly in Amber* (London, 1964), 44; A. J. Jex-Blake (ed.), *Gardening in East
Africa* (London, 1934), chs. by H. B. Sharpe, G. S. Huggan, H. M. Gardner, Mrs E. L. Grant.
[22] St Andrew's Church Women's Guild, *The Kenya Settlers' Cookery Book* (Nairobi, [1928]
1958), 125–31; Wheeler, *Too Close*, 56; quotations from Jennifer Riggs, ketchup from Isabel
Nanton, in emails, May 2006. M. G. Vassanji, *The In-between World of Vikram Lall* (Toronto,
2004), a historical novel; Stephanie Jones, 'Merchant-Kings and Everymen: Narratives of the
South Asian Diaspora of East Africa', *Journal of Eastern African Studies*, 1/1 (2007), 16–33.

strain of high altitude, farmers could choose coastal hotels like The Manor or Tudor House. Townspeople could also holiday at home in highland fishing inns like The Brown Trout on the Kinangop plateau, that fabulous 'Katmandu in Devon', or The Izaak Walton and Pig and Whistle beneath Mount Kenya. Other names captured the frontier, The Outspan and White Rhino hotels at Nyeri or the Muthaiga Club for smart Nairobi.[23]

Class, Race, and Sex

The settlers' culture hero was Lord Delamere, 'D', who ruined his English inheritance for Kenya's sake and soiled his hands with trade at a time when falling rents and rising taxes forced barons into business, if only by marrying it. That Africans named the lead ox in farm teams 'Dalmia' and a notorious stockthief called himself 'Delamere' even made him a cross-racial hero, of sorts. Aristocrats at home joked about their new poverty. In Kenya 'poor whites' were no laughing matter. Poverty was less dangerous among 'Dutchmen'; some ox-drivers lived no better than squatters. But Britons had to discipline a racial identity that could, confusingly, blur class distinction and confer upward mobility; railway guard's sons went to boarding school. At home family honour had often been enough. Public sanctions were needed in Kenya, exercised by 'calling' on new arrivals and the peer pressure of sports clubs, masonic lodges, and churches. English-speaking fecklessness, often with 'a history of whisky behind it', made for squalid familiarity with Africans. Poor whites—the enemy within, unemployable by railway or police—could be repatriated as Distressed British Subjects, at public expense, away from African eyes.

Settler views on class and race focused on sex and reproduction. Until white women equalled men in number in the late 1930s, males could with little censure consort with African, especially Somali, women, even keeping them in potentially companionate concubinage. For white women, however, it was a taboo, generally observed, to taste black flesh. House servants accordingly were not female but male—even if, as an added precaution, they were seen to be 'boys'. Indeed Davis and Robertson thought feminine frailty to be the settlers' weakest link. Two of their *Chronicles* contrasted the wifely

[23] F. H. Le Breton, *Up-Country Swahili* (Richmond, [1936, 1937, 1940, etc.]; 13th edn., 1956), 16, 19, 23, 26, 37, 39, 45; C. S. Nicholls, *Red Strangers: The White Tribe of Kenya* (London, 2005), 199; T. L. Hately and Hugh Copley, *Angling in East Africa* (London, 1933); Hewitt, *Cowboy*, 31.

devotion on which prestige rested with the female folly by which it might be destroyed. The first episode imagined a ship bound for Mombasa on which society ladies—vamps, pussies, a lesbian tomboy—all pursued pleasure. None found happiness. 'The real thing in girls', 'happiest of their sex', were 'young matrons with families under their wing', sensibly dressed, perambulating infant white Kenya. A fantasy of racial degradation followed this patriarchal idyll. Four white men and a white woman on safari encountered a large ape, almost human and able to speak. His companions, he said, had been studying the watching whites. The terrified woman became separated from her friends. Weeks later they found her with the apes, the latter now shaven, clothed, and 'nearly white'. The woman, married to the chief ape, had become an idiot, 'not a white woman now'. The fable ended with the reflection that a savage environment could make men brutish, but it took an unattached woman to provoke that nightmare.[24]

Apes watched men. Mrs Carnegie's Okiek knew settlers better than settlers knew them. Kenya was a 'whispering galler[y]' for African tales of settler scandals. Harsh employers found it difficult to get workers; good employers with cross-border connections did not. All whites had African nicknames, often crude like Mrs Watkins's spinster friend *kabithu*, 'the cow that refuses the bull'. Settlers could feel haunted by the same unseen dangers as Africans, revealing their moral anxiety. Nakuru residents were not greatly surprised when Charles Ross was hanged for murdering two white women on the Menengai crater; Maasai had told them the mountain was accursed. When Diana (formerly Broughton, soon to be Delamere) Colvile's infant child died some blamed the sorcery of Waweru, servant to her former lover, the murdered Lord Errol. Others thought Happy Valley's promiscuity provoked Mau Mau, that lethal African disrespect. Still others blamed it on post-war settlers who did not know how to treat servants with a properly distant courtesy. Middle-class emotional discipline was what protected

[24] Redley, 'Predicament', and Kennedy, *Islands*, for my general approach in these two paragraphs; also, David W. Cohen and E. S. Atieno Odhiambo, *Siaya: The Historical Anthropology of an African Landscape* (London, 1989), 113; Richard Waller, 'Rough and Ready Injustice? Stock Theft Legislation in Colonial Kenya' (unpublished, 2007); Archibald Lyall, *It isn't Done: The Future of Taboo among the British Islanders* (London, 1930), 125–30; Ross, *Kenya from Within*, 120; Huxley, *Nellie*, 36; Blundell, *Wind*, 23; Denis Holman, *Bwana Drum* (London, 1964), 9–10; Watkins, *Olga*, 115; F. S. Joelson (ed.), *Eastern Africa Today* (London, 1928), 177, 179, 191; C. J. Duder and C. P. Youé, 'Paice's Place: Race and Politics in Nanyuki District, Kenya, in the 1920s', *African Affairs* 93 (1994), 253–78; Nicholls, *Red Strangers*, 29, 42, 177, 197, 246; Davis and Robinson, *Chronicles*, chs. 19–21.

white prestige. History was a personal responsibility. One either kept up standards on stage or let them slip. The academic historian's dialectics, trends, or cycles offered settlers no comfortable alibi, for the stage of supremacy was set in every home.[25]

Private lives were enacted in front of servants who brought tea in bed, even in the undressed state some Africans at first thought more manly than the Islamic robe, *kanzu*, that became houseboy uniform. Karen Blixen called this on-stage life 'brass-serpenting', after the snake Moses had lifted in the desert to save Israel from plague. She felt it lent magic to existence. George Orwell in Burma was not so sure. His need to preserve a hated authority seemed to make him the plaything of native opinion, not its master. Sir Edward Grigg (1925–30), governor and friend to settlers, was equally doubtful. He thought contact with Africans 'on a lower plane of life' tempted whites to lose 'patience and gentleness'. Michael Blundell agreed that privilege made whites careless of the self-restraint that was their best protection.[26]

Grigg echoed popular opinion. 'Are you married or do you live in Kenya?' was a chat-up line known even to the formidable Miss Perham. That Kenya was 'a place in the sun for shady people' was commonplace, thanks to the 'Kenya novel', pulp fiction of its day, in which native gossip turned white adultery into racial treachery. Settlers resented all this. A guidebook protested that Nairobi life was not as painted by 'sensationalist novelists' who raked up 'the sordid side of divorces'. Conversely, fear of black sexuality made whites worry about their children. Sexual assault by black youths on white children lent occasional proof to such prejudice. While one in seven of all employed Africans was a domestic servant the wealthy protected their young by employing white nannies; in the 1930s 4 per cent of whites were 'in service'. By contrast, officials were ready to blame settlers 'of low social

---

[25] Carnegie, *Diary*, 17; Norman Leys, *Last Chance in Kenya* (London, 1931), 80; Watkins, *Olga*, 164, 171; Blundell, *Wind*, 41–2, ch. 6; Scott, *Nice Place*, 142; W. J. Wright, *Their Excellencies* (Leicester, 1953), ch. 8; Erroll Trzebinski, *The Life and Death of Lord Errol: The Truth behind the Happy Valley Murder* (London, 2000), 231; James Fox, *White Mischief* (London, 1982), 31–2. Compare Florence Bernault, 'Body, Power and Sacrifice in Equatorial Africa', *Journal of African History*, 47/2 (2006), 207–39.

[26] Watkins, *Olga*, 91; Blixen, *Out of Africa*, 115–17 (and Numbers 21:5–9); George Orwell, *Shooting an Elephant: And Other Essays* (London, 1950); Sir Edward Grigg, *Speeches* (Nairobi, 1930), 155–6; Blundell, *Wind*, 39; also Farson, *Last Chance*, 175–6.

standing', either too familiar or too severe with their houseboys, for African assaults—a constant theme.

The wealthy also sent children home to boarding school and often the unhappiest years of their lives, deprived of open-air freedoms and black playmates. Mothers wept at this 'awful price of empire'. Since few settlers could afford to exile their young, fear for the future of illiterate whites caused government to subsidize school fees at local boarding schools, to which upcountry children travelled on chaperoned school trains. When opening the Prince of Wales School on Queen Victoria's birthday in 1928, Grigg added a colonial twist—and unrealistic hopes for minority rule—to schoolmasterly platitudes. He told the boys to prepare for an unusually exacting manliness, under the anxious gaze of other races. 'Though your destiny is in many ways to be rulers, you must learn from the outset to rule yourselves.'[27]

The Force of Obedience

Self-control upheld mastery over others. Mastery gave one the confidence to turn bush into a garden, to enter into labour-recruiting deals with chiefs, accept squatter tenant-workers whose elders spat, for good luck, on one's infant child, or a naked Luo cook in the kitchen. Beryl Markham's father made his farm out of the bush because 'you could feel the future of it *under your feet*'.[28] But mastery required force, military, legal, and personal, to reinsure prestige. No memoir admitted as much. The daily vocabulary of mastery made force seem so unremarkable.

It was with *kupiga*, to hit, that *Up-Country Swahili* explained Swahili verbs. *Kupiga* served many purposes, not only to hit a disobedient servant but to ring a bell, blow a whistle, fire a gun, iron clothes, and more. Force

---

[27] For these two paragraphs, Perham, *Journey*, 157; Florence Riddell, *Out of the Mist* (New York, 1926), 105, 251, 256–7; C. J. Duder, 'Love and the Lions: The Image of White Settlement in Kenya in Popular Fiction, 1919–1939', *African Affairs*, 90/360 (1991), 427–38; Joelson, *Eastern Africa*, 183; H. O. Weller, *Kenya without Prejudice* (London, 1931), 84; David Anderson, 'Sexual Threat and Settler Society in Colonial Africa' (unpublished); L. S. B. Leakey, *White African* (London, 1937), 83–9; Scott, *Nice Place*, 17, 89–97; Watkins, *Olga*, 169; Nicholls, *Red Strangers*, 102, 172–5; Grigg, *Speeches*, 283.

[28] Beryl Markham, *West with the Night* (London, [1942] 1984), 67; my emphasis. Shelagh Hill (ed.), *Early Memories of Settlers in Machakos, Kenya* (privately printed, ?2006), 37. I owe my subtitle to Béatrice Hibou, *La Force de l'Obéissance: Économie politique de la répression en tunisie* (Paris, 2006).

helped settlers possess Kenya. When botched or abused it could also signal an end to mastery, personal or political. Gerald Hanley, who knew Kenya, had a fictional settler first reflect on mortality when he failed to strike an African who answered back. Criminal responsibility for beating eleven Mau Mau detainees to death at Hola camp in 1959—the single most important event in persuading the British to leave Kenya, fast—turned on the degree of violence authorized by the commandant. What did he mean when in upcountry Swahili he told his warders they could hit a recalcitrant detainee, *piga yeye*, but not 'utterly'—*lakini hapana piga kabisa?*[29]

The degree of violence permissible against Africans was contentious from the start. The British used as little force as they could get away with but conquest became bloodier, and London more critical, as time went on. Most 'punitive expeditions' occurred before the first wave of settlers arrived in 1903–4. A mutually rewarding politics of collaboration followed, between district officers and Africans called chiefs. The British never allowed settlers to break this alliance, however much it was tested by white demands for land, cheap labour, and other subsidies. But archaic Master and Servant laws favoured employers over workers and, until the late 1920s, permitted judicial floggings. Pass controls also lent employers much power.

Settler memoirs say little of these helpful coercions. They say nothing of the collective fines, of dubious legality, imposed on Africans believed to harbour stockthieves, the bane of settler life. They reveal little of what became scandalous, the illegal use of the whip by employers who felt rough justice best suited raw natives even if it killed them—as it did more than once in the 1920s. If murder charges were brought white juries, notoriously, refused to convict. But London could nonetheless insist on reform. In the 1930s corporal punishment was dropped from the penal code. Workers began to sue; magistrates sometimes fined abusive employers. A jury convicted the widowed Mrs Selwyn of manslaughter when a farm-worker died after a beating.[30]

---

[29] Le Breton, *Swahili*, 17–22; Gerald Hanley, *The Year of the Lion* (London, 1953), 29; Colonial Office, *Record of Proceedings and Evidence in the Inquiry into the Deaths of Eleven Mau Mau Detainees at Hola Camp in Kenya* (Cmnd. 795, 1959), 41.

[30] For these two paragraphs, John Lonsdale, 'The Conquest State of Kenya 1895–1905', in Bruce Berman and John Lonsdale, *Unhappy Valley: Conflict in Kenya and Africa* (London, 1992), ch. 1; John Lamphear, *The Scattering Time: Turkana Responses to Colonial Rule* (Oxford, 1992); David Anderson, 'Master and Servant in Colonial Kenya, 1885–1939', *Journal of African History*, 41/3 (2000), 459–85; David Anderson, 'Black Mischief: Crime, Protest and Resistance in Colonial

Mastery, then, remained in flux as the colonial administration—never a
settler regime—juggled its dialectics of control under the eyes of New Delhi
and Whitehall.[31] A brief history must show how settlers conducted themselves, at first in order to possess, to master, and then, later, to lead, to stay.
Many remained migrant, unconvinced by a settler future, or broke. Starting
as adventurers, in two world wars settlers won a local indispensability while
exposing their global insignificance. Peace proved equally deceitful when the
state's support for white farming obliged it to repair African land usage too.
The more settlers fenced in their home county the less chance they had to
lead Kenya. The more Africans entered civilization's frontier the less settlers
agreed on how to renew the art of domination and, as Grigg well knew, at
times refused to be taught.

Rhinoceros Questions

In 1907 Winston Churchill, under-secretary of state at the Colonial Office,
visited East Africa. He thought the few white settlers there to be 'ruffians'; a
CO official later wanted to repatriate them. But the settler 'outrages' that
upset London showed only how hard it was to turn an African province of
India into a white man's country. Churchill called such conflicts of interest
'rhinoceros questions—awkward, thick-skinned, and horned, with a short
sight, an evil temper, and a tendency to rush upwind upon any alarm'.[32]

To limit its responsibilities to the settlers the CO gave no assisted passages
and after 1905 insisted that immigrants had capital. They differed in wealth
from the start. In 1912 six men or syndicates, 'D' among them, held one-fifth
of all alienated land. Such concentration of ownership was contrary to
policy but followed an inexorable logic. The railway had to pay. Officials
did not trust black peasants with penny packets of grubby produce to

Kenya', *Historical Journal*, 36/4 (1993), 851–77; Waller, 'Rough and Ready Injustice?'; Nicholls,
Red Strangers, 56; Patrick Collinson, 'The Cowbells of Kitale', *London Review of Books* (5 June
2003), 15–20; generally, Jean-François Bayart, *Le Gouvernement du monde* (Paris, 2004), 230–44.

[31] Bruce Berman, *Control and Crisis in Colonial Kenya: The Dialectic of Domination* (London,
1990).

[32] Ronald Hyam, *Elgin and Churchill at the Colonial Office 1905–1908* (London, 1968), 405–25;
Edward Paice, *Lost Lion of Empire: The Life of 'Cape to Cairo' Grogan* (London, 2001), ch. 14;
M. P. K. Sorrenson, *Origins of European Settlement in Kenya* (Nairobi and London, 1968), 65, 150–2;
Winston Churchill, *My African Journey* (London, 1908), 41, and compare Hilary Hook, *Home from
the Hill* (London, 1987), 187.

generate enough traffic. That needed investment, and big men. The colony, drip-fed by the British treasury until 1912, was too weak to help small fry who in any case could not compete with Indians living on 'the smell of an oil-rag'. Banks would not lend on land hedged with development conditions. To attract 'men of means' the CO had to relax its rules and permit unfettered concessions of cheap land on 999-year leases. This logic bore fruit. Shortly before 1914 'D' sold the first wool, mutton, and cereals off his Rift Valley estate. Subdivision of estates on a rising land market then made room for new farmers, with wives. In 1904 one in five whites was female; in 1914, one in three. Speculation began to pay. Settlers became more settled.[33]

Speculative origins shaped and stifled white Kenya. They burdened farmers, retarded profits, divided opinion, and opened the highlands to black colonization. Yet concessionaire development was inevitable, not only because Britain offered no choice. For half the 12,000 square miles reserved to whites was dry, not farmland but pasture, on Maasailand's high prairies. Of rain-fed Gikuyuland only the southern fringe was alienated, after its partial depopulation by famine. This area, 6 per cent of the Gikuyu sphere and 1 per cent of the white highlands, became the main coffee belt. Many whites settled here in small homesteads. But cattle country was big-man territory. Speculative land-hoarding raised costs further. Many immigrants lived on family funds and service pension, for want of profit. Concessionaire gains were the more resented. White Kenya became a polemical arena.

Far from reducing African farming, white settlement enlarged it. Peasants wanted pasture for the stock they accumulated as their crop sales grew—and the vast size of some estates allowed many squatters to 'creep on all unbeknown'. Maasailand became a magnet for black colonists. Chiefs, recruiting sergeants for whites, became African land agents. Karen Blixen's friend Kinyanjui rewarded his clients with squatter rights to the land of 'Delamere', the white tribe. His enemies he kept at home, to pick on whenever his district officer wanted labour or tax. Inter-racial alliances rested on a trade in African clients for other Africans' land. Here was the settlers' dilemma: were they a separate clan, or among the upper classes of a plural society? In the New Year of 1914 some answered that question by

---

[33] For these two paragraphs, Hately and Copley, *Angling*, 22–3; Paice, *Lost Lion*, 190–1; Huxley, *White Man's Country*, i. 158; generally, Sorrenson, *Origins*, ch. 9.

opening the Muthaiga Country Club, with the 'best cellar in Africa', exclusively for the upper class of their own kind.[34]

War and Peace

War was the handmaid of imperial reform as Britain repaid debts to colonial blood and treasure. Here the Great War was a problem for settlers. Victory owed more to Indians and Africans—and America—than to them. Thirty were killed, one by a lion. More were ruined by malaria and dysentery. Their Mounted Rifles, always 'a small unit in a large army', withered away as other units recruited its local knowledge. Despite this omen of expendability on the imperial stage, the settlers' wartime political gains far exceeded their military weight. Indeed, in 1915 the CO had to order them back to the colours from their farms. They went back, but on terms: seats on an executive war council, with their representatives popularly selected. Settlers obeyed Whitehall when it suited them.[35]

Women also fought to profit from war. Olga Watkins's first husband was killed early on. Her bachelor neighbours told her to leave his farm. A lone woman would tempt Africans to 'worse than murder'. Her bank wanted to foreclose. But the war went on. 'Lady farmers' became stock figures in Kenya novels. Male prejudice made women organize. Delamere demanded an electoral constitution to succeed the *ad hoc* war council but called female suffrage 'one of the greatest dangers to the Empire'. The East African Women's League arose in protest. After the war Northey decided in their favour, reassured that they were 'practically all wives'. They got the adult franchise before their British sisters.[36]

After the war men had to mobilize too, to recapture the empire story, only to find that to defeat one competitor, British Indians, they had to

---

[34] Paul Mosley, *The Settler Economies: Studies in the Economic History of Kenya and Southern Rhodesia 1900–1963* (Cambridge, 1983), 73; Thomas Spear and Richard Waller (eds.), *Being Maasai: Ethnicity and Identity in East Africa* (London, 1993); Lotte Hughes, *Moving the Maasai: A Colonial Misadventure* (Basingstoke, 2006), 27–9; Rebmann Wambaa and Kenneth King, 'The Political Economy of the Rift Valley: A Squatter Perspective', in B. A. Ogot (ed.), *Hadith 5: Economic and Social History of East Africa* (Nairobi, 1975), 195–217; Paice, *Lost Lion*, 257.

[35] George Bennett, *Kenya: A Political History, the Colonial Period* (London, 1963), 35; C. J. Wilson, *The Story of the East African Mounted Rifles* (Nairobi, 1938), 100, 120–36; R. Meinertzhagen, *Army Diary 1899–1926* (Edinburgh, 1960), 150; Maxon, *Struggle*, 79–127.

[36] Watkins, *Olga*, 56–9, 71–2; Elisabeth Hunt, 'A Voice in the Wilderness: European Settler Women in Kenya 1917–39' (Syracuse University Graduate Term paper, 1975).

champion the other, Africans. The war had helped them as farmers. The army bought their cereals, the navy their sisal, South Africa their coffee. Settlement became a fact.[37] But Britain owed so much to India in the war that it promised Indians equality of status throughout the dependent empire. Indian nationalists saw Kenya as the test of Britain's word. But the Devonshire Declaration gave an African answer to the 'Indian question'. Black loyalty had to be recognized, too. For the King's African Rifles, 10,000 of them from Kenya, had also helped win the war.

KAR dead, from East and Central Africa, were almost half the 11,000 empire troops killed in 'German East'. Kenya's 190,000 Carrier Corps porters suffered more terribly, with nearly one-quarter dead. Britain's War Office, remorseless by habit, refused for years to pay what it owed the dependants of 10,000 missing carriers. White Kenya, itself in mourning, was also unashamed. It welcomed white soldier-settlement after the war partly to allay fear of natives who had learnt the civilized way to kill. The labour demand was such that in 1923 one in eight employed Africans was coerced. Hut tax rose. Settlers blamed hardship on post-war slump. Africans blamed settlers.[38]

What made African resentment count was its connection with the 'Indian question'. This, at bottom, was about the security of white property. Smaller settlers liked cheap Indian credit, however much it weakened the case for proprietary segregation. Small men won the first legislative council election. Big men, lenders at higher interest, had to teach them a lesson. White supremacy, prerequisite for survival, needed solidarity whatever the price. And only natural leaders could cloak economic weakness in the civilizing mission, picturing plucky little Kenya as the Thermopylae of Christian white Africa, facing Asiatic hordes.[39]

Delamere and friends won their by-elections. London was harder to persuade. Why could not Kenya flourish on peasant production and Indian commerce? Settlers reacted by claiming a share in trusteeship. Missionaries backed them, fearing an advancing Islam. In coarser terms than any applied to Africans, whites deplored Asiatic filth and perversion. Whites accepted

---

[37] Huxley, *White Man's Country*, ii. 26–35, 50; contradicted by John Overton, 'War and Economic Development: Settlers in Kenya 1914–18', *Journal of African History*, 27/1 (1986), 79–104.

[38] Geoffrey Hodges, *The Carrier Corps: Military Labor in the East African Campaign 1914–1918* (New York, 1986), 110–11, 211; Edward Paice, *Tip and Run: The Untold Tragedy of the Great War in Africa* (London, 2007), 392–9; Huxley, *White Man's Country*, ii. 54. 58: Clayton and Savage, *Government and Labour*, ch. 4.

[39] Redley, 'Predicament', 64–119; Maxon, *Struggle*, 128–70; Paice, *Lost Lion*, 288–307; E. Powys Cobb, *The Thermopylae of Africa: Kenya Colony* (Nairobi, 1923).

the Protestant missionary alliance's desire for a secondary school to teach Africans the skills they now hired from Indians. The Alliance High School was born, helped by an unexpended KAR welfare fund. Twenty years later its boys beat white schools in examinations while, prophetically, adding the folksong 'English Country Garden' to their choral repertoire. Twenty years later still, in 1963, Alliance furnished half Jomo Kenyatta's first cabinet.[40]

This grappling of trusteeship to the settler cause, and its outcome, was an allegory of the times. In face of crisis, segregated privilege was repeatedly urged into responsible leadership by a government learning to see Kenya whole, not divisible into raw frontier and home county. This process hinged on 1929. Before then settlers grew in confidence; tripled their cultivated acreage with their first tractors; produced 90 per cent of Kenya's exports and got their 'burgher' Defence Force. Delamere dreamt of a settler-led federation with Uganda and Tanganyika, an East African dominion.

Such ambition crashed with Wall Street. Its foundations were never firm. Kenya offered settlers less than Australasia or Canada, more expensively. In 1926, a boom year, most farms earned under £300 (£13,000). There were only 17,000 whites by 1931. Barely half had lived in Kenya more than five years. 2,000 farms supported twenty-seven local associations with differing interests. Fewer than half eligible whites registered to vote. Under half the legislative council elections were contested.

Nairobi—Nairobbery—was only precariously white. Private covenant, not law, secured residential segregation from Indians. Business boundaries were blurred. Mohamed Ahmed, who safari-suited the Prince of Wales, flaunted his symbol, the three feathers, for forty years in the main street, Sixth Avenue, later Delamere, and now Kenyatta Avenue. The Jami'a mosque was not one hundred yards from the settlers' Memorial Hall. Courts upheld the Indian right to bid for any commercial property until in 1931 London's Privy Council overruled them, accepting what the CO denied but colluded in, the legality of urban property segregation. All Saints cathedral, white Nairobi's war memorial, embodied these ambiguities in Anglican style. A non-racial house of prayer, it segregated believers by the clock. Whites vacated pews before black buttocks sat on them. Stained-glass

---

[40] H. C. Delamere and C. Kenneth Archer, *Memorandum on the Case Against the Claims of Indians in Kenya* (Nairobi, 1921), 8; B. E. Kipkorir, 'The Alliance High School and the Origins of the Kenya African Elite 1926–1962', Ph.D. thesis (Cambridge, 1969), 44–82, 213–14, 249, 382; Atieno Odhiambo's reminiscence.

images nonetheless presented colonists with their faith's most awkward demand. Four British saints shone down from the windows. So too did four local heroes. Three were white missionaries. One was black, Apolo Kivebulaya, 'apostle to the pygmies'.[41]

Delamere died in 1931, his dreams in ashes. At home the Labour government stated that any future self-rule must represent all races; the next Tory colonial secretary confirmed that decision. The world depression made exports unprofitable; the home county returned to bush. By 1934 one in five farms was left abandoned to squatters and stockthieves. Government could do little to help. In 1932 one-third of its shrivelled revenue went to repay London bankers—at 5 per cent, the highest rate in British Africa—for the branch lines and other 1920's investments. Hard times sharpened white conflicts; planters refused to buy from farmers the maize to feed their large workforces when peasants sold it more cheaply. Farmers had to survive on cross-border deals of their own. Their Farmers Association traded in African maize while its members' own acreage halved. Ranchers waged range-wars with black pastoralists equally hit by drought and locusts, but also patched up compromises. For a fee, farm guards winked at African trespass; whites hired out pasture to Africans in defiance of the law and their neighbours. In Nairobi a down-and-out begged for 'any employment to keep me white'. Poverty could cause the abuse of half-starved white children and parental suicide. In his foreword to a glossy promotional book the governor praised Kenya as a winter resort, not as a home. It was almost as if 'D' had never been.[42]

---

[41] For these three paragraphs: Redley, 'Predicament', chs. 6–11; Waller, 'Clean and Dirty'; Paice, *Lost Lion*, 341; Salvadori, *Colonisation*, 118–19, 131–2; Errol Trzebinski,. *The Kenya Pioneers* (London, 1985), 193; Huxley, *White Man's Country*, ii, ch. 22; Kennedy, *Islands*, 195; Leonard Weaver, 'The Origins, Record, and Historical Significance of the Kenya Regiment' (unpublished, 2004), 68–74; Anthony Lester and Geoffrey Bindman, *Race and Law* (Harmondsworth, 1972), 42–6; Grigg, *Speeches*, 110–19, 156; observations of David Anderson and Sloane Mahone in All Saints, 2006.

[42] Redley, 'Predicament', 200–2; Paice, *Lost Lion*, 343–5; Berman, *Control and Crisis*, 183–4; John Lonsdale, 'The Depression and the Second World War in the Transformation of Kenya', in David Killingray and Richard Rathbone (eds.), *Africa and the Second World War* (Basingstoke, 1986), 104–19; Huxley, *Nellie*, 85–113; David Anderson, *Eroding the Commons: The Politics of Ecology in Baringo, Kenya 1890–1968* (Oxford, 2002), ch. 4; Kennedy, *Islands*, 168; Watkins, *Olga*, 166–8; Nicholls, *Red Strangers*, 182; R. F. Mayer, *Kenya Camera Studies* (Nairobi, 1934), pp. iii–iv.

But not quite. In the 1920s government had courted producer interests—cereal, dairy, plantation—to divide the politics Delamere tried to unite. These now emerged to coordinate white survival. Depression saw off the incompetents, Baroness Blixen among them. Corporate discipline, farm sector by sector, became the watchword. It lent an appropriate structure to the fascism that briefly entranced settler politics—until Hitler tried to reclaim Tanganyika for the Reich. And efficiency worked. Coffee yields compared with Brazil's. Surviving maize farmers were twice as productive as white South Africans. Some thought them 'maize miners', ruining the land.

It was here that government began to see Kenya whole, in tune with a worldwide fear that impoverished cultivators were flogging farmlands into dust-bowls. Africans with scrub cattle were as bad as maize miners. Government determined that both must mend their ways. As settlers left the land and sacked workers, government also had to find new ways for Africans to earn a taxable income—as producers. A few were permitted to grow coffee, breaching the whites' most valuable monopoly. The CO had long advised Kenya to enlarge its exports by adding black production to white. London similarly exploited Mussolini's invasion of Ethiopia in 1935 to replace the Kenya Defence Force, the arm of colonial segregation, with the Kenya Regiment, an imperial unit for training officers. White youths now learnt not how to kill native rebels but to lead black fellow subjects against a common enemy, should war again swell the KAR. White politicians walked out of the governor's executive council.

The boycott was brief, symptom of uncertain times. Ambivalence marked all change. Imperial Airways started an eight-day service from London by air and rail; Hemingway came on safari; the market town of Nakuru boasted an amateur orchestra; farmers employed refugee German Jews; pyrethrum, an insecticidal daisy, pulled many out of debt. But air travel also brought in the Happy Valley crowd, making Kenya seem 'a debauched purlieu of Mayfair'. A land commission cleared the way for the legal segregation of white highland property but put an end to its further expansion. Over the frontier chiefs grew carnations. London companies bought up bankrupt farms; settler society was becoming planter economy. Edward Bovill thought this transition essential but accepted that any farmer would think his loss of independence a 'foul heresy', with 'his cherished homestead become a mere manager's house'. Sir Robert Brooke Popham (1937–9), horseman, airman, governor, was unperturbed. He thought Kenya was not 'primarily a money-making organisation.... [T]he main object of most people in coming out here is to live in fine scenery, a good climate, and amongst friends.'[43] The next war put paid to such fantasies. Mere management was at hand.

Ruling, Leading, Fighting, Quitting

In 1939 'Signifer', long-settled, published an essay in the local press.[44] His premise was that Kenya offered whites 'no alternative between ruling and quitting'. World opinion required them to lead Africans; settlement had no other justification. But with another war in the offing settlers would have to convert African discontent into cooperation. Whites must 'lead this land or, sooner or later, they must quit this land'. Ruling and leading meant the same to Signifer. The colony's last years were to expose their contradictions.

The Second World War, like the First, summed up the complexities to come. Settlers became managers of the war economy and so, paradoxically, evaded the fate Bovill had foretold. Family farmers became solvent, confident, joint rulers of what seemed to be a white man's country at last. But 2,000 of their sons learnt respect for Africans when leading KAR platoons in Ethiopia, Madagascar, and Burma. After 1945 a second post-war settlement scheme brought in 300 men as state-assisted tenants, not pioneers. More arrived on passages paid by their Nairobi employers, to enjoy better living than in weary, rationed, Britain. No mud huts or pit-latrines for them, unlike the 1920s. Official enthusiasts swelled government's field services, to cajole African conservatism into the labour of reform. Many were transient, as before, not intending to lay their bones in Kenya. The seasoned, settled, minority, increasingly in business, provided their post-war leadership. Some even tried to lead Africans.

War brought profitable self-rule to white farming as the export market came to Kenya. In 1943 farm sales tripled 1935's exports. Kenya became more of a farmer's country, reversing the 1930s, from feeding both the multi-racial

---

[43] For these three paragraphs: Redley, 'Predicament', 32–3, 203–37; Mosley, *Settler Economies*, 172–6; Trzebinski, *Life and Death*, ch. 7; Blundell, *Wind*, ch. 3; Anderson, *Eroding the Commons*, ch. 6; Weaver, 'Kenya Regiment', ch. 2; Nicholls, *Red Strangers*, 185–6, 207–8; Edward Steinhart, *Black Poachers, White Hunters* (Oxford, 2006), 128–30; Paice, *Lost Lion*, 346–8; Huxley, *Nellie*, 132–4; R. Breen, 'The Politics of Land: The Kenya Land Commission (1932–33) and its Effects on Land Policy in Kenya', Ph.D. thesis (Michigan State University, 1976); L. S. B. Leakey, *Kenya Contrasts and Problems* (London, 1936), 13; Watkins, *Olga*, 218–19; E. W. Bovill, 'Economic Development in East Africa', Nov. 1938, with Governor's minute, 25 Jan. 1939: Kenya National Archives: SC/AGR.56/4.

[44] Signifer, 'Conversation Piece', *East African Standard* (27 Jan. 1939), 11.

Commonwealth army that conquered Italian Ethiopia and the 55,000 Italians made prisoner. Farmers also earned a more lasting maize premium as Kenya's famine reserve, after a fall in African sales, and hunger, in 1943 confirmed a view that it was African greed that impoverished the soil, not poverty. Under Ferdinand Cavendish-Bentinck, 'C-B', aristocrat and businessman, settlers became economic managers.

But many refused to count their 250,000 African squatters among their responsibilities. White district councils moved to reduce squatter entitlements. They had three reasons. First, patriotic profit enabled settlers to farm the many acres previously held by squatters. Next, councils feared that a Labour government at home might support Kenya's labour officers in a policy that would permit former squatters to stay on as villagers with kitchen gardens, free to work for any farmer they chose. But an African title to highland land, not conditional on a work contract, would breach the settlers' only security, their sole right to lease land in the scheduled highland area. Finally, to rebut the belief that the settler was 'an idle man occupying idle acres', the new settlement scheme subdivided existing farms for more intensive use. Intensive mixed farming had no room for squatters. They must become labourers. But farmers failed to pay the higher wages needed to compensate for the loss of domestic production. A government that still relied on settlers to finance native trusteeship failed to redress this African grievance. Farmers most reluctant to close the home county's gate on their clients included veterans from the KAR.[45]

As on the frontier, war had taught whites to trust Africans, 90,000 of whom from Kenya had volunteered for military service. Over 100 settler officers and at least 2,000 Kenyan *askari* died, more to dissolve the empire than defend it. They got Haile Selassie back on his throne and in the Burma campaign helped clear the way for Nehru to inherit the viceroy's duty to Indians overseas. Many encountered cross-racial, self-sacrificial loyalty. After battle they had lain exhausted, white and black 'all twisted up together', as was unthinkable back on the farm. The army's Swahili textbook had prepared the way. Its 'good morning' was a greeting not found in

[45] For these two paragraphs, J. F. Lipscomb, *We Built a Country* (London, 1956), 102, 104; Lonsdale, 'Depression and War', 119–33; Clayton and Savage, *Government and Labour*, 246, 305–11; Richard Frost, *Race against Time: Human Relations and Politics in Kenya before Independence* (London, 1978), 21–2; David Throup, *Economic and Social Origins of Mau Mau 1945–53* (London, 1987), ch. 5; Joanna Lewis, *Empire State-Building: War and Welfare in Kenya 1925–52* (Oxford, 2000), 261–3.

Up-Country Swahili. Still more subversively the army taught many Africans English. After the Great War settlers had got the vote. Now, before the *askari* came home, the governor thought it wise to nominate the first African legislative councillor, Eliud Mathu, witchdoctor's son, schoolteacher, and Balliol man.[46]

Kenya clearly faced a discordant post-war future. Sir Philip Mitchell, the new governor (1944–52), came as an old East Africa hand, believer in trusteeship and allergic to obstinate settler, excitable Hindu, and half-educated native alike. So he tried to coax settlers, lords now of their home county, into a cross-racial leadership of all Kenya. Initiating a quasi-ministerial regime, he made C-B 'member' for agriculture, to teach whites care for African as well as settler lands. Mitchell also gave settlers what some had long demanded, an unofficial majority in legislative council within a closer union of the three East African territories—but in a nightmare version of Delamere's dream. The new inter-territorial assembly was to be elected on a racially balanced formula that would one day see Africans predominate. Kenya's own unofficial majority was multi-racial too. If settlers wished to outvote government they had to bring the elected Asian legislators and the unelected, nominated, Africans with them. Mitchell had at last invited settlers to become associate trustees with Britain in building the future.[47]

Few accepted the challenge. Bovill's company gave bursaries to Africans at Uganda's Makerere College. A handful of officials and professionals opened the multi-racial United Kenya Club. Cultural initiatives were rare and their jollity forced, unable to bridge the frightful discrepancies in income between whites and Indians on the one hand, and Africans, even white-collar workers, on the other. Boy Scouts obeyed their fourth law, that all scouts were brothers, only on ceremonial occasions. But inter-racial sport flourished, especially cricket with its lack of bodily contact. Asian cricketers noted with interest the class distinctions between white teams.

---

[46] John Nunneley, *Tales from the King's African Rifles* (London, 1998); Blundell, *Love Affair*, 67, and cf. Waruhiu Itote, *'Mau Mau' General* (Nairobi, 1967), 27; Le Breton, *Swahili*, 70; East African Army Education Corps, *KiSwahili* (Nairobi, 1942), 42, 125, 137; Timothy H. Parsons, *The African Rank-and-File: Social Implications of Colonial Military Service in the King's African Rifles, 1902–1964* (Portsmouth, NH, 1999), 114–17.

[47] Bennett, *Kenya*, 99–109; Berman, *Control and Crisis*, 283–5; Richard Frost, *Enigmatic Proconsul: Sir Philip Mitchell and the Twilight of Empire* (London, 1992), 174–201; Farson, *Last Chance*, 28.

More saw Mitchell's offer as a trap, the *East African Standard* warning that whites would one day become 'constitutionally a racial minority'. Mitchell was unsympathetic, calling their leaders 'little, frightened, narrow, heathen men ... full of racial bitterness'. Michael Blundell, back from the KAR, sought election to legislative council in 1948 on the contradictory slogan 'European leadership, reservation of the European highlands and a communal or racial [voters'] roll'. Whites refused to pay for services that met mainly African needs. In Britain the state taxed the rich to fund benefits for the poor. Not in Kenya. Each community paid largely for its own services—Africans mainly through local government rates. 'God preserve us from ... a welfare state', Lady Shaw exclaimed in committee, early in 1952. Such a fate was unlikely in a poor colony but worse was to befall before the year was out.[48]

Settlers were in two minds. Most clung to what they had, the home county. A few edged towards the unmapped frontier of national leadership, meeting racial strangers who must in time dominate by number, not by fitness. There seemed no hurry to decide. The assisted-settlement scheme assumed a forty-four-year term of repayment to a still-colonial state; Kenya's wisest critic, Margery Perham, thought any African share in power was two generations away; the white population grew. The 1948 census counted 30,000 Europeans, a quarter locally born. 3,000 adults were in agriculture, including managers. Government employed similar numbers. 5,000 were in business, 1,500 of them female secretaries. 6,600 unpaid housewives had only 7,400 dependent children. The middle classes had learnt to travel light and many teenagers were absent, earning in Britain the qualifications that mobility required. While many called Kenya 'my country'—not, as in Rhodesia, 'my nation'—Britain remained 'home'.[49]

Nairobi cinemas used four times more energy in 1945 than in 1932. Postwar prosperity brought in light-brown Seychelloise nannies and modernist

[48] Timothy H. Parsons, *Race, Resistance, and the Boy Scout Movement in British Colonial Africa* (Athens, Ohio, 2004), 113–90; reminiscences of Ali Rattansi; *East African Standard* (4 Apr. 1947) and Mitchell, diary entries Dec. 1951 and Aug. 1946, all quoted in Frost, *Race*, 47, 56 (see also pp. 255–6); Blundell, *Wind*, 70; Low and Smith, *History of East Africa*, iii. 603–4; Bennett, *Kenya*, 104; Lewis, *Empire State-Building*, 357–8.

[49] Huxley and Perham, *Race and Politics*, 240; Fabian Colonial Bureau, *Kenya: White Man's Country?* (London, 1944), 31; Farson, *Last Chance*; Elspeth Huxley, *The Sorcerer's Apprentice: A Journey through East Africa* (London, 1948); J. E. Goldthorpe, *Outlines of East African Society* (Makerere University College, 1959), 129–43.

architecture, assurances of an orderly future. Plate-glass and concrete made upcountry farmers in muddy pick-ups seem burnt-out cases from another age but also insulated white townsfolk from Africa. Upcountry life changed too, but differently. Hunting and polo flourished; in far Kitale colonels 'clustered like grapes'; butchers sold boys' meat (houseboy's rations) as cheaply as dogs' meat; white primary schoolboys went naked on runs. But local drama societies also built theatres; farmers' wives ran clinics and schools for their workers; sons and daughters returned from overseas as lawyers and doctors; settler and official families intermarried. Conventional piety moved out of the club—where an altar cloth had masked the bar—as farmers built churches in upcountry-gothic, with memorials to sons killed on imperial service. Introspective piety also grew. Many whites joined Moral Rearmament's house-parties to confess their sins, racial arrogance not least. But Kenya's history, to whites a self-regarding myth of beneficent progress, had already spawned disaster.[50]

1947, so soon after the war, was a year of tumult in which settlers lost any chance to lead. Squatters rejected their new labour contracts. Ex-squatters resisted, with an oath of solidarity, land-husbandry rules designed to turn them into improving smallholders on a pilot settlement scheme. Kenyatta, back after sixteen years in Britain, became president of the new Kenya African Union. His hopes of national leadership were as doomed as the settlers', in his case by the gulf between Gikuyu militants and elders of their own and other ethnic groups. Of Kenya's Africans Gikuyu had gained most from colonial rule and so were the most divided. Gikuyu gentry, Kenyatta among them, tried to lead a conservative, propertied, nationalism. Their impatient juniors became Mau Mau—which means 'the greedy eaters [of elders' authority]'. The failure of Mitchell's multi-racialism to deliver any improvements visible to Africans, combined with the hard labour of saving

---

[50] L. W. Thornton White, L. Silberman, and P. R. Anderson, *Nairobi: Master Plan for a Colonial Capital* (London, 1948), 83; cf. Rhodri Windsor Liscombe, 'Modernism in Late Imperial British West Africa: The Work of Maxwell Fry and Jane Drew, 1946–56', *Journal of the Society of Architectural Historians*, 65/2 (2006), 188–215; Nicholls, *Red Strangers*, ch. 10; Clayton and Savage, *Government and Labour*, ch. 9; Frederick Cooper, *Decolonization and African Society: The Labor Question in French and British Africa* (Cambridge, 1996), 348–60; Farson, *Last Chance*, 83; personal observation; URL: <www.oldcambrians.com>, accessed Sept. 2009; Alan Knight, oral interview 15 Mar. 1994; Philip Boobbyer, 'Moral Re-Armament in Africa in the Era of Decolonization', in Brian Stanley (ed.), *Missions, Nationalism, and the End of Empire* (Grand Rapids, Mich., 2003), 212–36.

the African reserves from soil erosion—and therefore the white highlands from African invasion—meant that the militants were bound to win.[51]

How far the violence of counter-insurgency was unusually atrocious and, if so, was specifically racist and colonial, are questions often addressed and in a social history of the settlers must take priority over other issues to do with Mau Mau.[52] This chapter concludes that, while the violence of the 'Emergency' was comparable to that of any peasant war, its spectacular nature owed much to its colonial context; and it divided settlers more decisively than ever before.

To settlers Mau Mau was 'a kick in the solar plexus'. Most reacted with the pained panic of paternalism betrayed. Graham Greene's comment that it was as if Jeeves had taken to the jungle was no joke. The first act to horrify, one to haunt the memory of some pastoral peoples still, was the hamstringing of ranchers' cattle. On the first day of the emergency, 21 October 1952, the *East African Standard* reported an arson attack on a polo club more prominently than an expected statement from the secretary of state. The first white murder set the tone of terror. Eric Bowyer, a lonely old man, met his end under the knives of Africans with whom he had traded, in his blood-filled bath. Thirty other farmhouse assaults followed before mid-1953, one-third of them fatal, often at supper with the complicity of servants coerced into killing their employers as much to enforce insurgent solidarity as to terrorize whites. If white supremacy was enacted in the home so too was its bloody rejection. Settlers saw in Mau Mau a contrivance of all their ancient enemies: a negrophile Colonial Office that raised foolish black expectation,

---

[51] Bruce Berman, 'Bureaucracy and Incumbent Violence: Colonial Administration and the Origins of the "Mau Mau" Emergency' (1976), in Berman and Lonsdale, *Unhappy Valley*, 227–64; for the large literature on the origins of Mau Mau see bibliography in Atieno Odhiambo and John Lonsdale (eds.), *Mau Mau and Nationhood* (Oxford, 2003), to which add David Anderson, *Histories of the Hanged: Britain's Dirty War in Kenya and the End of the Empire* (London, 2005), 9–86, 119–51.

[52] Addressed in sequence by: Evans, *Law and Disorder*; Josiah Mwangi Kariuki, 'Mau Mau' *Detainee* (London and Nairobi, 1963); Carl G. Rosberg and John Nottingham, *The Myth of 'Mau Mau': Nationalism in Kenya* (New York and London, 1966), 320–47; Anthony Clayton, *Counter-Insurgency in Kenya 1952–1960* (Nairobi, 1976); Robert B. Edgerton, *Mau Mau, an African Crucible* (New York and London, 1989); Berman, *Control and Crisis*, 347–71; Tidrick, *Empire and the English Character*, 156–71; Frank Furedi, *Colonial Wars and the Politics of the Third World* (London, 1994); Mark Curtis, *Web of Deceit: Britain's Real Role in the World* (London, 2003), ch. 15; Anderson, *Histories*; Caroline Elkins, *Britain's Gulag: The Brutal End of Empire in Kenya* (London and New York, 2005).

salaried officials ignorant of the native mind, Indian intrigue, and the abuse of British freedoms by half-educated Africans. Any agrarian notables anywhere, in any age, would have expressed similar sentiments in face of peasant revolt.[53]

Not many police recruits, however, start training in identification procedure with a pair of human hands, severed from an insurgent killed that morning. The Emergency's violence was particular to its time and place, in two respects. First, while all attempts to subvert or defend existing distributions of power necessarily engage in spectacular force, in Kenya there were two such social orders under attack, one Gikuyu, the other racial. Each struggle inflamed the other. In Gikuyuland mission literacy, population growth, the Nairobi food market, loss of land, had all spurred a new gentry to convert its kin seniority into power over markets, land, and labour. Militants had to overturn this order to win their own self-mastery. Mau Mau's initial outrages against fellow Gikuyu showed how hard it was—as settlers had found years before—to overturn a colonial politics of collaboration. Whites responded with equally spectacular violence. They had property to defend, their only capital; a racial solidarity with which to conform; and a racial imbalance of force to restore. Class hatred was also at work. A notoriously murderous army officer had seen his horses mutilated. The part-time Kenya Police Reserve by contrast, the body with the worst reputation for killing prisoners, relied much on insecure men not of the officer class. While the often atrocious violence unleashed in 1952 was specific to Kenya, however, one may still question how far the white treatment of black captives was worse than more easily concealed villainy in the more formal frontlines of modern war.[54]

What made the violence still more distinctively Kenyan was the reaction of the colonial state. Like any *ancien régime* with little force at central command, the government tried to suppress rebellion without permitting its own indispensable allies, white and black, settler and 'loyalist', to become over-mighty subjects, each dictating incompatible terms. The state had therefore

---

[53] Holman, *Bwana Drum*, 17; John Lonsdale, 'Mau Maus of the Mind: Making Mau Mau and Remaking Kenya', *Journal of African History*, 31/3 (1990), 393–421; Graham Greene, *Ways of Escape* (London, 1980), 188; Anderson, *Histories*, 86–95.

[54] Hewitt, *Kenya Cowboy*, 11–12; for killing prisoners, John Keegan, *The Face of Battle* (Harmondsworth, 1978), 47–50; Joanna Bourke, *An Intimate History of Killing* (London, 2000), 165–6, 183–92, 255–6, 293; Niall Ferguson, *The War of the World: History's Age of Hatred* (London, 2007), 125–30, 541–52.

to take more power itself, to protect their interests but not at their behest. Government had pre-empted white vigilantism more than once before, by moving the Maasai, by conceding the communal roll in 1923, by replacing the local Defence Force with the imperial Kenya Regiment. It did so now.

To silence settler calls for vigilante 'justice', the government multiplied capital offences and pruned legal procedures designed to protect defendants. Over 1,000 Mau Mau were hanged, twice the number the French guillotined in Algeria. But not all suspects could be brought to court. Legal due process, however abbreviated, was often impossible. Many witnesses were intimidated or murdered by Mau Mau. Mass detention without trial, a breach of the rights of even native subjects, became a necessary instrument of repression. Still more disruptive of life, with harsh effects in malnutrition, disease, and exposure to cruelty, was the enforced concentration of previously dispersed rural populations into 850 wired-in strategic villages. Terror succeeds by stampeding rulers into substituting coercion for consent. Settlers became complicit in arbitrary rule, never a route to legitimate leadership.[55]

Mau Mau imposed heavy costs on Gikuyu. Terror and counter-terror killed many. Gikuyu and related peoples totalled 1.5 million; their normal annual mortality was around 28,000; in the Emergency they lost around 50,000 'extra' persons, half of them children. But some 'missing' children were simply delayed, since more Gikuyu young women were at school, unmarried, than among other ethnic groups. Gikuyu entrants to Makerere University were 45 per cent of Kenya's admissions through the 1950s, twice the Gikuyu share of Kenya's population. Here were deep-seated advantages uninterrupted by war, thanks to missionaries who had not set the tone for white Kenya. A new opportunity took root too—a smallholder cash-crop programme that government saw as the 'second prong' of counter-insurgency. Smallholder production, 16 per cent of Kenya's output in the mid-1950s, rose to over 40 per cent by 1964, the first year of independence. Gikuyu again took the lead, but war and recovery sharpened the differentiation that had provoked Mau Mau. Loyalists—conservative patriots who accounted for 40 per cent of insurgent deaths in action—often did well at

---

[55] My analysis of the regime's problems follows that of Philip Rogers at the Colonial Office, minute to W. Gorell Barnes, 24 Oct. 1952: TNA, CO 822/444/195; for other sources see n. 52 above, esp. Anderson, *Histories*, 111–18, 151–80, 200–24, 289–327, and Elkins, *Britain's Gulag*. Clayton's *Counter-Insurgency* owes much to personal experience and to the views of the then Attorney-General, Sir John Whyatt.

the expense of absent detainees. The agrarian revolution was intended to protect the settler future by dividing a hungry peasantry into sturdy black yeomen and urban workers now permitted to organize as a class. If such a social order was ever sustainable it was too late now.[56]

Mau Mau divided whites no less. Their political leader Michael Blundell was on the governor's war council; Kenya Regiment personnel were used, as in the Second World War, to sharpen British battalions with local skills and lead black loyalists, incorporated into the Kikuyu Guard. Such appearances were deceptive. British troops and British money took Kenya's future out of local hands, for reasons 'Signifer' had not foreseen. British policy was to make Kenya governable again and potentially, therefore, disposable. The means were plain but impossible, to 'build up a substantial "middle class" of *all* races to be the backbone of the country'. White supremacy was finished; class interest must replace racial antagonism. Few whites could rise above the racial anger of war to grasp at what in distant Whitehall seemed the only promise of peace. In 1954, faced with staff shortages, it did not occur to the Kenya Co-operative Creameries, a true backbone, to recruit non-white managers. But, again, some whites took up the challenge, and divided settler opinion further. A minority, with the bravest joining the all-race Capricorn Africa Society, dared to ride the tide of multi-racial politics, in the belief that the self-evident need for European 'standards' would ensure that, as the colonial government paid ever more heed to racial arithmetic, a qualified franchise would continue to reflect peoples' supposed 'fitness to rule'. The majority argued, correctly, that retention of white leadership down that slippery slope was wishful thinking. If settlers could not continue to rule Kenya by hectoring its officials then they must split it, with a white-highland island to call their own, separate from its black surroundings. 'Parity [in legislative council] or partition' became their still more wishful cry, heedless of their white highlands' arithmetical blackness. If partition was impossible there was always resistance. White opposition prevented Oliver Lyttelton, Churchill's secretary of state, from bringing as many Africans as he wanted into government in 1954. White fear of their black allies led them to

[56] John Blacker, 'The Demography of Mau Mau: Fertility and Mortality in Kenya in the 1950s, a Demographer's Viewpoint', *African Affairs*, 106/423 (2007), 205–27; J. E. Goldthorpe, *An African Elite: Makerere College Students 1922–1960* (Nairobi, 1965), 28; Goldthorpe, *Outlines*, 235; Judith Heyer, J. K. Maitha, and W. M. Senga (eds.), *Agricultural Development in Kenya: An Economic Assessment* (Nairobi, 1976), 81, 89, 90, 196; Daniel Branch, *Defeating Mau Mau, Creating Kenya: Counterinsurgency, Civil War, and Decolonization* (Cambridge, 2009).

publicize loyalist atrocity by circulating a critical court judgment under the title 'Kenya's Belsen?'[57]

Younger whites, many fresh from school, bore the brunt of the war, seconded from their training unit, the Kenya Regiment, to the British army, the police, or Kikuyu Guard. In the last they were members of the otherwise all-African small platoons whose comradeship is always the key to fighting spirit. Leadership's demands led in different directions. Some dodged the draft; others broke down when put to the test. There was always the dread of appearing weak in front of one's men. How often that racial dynamic tempted young whites to initiate or wink at illegal violence one cannot tell. A Kenyan officer in the KAR had to be posted elsewhere after his refusal to hand Gikuyu prisoners over for rough treatment forfeited his soldiers' respect. Restraint was difficult when in command of Kikuyu Guard eager to wreak vengeance on Mau Mau, often their neighbours. But leadership also brought cross-racial friendship and astonishing trust. Young whites put their lives in the hands of African trackers, as their grandfathers had done on the frontier. They went into the forest in the company of former Mau Mau, as prisoners 'turned' against their comrades and led 'pseudo gangs' to 'track down and shoot' the human 'shy game' that clumsy British troops, *WaJohnny*, found so hard to hunt. Blackening one's skin with Zebo stove polish was nothing compared to trusting the gangster captured in the morning to be one's guide that night, gun in hand. Similar courage and trust, on both sides, was evident elsewhere. A cook refused to kill his white employers, at risk of his life; a Mau Mau leader spared a farmer who had cared for him as a child; white employers negotiated elaborate evasions with their servants to avoid the risk of either having to kill the other; one farmer even sued the press for calling his farm headman—correctly as it turned out—a Mau Mau treasurer; penitent 'Kenya cowboys' ran reform schools for Mau Mau young; in the detention camps some locally recruited commandants confessed white guilt; others resisted the abuse of detainees; many farmers refused to get rid of their Gikuyu squatters. Mau Mau, sworn to drive settlers from Kenya, could recreate the cross-racial loyalties of the

---

[57] Sir Charles Jeffries, minute, 17 Feb. 1953 (emphasis in original): TNA, CO.822/440; M. F. Hill, *Cream Country: The Story of Kenya Co-operative Creameries Limited* (Nairobi, 1956), 103; Richard Hughes, *Capricorn: David Stirling's Second African Campaign* (London and New York, 2003); Blundell, *Wind*, 114–220; Bennett, *Kenya*, 135–40; Anderson, *Histories*, 273–9, 281, 297–307.

frontier and paradoxically, turn some whites into Kenyans with no other home.[58]

When Britain decided in 1960 that Kenya could not be excluded from decolonization, with its neighbours independent or about to be, white society retained its divisions to the last. Nellie Grant saw clearly how whites would go their separate ways. 'Of course settlement is killed stone dead; a lot of people, those who can, will go: commercials etc will stay on and no doubt Kenya will eventually flourish but we settlers have had it.' That point was driven home when Peter Poole died a few months later, the first, and only, white man to be hanged for the murder of an African in Kenya's colonial history. Mastery was no more; possessive confidence collapsed, capital flowed out like water; farm development ceased; black unemployment soared. Decolonization turned into a salvage operation, made the more urgent by the flood of Belgian refugees from the Congo, and peasant occupations of deserted farms, reminiscent of the 1930s. Most settlers left, especially those with children, so that white Kenya still flourishes on the internet, as people now retired in Natal, Queensland, or Canada seek to recall the highland friends of their youth. The British taxpayer, having paid for the railway that brought the settlers in, now paid to buy them out.

But many stayed, surprised at how the social distance of race could shrink into a tolerant neighbourliness. The dread Kenyatta became the 'old man' as much for white Kenyans as for black. For Kenya Regiment veterans Kenya remains their most popular home; several Mau Mau hunters became game wardens, helped by their former enemies. As Nellie foresaw, 'commercials' stayed most of all, both urban businessmen and plantation managers who felt no great pangs of political betrayal for generations of mud and sweat. Families stayed too, including the largest owners, the Delameres. When those longest settled did finally sell up, patrons to the last, they saw to it that those who had been with them longest, their squatters, were provided for. Pam Scott handed over her father's estate, Deloraine, to a local co-operative. Its name, a corruption of the family's old Scottish estate given by a queen, 'Delareine', became still further

---

[58] Gill, *Military Musings*, 33, 35–8, 41–4, 48, 61; Leonard Gill, *More Military Musings* (Victoria, BC, 2004), *passim* for tracker Ngalu; Leonard Gill, *Remembering the Regiment* (Victoria, BC, 2004), 81–7; Holman, *Bwana Drum*, 87–9, 90–2; Weaver, 'Kenya Regiment', 158–237; David Lovatt Smith, *Kenya, the Kikuyu and Mau Mau* (Herstmonceux, 2005), 128, 155, 159–228; GHQ East Africa, *A Handbook on anti-Mau Mau operations* (Nairobi, 1954), 11, for shy game; Lander, *My Kenya Acres*, 15–17; Huxley, *Nellie*, 178–215; Nicholls, *Red Strangers*, 264; Evans, *Law and Disorder*, 157–8.

corrupted, which is to say naturalized, as *Derorini*. Nellie Grant's squatters, who bought her farm, had good reason to call it *Mataguri*, 'we have been here a long time'.[59]

How white Kenya changed at independence is best seen in the domestic guidance that women offered. The Scots ladies of Nairobi's St Andrew's Church Women's Guild first brought out the *Kenya Settlers Cookery Book* in 1928. The twelfth and final edition appeared in 1958, still full of frugal tips on how to use sour milk, make jam, bottle fruit or concoct soft drinks, how to knit laddered stockings into floor rugs or stir beeswax and turpentine into floor polish, how to boil maize meal and pork fat into soap, how to destroy cockroaches and rats, treat chickens for scaly leg and talk to servants in Swahili or Gikuyu. Its useful phrases gave a sense of how the trans-racial negotiation of household duties might create a nightmare of misunderstanding: 'I will explain to you again. Answer me when I speak to you. Speak slowly. Speak softly. Be quiet. Leave off talking. Enough of words. . . . Do not be sulky. You are insolent! You must look pleasant (or pleased). It is better not to be sulky.' Cooks had a Swahili version, with eleven editions of their *Kitabu cha Upishi* appearing before 1958. This literacy of domestic service showed how far some Africans had redefined their masculinity since the proud nudity of Olga Watkins's cook. These two books were the hidden props of colonial Kenya. An entirely new *Kenya Kitchen Cookery Book* appeared in 1964, a year after independence. It said little of local materials and nothing about servants, advertising electrical appliances instead. That white Kenya was changing from a conservative local paternalism to post-colonial mobility was plain from a section entitled 'Beware! Bachelors at work' in which the (white) bachelor was advised to 'flatter the girl friend' by asking her for help when in difficulty—after serving her continental breakfast. White domesticity had descended from a highlands farmhouse with servants at the back to a city flat with no room for a cook-houseboy but with all modern conveniences, not least an expatriation allowance.[60]

---

[59] Huxley, *Nellie*, 235, letter of 6 Feb. 1960, and 270 for *Mataguri*; Nicholls, *Red Strangers*, 270–1; Garry Wasserman, *Politics of Decolonisation: Kenya Europeans and the Land Issue* (Cambridge, 1976); Weaver, 'Kenya Regiment', 275–6; Lovatt Smith, *Kenya*, 305–8; Thesiger, *My Kenya Days*, 170; Scott, *A Nice Place to Live*, 179–95.

[60] St Andrew's Church Woman's Guild, *The Kenya Settlers Cookery Book and Household Guide* (Nairobi, 1958), 292–314; Elizabeth M. Giles, *The Kenya Kitchen Cookery Book* (Nairobi, 1964), 67–70.

Select Bibliography

DAVID ANDERSON, *Histories of the Hanged: Britain's Dirty War in Kenya and the End of the Empire* (London, 2005).

MICHAEL BLUNDELL, *So Rough a Wind* (London, 1966).

RICHARD FROST, *Race against Time: Human Relations and Politics in Kenya before Independence* (London, 1978).

ELSPETH HUXLEY, *White Man's Country: Lord Delamere and the Making of Kenya*, 2 vols. (London, 1935).

—— (ed.), *Nellie: Letters from Africa* (London, 1980).

TABITHA KANOGO, *Squatters and the Roots of Mau Mau 1905–1963* (London, 1987).

DANE KENNEDY, *Islands of White: Settler Society and Culture in Kenya and Southern Rhodesia, 1890–1930* (Durham, NC, 1987).

NORMAN LEYS, *Kenya* (London, 1924).

JOHN LONSDALE, 'The Depression and the Second World War in the Transformation of Kenya', in David Killingray and Richard Rathbone (eds.), *The Second World War and Africa* (Basingstoke, 1986), 97–142.

PAUL MOSLEY, *The Settler Economies: Studies in the Economic History of Kenya and Southern Rhodesia 1900–1963* (Cambridge, 1983).

C. S. NICHOLLS, *Red Strangers: The White Tribe of Kenya* (London, 2005).

M. G. REDLEY, 'The Politics of a Predicament: The White Community in Kenya 1918–32', Ph.D. thesis (Cambridge, 1976).

M. P. K. SORRENSON, *Origins of European Settlement in Kenya* (Nairobi, 1968).

RICHARD WALLER, '"Clean" and "Dirty": Cattle Disease and Control Policy in Colonial Kenya, 1900–40', *Journal of African History*, 45/1 (2004), 45–80.

GARRY WASSERMAN, *Politics of Decolonisation: Kenya Europeans and the Land Issue* (Cambridge, 1976).

5

Rhodesia 1890–1980
'The Lost Dominion'

Donal Lowry

Prologue: UDI and the Battle of Britishness

On 11 November 1965, following failed negotiations with the British government led by Prime Minister Harold Wilson, members of the Rhodesian cabinet gathered in the aptly named 'Phoenix Room' at Government Buildings, Salisbury, in the full photographic blaze of world publicity. Here they signed a Unilateral Declaration of Independence (UDI) from the United Kingdom, couched in archaic clauses recalling the American declaration of 1776, triggering the most protracted crisis of British decolonization. On the face of it this was a most unlikely putsch, for revolutionary allegory ended there.[1] Indeed, this was an avowedly imperialist gathering, seemingly out of place in an era of rapid decolonization. Annigoni's famous portrait of a youthful Elizabeth II in Garter robes presided as her ministers endorsed the elaborately illuminated scroll which—echoing previous Scottish and Ulster covenants and a threatened Kenyan settler revolt of 1921—concluded with the conventional salutation, 'God Save the Queen'.[2] As it transpired, it was signed at 11 o'clock British time on Armistice Day, adding poignancy to the proclamation's accusatory recollection of Rhodesian martial loyalty to the Crown and to 'kith and kin' in Britain and the Commonwealth in two world

---

[1] J. R. T. Wood, *So Far and No Further! Rhodesia's Bid for Independence during the Retreat from Empire, 1959–1965* (Crewe, 2004), ch. 27.

[2] David Armitage, *The Declaration of Independence: A Global History* (Cambridge, Mass., 2007), 135–6; Donal Lowry, 'Ulster Resistance and Loyalist Rebellion in the Empire', in Keith Jeffery (ed.), *'An Irish Empire'? Aspects of Ireland and the British Empire* (Manchester, 1996); Christopher P. Youé, 'The Threat of Settler Rebellion and the Imperial Predicament: The Demise of Indian Rights in Kenya', *Canadian Journal of History*, 12 (1978), 347–60.

wars. Somewhat incongruously, this 'revolutionary' cabinet included an English county solicitor and an accountant, an ex-Hussar officer, and a leading Scottish duke, all of whom protested their continuing allegiance to the 'Queen of Rhodesia', whom they now distinguished constitutionally from the 'Queen of the United Kingdom', who was Harold Wilson's legislative instrument.[3]

In accordance with assurances highlighted in an accompanying broadcast by Prime Minister Ian Smith, himself a former wartime RAF fighter pilot, the blue Rhodesian ensign, still quartered by the Union Jack, together with the British flag itself, continued to be flown across the territory, while magistrates dispensed justice in the monarch's name.[4] Air force and army regiments preserved their royal prefixes and insignia, officers retained their commissions by Crown warrant, and the police maintained the historic title of the 'British South Africa Police' (BSAP), of which force the Queen Mother remained honorary colonel. Nonetheless, following instructions from Wilson, Governor Sir Humphrey Gibbs sacked the cabinet, which in turn no longer recognized his legitimacy, replacing him with an English-born Rhodesian Front party stalwart, Clifford Dupont, as 'Acting Officer Administering the Government', the traditional titular designation of an acting governor *ad interim*. Crucially for the success of this peculiar *coup*, no new oath of allegiance was yet demanded by the regime. Indeed, Dupont, in keeping with dominion practice, maintained the metaphysical fiction that he fully represented his Rhodesian sovereign, even if she was 'temporarily prevented' by her British cabinet from acting directly on the constitutional advice of her Rhodesian ministers, in the way that she discharged her duty to her other realms. Such pretensions to monarchical continuity, condemned as insolent by Whitehall officials, were in fact imperative in retaining initial settler support for this drastic action.[5]

In response to UDI, the British government immediately proclaimed Rhodesia to be in a state of rebellion, while requesting the United Nations to apply sanctions against the 'rebel regime'. The Chief Justice, Rhodesian-born Sir Hugh Beadle, moved in solidarity into Government House, where Gibbs maintained an alternative if skeletal vice-regal court. There, however,

[3] Phillipa Berlyn, *Rhodesia: Beleaguered Country* (London, [1966]), chs. 1–3.
[4] Peter Joyce, *Anatomy of a Rebel: Smith of Rhodesia* (Salisbury, 1974), 233–5.
[5] Clifford Dupont, *The Reluctant President: The Memoirs of the Hon. Clifford Dupont* (Bulawayo, 1978).

the conventional response to rebellion substantially ended. Brigadier Andrew Skeen, Rhodesian High Commissioner in London, himself a former British army officer, was declared *non grata* but, in a tacit recognition of his singular status, he was allowed to leave Rhodesia House unhindered and to return home, as though he were an envoy of a sovereign state possessing diplomatic immunity, rather than the treacherously criminal agent of a rebellious regime.[6] Rhodesian civil servants and security officials were advised by the British somewhat confusingly not to aid the regime, but crucially they were not ordered to leave their posts. The British government meanwhile had counselled its missions abroad to assert that Rhodesia was a 'unique situation [in which there was] not a single British soldier, not a single British policeman, not a single British administrator in the Rhodesian services responsible to the British government', so that Britain had 'no direct means of making her views prevail'.[7] The British government thus sought to disarm any suggestion that it use force against Rhodesia, by emphasizing, if not exaggerating, its powerlessness, for it had tried to extricate itself from Africa rather than be drawn further into the continent. Its response to the crisis nevertheless revealed the historic limitations on British authority in the colony. Indeed, the farcical side of these constraints was encapsulated in Gibbs advising the army commander that he should attend the formal opening of parliament, but that he should ensure that he did not look as though he was enjoying the occasion.[8]

Rhodesia's singular status continued to be recognized tacitly by Britain even after UDI, when junior diplomats were retained at Rhodesia House in London and at the British High Commission in Salisbury to facilitate continuing bilateral communications and consular care, until these were severed following a vote of the Rhodesian electorate in a referendum in 1969 to declare a republic. Thus the white Rhodesians became, however reluctantly, the first people of largely British origin to throw off the Crown since the American Revolution.[9] By then, rebel Rhodesia's unrequited monar-

---

[6] Brigadier Andrew Skeen, *Prelude to Independence: Skeen's 115 Days* (Cape Town, 1966), 148–50.

[7] FO/CRO outward telegram no. 418 to British missions overseas, 19 Oct. 1965: National Archives, Kew (TNA), PREM 13/542.

[8] Ken Flower, *Serving Secretly: An Intelligence Chief on Record. Rhodesia into Zimbabwe 1964–1981* (London, 1987), 82.

[9] Ben Pimlott, *The Queen: A Biography of Elizabeth II* (London, 1996), 345–54; Robert Blake, *A History of Rhodesia* (London, 1977), 374–86.

chism had worn thinner, particularly when the regime proceeded with executions of three African guerrillas condemned to death for murder before UDI, with the Appellate Division declaring by majority decision that the regime was not only a *de facto* but a *de jure* government. The Chief Justice, Beadle, who upheld this decision, was ordered by Gibbs to leave Government House, although, tellingly, in this strange 'revolution', Beadle retained both his knighthood and his privy councillorship for the rest of his life.[10]

Even the reluctant republic that emerged in 1970 was bizarrely British: Dupont became president, but gubernatorial rather than presidential protocol was maintained and there was little republican fanfare. Air force and army formations regretted the loss of their royal titles, but emblems, uniforms, and rituals remained substantially unchanged, while the BSAP retained its name and the monarchical motto: 'Pro rege, pro lege, pro patria' ('For King, For Law, For Country'). The Union Jack-quartered flag had already been replaced by an initially controversial green-and-white ensign, but this nonetheless displayed the traditional Rhodesian crest incorporating the lion and English rose—a heraldic pun on Rhodes—and the eponymous motto, 'Sit nomine digna': 'May she be worthy of [Rhodes's] name'. The Union Jack continued until 1979 to be raised solemnly at the annual Pioneer Day ceremony by a BSAP trooper on the site of the original hoisting of the flag in 1890, before the prime minister and assembled dignitaries. In parliament and other public buildings, the sovereign's portrait was transferred, but generally retained in positions of prominence, to be replaced only by portraits of 'The Founder', Cecil Rhodes, whose cult was now even more pervasive than ever. 'You can call us rebels, and you can call us rogues', protested a popular balladeer: 'but we were founded by an Englishman by the name of Cecil Rhodes.'[11] It was symbolically, if strangely, a very British imperialist republic.[12]

The white Rhodesian leadership had been long concerned about its limited leverage and declining influence in Britain, particularly after the Second World War, when fear of the consequences of decolonization and

---

[10] Manuelle Facchini, 'The "Evil Genius": Sir Hugh Beadle and the Rhodesian Crisis, 1965–72', *Journal of Southern African Studies*, 33/5 (2007), 673–89.

[11] John Edmond, *The Story of Troopiesongs and the Rhodesian Bush War* (Johannesburg, 1982), 16.

[12] Peter Godwin and Ian Hancock, *'Rhodesians Never Die': The Impact of War and Political Change on White Rhodesia, c.1970–1980* (Harare, 1996 edn.), 51.

a determination to achieve dominion status or independence became acute. They retained vociferous support among the back benches of the Conservative Party and at annual Tory party conferences, but never nearly enough to sway the front benches into total support. In the interwar period, but particularly after 1945, they increasingly felt that they resembled embarrassing relatives that the metropolitan British would rather forget.[13] The Rhodesian Front emerged as a 'grassroots party' resentful of the dominant Anglo-Rhodesian political establishment, and sought to recruit heavily among those who had felt socially, or—chiefly in the cases of Afrikaners and Greeks—ethnically excluded by this elite. The Rhodesian Front further capitalized on a widespread disillusionment with Britain, and increasing admiration for right-wing elements in America was encapsulated in the designation of the new decimalized unit of currency as a 'dollar'. Nonetheless, white Rhodesians could never quite escape their imperial origins in the dreams of the Englishman, Cecil John Rhodes.[14] A coherent anti-Britishness never quite emerged, even after the declaration of a republic. To the extent that a form of anti-Britishness began to develop, accompanied by an intensified Rhodesian identity based largely around UDI, it appeared to be a denial of the very origins of the colony.

Even after UDI, the territory continued to be regarded by elements of the British right, including A. K. Chesterton's League of Empire Loyalists and the Candour League, as well as the somewhat eccentric British Israelite cult, as upholding what remained of the British imperial mission against its enemies on the frontier and metropolitan abdication. To more mainstream but sympathetic Conservatives, Rhodesia was a slice of the Home Counties in Africa, variously described as '1912 Cheltenham', and 'Surbiton', or 'Basingstoke in the bush'.[15] While leading members of the British Labour Party castigated the white Rhodesians as embarrassing reminders of an unjust imperial past, Harold Soref, Conservative MP and Monday Club activist, was mindful of Rhodesia's disciplined and obedient schoolchildren. He regarded Rhodesians as beacons of true if unrequited loyalty. 'Rhodesia

---

[13] Philip Murphy, *Party Politics and Decolonization: The Conservative Party and British Colonial Policy in Tropical Africa, 1951–1964* (Oxford, 1995), 10, 25–6, 58–60, 69, 160–5, 208.

[14] Michael Evans, 'The Role of Ideology in Rhodesian Front Rule, 1960–1980', Ph.D. thesis (University of Western Australia, 1993).

[15] Dominic Sandbrook, *A History of Britain in the Swinging Sixties* (London, 2008), 127.

represents Britain at its best', he reflected: 'patriotic, self-reliant, self-supporting, with law and order and a healthy society'.[16] Douglas Bader, wartime fighter ace, and SAS Brigadier Mike Calvert were among those prominent veterans who regarded the Rhodesians as 'kith and kin', embodying the truest of true Britishness, while entertainers such as Eric Sykes and Jimmy Edwards regularly arrived on morale-boosting tours of the rebel colony, to cheer the frontline troops in the operational areas. There were supportive 'friends of Rhodesia' scattered from Australia to Canada, but there were also those both in Britain and Rhodesia who disputed this definition of Britishness, so that at a time of cultural changes UDI became a defining battle in an ideological war about Britishness itself.[17] Indeed, it was this sense of a shared Britishness that had made British ministers hesitate in using force to crush Rhodesian recalcitrance.[18] It was, nonetheless, a powerful myth for its adherents. Ian Smith frequently stated that he believed that, had Churchill lived on, he would have settled in Rhodesia in order to feel at home. The British had identified him as possessing a dated *Boy's Own Paper* form of patriotism, a view confirmed when he told Harold Wilson that Britain appeared 'hell-bent on appeasing the cult of Marxism Leninism, at the expense of the old traditional values of the British Empire'.[19] Sir Robert Tredgold, a liberal-minded Rhodesian opponent of UDI, lamented the ease with which most white Rhodesians believed that they embodied the 'repository' of those qualities which had made Britain great, but which the metropolitan British and even the white dominions had wilfully and culpably abandoned.[20] Following UDI, with their loyalty unrequited and Britain no longer seemingly resembling the metropolis of their

---

[16] J. Taylor, 'Memory and Desire in *Going Home*: The Deconstruction of a Colonial Radical', in Eve Bertelsen (ed.), *Doris Lessing* (Johannesburg, 1985), 60.

[17] Bill Schwarz, 'Reveries of Race: The Closing of the Imperial Moment', in B. Conekin, F. Mort, and C. Waters (eds.), *Moments of Modernism: Reconstructing Britain, 1945–1964* (London, 1999), 189–207; St. J. and G. Barclay, '"Friends in Salisbury": Australia and the Unilateral Declaration of Independence', *Australian Journal of Politics and History*, 29/1 (1983), 38–49.

[18] Carl Watts, 'Killing Kith and Kin: The Viability of British Military Intervention in Rhodesia, 1964–5', *Twentieth Century British History*, 16/4 (2005), 382–415; Philip Murphy, '"An Intricate and Distasteful Subject": British Planning for the Use of Force Against the European Settlers of Central Africa, 1952–65', *English Historical Review*, 121/492 (2006), 746–77.

[19] Wood, *So Far and No Further!*, 70.

[20] Robert Tredgold, *The Rhodesia that was my Life* (London, 1968), 255.

ideals, it became increasingly difficult for the bulk of white Rhodesians to identify themselves convincingly as British.

The Constitutional Uniqueness of Rhodesia

For scholars of the British empire, too, Rhodesia had always been a peculiar possession. In 1974, the historian J. D. B. Miller, writing in the *Survey of Commonwealth Affairs*, titled his Rhodesian chapter, 'The Lost Dominion', in an allusion to William Keith Hancock's *Survey* of 1942, which had predicted that Southern Rhodesia would inevitably progress from responsible government, granted in 1923, to full dominion status.[21] Ultimately, of course, Rhodesia never attained such constitutional recognition and, as Miller himself recognized, the notion that Rhodesia under European rule would follow the route of New Zealand to dominionhood had since become untenable. Nevertheless, it is this partially realized but profoundly felt ambition that to a considerable extent marks the white Rhodesians out from the other British communities in this volume, for British governments had long been aware of Rhodesian exceptionalism. In 1944, Lord Harlech, British high commissioner in the Union, warned the Rhodesian governor that the Rhodesians were 'essentially permanent colonists, bringing up their children as Rhodesians and nothing else'. They demonstrated 'not a few signs of the outlook of the several North American colonies before the Declaration of Independence . . . the same impatience at criticism or control from those outside the country'. They were, he concluded, 'emphatically not a country of planters like Malaya or Ceylon or even the West Indies other than Barbados'.[22] 'Rhodesia [had] never been administered by the British Colonial Service, or, to use a common term, by "expatriates"', declared Desmond Lardner-Burke, Rhodesian Minister of Law and Order, in 1966; the fact that he himself was South African-born and therefore an expatriate encapsulates the constitutional allegiances of white Rhodesia.[23]

Rhodesian settlement patterns were in reality far less stable than Harlech thought, as we shall see. Nevertheless, it is essential to keep in mind those constitutional and demographic characteristics that distinguished Rhodesia

[21] J. D. B. Miller, *Survey of Commonwealth Affairs: Problems of Expansion and Attrition, 1953–1969* (London, 1974), 167.

[22] Charles Douglas Home, *Evelyn Baring: The Last Proconsul* (London, 1978), 112, 133–4.

[23] Desmond Lardner-Burke, *Rhodesia* (Cape Town, 1966), 10.

in the minds of contemporary observers from the other British-derived societies discussed in this volume. All of those communities evolved to varying degrees distinctive local identities, linked in several cases to political aspirations. Two of these, the white settlers of Natal and Kenya, shared much of the white Rhodesian ambition for greater constitutional autonomy; indeed Natal had possessed responsible government before 1910. Nevertheless, the Natal British, ultimately, if grudgingly, joined the Union, where they felt increasingly controlled by predominantly non-British, Afrikaner-led and even anti-British governments in Pretoria. Following the Great War, the Kenyan settlers also found their political aspirations blocked by the imperial government's declaration of African paramountcy, as well as circumscribed by pressure from the British Government of India in support of Asian immigrants, but ironically these restraints occurred at the very time of Southern Rhodesia's achievement of a generously defined measure of responsible government in 1923, which included fiscal autonomy and effective control of native affairs.

It may be helpful to provide a brief outline of the political and constitutional evolution of the territory, before discussing its implications in greater detail. Northern and Southern Rhodesia were both named after Cecil Rhodes, but we are chiefly concerned here with Southern Rhodesia. From 1890 until 1923, its government, together with its northern namesake, was in the hands of Rhodes's chartered British South Africa (BSA) Company. In 1898, following the Jameson Raid fiasco and two major uprisings in Matabeleland and Mashonaland, its rule was restrained by a British-appointed resident commissioner and the election, at British insistence, of a handful of members of the Legislative Council.[24] Settler representatives became more assertive and distrustful of the Company following the death in 1902 of Rhodes, whose personalized style of government— 'cheque-book imperialism'—had done much to allay their anxieties. It was then widely envisaged that the territory would become a fifth province of the Union of South Africa, where politically it might bolster pro-imperial elements against a resurgent Afrikaner nationalism, as well as secure markets for its agricultural goods. Southern Rhodesia was represented in the negotiations leading to the unification of South Africa in 1908–9. During the Great War, however, despite a political truce, the Company

---

[24] M. C. Chanock, *Unconsummated Union: Britain, Rhodesia and South Africa, 1900–1945* (Manchester, 1977).

antagonized settler opinion by toying with schemes to amalgamate the Rhodesias and, later, to encourage its entry into the Union. The settlers suspected a cynical manœuvre, fearing that such an amalgamation would diminish their ratio to the African majority still further and weaken their chance of either entering the Union or gaining responsible government. The Company began to consider again the option of incorporation in the Union, now backed by the imperial and Union governments, as well as powerful local mining and capitalist interests in the territory and all but one of its newspapers.[25]

These schemes antagonized settler opinion, however, and their political confidence was further encouraged by a Privy Council judgment in 1918 which ruled that the Company did not own all of the unalienated land of the territory. This made responsible government seem a viable alternative, which was exploited effectively by the newly formed Responsible Government Association (RGA), led by Sir Charles Coghlan and Ethel Tawse Jollie, an experienced veteran of pre-war Radical Right politics in Britain.[26] The political mobilization of the white electorate on this issue proved to be a defining moment in the constitutional and cultural history of the community. In a crucial referendum in 1922, 8,774 white voters chose responsible government, while 5,989 opted for provincial incorporation in the Union. Responsible government was granted in the following year, but the territory could never entirely escape the orbit of its larger southerly neighbour. Southern Rhodesia's franchise was modelled on the 'colour-blind' regulations of the Cape Colony, and its Roman-Dutch legal system, together with strong economic, educational, and sporting ties, continued to link it to the Union. Until the Second World War, a majority of its immigrants originated in South Africa. Equally, however, there were continuing ties to the mother country, as well as a growing confidence in their institutions of self-government. In contrast to Kenya and Natal after union, the Southern Rhodesian government gained control over its own

---

[25] M. E. Lee, 'The Origins of the Responsible Government Movement', *Rhodesian History*, 6 (1975), 33–52; J. M. Mackenzie, 'Southern Rhodesia and Responsible Government', *Rhodesian History*, 9 (1978), 41–62.

[26] H. C. Hummel, 'Sir Charles Coghlan: Some Reflections on his Political Attitudes and Style', *South African Historical Journal*, 9 (1977), 59–79; R. Hodder-Williams and P. Whitely, 'The Rhodesian Referendum of October 1922', *Zimbabwean History*, 11 (1980), 56–74; Donal Lowry, '"White Woman's Country": Ethel Tawse Jollie and the Making of White Rhodesia', *Journal of Southern African Studies*, 23/2 (1997), 259–82.

defence force, including, on the eve of the Second World War, a small air force. By the 1930s it had already become virtually an honorary dominion with, crucially, effective control over native policy and after 1927 it came under the remit of the Dominions Office rather than the Colonial Office. The colony's prime ministers were customarily invited to Imperial and later Commonwealth conferences, and it was represented diplomatically by high commissioners in London and Pretoria. Self-government, moreover, enabled the Southern Rhodesians to act more as sub-imperial agents than conventional colonists, particularly in their new ambitions in the interwar period when they sought closer association with Northern Rhodesia and its mineral-rich Copper Belt.[27]

After 1953, when Southern Rhodesia joined in a federation with the protectorates of Northern Rhodesia (now Zambia) and Nyasaland (now Malawi), the Rhodesians established their own department of external affairs, served by high commissioners, military attachés, consular officials, and envoys possessing the diplomatic rank of minister. They also pursued a quasi-autonomous foreign policy on such issues as Katanga and the Belgian Congo, supported by modernized armed forces which now included jets and SAS-modelled commando units. This expansion in diplomatic functions and military capability survived the end of the federation in 1963. Using the precedent of continuing separate representation in Pretoria following the declaration of a republic in 1961, a Rhodesian legation separate from the British embassy was established in Lisbon as an obvious precursor of UDI in 1964, despite British objections, and accorded honorary diplomatic status just short of full recognition. In common with the dominions, Southern Rhodesia enacted separate citizenship legislation in 1949, while in the following decade British governments were effectively powerless to prevent the deportation of British citizens deemed by Rhodesian governments to be threats to public order. Even though they possessed discretionary powers that were theoretically wider than those of dominion governors-general, Southern Rhodesian governors conventionally acted on the advice of their prime ministers and cabinets rather than that of British governments, particularly after the introduction of a new constitution in 1961.[28] On the eve of UDI, for example, Governor Gibbs

---

[27] Kenneth Good, 'Settler Colonialism in Rhodesia', *African Affairs*, 73/290 (1974), 10–36; H. I. Wetherell, 'Britain and Rhodesian Expansionism', *Rhodesian History*, 8 (1977), 115–28.

[28] See D. J. Murray, *The Governmental System in Southern Rhodesia* (Oxford, 1970).

felt compelled to comply with the constitutional advice of his prime minister, Ian Smith, in declaring a state of emergency, even though he suspected that this might well be followed by a unilateral declaration of independence.[29]

Settlers and Migrants

In population patterns as in constitutional status, Rhodesia also occupied a unique place among Britain's settler possessions. Its founder, Cecil John Rhodes, together with those who conquered it in the 1890s, was self-consciously aware that this was the last great adventure of the scramble for Africa, before the final closure of colonial frontiers, and hoped that it would create a great colony of permanent settlement for the British race.[30] The conquest resulted in the largest of the late-Victorian settler societies with an unquestionably keen ambition to permanence, either by adoption or birth, a fundamental objective so often articulated in fiction. 'I was a Devonshire man', the policeman-hero of Gertrude Page's 1912 novel, *The Rhodesian*, responds defensively to a query about his origins: 'I *am* a Rhodesian'; while in a children's novel of 1922, the chief, Rhodesian-born character, Gwenda, is reassured on the eve of her emigration to the Cape Colony that she will 'remain a little Rhodesian' on the grounds of her country of birth.[31] Such permanence remained elusive, however, for although white Rhodesians constituted the most numerous settler community after the white dominions, throughout their history a majority of them were born outside the territory, and in this respect at least, Rhodesia may be compared with white societies in West Africa or India.[32] The white population increased considerably, from approximately 1,500 in 1891 (out of a total population of 500,000 Africans), to 23,606 in 1911, when the African population numbered 752,000. By 1941 there were 69,370 Europeans and 1,425,000 Africans. In 1969, there were 228,296, rising to approximately 277,000 by 1977, when Africans numbered just under five million. During these decades the ratio of male to female rose from almost two to one to roughly equal

---

[29] See Claire Palley, *The Constitutional History and Law of Southern Rhodesia, 1888–1965* (Oxford, 1966), for constitutional limitations on Rhodesian autonomy.

[30] Arthur Glyn Leonard, *How we Made Rhodesia* (London, 1896), 356.

[31] Gertrude Page, *The Rhodesian* (London, 1912), 16; Margaret Bachelor, *A Little Rhodesian* (London, 1922), 27.

[32] Frank Clements, *Rhodesia: The Course to Collision* (London, 1969), 93.

numbers. The period of fastest population growth was the 1940s, when many British servicemen who had been stationed in the wartime colony returned to settle in substantial numbers.

More significant than these somewhat modest gains was the high turn-over rate of European population. From 1921 to 1926, for every ten immi-grants, there were seven emigrants; from 1931 to 1936, there were nine immigrants to seven emigrants. After UDI, some 103,000 emigrated and 127,000 immigrated.[33] These figures can be partially explained by the terri-tory's vulnerability to international economic fluctuations, as well as the fact that many English-speaking South Africans regarded Southern Rhode-sia as the forward frontier of British South Africa, an imperial redoubt unadulterated by Afrikaner republicanism, where they might try their luck for a while and to which they might return. The fact that the territory was so staunchly British also made it easier for metropolitan migrants to feel they were simply moving from one British possession to another, without having to make a once-and-forever decision to settle and abandon previous alle-giances. Nevertheless, the issue of population stability remained acutely at the heart of settler politics from beginning to end. During the uprisings of the 1890s, a significant proportion of the white community was killed, leading to demands to encourage immigration. Resentment against the BSA Company in these years was fuelled not least by the perception that it was 'locking up' vast tracts of land for speculation which might otherwise be used to encourage immigration. Moreover, they were concerned by the growing minority of Afrikaners settled in the territory, many of whom were poverty-stricken and had a higher birth rate, an awareness which fuelled the opposition to incorporation in the Union. In the 1920s, the white Rhodesians themselves had one of the fastest rates of increase in the world. The ratio of males to females became more equal and the birth rate was far higher than that of northern European countries.[34] It remained a young population, with few grandparents and, even in the late 1950s, it still

[33] R. S. Roberts, 'The Settlers', *Rhodesiana*, 39 (1978), 70. A. S. Mlambo, *White Immigration into Rhodesia: From Occupation to Federation* (Harare, 2002), 1–2; Barry M. Schutz, 'Homeward Bound? A Survey Study of the Limits of White Rhodesian Nationalism and Permanence', *Ufahanu*, 5/3 (1975), 81–117; P. J. M McEwan, 'The European Population of Southern Rhodesia', *Civilizations*, 13/4 (1963), 438.

[34] Lewis Gann, *A History of Southern Rhodesia* (London, 1965), 313.

possessed one of the highest birth rates in the European world, fluctuating annually between 2.1 and 2.2 per cent between 1956 and 1958.[35]

On the other hand, the highly effective RGA, formed in 1917, heightened fears that incorporation would import the white labour crises of the Rand, bilingualism, and Afrikaner republicanism in the form of large numbers of Afrikaner 'poor whites'. These, according to one RGA woman activist, were 'neither black nor white but really worse than animals, and in addition they were mentally deficient'.[36] At this time, it should be stressed, Indians and Coloureds, who possessed the franchise on the same terms as Europeans, were not perceived as posing a political menace. The African majority, though ever present, was not regarded as immediately threatening: it was described as the 'Native Question', to be distinguished from the 'Race Question' and 'racialism', which almost invariably referred to divisions between Afrikaners and Rhodesians of British origin. Afrikaners who lived in Southern Rhodesia were widely depicted as illiterate or indigent and were often treated by magistrates more severely than Anglophone settlers or even Africans.[37] It was noted that a growing percentage, almost a quarter, of all white births was to Afrikaner families.[38] These allegedly constituted a potential Trojan horse within the territory. Anti-Afrikaner feeling proved to be an enduring feature of Rhodesian public culture, at least until the 1960s. As the novelist, Doris Lessing, puts it: '[The] phrase "poor whites"... caused disquiet... [T]here was certainly a race division. The small community of Afrikaners had their own lives, and the Britishers ignored them.'[39] The implication was that poor whites were always Afrikaners, who provided a warning of what happened when 'standards' were compromised, but this was a fond myth, for there were always numbers of English-speakers who lived in squalor on the edges of settlements or in remote areas, often ruined by alcohol and a high rate of child malnutrition and illiteracy.[40] A similar admonition was provided by the small community, numbering several thousands, of mixed race or 'Coloured' people. By the 1950s, it was common for white

[35] L. H. Gann and Peter Duignan, 'Changing Patterns of a White Elite', in Gann and Duignan (eds.), *Colonialism in Africa*, ii (Cambridge, 1970), 123 n. 3.

[36] J. M. Mackenzie, 'Responsible Government', *Rhodesian History*, 9 (1978), 36 n. 66.

[37] Richard Hodder-Williams, 'Afrikaners in Rhodesia: A Partial Portrait', *African Social Research*, 18 (1974), 621.

[38] Ethel Colquhoun Jollie, *The Future of Rhodesia* (Bulawayo, 1917), 9.

[39] Doris Lessing, *The Grass is Singing* ([1950]; London, 2007), 10–11.

[40] Daphne Anderson, *The Toerags: A Memoir* (London, 1989), 216–18.

Rhodesians to attribute these to miscegenation with undiscerning wartime RAF serviceman, whereas many in fact could trace their origins to early colonial liaisons and some of the most illustrious of pioneer heroes. These, together with small numbers of Asians, lived in modest segregated areas. They lapped the shores of what Prime Minister Sir Godfrey Huggins once described as a white island in a sea of blacks, occupying a position just below shopkeepers engaged in 'kaffir trade': Greeks, Jews, and others, pejoratively called 'dagoes'.[41]

The colony remained dependent on immigration, however, for its chief source of population. The settlers gained control of immigration in 1923, but there remained a fundamental tension in policy. They wanted settlers of the 'right sort', that is, with capital and skills, few of whom were available in the years of the Depression, when many whites were reduced by unemployment to working on the roads of the colony. If, on the other hand, as some suggested, they were to allow the immigration of larger numbers of immigrants of modest means; the cost of living would go up, as more whites took on more menial tasks hitherto done by Africans for lower wages. The white population was, moreover, socially more diverse than Kenya, and divided not only ethnically, between the British-descended majority and Afrikaners, Jews, Greeks, and other 'outsiders', but occupationally as well. In 1919, 12 per cent of males were employed by the public service, 3 per cent were professionals, 15 per cent in mining, over 27 per cent in agriculture, 11 per cent in industry, 16 per cent in commerce, 12 per cent in railways and communications, and 4 per cent in commercial services. By 1941, agriculture, mining, and railways had declined to 14 per cent, 11 per cent, and 8 per cent respectively, while those engaged in commerce and the professions had increased to 19 and 27 per cent, trends which would largely continue until the end of white rule. By 1969, only 7 per cent were engaged in agriculture, 22 per cent were professional or managerial, and almost a third were employed in clerical and security jobs.[42] In the 1930s, white artisans achieved legislative security from African competition, and it was not difficult to fuel paranoia about poor whites, trade unionism, and 'bolshevikism'.

---

[41] H. H. Patel, 'Asian Political Activity in Rhodesia', *Rhodesian History*, 9 (1978), 63–82; Fay Chung, *Reliving the Second Chimurenga: Memoirs from the Liberation Struggle in Zimbabwe* (Uppsala, 2006), 31–4.

[42] Dane Kennedy, *Islands of White: Settler Society and Culture in Kenya and Southern Rhodesia, 1890–1939* (Durham, NC, 1987); Central Statistical Office, *Census of Population* (Salisbury, 1969).

Similarly, following the Second World War, there were those who advocated the mass immigration of non-British Europeans, but such schemes
foundered on ethnic concerns about maintaining the British character of the
community, already anxious about the resurgence of Afrikaner nationalism
in the Union. Charles Olley, right-wing champion of lower-middle and
skilled working-class whites and president of the White Rhodesia Council,
precursor of the Rhodesian Front, opposed the importation of Polish workers. Not surprisingly for a Belfast-born Orangeman, he argued that Roman
Catholic immigrants would be the ruination of the country. Czech, Jewish,
and Greek immigration met with similar hostility.[43] Neil Wilson, populist
editor of the *New Rhodesia*, warned in 1949 that the immigration rate was
too slow to secure the white Rhodesians' long-term political future. He
estimated that the African population would double in twenty-five years.
Assuming a white population of 120,000 by 1950, 15,000 immigrants in that
year increasing by 1,000 annually, together with a healthy excess of births
over deaths, then the Europeans would reach 600,000 by 1968 and one
million by 1975, when he estimated that the African population would
have reached three million. If there were only 600,000 whites to five million
blacks by 1975, then Southern Rhodesia was finished as a white man's
country and they might as well 'pack up and leave'.[44]

White Rhodesia always, however, chose short-term prosperity, low wage
costs, cultural compatibility, and, therefore, selective settlement of largely
British-derived settlers, over higher wage costs and the immigration of
larger numbers of poorer and non-British immigrants. Rhodesia's immigration propaganda emphasized more than most the material benefits of
settlement, but, against a background of growing political assertiveness by
the black majority, successive governments would find it a growing challenge to persuade immigrants to remain permanently. By the 1970s, when
more Africans were born annually than the total number of Europeans in
employment, and white emigration was adversely affecting Rhodesian military and economic endurance, this quandary would ultimately ensure the
failure of white supremacy. Indeed, fear of a haemorrhage of population was

[43] Charles Olley, 'Another View of Poles', *New Rhodesia* (13 Dec. 1946); Richard Gray, *The Two Nations: Aspects of the Development of Race Relations in the Rhodesias and Nyasaland* (London, 1960), 310–13.
[44] N. H. Wilson, 'Expectation of Population', *New Rhodesia* (19 Aug. 1949), 3.

a key factor in Smith's decision to declare UDI, in the hope that such a stand would solidify the community at last.[45]

In such a transitory society, behind the myth of a 'Rhodesian nation', there lay ultimately the impossibility of sustaining a stable sense of community. In the 1970s, even right-wing Rhodesians continued to be unsure whether such a nation had already been formed before UDI, or as a result of it, or following republican status, or indeed whether it had still yet to be formed, an uncertainty which also pervaded much of the fiction written about the country.[46] Yet it is not sufficient simply to conclude that Lord Harlech's 1944 estimation of settler durability should be dismissed and that the Rhodesian aspiration to permanence was simply as vain and inconsequential as it was vociferous. Given the manifest instability of the white population, it is surely all the more remarkable that *in extremis* white Rhodesians defied international pressure for as long as they did and that they caused such disruption to British decolonization. These larger statistical trends do not, moreover, entirely explain important individual exceptions. It is true that when, in the 1970s, the going became tough, despite popular protestations of fighting 'through thick and thin', many Rhodesian-born whites left; yet many non-Rhodesian-born stayed, and not always for material reasons. In 1975, for example, one South African-born settler returned after only a year of having emigrated home, feeling guilty for having left and even occupying a remote farm whose owners had recently been murdered in a guerrilla attack. He was, his daughter recalls, 'Rhodesian from the moment he set foot in the country', and such stories were by no means unique.[47] The parents of journalist Peter Godwin, both post-war immigrants, were equally determined to stay; he only later discovered that his English middle-class father was in fact a Polish Jew and survivor of the Nazi genocide.[48] Gender also appears crucial, with the endurance or

[45] John Parker, *Rhodesia: Little White Island* (London, 1972), 162; Josiah Brownell, 'The Hole in Rhodesia's Bucket: White Emigration and the End of Settler Rule', *Journal of Southern African Studies*, 34/3 (2008), 591–610.

[46] Barry M. Shutz, 'The Theory of Fragment and the Political Development of White Settler Society in Rhodesia', Ph.D. thesis (California), 170–80, 216–26; Anthony Chennells, 'Settler Myths and the Southern Rhodesian Novel', D.Phil. thesis (University of Zimbabwe, 1982), 221–7.

[47] Lauren St John, *Rainbow's End: A Memoir of Childhood, War and an African Farm* (London, 2007), 3.

[48] Peter Godwin, *When a Crocodile Eats the Sun* (London, 2006).

withdrawal of white farmers in rural areas largely determined by the attitudes of white women.[49] While many right-wing, even Rhodesian-born, settlers contemplated emigration rather than military service, liberal-minded opponents of UDI could feel a larger pull of loyalty to serve in the security services.[50] White Rhodesia certainly embodied four key elements of a collective political identity pinpointed by Jack P. Greene, notable historian of the settler empire: a sense of place, a belief in destiny, an insistence on a high standard of government, and an awareness of history.[51]

Rhodesia's Britishness

As highlighted at the beginning of this chapter in relation to UDI, for many observers, the most striking aspect of Rhodesia remained its Britishness, and until the late 1950s, most whites appear to have identified themselves primarily as British rather than Rhodesian.[52] Indeed, that acute observer of imperial Britishness, Rudyard Kipling, had once foretold with a peculiar prescience that Rhodesia would be 'the last loyal white colony', while Cecil Rhodes reputedly prophesized that the territory would 'remember the rock from which she was hewn, and the Empire of which she is one of the outposts'.[53] 'A little bit of England', remarked Lord Buxton, British high commissioner in South Africa, following a visit to the territory in 1916, adding that the settlers were 'proud of being purely British, and that they form a part of the Empire; and they crave for public recognition of this

---

[49] Deborah Kirkwood, 'Settler Wives in Southern Rhodesia', in Hilary Callan and Shirley Ardener (eds.), *The Incorporated Wife* (London, 1984), 161.

[50] Luise White, 'Civic Virtue, Young Men, and Family: Conscription in Rhodesia, 1974–1980', *Journal of African Historical Studies*, 37/1 (2004), 103–21.

[51] J. H. Elliott, 'Introduction', and Jack P. Greene, 'Changing Identity in the British Caribbean: Barbados as a Case Study', in Nicholas Canny and Anthony Pagden (eds.), *Colonial Identity in the Atlantic World* (Princeton, NJ, 1987), 9, 214; H. C. Hummel, 'The Growth of White Rhodesian Nationalism: A Critical Appraisal', *Zimbabwean History*, 11 (1980), 75–86; W. D. Gale, *The Years Between, 1923–1973: Half a Century of Responsible Government in Rhodesia* (Salisbury, [1973]).

[52] C. A. Rogers and C. Franz, *Racial Themes in Southern Rhodesia: The Attitudes and Behaviour of the White Population* (Port Washington, 1973 edn.).

[53] Kipling to H. A. Gwynne, 1907, quoted in Charles Carrington, *Rudyard Kipling: His Life and Work* (London, 1978), 454; Cecil Rhodes quoted in 'Manifesto to the People of Rhodesia and a Statement of Policy', *The Independent* (Rhodesia, 26 Aug. 1922).

fact'.[54] 'The average British-born Rhodesian feels that this is essentially a British country, pioneered, bought and developed by British people, and he wants to keep it so', declared Tawse Jollie, 'Rhodesians, as a rule, are intensely imperialistic.'[55] She became the chief articulator of a nascent Rhodesian identity and was one of the first to attribute a time-warped quality to the territory's Britishness. 'Rhodesian [conveyed] a sort of super-British Imperialism', she reflected in 1930, 'a loyalty to the Flag and Empire which appears to be old fashioned in Great Britain today'.[56] She believed that the Great War had shattered British moral values and self-complacency, but only in Southern Rhodesia 'there still linger[ed] a little of the old faith; the old religious sentiment about the Flag, the Empire and the Traditions of our Race'.[57] The Englishness or Britishness of Rhodesia was a key marketing factor in immigration, its high commission in London proclaimed in 1935. The colony was 'an England freed from the burden of income tax, the high cost of living, the children's school bills and the depressing vagaries of climate . . . Yet [it was also] an England where life runs smoothly and happily, amid ideal surroundings, among British people'.[58] Such propaganda was often complemented by images of newly built houses which were 'reminiscent of an English country home'.[59] The Church of England was the largest denomination among whites, at almost half of the population, followed by significant numbers of Dutch Reformed Church members, Presbyterians, Methodists, Roman Catholics, and Jews. While only 1 per cent in 1936 defined themselves as agnostic, most whites, like their metropolitan cousins, were only occasional churchgoers, but the community remained culturally predominantly Protestant.[60]

These affiliations appeared to be reinforced by the Second World War, when the colony boasted that it was 'second to none in loyalty to the Crown',

---

[54] 'Report by Lord Buxton of a visit to Rhodesia' (14 Aug. 1916, TNA, CAB37/152/34), in I. M. Cumpston (ed.), *The Growth of the British Commonwealth, 1880–1932* (London, 1973), 158–9.

[55] Ethel Tawse Jollie, 'Southern Rhodesia', *South African Quarterly*, 3 (1921), 10–12.

[56] Ethel Tawse Jollie, *The Real Rhodesia* (London, 1924), 7, 102.

[57] Ethel Tawse Jollie, 'The Rhodes Idea: Portrait of a Great Imperialist', *Review of Reviews*, 90 (1930), 722.

[58] *Overseas: The Monthly Journal of the Overseas League*, 20/235 (1935), p. iv.

[59] 'Rhodesian Homestead and Garden', *Rhodesian Annual* (1932), 26.

[60] Gann, *History of Southern Rhodesia*, 319.

a 'Bastion of Empire', with a proud record of British-style government.[61] Governor Sir John Kennedy highlighted in 1950 the enormous degree of settler affection for 'the Throne and the motherland'.[62] Even non-British settlers stressed their Britishness. Rhodesian-born Sir Roy Welensky, federal prime minister from 1956 to 1963, emphasized that though he was half Jewish and half Afrikaner, he was '100 per cent British'. Following Britain's humiliation in the Suez Crisis of 1956, he was swift to declare that their 'loyalty to the Crown [was] unquestioned [and that] as a people whether black or white, [they were] British'.[63]

The Evolution of a Rhodesian Identity

Of course, Rhodesians had never been British in the metropolitan sense of the word, but combined a wider Britishness with a degree of local patriotism. They shared with other British communities an expectation of responsible government—the concession of the 'Durham Formula' so cherished by white settlers—combined with a profound contempt for metropolitan interference in local affairs. The 1890s was crucial in providing the white community with a powerful foundation myth of sacrifice, based around key events in the Matabele War of 1893 and the uprisings in Matabeleland and Mashonaland in 1896–7. Chief among these were the Shangani Patrol of 1893, which shielded the Last Stand of Major Allan Wilson and his patrol of thirty-three troopers, who were cut off and killed during an attempt to capture Lobengula, the King of the Ndebele. The posthumous tribute of an enemy chieftain that 'they were men of men' and the epitaph, 'there were no survivors', were often repeated. On Rhodes's instructions, the remains of the Patrol were ultimately housed in a Grecian mausoleum close to his own grave in the Matopos, which he had designated to be the Valhalla of Rhodesia, like hoplites attending their dead king. The Patrol itself provided the central tableau of early Rhodesia, celebrated in paintings and in Boy Scout re-enactments. A secondary epic was provided by the Mazoe Patrol of

---

[61] *Rhodesian Graphic Annual* (1947), p. i; L. H. Gann, 'The White Settler: A Changing Image', *Race*, 2/2 (1961), 28–40.

[62] Sir John Kennedy to Sir P. Liesching, 11 Jan. 1950, DO35/3681, no. 22, in Philip Murphy (ed.), *Central Africa British Documents on the End of Empire*, part 1: *Closer Association* (London, 2005), 129.

[63] Colin Leys, *European Politics in Southern Rhodesia* (Oxford, 1959), 247.

1896, centred on the gallantry of two telegraphists, Blakiston and Routledge, who lost their lives in an attempt to save settlers besieged at Mazoe during an uprising.[64] These, too, were soon revered as paladins of early Rhodesia, saviours not least of white womanhood from the 'black peril' of African men. As a medievalist balladeer extolled:

> A chivalrous and knightly deed
> Rhodesian annals tell
> Of Blakiston and Routledge, who
> In honour's tourney fell
> To save Mazoe's women from
> The gaping jaws of Hell ...[65]

Central to the epic of conquest, of course, was Rhodes himself, around whom a cult developed in his own lifetime. He became central to the Rhodesian legend, a fact constantly recalled by the country's name, prominent statues and portraits displayed in official buildings and town halls across the country, as well as by the annual Rhodes and Founders public holiday. Using his charisma and personal largesse to appease disgruntled settlers, he also came to be regarded by the Ndebele chieftains whom he had conquered and entertained with Homeric cattle feasts as a protector against further European encroachment. He played a crucial role in constructing his own myth, which was given powerful architectural character by Herbert Baker and poetic form by Rudyard Kipling, as well as further embellishments by heroic biographers. He chose as his pantheon a mountain-top in the Matopo Hills, where Mzilikazi, warrior-king of the Ndebele, was buried, setting it aside for 'those who deserved well of their country'. At his dramatic funeral in 1902, a pantheist poem of Kipling was read, the final lines of which would often be recited: 'Living he was the land, and dead, his soul shall be her soul'. His chosen epitaph, engraved on a plain brass plaque, was deliberately minimalist: 'Here lie the remains of Cecil John Rhodes'. Place of origin and dates of birth and death were deemed superfluous and pilgrims to the grave were invited to look about them to the

---

[64] See *Matabeleland, 1893–1933: An Illustrated Record of the Fortieth Anniversary of the Occupation* (Bulawayo, 1933); *The Occupation of Matabeleland: A Souvenir* (Bulwayo, 1933); 'The Story of Shangani', *Rhodesian Annual* (1927), 29.

[65] Lynn Lyster, 'The Mazoe Patrol', in *Ballads of the Veld-Land* (London, 1913), 89.

furthest horizons to seek his monument.[66] Apart from the sepulchre to the
Patrol, only two other individuals were honoured by burial near to Rhodes:
Sir Leander Starr Jameson, his loyal lieutenant, and Sir Charles Coghlan, the
first prime minister of Southern Rhodesia. After 1935 the Matopos site was
closed to further burial and this appeared to separate further the era of the
pioneers from those of later—implicitly lesser—mortals. The apotheosis of
Rhodes and his pioneers remained an enduring feature of white Rhodesian
identity. Descendants of pioneers, together with those who had settled in
earlier decades, continued to constitute a local elite to which later generations largely deferred. The 'mantle of the Pioneers' was also explicitly
invoked and linked by Ian Smith to the Rhodesians' 'heroic role' in his
UDI broadcast in 1965, while Rhodes's grave proved to be a popular setting
for advertisements stating that this was 'just the beginning' of Rhodesia's
greatness.[67]

A Pioneers and Early Settlers Society developed soon after the period of
conquest, which preserved the cult of the pioneers, and this became the
equivalent of South Africa's 1820 Settlers, Canada's United Empire Loyalists,
and America's Pilgrim Fathers Society.[68] White women were especially
prominent during the conquest of the territory and in keeping alive the
memory of the pioneers. Conservative in outlook but highly assertive, they
were to prove crucial in gaining much of the women's vote in the referendum of 1922 against Union, led by Ethel Tawse Jollie, who became the first
woman parliamentarian in Southern Rhodesia, as well as in the overseas
British empire. Their early political prominence was emphasized by an
elaborate tapestry hanging in parliament, modelled on its ancient Bayeux
predecessor.[69] After self-government was achieved, however, they appeared
satisfied to take a secondary role, exercised through the Women's Institutes
and the Guild of Loyal Women. Marriage remained women's normative

[66] Donal Lowry, 'Race, Nation and Empire at Rhodes's Mountain Mausoleum', in Richard
Wrigley and Matthew Craske (eds.), *Pantheons: Transformations of a Monumental Idea* (London,
2004).
[67] Joyce, *Anatomy of a Rebel*, 234; *Seventy Five Proud Years* (Salisbury, 1965).
[68] Neville Jones, *Rhodesian Genesis: The Story of the Early Days of Southern Rhodesia from the
Reminiscences of Some of the Pioneers* (Bulawayo, 1953); J. A. Edwards, 'Southern Rhodesia: The
Response to Adversity, 1935–1939', Ph.D. thesis (London, 1978), 14–17, 213–14.
[69] Donal Lowry, 'Making Fresh Britains across the Seas: Women's Suffrage and Anti-
Feminism in Rhodesia', in Ian C. Fletcher, Philippa Levine, and Laura Nym Mayhall (eds.),
Women's Suffrage and the British Empire (London, 1999); *Rhodesian Tapestry: A History in
Needlework* (Salisbury, 1963).

ambition with only 10 per cent of women in full-time employment and only one woman member of parliament in the 1950s. This apparent acceptance of domesticity was later dramatically transformed by the manpower needs of the UDI era and a soaring divorce rate linked to a widening conscription and militarization of white males. It was widely believed, however, that wives continued to exercise an inordinate and right-wing influence on the men of the Rhodesian Front.[70]

Rhodes's death in 1902 inaugurated a new era of settler militancy against what many now saw as an impersonal company. 'Would you have your Wardens bound by Coward Traitor Hands?', a leading early Rhodesian balladeer asks accusingly: 'Shame upon Little England / While Greater England Stands!'.[71] Such sentiments were articulated outside the Legislative Council. In 1911, the Colonial Office feared an Ulster-style resistance to the British South African Company's monopoly of African labour recruitment, with settler militants invoking the seventeenth-century spirit of parliamentarian advocate, John Hampden.[72] Since the Legislative Council appeared somewhat moderate, the annual congress of the Rhodesian Agricultural Union served as an alternative 'settler parliament'. This body discussed not only issues of agriculture and infrastructure, but the lack of educational facilities for settler children and the increasing emphasis being placed by Woodrow Wilson and others on the right of self-determination.[73]

The RGA sought to harness and mobilize settler grievances in support of a grant of responsible government.[74] The material interests of various

---

[70] Susie Jacobs, 'Gender Divisions and the Formation of Ethnicities in Zimbabwe', in Daiva Stasiulis and Nira Yuval-Davis (eds.), *Unsettling Settler Societies* (London, 1995), 241–62; Ethel Tawse Jollie, 'The Women of Rhodesia: Civil Service, Professions and Trades', *African World*, 97 (1926), 249; Colin Black, 'The Woman behind Ian Smith', *Illustrated Life Rhodesia* (27 Feb. 1969).

[71] Henry Cullen Gouldsbury, *Rhodesian Rhymes* (Bulawayo, 1923), 251; Donal Lowry, 'Southern Rhodesia and the Imperial Idea', in Andrea Bosco and Alex May (eds.), *The Round Table: The Empire/Commonwealth, and British Foreign Policy* (London, 1998), 305–42.

[72] Ian Henderson, 'White Populism in Rhodesia', *Comparative Studies in Society and History*, 14/4 (1972), 393.

[73] Rhodesia Agricultural Union, *Report of Proceedings at the Thirteenth Annual Congress* (Salisbury, [1916]), 41–52, 84–138.

[74] See M. Elaine Lee, 'The Origins of the Rhodesian Responsible Government Movement', *Rhodesian History*, 6 (1975), 33–52; M. Elaine Lee, 'An Analysis of the Rhodesian Referendum, 1922', *Rhodesian History*, 8 (1977), 71–98; John M. Mackenzie, 'Southern Rhodesia and Responsible Government', *Rhodesian History*, 9 (1978), 23–40; R. Hodder-Williams and P. Whiteley, 'The Rhodesian Referendum of October 1922: Some Further Reflections', *Zimbabwe History*, 11 (1980),

pressure groups played a crucial role, but the campaign for responsible government emphasized the distinctiveness of the Rhodesian settler community, both drawing on and giving focus to an existing nascent white Rhodesian identity, and it was presented heroically as the 'liberation of Southern Rhodesia', with 'Rhodesia for the Rhodesians; Rhodesia for the Empire', as its catchphrase. There was even a public competition for a 'Rhodesian National Anthem' to complement 'God Save the King'.[75] There was already a militancy about this loyalty which would anticipate the UDI mentality by several decades. When George V met a settler delegation in 1921, he remarked to Coghlan that, in objecting to Union, Rhodesia appeared to be 'the Ulster of South Africa', a common analogy at that time, to which the settler leader responded ominously that Rhodesia would prove to be 'just as loyal as Ulster'. 'We will not part from the British flag without fighting', he declared. 'If 10,000 [Kenyan settlers] can give all that trouble [to the imperial government], what can we with 35,000 do if need be', he remarked to a colleague, referring to the threatened Kenyan revolt over Indian immigration.[76] Supporting such sentiments was also a growing body of popular settler literature and ballads of varying quality self-consciously celebrating the 'romance' of the Rhodesian frontier and its landscape and the sacrifices made to conquer the country.[77] It was said of the Rhodesians in the Union that they were 'not only "intensely British" but quite "intolerably Rhodesian"'.[78]

Meanwhile, the central Rhodesian ambition to permanence was given a fillip by the achievement of responsible government in 1922–3. Possession of their own parliament provided Southern Rhodesians with a more effective forum for the control of Africans, the reconciliation of various occupational interest groups, as well as the encouragement of selective immigration. Most crucially, it enabled the safeguarding of white agricultural and artisan interests from African competition, through the passing of the Land Apportionment Act of 1931 and the Industrial

56–84; H. C. Hummel, 'The Growth of White Rhodesian Nationalism: A Critical Appraisal', *Zimbabwe History*, 11 (1980), 75–86.

[75] J. P. R. Wallis, *One Man's Hand: The Story of Sir Charles Coghlan and the Liberation of Southern Rhodesia* (London, 1950).

[76] Sir Charles Coghlan to Sir Francis Newton, 5 Apr. 1923, National Archives of Zimbabwe, Newton Papers, Correspondence NE1/1/1.

[77] Jollie, *Real Rhodesia*, 85.

[78] Ibid. 7.

Conciliation Act of 1934. The first of these became 'the Magna Carta of white Rhodesia'. It granted roughly half of Rhodesia to white farmers and it was invested with a fundamental political symbolism which reached far beyond the farming population to the increasingly urbanized community at large. White politicians questioned it at their political peril and the question of land tenure remained central in settler politics, down to the even more stringent Land Tenure Act of 1969 and beyond.[79] Government support to agriculture generally, but particularly the inter-war encouragement of tobacco, proved to be the engine of much Rhodesian prosperity.[80] Representing such a tiny electorate, it was, moreover, a highly responsive assembly. After early toying with uneconomic schemes for mass white immigration, Rhodesian politics was dominated by an essentially conservative establishment, whose values were embodied by Sir Godfrey Huggins, their long-serving prime minister. Parties to the right or left of this establishment were largely confined to the political margins. Only in the early 1960s, amidst wider anxiety about Britain's colonies in Africa, did this establishment begin to lose its political grip to the avowedly populist and hardline Rhodesian Front.

Egalitarian Myths and Snobbish Realities

Imperial loyalties, reinforced not least by settler service in the Great War, gave to the community a sense of cohesion, masking differences of class, economic interests, and culture. The MOTHs, or 'Memorable Order of Tin Hats', was an especially prominent ex-servicemen's association which transcended other, largely ethnically or religiously based organizations, in a colony where a particularly high proportion of settlers were ex-servicemen.[81] Rhodesia possessed a more diverse settler population than Kenya, with significant numbers drawn from the lower-middle and skilled

[79] M. L. Rifkind, 'Land Apportionment in Perspective', *Rhodesian History*, 3 (1972), 53–62; Allison K. Shutt. '"The Natives are Getting Out of Hand": Legislating Manners, Insolence and Contemptuous Behaviour in Southern Rhodesia, c.1910–1963', *Journal of Southern African Studies*, 33/3 (2007), 653–72.

[80] Frank Clements and Edward Harben, *Leaf of Gold: The Story of Rhodesian Tobacco* (London, 1962), chs. 10–11; Ian Phimister, *An Economic and Social History of Zimbabwe, 1890–1948: Capital Accumulation and Class Struggle* (London, 1988), ch. 1; Robin Palmer, *Land and Racial Discrimination in Rhodesia* (London, 1977), chs. 2–4.

[81] Peter McLaughlin, *Ragtime Soldiers: The Rhodesian Experience in the First World War* (Bulawayo, 1980), chs. 6, 8.

working classes. While there was always a leavening of well-connected upper-middle and aristocratic settlers, the white Rhodesian community lacked the reputation of a racy 'Happy Valley' kind of elite. The social mores of the white Rhodesians were largely middle class in tone, so that upper-class settlers and white artisans largely deferred to this image, at least until the 1960s.

The myth of white Rhodesian egalitarianism was a powerful one.[82] 'In all old civilizations life gets into a ... hereditary rut', reflected Tawse Jollie, the chief publicist of the colony in the 1920s, 'in Rhodesia one ... is never debarred from climbing out of it'. She noted that an ex-colonel might be seen driving a railway engine, or acting as a blacksmith and storekeeper. Ex-officers did not as a rule use their hard-won titles.[83] Novels frequently emphasized that this was a 'new country', where background did not matter so much. 'There is not in the colonies the same gulf between the classes as in Britain, the *Bulawayo Chronicle* asserted in 1924. 'European status marks the general level.'[84] There were, nevertheless, ethnic and regional differences stemming from the metropolitan state, which continued to manifest themselves through cultural organizations in the Colony. There were also provincial distinctions and loyalties such as between Matabeleland and its mining and railway interests and its closer proximity to the Cape Colony, and Mashonaland, dominated by its civil service, and agricultural sectors, while those former pioneers who remained in the territory soon acquired a self-conscious 'founding fathers—and mothers' identity.

For all the settlers' egalitarian self-image, however, the capital of Salisbury soon acquired a reputation for stuffiness, hierarchy, and convention, in keeping with its municipal motto—'Discrimine Salus' ('In discrimination there is safety'). As in all Rhodesian towns, the comparatively small African population in the early decades of the century was confined to locations on its outskirts, largely out of sight to all but a handful of officials. Salisbury had an informal social segregation of its own based not so much on money but on social background. Broadly speaking, 'trade'—minor shopkeepers, clerks and artisans, railwaymen, and the semi-skilled—lived in the southern districts of the town. Like their British counterparts, those of the lower-

---

[82] Patrick Keatley, *The Politics of Partnership: The Federation of Rhodesia and Nyasaland* (Harmondsworth, 1963), 273.

[83] Jollie, *Real Rhodesia*, 8.

[84] *Bulawayo Chronicle* (8 Sept. 1924).

middle classes craved respectability and were in many ways the most xenophobic, anti-Afrikaner, and jingoistic in the territory.[85] Similarly, because of their vulnerability to African competition, as elsewhere in the Empire, white workers were often attracted to a nationalist brand of socialism, although ultimately choosing racial security over solidarity with African workers.[86] Some white artisans who had left the metropolis did so to escape persecution for trade union activity. A later Rhodesian Labour Party leader, Jack Keller emigrated following his involvement in the British railway strike of 1911. He rejoiced in the nickname of 'the Lenin of Rhodesia', and in 1926 in a pamphlet accusing the government of plotting to use the defence force to break white worker strikes, referred to the government as 'The fascists of Southern Rhodesia'.[87] The poorest whites lived in one of the oldest districts of Salisbury, aptly named Pioneer Street, where white destitutes, alcoholics, and prostitutes lived cheek-by-jowl with Greeks, Asians, and Coloureds. It was here that Sir Roy Welensky, a future federal prime minister, was born the thirteenth of fourteen children to an elderly Lithuanian-Jewish owner of a dosshouse and his Afrikaner wife. Leaving school at 11, he became in turn a storeman, a boxer, a locomotive fireman, and a trade union organizer and married a local waitress. He rejected socialism, and became politically moderate by general white Rhodesian standards, but he embodied the culture and the fears of the white working class, and maintained a bluntness of manner uncommon in a political system culturally dominated by the upper-middle class.[88]

North of Salisbury was a very different world from that of the artisans, out of residential reach to all except higher civil servants, professionals, retired officers, and well-connected landowners. 'Society' centred on Government House parties, the Salisbury Club, and the lounge of Meikles Hotel. Wives imported the English custom of calling cards, insisted on their husbands dressing for the occasion, and exchanged petty snobberies and

---

[85] See T. Tanser, *A Sequence of Time: The Story of Salisbury, Rhodesia, 1900–1914* (Salisbury, 1974).

[86] Jonathan Hyslop, 'The Imperial Working Class Makes itself White', *Journal of Historical Sociology*, 12/4 (1999), 398–421; Ian Henderson, 'British Working-Class Immigrants to Rhodesia', in Ian Henderson and Philip Warhurst (eds.), *Revisions in Central African History* (Salisbury, 1965); M. C. Steele, 'White Working Class Disunity: The Southern Rhodesian Labour Party', *Rhodesian History*, 1 (1970), 59–81.

[87] Jack Keller, *The Fascists of Southern Rhodesia* (Bulawayo, 1926).

[88] G. Allingham, *The Welenksy Story* (London, 1962).

gossip at parties and polo matches.[89] Both upper- and lower-class whites aspired to this middle-class norm. Dornford Yates, a novelist whose writings embodied upper-middle-class values, settled comfortably in the border town of Umtali. But it was, of course, impossible to reproduce England in the heart of Africa, except in caricatured form. In the late 1950s, the novelist Evelyn Waugh, himself a noted expert in snobbery, opined disdainfully that

The whites are (a) Old Rhodesians—that is to say families dating from 1890, survivors and descendants of the riff-raff who came up from the Cape with Jameson & Rhodes... Dreadful people rather stuck up [and] (b) English county families who came there in 1946 to escape the Welfare State. They are rapidly becoming middle class... Every white man has a motor car and a dinner jacket and goes to bed at 9. The women drink tea all day long.[90]

Bulawayo, the largest Rhodesian town until the 1930s, provided perhaps a more accurate barometer of the community's character. It was the centre of transport, mining, and industry and seemed unmistakably a town of the newly colonized world. Where Salisbury represented stuffed shirts and snobbery, Bulawayo seemed to epitomize colonial egalitarianism, a town of shorts, bush hats, and open-necked shirts, flatter vowels, and, it seemed, an almost Australian disdain for snobbery, where conversation was believed to be racier and club membership was reputedly far less snooty. Unlike Salisbury, it romanticized its pre-colonial past, incorporating Lobengula's elephant in its city crest. Local whites unveiled a monument in the 1920s to Mzilikazi, founder of the Ndebele, whom they deemed a warrior race. The first premier, the convivial Sir Charles Coghlan, escaped to Bulawayo from Salisbury whenever he could. By the 1930s, however, Bulawayo also developed its own petty conventions. The novelist Muriel Spark noted that wives of the pharmacist, the doctor, the vicar, and the schoolmistress left their calling cards with the corner turned down, in an imitation of English village life.[91] Margery Perham, however, was unconvinced. 'English as white Rhodesians are', she reflected in 1930: 'they have already grown away from us, and the language talked by the upper-class Englishwoman is peculiar to her kind and has little in common even with her cousins over here'.[92]

[89] Hardwicke Holderness, *Lost Chance: Southern Rhodesia 1945–58* (Harare, 1985), 9–18.
[90] Evelyn Waugh to Laura Waugh, 6 Feb. 1958, Mark Amory (ed.), *The Letters of Evelyn Waugh* (London, 1980), 504.
[91] Muriel Spark, *Curriculum Vitae* (London, 1992), 125.
[92] Margery Perham, *An African Apprenticeship* (London, 1974), 257.

The differences between the two towns were more than social, however. Industrial Bulawayo, with its Raylton suburb constituting effectively a white railwaymen's town in itself, contrasted with Salisbury, the capital of the farming interest concentrated in Mashonaland which felt neglected. These factors influenced political attitudes in the years leading to the 1922 referendum. Within these provincial divisions, there were other strong sub-identities, such as that of the Eastern Districts or Gazaland settlers, local attachments common in British communities throughout the subcontinent.[93] Farmers were increasingly divided between cattle ranchers in Matabeleland, who had relatively better rail access to the markets of the Union, and crop farmers of Mashonaland and Manicaland, who were generally more remote from railway lines. The mining sector was divided between comparatively large companies, often with South African connections, and small miners and prospectors. Generally, agricultural and mining sectors competed for labour. The white working class was generally more homogeneous, being concentrated in the railway yards of Bulawayo, but they lived with the constant fear of destitution and deportation as a 'DBS'—a 'distressed British subject'. In common with settler societies in Australasia and North America, the legends of the society were rural, with the typical white Rhodesian being depicted as a lone, sun-tanned, and broad-brimmed rancher embodying the virtues of the English public schoolboy adapted to the African veldt.[94] Like Australia, whose myths were pastoral, in reality, white Rhodesia was increasingly an urbanized community, but the greater tendency of farmers to remain on the land in an otherwise somewhat transitory community gave them an image of integrity and rootedness and therefore a disproportionate political influence. This was evident in the prominence of farmers in both the movement for responsible government and the later campaign for independence.[95]

Schools, Defence, and Rhodesian Identity

Self-government also gave the settler crucial control of health and education, which they were able to make compulsory for whites and thus protect them from African competition, policies which bore the collectivist

[93] Andrew Thompson, 'The Language of Loyalism in Southern Africa, c.1870–1939', *English Historical Review*, 118 (2003), 617–50.

[94] See e.g. Sheila Macdonald, *Martie and Others in Rhodesia* (London, 1927).

[95] H. I. Wetherell, 'Populism in Rhodesian Politics', *Rhodesian History*, 6 (1975), 53–76.

hallmarks of pre-war metropolitan concerns about 'National Efficiency'. The settlers were also able to shape the character of the educational system. Although many whites were lower-middle and working class in background, the English public school model was chosen, not only for private institutions, but for government schools as well. As Godfrey Huggins put it graphically: the country needed 'young men who had fagged at school and had been flogged at school, people who knew how to command and obey and knew how to handle their black labourers'.[96] The privately owned Ruzawi School embodied these ideals, but so, too, did government schools such as Prince Edward in Salisbury. Even the equivalent of a state vocational or 'secondary modern' school could exemplify these ideals. Allan Wilson High School, founded in Salisbury in the interwar period, and catering largely for the artisan classes, had boatered and blazered pupils, a chapel, and houses named for members of the Shangani Patrol whose ideals were celebrated in the school hymn.[97] Central to the system too, of course, was sport, which also served greatly to heighten local attachments.[98] 'We are attempting what has never been done before', R. A. Hammond, a leading educationalist noted: 'the founding of a white nation wholly within the tropics and containing a native population preponderating in numbers'.[99] It should be noted that boarders constituted a higher proportion of pupils than any other community in the world, which explains the exceptionally high degree of identification with school affiliations which, together with military and sporting ties, continues to define white Rhodesians both at home and in exile.[100] The education department noted as early as 1911 that the children of settlers were already evolving a Rhodesian variant of South African speech.[101] This accent could not be suppressed, however, and as a measure of belonging it continued to have both a conformist as well as exclusionary impact on new immigrants to the end of white rule, as the future British politician and journalist, Matthew

---

[96] Lewis Gann and Michael Gelfand, *Huggins of Rhodesia* (London, 1964), 70.

[97] Noel Brettell *et al.*, *Ruzawi: The Foundation of a School* (Salisbury, 1968), 3–4; I. P. MacLaren (ed.), *Some Renowned Rhodesian Schools, 1892–1979* (Bulawayo, 1981).

[98] J. de L. Thompson, *A History of Sport in Southern Rhodesia* (Bulawayo, 1935).

[99] R. A. Hammond, *Education for Rhodesia: Address to the Rhodesia Scientific Association* (Bulawayo, 1925), 2.

[100] R. J. Challis, *The European Educational System in Southern Rhodesia, 1890–1930* (Salisbury, 1980).

[101] National Archives of Zimbabwe: Director of Education to Parents and Guardians, 10 May 1912, circular no. 112 in E2/5.

Parris, found as a Rhodesian schoolboy in the 1950s.[102] Rhodesia's heroic past was continually invoked, based on Rhodes, Jameson, and other pioneers, who were depicted as the paladins of early Rhodesia. These myths were propagated by schools and cadet corps, assimilating later generations of Rhodesians, the children of even non-British immigrants, who had no direct link to the 1890s, and they could be used to bolster the egalitarian aspects of their society. These were 'ordinary men ... not kings, cabinet ministers, generals or even professional soldiers, but clerks, miners, store-keepers, even servants ... who laid the foundations of our country's greatness', the headmaster of Blakiston Junior School, himself of Afrikaner descent, advised his pupils, who were of largely immigrant origin, in 1956.[103]

The foundations of the educational system were laid in 1929 when a government commission advocated combining a sense of loyalty to the wider empire, with a local patriotism, based on a love of the land and a benevolent attitude towards its local people. These sentiments were fostered by the Boy Scout movement, which was keenly aware that Rhodesia provided Baden-Powell with his original inspiration for the movement. The country's unique character was also related to the story of David Livingstone, and the beauty of local attractions such as the Victoria Falls, Inyanga, which was likened to the Scottish highlands, as well as the 'mysterious' Zimbabwe Ruins, believed by many to have been the source of King Solomon's Mines.[104] The inculcation of a Rhodesian identity was further facilitated by the introduction of compulsory military service in the 1926 Defence Act. T. G. Standing, a senior educationalist, encouraged the holding of annual cadet camps to promote the teaching of shooting, veldt-craft, drill, and discipline, held to be essential to the vigour of the country's youth. He believed that Rhodesians made better soldiers than their metropolitan counterparts and that they resembled medieval Norman barons. Although trained to defend the wider empire, Standing believed that the time may come when 'the youth of the whole small nation, gathered together, in a common life and under common influences' might have to defend the colony itself. He thought such camps meant 'more than in England' and that here was 'one of the forces moulding the Rhodesian national

---

[102] Matthew Parris, *Chance Witness: An Outsider's Life in Politics* (London, 2002), 44.

[103] H. Rousseau, 'Blakiston Day Address, 1956', Blakiston Junior School Archives, Harare.

[104] E. C. Anderson, 'Among the Mountains of the Beautiful Eastern Districts', *Rhodesian Annual* (1938), 3, 57, 99.

character'.[105] Significantly, decades later, the army high command drew on
such sentiments in formulating a 'flexible response to the terrorist threat'.
It recommended incorporating 'Rhodesian tradition in order to preserve
the cavalry of the old Rhodesian units', including such titles as 'patrols,
troops, squadrons and commandos'.[106] These suggestions were taken up in
the 1970s, with the raising of a mounted infantry unit named the Grey Scouts,
as well as the undercover Selous Scouts, pioneer connections which were
further highlighted by popular ballads.[107]

Conservatism and Liberalism

Rhodesians, being small in number, tended to emphasize unity rather than
division, particularly in times of insecurity. Until the 1950s, Afrikaners,
particularly poor whites and those believed to have republican sympathies,
were the primary 'Other' against whom most Anglophone white Rhodesians identified themselves. Rhodesians also distinguished themselves from
Portuguese and Belgian colonial communities in the region, but these did
not of course pose any political threat. Despite their preponderance in numbers, Africans were not perceived to be an urgent threat, at least until the 1950s,
and attitudes towards them proved to be more complex than might be
expected. There was certainly a right-wing element in Rhodesian politics
and conservatism tended to be linked to length of residence. The outbreak
of war in 1939 brought debates about race into sharp focus. Henry Hamilton
Beamish, a self-confessed fascist and anti-Semite, was briefly elected to
Parliament in the late 1930s, before being interned. The Atlantic Charter
of 1941, with its promise of self-determination, prompted heated discussions
about citizenship both inside and outside parliament and across the racial
divide. Partly, perhaps, to appease opponents of Rhodesian racial policies in
Britain, Prime Minister Godfrey Huggins stunned critics by affirming that
Africans and Europeans shared a common ancestry, while some members of
parliament accepted that the conflict would necessitate greater participation
of Africans after the war.[108] The enlightened Mayor of Salisbury and Labour

---

[105] T. G. Standing, 'The Youth of a Nation', *Rhodesian Annual* (1928), 67.
[106] 'A Flexible Response to the Terrorist Threat, 7 July 1964', Rhodesian Army Archives,
Empire and Commonwealth Museum Bristol: Chiefs of Staff Committee, JP110/JPS/1/4.
[107] Edmond, *Story of Troopiesongs*, 6–13.
[108] Southern Rhodesia, *Debates of the Legislative Assembly*, 21/32, 19 June 1941, col. 1528.

Party activist, Gladys Maasdorp, attempted to move her white artisan-dominated party in a non-racial direction, which ultimately occasioned a split. Under Huggins, despite his protestations, segregationism was, if any-thing, tightening. Charles Mzingeli, chairman of the Labour Party's African branch, cited the Charter in support of African rights.[109] The traditionally conservative African elite also set much store by their rights under the Crown. This was in spite of periodic settler demands, championed not least by Prime Minister Huggins, to remove the 'anomaly' of a tiny African electorate from the voters' roll altogether. It is, perhaps, important to note, in a volume dealing with 'British communities', that the white Rhodesians, largely British or British South African by descent, were constantly challenged for this status by the traditional leaders of the black majority. 'We Africans have proved our loyalty to the Empire and the King by our own blood', Esau Nemapare declared in September 1945. 'The Empire is our house...We fought for Empire, King and Peace...'[110]

Until the radicalization of African politics in the late 1950s, traditional black Rhodesian leaders could also claim therefore to be a British community, although in a civic rather than ethnic sense, owing allegiance to a common sovereign and claiming equal rights, whether under the Atlantic Charter, or under Cecil Rhodes's disingenuous dictum, 'Equal rights for every civilized man'. In contrast to Afrikaner nationalists in the Union, who at times scarcely conceded that even their English-speaking white compatriots were part of a white South African 'nation', many white Rhodesians conceded that black Rhodesians formed a part, however subordinate, of a composite polity. These ideals were particularly manifested in the Central African Rhodes Centenary Exhibition of 1953, the colony's showcase at the beginning of federation and propagated by the newly founded university and the liberal-minded if somewhat paternalistic Capricorn Africa Society. This was an uphill battle in a society that had inherited a metropolitan anti-intellectualism and valued practical achievement over philosophical reflection.[111]

---

[109] Lawrence Vambe, *From Rhodesia to Zimbabwe* (London, 1976), 119; T. Scarnecchia, *The Urban Roots of Democracy and Political Rights in Zimbabwe: Harare and Highfield, 1940–1964* (Rochester, 2008), 32–3; Doris Lessing, *Under my Skin* (London, 1995), 304–5.

[110] Terence Ranger, *Are we Not Also Men? The Samkange Family and African Politics in Zimbabwe, 1920–64* (London, 1995), 103.

[111] Allison K. Shutt and Tony King, 'Imperial Rhodesians: The 1953 Rhodes Centenary Exhibition in Southern Rhodesia', *Journal of Southern African Studies*, 31/2 (2005), 360. Ian Hancock, *White Liberals, Moderates and Radicals in Rhodesia, 1953–1980* (London, 1984); John

The view that Africans could also form a subordinate part of a British-Rhodesian community continued under Sir Edgar Whitehead, the Southern Rhodesian prime minister. His 'Build-a-Nation' publicity campaign in the early 1960s, was designed to woo moderate African support for a common 'British' Rhodesian nation, which owed allegiance to their common sovereign. On the other hand, the continuing regional and educational links of the colony kept it within a South African orbit, where, in sporting terms, so pervasive to white identity, Southern Rhodesia constituted a provincial side. Indeed, in some respects, Rhodesia was thus a kind of self-governing English-speaking South African frontier, whose autonomy and unchallenged Britishness was envied by English-speaking South Africans in the Union, particularly in Natal. White Rhodesians were encouraged to think of themselves as harbingers of civilization among the black majority, but there was also a white Rhodesian tradition of romanticizing the Ndebele or 'Matabele' section of the African population, defined as 'martial' and 'noble'. Such archetypal virtues were believed to be embodied in the 'traditional' chiefs and headmen, as well as in the *askaris* and regimental ethos of the Rhodesian African Rifles.[112] Similar considerations ensured that a residual African representation continued in parliament even after the introduction of an overtly racialist constitution in 1969, despite calls for its abolition. During the 1960s, conscripted white servicemen began to incorporate African and creolized words into their distinctive patois.[113] Such benevolence did not, of course, preclude a ruthless defence of the white-ruled state, or the popularity in Rhodesia of the patronizing humour of racist comedian Wrex Tarr. Nevertheless, there was a wide measure of collaboration from the African population. The dominance and control of the small white minority for so long cannot be otherwise explained.

A Sense of False Security

White Rhodesians had an 'infinite capacity for self deception'.[114] This helps to explain how such a minority came to believe that they could hold power

Snelling, 'Rhodesian Verse', *Trek*, 15/5 (1951), 4–10; M. Gelfand, *A Non-Racial Island of Learning: A History of the University College of Rhodesia from its Inception to 1966* (Gwelo, 1978).

[112] See e.g. John Lovett, *Contact: A Tribute to Those Who Serve Rhodesia* (Salisbury, 1977), 86–8, 100–1; Women for Rhodesia, *Rhodesia as it Really is* (Salisbury, 1978), 1, 5.

[113] Edmond, *Story of Troopiesongs*, 29, 59.

[114] Godwin and Hancock, *Rhodesians Never Die*, 11.

indefinitely. The post-war world was a confusing time for them. There were growing anxieties about the security of the wider empire, as well as cultural and political changes in both the motherland and the Union and there continued to be a high turnover of settlers. Immigrants were nevertheless arriving and staying more permanently in unprecedented numbers: metropolitan arrivals outnumbered those from the Union for the first time. Local construction companies could not keep pace with the demands for European housing, and many immigrants had to be accommodated in prefabricated suburbs, but American-style high-rise corporate buildings proliferated in Salisbury and Bulawayo, built on the boom resulting from federation with the two northern territories. The opening of a multi-racial university and the Kariba hydroelectric dam added to this sense of security. Still, despite the growth of African trade unionism, manifested in the strike of 1948, and the beginnings of militant nationalism elsewhere in Africa, newsreels narrated in confident and authoritative voices the continuing strength of the Empire–Commonwealth and the new federation's contribution to its defence. The Rhodesian forces were rapidly expanded and modernized in these years, serving alongside British and Commonwealth armies in such trouble spots as Aden, Cyprus, and Malaya, and heightening the colony's sense of its importance in the global struggle against communism. Fatefully, the white Rhodesians shared, moreover, a traditional illusion of imperial invincibility, perpetuated by the V-bomber strategic force and Britain's apparent ability in the 1950s to remain a superpower, however subordinate. Added to this was a belief that they would never be displaced, as other peoples had been, not least in the Second World War. Even the architecture of the society, whether the art-deco-influenced, international style of commercial buildings and American grid-patterned street planning, or the 'stockbroker tudor' of residential suburbs, appeared to reinforce a sense of optimism, permanence, modernity, and Rhodesia's membership of the Western world. This illusion had been heavily reinforced by Britain's survival in the Second World War, which victory was perpetuated by such cinema films as *The Dam Busters* and *Ice Cold in Alex*, both highly popular in the colony. The establishment of two new high schools in Salisbury, named respectively for Churchill and Roosevelt, reflected this vain optimism and faith in the decisiveness of military and technological modernity.[115] The

---

[115] Donal Lowry, 'Southern Rhodesia and the Imperial Idea', in Andrea Bosco and Alex May (eds.), *The Round Table The Empire/Commonwealth and British Foreign Policy* (London, 1997),

conviction that Rhodesia was destined to be a 'white man's country' was also largely sustained by the settlers' high level of visibility. As late as 1969, the white Rhodesians made up more than one in four of the urban population of the territory, including more than one in three residents of the capital, Salisbury. The white population of the city was just under 100,000, most of whom lived in sprawling suburbs, whose visible presence could create an illusion of white preponderance, while the bulk of the black municipal majority of 280,000 was largely confined after working hours to remotely situated townships.[116]

The End of White Rhodesia

The 1960s witnessed a coarsening of white politics, as the Rhodesian Front consolidated its hold on all levers of power in the name of the struggle against communism. This suited the white electorate, apart from the 15–25 per cent who did not vote for it, because they were told that they were not fighting African nationalism but international communism, a myth the regime itself believed.[117] This illusion of invincibility was initially reinforced by the country's effective circumvention of sanctions, as well as early military successes against guerrilla incursions. The regime, like most of the electorate, believed its own propaganda, however, ever mistaking tactical success for strategic security. The Rhodesia Front was politically reminiscent of the RGA of the 1920s, forming an alliance of white farmers, locally based capital and the white working class, as well as previously largely excluded ethnic groups such as the Greeks and Afrikaners. Its election in 1962 was, as Lord Blake points out, virtually a class revolution.[118] Immigration increased and tourism boomed, as did interest in Rhodesian pioneer history, but this evident optimism was short-lived. The 1974 Lisbon *coup* sealed the fate of the Portuguese empire in Africa and with it that of white Rhodesia. With questionable support from South Africa, and the exposure of its entire eastern frontier, the Rhodesians could not long prevail. The growing guer-

329–32; Charles A. Frantz and Cyril A. Rogers, 'Length of Residence and Race Attitudes of Europeans in Southern Rhodesia', *Race*, 3/2 (1962), 53.

[116] Central Statistical Office, *Census of Population* (Salisbury, 1969); Kenneth Young, *Rhodesia and Independence* (London, 1969), 11.

[117] Donal Lowry, 'The Impact of Anti-Communism on White Rhodesian Political Culture, ca.1920s–1980', *Cold War History*, 7/2 (2007), 169–94.

[118] Blake, *History of Rhodesia*, 343.

rilla war put an increasing strain on white manpower and encouraged 'white flight', known pejoratively as the 'Chicken Run'. Still, many put their faith in Smith and his Rhodesian Front, believing that Africans needed to be protected from communist intimidators. This made Robert Mugabe's election victory in 1980 seem all the more perplexing to them.[119]

Soon after independence in 1980, the white community of Zimbabwe shrank to less than 70,000, with an average age of 59. Perhaps predictably, South Africa was the favoured and most proximate destination for many Rhodesian emigrants, but significant numbers settled in Australia and New Zealand, Britain, and North America, taking advantage of their skills and proficiency in the English language. Initially, a high proportion of white farmers remained and in many cases these became even more prosperous in the 1980s. Unlike exiled 'Rhodies', mocked in South Africa as 'Whenwes' for their habitual telling of nostalgic tales of life in Rhodesia, most whites who stayed readily made the transition to the new dispensation, relating to it apolitically as a tourist playground they now commonly called 'Zim'. Politically recused and abandoning the swaggering identity of white Rhodesia, they concentrated on economic rather than political success. Their optimism was short-lived, however, as the British government failed to provide promised funds for buying white farmland and the Mugabe government made them a scapegoat for economic failure. In the 1990s government-fomented waves of farm seizures by supposed war veterans reduced white farmers to a few hundred. Some white farmers were enthusiastically re-cruited by Mozambique, Zambia, the Congo, and Nigeria. By 2009, perhaps only 40,000 whites in total remained, an ageing shadow of the confident community that once designed and dominated the country's towns and farmlands. Nevertheless, their political legacy was indelible; Zimbabwe may well never have existed as a separate state from South Africa but for the 1922 referendum vote. Residual if tenuous respect for due legal process, as well as some strands of the Movement for Democratic Change and organizations opposed to the Mugabe government such as the Catholic Commission for Justice and Peace, can be traced to the extra-parliamentary and non-violent opposition to the Smith government. The cultural legacy of the settlers has also been as profound as their impact on the urban and rural landscape, not

[119] Paul L. Moorcraft, *A Short Thousand Years: The End of Rhodesia's Rebellion* (Salisbury, 1979); Julie Frederickse, *None But Ourselves: Masses Versus Media in the Making of Zimbabwe* (Johannesburg, 1973); David Caute, *Under the Skin: The Death of White Rhodesia* (London, 1983).

least in the area of education. The traditionally white schools, both government and private, for example, have perpetuated many of the attitudes,
some of the identities and sometimes even the distinctive white Rhodesian
accent among sections of the post-independence African elite, and these
developments have occurred, ironically, at the moment of near-extinction
of the white community. Published memoirs of life in Rhodesia, some of
them critical, proved popular beyond an ethnic audience.[120] Appropriately
enough for a community which generally equated modernity with technical
advances rather than social progress, the internet allowed white Rhodesians
settled largely in the old white Commonwealth and the USA to reconstitute
Rhodesia in cyberspace, and to facilitate local organizations, where friend-
ships could be revived and memories shared, with the aid of YouTube films
and musical material.[121] With time, however, as direct recollections of life in
Rhodesia fade, it must be expected that these remnants too must melt into
the societies in which they have settled, and this unforeseen afterlife of 'the
Lost Dominion' will thus finally come to an end.[122]

Select Bibliography

ROBERT BLAKE, *A History of Rhodesia* (London, 1977).

JOSIAH BROWNELL, 'The Hole in Rhodesia's Bucket: White Emigration and the End of
   Settler Rule', *Journal of Southern African Studies*, 34/3 (2008), 591–610.

L. H. GANN and PETER DUIGNAN, 'Changing Patterns of a White Elite: Rhodesian
   and Other Settlers', in L. H. Gann and Peter Duignan (eds.), *Colonialism in Africa
   1870–1960*, ii. *The History and Politics of Colonialism* (Cambridge, 1970).

PETER GODWIN and IAN HANCOCK, *'Rhodesians Never Die': The Impact of War and
   Political Change on White Rhodesia, c.1970–1980* (Harare, 1996 edn.).

RICHARD GRAY, *The Two Nations: Aspects of the Development of Race Relations in the
   Rhodesias and Nyasaland* (London, 1960).

H. C. HUMMEL, 'The Growth of White Rhodesian Nationalism: A Critical Appraisal',
   Zimbabwean History, 11 (1980), 75–86.

[120] Peter Godwin, *Mukiwa: A White Boy in Africa* (London, 1996); Alexandra Fuller, *Don't
Let's Go to the Dogs Tonight* (London, 2002); Dan Wylie, *Dead Leaves: Two Years in the Rhodesian
War* (Johannesburg, 2002); Chris Mears, *Goodbye Rhodesia* (Eastbourne, 2005); Anthony Chen-
nells, 'Rhodesian Discourse; Rhodesian Novels and Zimbabwe Liberation War', in Ngwabi
Bhebe and Terence Ranger (eds.), *Society in Zimbabwe's Liberation War* (London, 1996).

[121] Tony King, 'Rhodesians in Hyperspace: The Maintenance of a National and Cultural
Identity', in Karim H. Karim, *The Media of Diaspora* (London, 2003), 177–88.

[122] Katja Uusihakala, 'Memory Meanders: Place, Home and Commemoration in an
Ex-Rhodesian Diaspora Community', Ph.D. thesis (Helsinki, 2008).

E. Tawse Jollie, *The Real Rhodesia* (London, 1924).

Dane Kennedy, *Islands of White: Settler Society and Culture in Kenya and Southern Rhodesia, 1890–1939* (Durham, NC, 1987).

Tony King, 'Rhodesians in Hyperspace: The Maintenance of a National and Cultural Identity', in Karim H. Karim (ed.), *The Media of Diaspora* (London, 2003), 177–88.

Colin Leys, *European Politics in Southern Rhodesia* (Oxford, 1959).

Donal Lowry, 'Making Fresh Britains across the Seas: Women's Suffrage and Anti-Feminism in Rhodesia', in Ian C. Fletcher, Philippa Levine, and Laura Nym Mayhall (eds.), *Women's Suffrage and the British Empire* (London, 1999), 175–90.

A. S. Mlambo, *White Immigration into Rhodesia: From Occupation to Federation* (Harare, 2002).

D. J. Murray, *The Governmental System in Southern Rhodesia* (Oxford, 1970).

John Parker, *Rhodesia: Little White Island* (London, 1972).

Ian Phimister, *An Economic and Social History of Zimbabwe, 1890–1948: Capital Accumulation and Class Struggle* (London, 1988).

6

'The Last Outpost'
The Natalians, South Africa, and the British Empire

John Lambert

In 1970 New Zealand's All Blacks toured South Africa. No Natal rugby player was chosen by the South African selectors to represent the country, even Tommy Bedford, one of Natal's iconic rugby heroes and vice-captain of the South African national team, was dropped. There was widespread anger in Natal and at a banquet for the All Blacks in Durban, Bedford welcomed the visitors not to the South African province, but to Natal, the 'last outpost of the British Empire'. Although this could be seen as a gesture of defiance to the South African selectors, it revealed a deeper reality. Natal's majority white group, the Natalians, were only too ready to see the omission of a Natal player as a slight on the integrity of their province and of their own identity. They consciously saw themselves as different to whites elsewhere in South Africa and the 'last outpost' was a defiant way of expressing that difference; of proclaiming their identity as an English-speaking, 'British' community, of South Africa, yet different from the rest of the country.

During Natal's imperial period (1843–1961), the Natalians were socially and culturally similar to British settlers elsewhere in the British empire, sharing a broadly common attitude to Britain, the empire, and the monarchy. Within white South Africa, British settlers were in a minority compared to Afrikaners. In Natal, however, they formed the white majority and dominated the region, politically, socially, culturally, and economically. Alone among South Africa's British communities they used their colonial name, Natalians, to distinguish themselves. During the imperial years they evolved as a distinctive, even idiosyncratic, British community, a South African Ulster and the 'last outpost of the Empire'.

I gratefully acknowledge the financial assistance of the University of South Africa. I am indebted for advice and criticisms from my fellow authors and from Alex Mouton and Peter Colenbrander. All opinions and conclusions, however, are those of the author.

The British presence in Natal began in 1824 when a few hunter-traders established an outpost at Port Natal. The Zulu king, Shaka kaSenzanga-khona, allowed them to exercise authority over nearby Africans and they established themselves as local chiefs, taking African 'wives'. By 1839, when Afrikaner voortrekkers created the Republic of Natalia, few hunter-traders remained and their legacy lived on as a Coloured or African community outside the settler identity.

The Republic had a short existence. In 1842 a small British force occupied Port Natal and on 31 May 1844, Natal was annexed to the Crown.[1] The new colony's future looked unpromising. Outside the narrow coastal strip and the midlands, Natal enjoyed few ecological advantages: the Drakensberg formed a formidable obstacle to contact with other white settlements; mail boats to England took over six weeks, and Natal's telegraph link came only in the late 1870s. Although the Zulu kingdom remained independent, many Africans lived in Natal. Their numbers grew rapidly, from under 100,000 in 1844 to over 950,000 in 1911, after the annexation of the rump of the Zulu kingdom and the Transvaal's New Republic district.[2] By contrast, white numbers remained small. Most Afrikaners left for the interior; by 1849 about sixty families remained, mainly in northern Natal where they became a distinctive minority.[3]

Natal also faced the British government's unwillingness to finance an effective administrative infrastructure or immigration schemes. The colony's first officials came from the Cape, including Theophilus Shepstone who dominated colonial life until the 1870s and posthumously influenced African policy into the twentieth century. The earliest British settlers came from the Eastern Cape or were drawn from the 45th Regiment which garrisoned Natal from 1843 until 1858. These soldiers were the real pioneers, building roads and providing Natal with its first skilled craftsmen.[4]

Immigration schemes were left to private enterprise. Between 1848 and 1852, approximately 4,800 settlers arrived in Natal, mainly under the

---

[1] Andrew Duminy and Bill Guest (eds.), *Natal and Zululand from Earliest Times to 1910: A New History* (Pietermaritzburg, 1989) provides a useful history of colonial Natal.
[2] P. S. Thompson, *Natalians First: Separatism in South Africa, 1909–1961* (Johannesburg, 1990), 1.
[3] Alan F. Hattersley, *The British Settlement of Natal: A Study in Imperial Migration* (Cambridge, 1950), 79–80.
[4] Ibid. 81, 82, 92.

auspices of the Byrne Emigration Company. Joseph Byrne brought settlers predominantly from northern England along with a Scottish contingent and a handful from Ireland. Byrne's scheme aimed at placing people of 'good character and industrious habits' on the land.[5] Without official financing, the scheme was largely affordable only to families able to pay between £10 (steerage) and £35 (cabin) per person for passage and twenty acres: middle-class, yeoman, and lesser gentry families. Few had farming experience, and twenty acres was too small for productive farming. By 1852, Byrne was bankrupt and the settlers' future was bleak. One-quarter soon emigrated. Those who remained on their allotments tended to be experienced Yorkshire farmers. Others with professional or commercial skills settled in Pietermaritzburg or Durban where they forged strong links between the towns and farming districts.[6]

The Byrne settlers and another 1,500 who arrived between 1858 and 1864 under their sponsorship[7] established a tightly knit, homogeneous settler society, strongly imbued with mid-Victorian bourgeois values of utilitarian individualism, self-discipline, and thrift.[8] They established an enduring settlement pattern: a colony in which middle-class values predominated and in which English were a majority over Celts, and 'loyal' Scots a majority over 'disloyal' Irish. There were few non-British white settlers and many, such as the Norwegians of Marburg, or the small influential Jewish community in Durban, became Anglicized. Only the small German communities of New Germany and New Hanover retained their distinctive identity and language. With few British settlers, Natal's white population grew slowly, reaching only 35,866 by 1887.[9] This growth resulted mainly from natural increase but was retarded by steady emigration. Severe depressions in the 1860s and 1880s encouraged emigration while the Kimberley diamond discoveries in the late 1860s, and the Transvaal gold discoveries in the 1880s, saw large numbers move inland.

Natal was a poor colony with no cash crop except sugar, which became a viable export crop after the introduction of Indian indentured labourers

---

[5] Alan F. Hattersley, *Portrait of a Colony* (Cambridge, 1940), 35.

[6] Hattersley, *British Settlement, passim.*

[7] Ibid. 223.

[8] John Comaroff identifies such values in 'Images of Empire, Contests of Conscience: Models of Colonial Domination in South Africa', in Frederick Cooper and Ann Laura Stoler (eds.), *Tensions of Empire: Colonial Cultures in a Bourgeois World* (Berkeley, Calif., 1997), 169–70.

[9] Edgar H. Brookes and Colin de B. Webb, *A History of Natal* (Pietermaritzburg, 1965), 158.

from 1860.[10] In the midlands and interior, farmers remained isolated and under-capitalized, seldom cultivating more than 10 per cent of their lands and dependent on unreliable supplies of African labour. Transport was mainly by ox wagon and bad roads, drought and heavy rains often made travel difficult. Letters and diaries describe evocatively how hard life was, particularly for women who often bore the brunt of farming and of supervising labour while men tried to earn money transport riding.[11] Many farms passed into the hands of speculators such as the Natal Land and Colonisation Company.[12] Economically, the colony survived on the through trade with the republics and on African taxes. In 1871 the Cape's *Graham's Town Journal* described Natal as 'a British colony, so-called, but in truth a native territory scantily occupied by Europeans'.[13] In the following years, as the population discrepancy between whites and Africans increased, the Natalians became ever more conscious of their position as a small minority surrounded by Africans.

Even after farming became commercially viable by the 1880s, the Natalians were essentially an urban community: over half lived in Pietermaritzburg and Durban. While other urban centres remained little more than villages, Pietermaritzburg and Durban became boroughs with mayors and town councils in the early 1850s. They retained the atmosphere of English market towns until the twentieth century. Pietermaritzburg was the administrative and military centre closely linked to the midlands farming community on which it depended commercially. Until Union the social and commercial life of the city centred on Government House and the Fort Napier military garrison while religious life focused on the Anglican bishopric, founded in 1853. The city was clique-ridden with clear divisions

---

[10] Peter Richardson, 'The Natal Sugar Industry, 1849–1905', in Bill Guest and John M. Sellers (eds.), *Enterprise and Exploitation in a Victorian Colony: Aspects of the Economic and Social History of Colonial Natal* (Pietermaritzburg, 1985), 181–98.

[11] R. E. Gordon (ed.), *Dear Louisa: History of a Pioneer Family in Natal, 1850–1888* (Durban, 1970); Eliza Whigham Feilden, *My African Home, or, Bush Life in Natal when a Young Colony 1852–8* (London, 1887); Daphne Child (ed.), *A Merchant Family in Early Natal: Diaries and Letters of Joseph and Marianne Churchill, 1850–1880* (Cape Town, 1979) and *Portrait of a Pioneer: The Letters of Sidney Turner from South Africa, 1864–1901* (Johannesburg, 1980); William Rees, *Colenso Letters from Natal* (Pietermaritzburg, 1958).

[12] John Lambert, *Betrayed Trust: Africans and the State in Colonial Natal* (Pietermaritzburg, 1995), 9.

[13] Bill Guest, 'The War, Natal and Confederation', in Andrew Duminy and Charles Ballard (eds.), *The Anglo-Zulu War: New Perspectives* (Pietermaritzburg, 1981), 55.

between officials and non-officials and between the military and civilians. Pietermaritzburg had a lower middle class mainly of civil servants and shopkeepers and there was constant friction between them and soldiers. The settlers had the Victorian social disdain for soldiering, a view reinforced by the soldiers' rowdy behaviour.[14] Durban's position meanwhile, as south-east Africa's most important harbour city, made it commercially important. It was a subtropical British city with very close ties with the Royal Navy. While Pietermaritzburg society was self-consciously genteel, Durban was brash and commercial, with its social and political life dominated by the merchant community. As the only town in Natal with an important white working-class community, it was more marked by class differences.[15]

From the earliest colonial days, the Natalians stressed what they saw as their superior antecedents. Over time a specifically British, essentially middle-class, mythology of settlement evolved. The Byrne settlers might not have had wealth but, the Natalians insisted, they had birth, intelligence, and education, good stock 'on which to engraft a respectable community'.[16] To Natal's first prime minister, Sir John Robinson, the Natalians had 'won... for the Empire and for themselves the country they inhabit... from barbarism, and have bequeathed it to civilisation... It is a goodly heritage, and they mean to pass it on as a homeland to their children and their children's children.'[17] An emerging sense of identity is implicit in Robinson's description, one that was essentially British and imbued with concepts of white racial and cultural supremacy, flourishing in contradistinction to both the African and Afrikaner presence in South Africa. This myth of Natalian superiority was nourished by a settler history that justified their dominance over other races, reinforced pride in British antecedents, and celebrated British values and institutions. Acceptance of British values is implicit in Alan Hattersley's books on Natal history and in the diaries and letters of the period. Imbued with colonial nostalgia, these writings portray a colonial setting that accepted the legitimacy of settler domination, ignored the Natalians' exploitation of blacks, and, by reinforcing stereotypes of

[14] John Laband and Robert Haswell (eds.), *Pietermaritzburg, 1838–1988: A New Portrait of an African City* (Pietermaritzburg, 1988), 102–9.

[15] Anna Christina Bjorvig, 'Durban 1824–1910: The Formation of a Settler Elite and its Role in the Development of a Colonial City', Ph.D. thesis (Natal, 1994).

[16] Gordon, *Dear Louisa*, 38.

[17] Sir John Robinson, *A Lifetime in South Africa: Being the Recollections of the First Premier of Natal* (London, 1900), 98.

their racial superiority, gave ideological justification to racism. They also, however, offer glimpses of the Natalians' endemic paranoia, particularly their fear of African uprisings, Zulu invasions, Indian competition, and miscegenation.

More recent Natal historiography, beginning with Brookes and Webb's 1965 classic *History of Natal*, places the Natalians in the context of their interrelationship with other races and offers a more rounded picture of the community and its identity, articulating voices suppressed in earlier work. The new historiography has also largely eroded the idealized myth of settler women and instead portrays them as both 'subordinate in colonial hierarchies and as active agents of imperial culture in their own right'.[18] Women lived socially restricted, home-bound lives, but they proved capable of taking the opportunities offered by colonialism and defining and imposing ideas of social status, culture, and Britishness in the home.[19] Both government and private girls' schools modelled themselves on their British counterparts and became important agents in reinforcing Natal's racial, social, and gender divisions.[20] Women's institutes and female patriotic societies like the Victoria League and the Daughters of the Empire became important agents reinforcing Britishness.[21]

The earlier historiography was, however, right to place Britishness at the core of the Natalians' identity. While there were always dissenting voices, Britishness legitimized the position of most Natalians and anchored their identity in a new 'savage' environment. Their ties with Britain remained strong. As late as 1911, 30.13 per cent were born in Britain[22] and continued to be influenced by families and friends 'back home'. Settler diaries and letters support Marjorie Morgan's argument that national identity should be understood 'in terms of everyday images and rituals to do

[18] Ann Laura Stoler, 'Making Empire Respectable: The Politics of Race and Sexual Morality in Twentieth-Century Colonial Cultures', in Louise Lamphere, Helena Ragoné, and Patricia Zavella, *Situated Lives: Gender and Culture in Everyday Life* (New York, 1997), 373.

[19] See Jo Beall, 'Class, Race and Gender: The Political Economy of Women in Colonial Natal', MA thesis (Natal, 1982), and P. L Merrett, 'Frances Ellen Colenso (1849–1887): Her Life and Times in Relation to the Victorian Stereotype of the Middle-Class English Woman', MA thesis (Cape Town, 1980).

[20] See Sylvia Vietzen, *A History of Education for European Girls in Natal with Particular Reference to the Establishment of Some Leading Schools, 1837–1902* (Pietermaritzburg, 1973).

[21] John Lambert, 'Britishness, South Africanness and the 1st World War', in Philip Buckner and R. Douglas Francis (eds.), *Rediscovering the British World* (Calgary, 2005), 288–9.

[22] Thompson, *Natalians First*, 2.

with landscape, religion, food and drink, recreation, manners, liberty, language and history'.[23] They reveal how the Natalians clung to old habits and traditions and tried to recreate their familiar way of life in a new environment, emphasizing the difference between savagery and order by cultivating English gardens and naming farms, homes, streets, and suburbs after British people and places. Most settlers handed a vision of Britain as 'the sweetest, and noblest and best of countries' down to their children and grandchildren.[24] Britain remained the epicentre of their world; fashions in dress, architecture, art, and literature followed those of Britain, as did the middle-class desire for self-improvement. Libraries and educational societies were founded and British books and journals were standard reading matter.

The colonial press served as a forum for imperialist ideology and was active in maintaining a British identity, reflecting and reinforcing ties of kinship and loyalty that bound the Natalians to Britain. The most important colonial newspapers, Pietermaritzburg's *Natal Witness* and Durban's *Natal Mercury*, were founded in the 1850s and still command a large place in Natalian affections. In their formative years their editors were forthright northerners who established a tradition of political independence and of opposition to those British policies seen as detrimental to settler interests. Editors like David Buchanan of the *Witness* and John Robinson of the *Mercury* were active political figures who used their newspapers in support of Natal's interests.[25]

The press seldom questioned the imperial ideal, however, and, until 1961, glorified British achievements and idolized the Crown and the royal family. To the Natalians, the Crown defined their Britishness. Queen Victoria's family life was seen to embrace the middle-class domestic virtues the Natalians were trying to recreate in their new home and identifying with royal activities was a way of buttressing their British identity. Settler letters and diaries reveal constant interest in the royal family while rituals associated with the Crown, such as the observation of the Queen's birthday and

---

[23] Marjorie Morgan, *National Identities and Travel in Victorian Britain* (New York, 2001), 219.

[24] Merrett, *Frances Ellen Colenso*, 206.

[25] Simon Haw, *Bearing Witness: The Natal Witness, 1846–1996* (Pietermaritzburg, 1996); Trevor Wilks, *For the Love of Natal: The Life and Times of the Natal Mercury, 1852–1977* (Durban, 1977). See also John Lambert, '"The Thinking is Done in London": South Africa's English-Language Press and Imperialism', in Chandrika Kaul (ed.), *Media and the British Empire* (London, 2006), 37–54.

the granting of honours made many Natalians feel part of what Cannadine describes as a pan-British imperial elite.[26] Royal visits also validated British rituals in the colony and reinforced colonial ties with the mother country, while statues of Victoria and other royal memorials provided physical reminders of the Crown. Churches of various denominations also promoted Britishness and loyalty to the Crown and empire. The settlers were predominantly Protestant and Catholicism was never more than a minority denomination. As elsewhere in the empire, Anglican and other Protestant clergymen were imbued with imperial pride and generally shared the settlers' segregationist and white supremacist views.[27]

The Natalians' sense of British identity was matched by an equally strong sense of belonging to Natal: while their sense of identity was British, their sense of place was Natalian. Settler writings reflect a love of place and identification with their surroundings. In 1857 Frances Colenso wrote from Bishopstowe to her sister: 'I wish you could see one of these summer evenings here, the sunset on these lovely hills, the fireflies in the grass ... I do so dote on these green hills.'[28] Twentieth-century poets like Roy Campbell and Roy McNab celebrated Natal's beauty, the most lyrical evocation being Alan Paton's famous opening lines of *Cry, the Beloved Country*: 'There is a lovely road that runs from Ixopo into the hills. The hills are grass-covered and rolling, and they are lovely beyond any singing of it.'[29] Landscape artists such as Cathcart Methven did much to give a visual identity to Natal in loving portrayals of the Drakensberg, the midlands, Durban bay, and the south coast.

Natalian identity was articulated by the colony's white elite, the major farming and coastal planter gentry and the officials and merchants of Pietermaritzburg and Durban, the so-called Old Natal Families.[30] These families believed as much in the social as in the racial hierarchical order. While some had an upper-class British background, others overcame initial hardships to become prosperous, gathering the trappings of gentility and building lavish urban and country houses where they replicated a British

---

[26] David Cannadine, *Ornamentalism: How the British Saw their Empire* (New York, 2001), 22.

[27] Brian Stanley (ed.), *Missions, Nationalism and the End of Empire* (Grand Rapids, Mich., 2003), 4.

[28] Rees, *Colenso Letters*, 41.

[29] Alan Paton, *Cry, the Beloved Country* (London, 1948), 1.

[30] Robert Morrell, *From Boys to Gentlemen: Settler Masculinity in Colonial Natal, 1880–1920* (Pretoria, 2001).

upper-class lifestyle. As in Britain, the gentry placed a priority on land as an inalienable asset and conformed to Cain and Hopkins's observation that gentlemen in the colonies 'took to paternalism as squires to the manner born, and they tried to recreate abroad the hierarchy they were familiar with at home'.[31] The Old Natal Families established a closely knit network that dominated Natal's political, social, and economic life and transformed colonial agriculture. Civically conscious, their male members played a role in the legislature and as justices of the peace and established a reasonably effective colonial bureaucracy. Aware of the social importance of the imperial connection they staunchly supported British traditions. Their social life revolved around the Durban Club and Pietermaritzburg's Victoria Club, institutions that were clearly designed to protect and further masculine interests and to exclude not only women but also 'undesirables' from access to power. These included the lower classes, other races, and, with few exceptions, Afrikaners and Jews. In rural areas, farmers' clubs and agricultural associations protected settler agricultural interests and worked rigorously to stamp out African or Indian competition.

By the end of the nineteenth century, a hegemonic masculinity had developed in Natal that embraced the middle class as much as the elite and was propagated by vigorously imperialist patriotic societies such as the Caledonian and the Sons of England, and Masonic lodges. This hegemonic masculinity reflected the creed of middle-class manliness that was being disseminated throughout the empire and dictated what was and was not acceptable masculine behaviour.[32] It was encouraged by the garrison and was particularly evident on the sports field. Hunting and shooting were popular colonial diversions while organized team sports were important indicators of race, class, and gender. Tennis and cycling were the only sports shared by men and women and all sports were strictly segregated racially until into the 1980s. Polo and golf were upper-class sports while football became divided along class lines by 1900 between 'middle-class' rugby and 'working-class' soccer. Cricket, played from the earliest colonial years, was popular among all classes and together with rugby was seen as embodying the best British values of team play and sportsmanship. Sports clubs, country clubs, and school old

---

[31] P. J. Cain and A. G. Hopkins, *British Imperialism, 1688–2000* (2nd edn. Harlow, 2002), 48.

[32] See Morrell, *From Boys to Gentlemen, passim.* For a discussion on English South Africa's patriotic societies, see John Lambert, 'Maintaining a British Way of Life: English-Speaking South Africa's Patriotic, Cultural and Charitable Associations', *Historia*, 54/2 (2009), 56–76.

boys' clubs were important social and sporting meeting places, rivalling urban 'gentlemen's' clubs in popularity if not prestige.[33]

As elsewhere in the empire, volunteering also provided an outlet for Natalian masculinity. Volunteer regiments like the Natal Carbineers, formed to supplement the imperial garrison, fought in the Anglo-Zulu War (1879), losing twenty-one men at Isandhlwana, and in the Anglo-Boer War (1899–1902). Natal families became associated with individual regiments, providing them with regional loyalties which lasted until the end of the twentieth century. In addition, the regiments established traditions linking them to the British military establishment and to the Crown.[34]

The settlers' hegemonic masculine and British ideology was passed from father to son by the colonial educational system. While those who could afford to, sent their sons to school in Britain, elite government schools such as Maritzburg College and Durban High School and private schools like Michaelhouse and Hilton College became prestigious institutions. They relied heavily on English public and grammar schools for their inspiration, traditions, syllabi, and teachers and established a code of conduct that, by training their pupils to fill leadership positions and become 'rulers of the natives', reinforced class and race prejudices.[35] The schools' ethos centred on sport: both team sports and boxing were believed to build up boys' characters and instil self-control, responsibility, and physical courage, essential to ensuring white supremacy. They also taught them to play the game and to 'take a licking like men'.[36] In a society in which white males often used violence to maintain their authority over Africans, many teachers believed that boys should know how to fight, encouraging them to sort out problems with their fists and often turning a blind eye when conformity or at least silence was thrashed into boys whose allegiance to hegemonic masculinity was suspect.[37] Settler masculinity also found a ready vehicle in the cadet

---

[33] Lambert, 'Maintaining a British Way of life'; John Lambert, 'South African British? Or Dominion South Africans? The Evolution of an Identity in the 1910s and 1920s', *South African Historical Journal*, 43/1 (2000), 210–11.

[34] National Archives, Pretoria, Governor-General 9/93; Alan F. Hattersley, *Carbineer: The History of the Royal Natal Carbineers* (Aldershot, 1950), and Morrell, *From Boys to Gentlemen*, ch. 6.

[35] *Pietermaritzburg College Magazine*, 3/26 (June 1908), 9.

[36] *The Durban High School Magazine*, 2/1 (Apr. 1902), 1.

[37] Morrell, *From Boys to Gentlemen*, chs. 3 and 4; John Lambert, '"Munition Factories... Turning Out a Constant Supply of Living Material": White South African Elite Boys' Schools and the First World War', *South African Historical Journal*, 51/1 (2004), 67–86.

system introduced from the 1860s. Cadets instilled military values in boys and provided a recruiting ground for volunteer regiments.[38] While scouting was introduced in the early twentieth century it never became as popular in the elite schools as cadets or as guides in girls' schools and drew mainly on lower class support.

In Natal, as in other European colonies where indigenous inhabitants outnumbered settlers, Britishness was as much a racial as a cultural definition, linked to social-Darwinist concepts of whiteness and the need to maintain social and cultural distance between the races, violently if necessary. Settler violence took many forms, ranging from physical force to interventions in African life and customs.[39] In an uneasy mix of paternalism and racism, Natalians stereotyped Africans morally and socially as children to be disciplined and whose way of life, from their clothes to the number of their wives, was legislated for. White arrogance and ignorance of African customs exacerbated relations between the races and were particularly evident in the ambiguous relationship between settler women and male African servants. Although there were remarkably few reports of African attacks on white women, periodic rape scares reflected settler fears of the virile 'savages' living among them and concerns about the sexual vulnerability of settler women.[40]

Feelings of insecurity and fear of the 'savage' African saw a particularly virulent and violent racism develop amongst Natalians, more extreme than amongst most other British South Africans and more akin to that of the Afrikaners. It was demonstrated in racist and restrictive laws that curtailed African freedom and in the ruthless crushing of all opposition.[41] Very few Natalians challenged this racism and those who did, such as Bishop Colenso and his daughters, were easily marginalized and ignored.[42] Insecurity and fear were interlinked with Natal's economic stagnation and constant labour shortages. The backwardness of settler agriculture saw many farmers rely on

---

[38] Hattersley, *Carbineer*, 46.

[39] See Ann Laura Stoler and Frederick Cooper, 'Between Metropole and Colony: Rethinking a Research Agenda', in Cooper and Stoler (eds.), *Tensions of Empire*, 7, 31.

[40] Norman Etherington, 'Natal's Black Rape Scare of the 1870s', *Journal of Southern African Studies*, 15/1 (1988), 36–53.

[41] Lambert, *Betrayed Trust*, passim.

[42] Jeff Guy, *The Heretic: A Study of the Life of John William Colenso, 1814–1883* (Johannesburg, 1983), and *The View across the River: Harriette Colenso and the Zulu Struggle against Imperialism* (Cape Town, 2001).

African tenants for labour and rents. African independence from settler control made this labour unreliable and the early colonial period was marked by settler attempts to end African independence. In 1856 Natal obtained representative government and, from the start, elected members on the Legislative Council tried to force the administration to limit Africans' independence and turn them into labourers.[43] Before responsible government was granted in 1893, they had limited success as British-appointed governors, and officials such as Shepstone, afforded Africans a measure of protection.

By the 1890s, however, the discovery of diamonds at Kimberley and gold on the Witwatersrand saw a rapid improvement in the farmers' position coupled with a diminished ability of African tenants to resist their demands. Land values rose, resulting in absentee-owned and Crown lands passing into settler hands. As the acreage available to Africans shrank, tenants had to accept more onerous labour contracts and became virtual serfs. In the towns, the attempts by the emerging African middle class of Christianized *amakholwa* to identify with British values and assimilate to Britishness were rebuffed, and there was also a growing demand for white control over both ex-indentured Indians and the growing class of Indian merchants and traders, all of whom threatened settler economic interests. Particularly in Durban, settler attitudes to Indians became nakedly racist. By the late 1880s there were almost as many Indians as whites in Natal and alarm was growing that the Natalians would be swamped politically and economically.[44]

British traditions of self-government meant that there had always been a strong sentiment in support of responsible government in the colony. Now, as settlers began flexing their economic muscles, they believed that only responsible government would enable them to control Africans and Indians. The small size of their community, however, made them acutely aware of their dependence on British military protection and many feared the consequences of responsible government. But by the early 1890s, these fears were balanced by growing resentment at the continuing neglect by successive British governments of Natal's interests in southern Africa. The

[43] Lambert, *Betrayed Trust*; Shula Marks, *Reluctant Rebellion: The 1906–1908 Disturbances in Natal* (Oxford, 1970); Robert Morrell (ed.), *Political Economy and Identities in KwaZulu-Natal: Historical and Social Perspectives* (Durban, 1996).

[44] Joy Brain, 'Natal's Indians, 1860–1910', in Duminy and Guest (eds.), *Natal and Zululand*, 249–74.

Natalians particularly resented Britain's non-support for their attempts to further Natal's economic interests in south-east Africa and the Transvaal. They had always wanted to see the Zulu kingdom brought under imperial rule to provide them with both land and labour but after the Anglo-Zulu War, vacillating British policies towards Zululand led by 1888 to the division of the kingdom between the Afrikaner-controlled New Republic (later part of the Transvaal) and a British colony.[45]

Natal's dependence on its import–export trade with the Transvaal made the settlers acutely aware of developments in the republic. In 1877 they had enthusiastically supported its annexation by Britain, and they had reacted with bitterness and humiliation when independence was restored in 1881 after the British defeat at Majuba. The discovery of gold in 1886 revolutionized the Transvaal's economic position and saw it poised to challenge British predominance in South Africa. To protect Natal's economic interests, the merchant leaders of Durban and their representatives in the legislature, Robinson and Harry Escombe, realized that a rapprochement with the republic would be in Natal's interests and they began wooing the Transvaal and distancing themselves from anti-republican imperial policies.

The desire to establish complete control over Africans and Indians and the belief that only responsible government would enable Natal to protect its interests in the Transvaal and south-east Africa, convinced Robinson and Escombe of the need for self-rule. After extensive negotiations with the British government, responsible government was granted in 1893 and the first ministry was sworn in under Robinson's premiership. With fewer than 10,000 voters, the new Legislative Assembly had only thirty-seven members. Party affiliations never took root and politics throughout the responsible government period tended to be parochial. After Robinson and Escombe's departure in the late 1890s, the legislators were of a poor calibre, 'governing themselves badly...and the native population worse'.[46] Responsible government succeeded in tightening settler control over Africans and Indians and saw the Colony of Zululand transferred to Natal in 1897, opening it to exploitation by sugar planters. The ruthless assertion of settler power over Zululand and over colonial Africans and Indians saw Winston Churchill

---

[45] John Laband, *Rope of Sand: The Rise and Fall of the Zulu Kingdom in the Nineteenth Century* (Johannesburg, 1995); Jeff Guy, *The Destruction of the Zulu Kingdom* (London, 1979).

[46] The Governor, Sir Matthew Nathan, in 1908. See Marks, *Reluctant Rebellion*, 19.

label Natal 'the hooligan of the British Empire'.[47] However, it ensured
white supremacy in south-east Africa until the 1980s. It was not uncon-
tested; racist legislation and increasingly onerous taxation saw widespread
uprisings in Natal-Zululand in 1906 which were ruthlessly crushed, leaving
Africans exhausted and sullen.[48]

With responsible government, the Natalians were also able to complete
the Transvaal railway and improve Durban harbour. They heavily mort-
gaged the colony doing so, in the process becoming dependent on Transvaal
trade at a time when the prospect of conflict between Britain and the
republic was looming. The Natalians were faced with the choice between
imperial sentiment and economic reality. Despite resentment at the detrimental effect of British policies on the colony, many were caught up in the
imperialist jingoism sweeping the empire and became increasingly vociferous in support of Transvaal *Uitlander* demands for British protection. By
contrast, successive Natal ministries realized the potentially disastrous economic implications of opposition to the Transvaal and cautiously distanced
themselves from British policies. Only in 1899, when it became obvious that
the high commissioner, Sir Alfred Milner, was determined to impose British
rule on the Transvaal, did the Natal ministry throw its support behind a
policy that led to the Anglo-Boer War.[49] With much of the early fighting
taking place in northern Natal, colonial volunteer regiments bore much of
the brunt of the initial attack. Although less than 25 per cent of white
Natalians of military age volunteered,[50] their services were invaluable in
northern Natal and the colony was rewarded after the war by being granted
the original New Republic Transvaal divisions.

The annexation of the northern districts and Zululand consolidated
settler control over south-east Africa. The exploitation of northern Natal's
coalfields played a vital role in the growth of the colonial infrastructure and
industries.[51] Railway lines now linked the colony to the interior, created new

[47] Martin Kitchen, *The British Empire and Commonwealth: A Short History* (New York, 1996), 57.
[48] Lambert, *Betrayed Trust*, chs. 10 and 11; Marks, *Reluctant Rebellion, passim.*
[49] Ritchie Ovendale, 'The Relations between Natal and the Transvaal during the 1890's', Ph.D. thesis (Natal, 1966).
[50] Brookes and Webb, *History of Natal*, 203, gives 2,710, while the *Natal Volunteer Record: Annals and Record of Service, Anglo-Boer War, 1899–1900* (Durban, 1900), p. x, lists 3,500 names.
[51] Ruth Edgecombe and Bill Guest, 'An Introduction to the Pre-Union Natal Coal Industry', in Guest and Sellers (eds.), *Enterprise and Exploitation*, 309–51.

villages, and brought many farmers into close contact with urban and overseas markets. Durban was becoming South Africa's favourite holiday resort and the subcontinent's premier port. By 1904, Natal's white population had increased to 97,109 and a new sense of settler self-confidence was reflected in a rash of building, including the exuberantly Edwardian baroque Durban town hall and impressive government and municipal buildings in Pietermaritzburg.[52] Despite this new self-confidence, the colony faced considerable problems. The growth of Durban had broadened the white urban working class and the appearance of trade unions and founding of the Labour Party in the early 1900s challenged the political and socio-economic hegemony of the Old Natal Families. Strikes, particularly among railway workers, became a new phenomenon. The post-war years also saw a severe economic depression that made Natalians aware of the fragility of their position. With annual expenditure exceeding revenue, the colony became more dependent economically on the now British Transvaal. British rule throughout South Africa offered the chance of closer cooperation between the four South African colonies that could alleviate some of Natal's concerns, including fear of another African rising and of Indian competition. In 1908, the Natalians agreed to take part in a National Convention to consider union.

The Natal delegates favoured a federation in which the colony would retain its identity. The other colonies, however, were intent on political union and carried the day. Natal's delegates were able to secure a number of concessions, including the establishment of provincial councils with limited powers over education, hospitals, roads, local public works, agriculture, and wildlife conservation.[53] These concessions, and the suicidal economic consequences of standing aside, saw the Natalians reluctantly accept the inevitable. In a referendum, they voted nearly four to one in favour of union.[54] They greeted the establishment of the Union of South Africa in 1910 with apprehension, however. The passing of political power from Pietermaritzburg to Pretoria had profound consequences for the new province and particularly for Pietermaritzburg. The departure of the King's last representative, and the transformation of the colonial parliament into a provincial

---

[52] *Twentieth Century Impressions of Natal: Its People, Commerce, Industries, and Resources* (London, 1906).

[53] Thompson, *Natalians First*, 1–5.

[54] Ibid. 6–8.

council, saw the city lose its status. The administrator, Charles Smythe, was a Union government appointee presiding over a small provincial administration with approximately 25 per cent of the city's civil servants transferring to Pretoria. Although the opening of the University College of Natal gave the city an educational importance, there was little else to compensate it for its loss in status, particularly after the imperial garrison left in 1914.

From 1910, Natal was ruled far more rigorously from Pretoria than it ever had been from London and the Natalians became very conscious of their political impotence. During the next half century they were to fight unsuccessfully to protect themselves from the realities of the changing constitutional position of South Africa and of the empire. Although Britain was replaced as the metropolitan power by the Union government, the Natalians resisted the loosening of imperial ties. Unlike their British compatriots in the other provinces who were cautiously accepting a common South Africanism uniting English- and moderate Afrikaans-speakers, the Natalians became more stridently British. Imperialism became all-pervasive in shaping their attitudes. For the remainder of the imperial period, Natal's newspapers retained their independence of the newspaper consortiums that were established elsewhere in the Union and continued to be bulwarks of imperialism and Britishness. As Horace Rose, the *Witness* editor, wrote, 'Heavy, indeed will be the responsibility upon us if it can be said by our posterity that we in this Province forgot that, whatever our South African nationhood may be, we are British first, and all the time.'[55]

The province gave the Natalians' Britishness a context and, despite its restricted powers, the provincial council gave their Britishness a voice. Thompson defines the province's civic culture as 'the sum of symbols and rituals which sustain authority and provide identity to a community'.[56] Until 1961, Britishness bound the Natalians together and gave them a sense of coherence. They deliberately used British symbols and imperial rituals to sustain their sense of identity and bitterly resisted all attempts to scrap them. The colonial mace was retained in the provincial council, the Union Jack continued to fly, and 'God Save the King' to be sung. These defined the Natalians and assured their position. Britishness became even

[55] P. S. Thompson, *The British Civic Culture of Natal, South Africa, 1902–1961* (Howick, 1999), 13.
[56] Ibid., p. iv.

more of an assertion of a separate identity than in the nineteenth century, distinct from Afrikaner identity.

In the nineteenth century relations between the Natalians and the colony's small Afrikaner minority had been cordial but the growth of imperialist jingoism in the 1890s encouraged anti-Afrikaner sentiments which were further stimulated when many Natal Afrikaners sided with the republican invaders in 1899. Despite being defeated, Afrikaners captured political control of the new Transvaal and Orange River colonies when responsible government was granted in 1907 and were the dominant political influence in the Cape. Fear of Afrikaner domination was an important reason for the Natalians' desire for federation and after 1910 they fought a long rearguard action to preserve their provincial liberties and British character. In doing so they lost sight of the larger picture, reducing their role in South Africa and, by their often vulgar jingoism, undermining the alliance between English-speakers and moderate Afrikaners that was essential for the continuation of British influence in South Africa.

Their attitude to Afrikaners was partly shaped by ignorance. Until after 1961, outside northern Natal, a Natalian seldom heard a word of Afrikaans.[57] Most Afrikaners they had contact with tended to be lower class, often railway workers or policemen transferred to the province after Union. Middle-class snobbery reinforced the Natalians' anti-Afrikaner sentiments, and, when the Transvaal leader, Louis Botha, was appointed prime minister in 1910, many felt bitter that an Afrikaner could dictate the future of a British community.

Despite being culturally and ideologically akin to English-speakers elsewhere in the Union, the Natalians were unable to form a cohesive block with the predominantly British Unionist Party. A legacy of economic rivalry with the Cape and rejection of the Cape's liberal franchise alienated them from the British in that province and they were equally unable to make common cause with the Transvaal British because the mining interests favoured using Mozambique's harbour facilities.[58] In the 1911 general election, only five Unionists and two supporters of Botha's South African Party (SAP) were elected in Natal compared to ten independents.[59] Botha

---

[57] Information received from Natalians who grew up in the province before the 1970s.

[58] The National Archives, Kew (TNA), CO 551/31, Gladstone to Harcourt, 16 Dec. 1912, p. 188; see also Thompson, *Natalians First*, 10.

[59] B. M. Schoeman, *Parlementêre Verkiesings in Suid-Afrika, 1910–1976* (Pretoria, 1977), 21–32.

capitalized on the Natalians' antagonism to the Unionists by appointing two independents to his cabinet. In 1912, Botha excluded the Orange Free State ex-Boer War general, Barry Hertzog, from his cabinet after Hertzog alien-ated English-speakers by advocating policies that they believed discrim-inated against their interests. His exclusion convinced many Natalians that their interests were safe in Botha's hands.[60] The SAP government's support for Britain during the First World War further consolidated their support for Botha and in the 1915 general election the province returned eleven SAP MPs compared to four Unionists, one Labour, and one Independent.[61]

The First World War brought out the best and the worst in the Natalians. They responded emotionally to what they saw as Britain's moral decision to protect Belgian neutrality. Like Britons elsewhere in the empire, they felt bound to support the mother country and 'proud of the high privilege of being called upon to play our part in the struggle'.[62] Schools, patriotic societies, churches, and Natalians of all political persuasions including Labour Party members, threw their weight behind the war effort. A steady stream volunteered with the South African forces while many, particularly from the elite schools, went to England to serve as officers in British regiments and in the Royal Flying Corps. Approximately 43 per cent of English-speaking South African men of military age fought and, although there are no figures for Natal, there is nothing to indicate that their response was less enthusiastic than elsewhere in the Union.[63] Negatively, the war evoked the Natalians' more jingoist and violent characteristics. Despite having lived harmoniously with their German fellow settlers since the 1840s, anti-German hysteria gripped the province, with Durban in particular being smitten by 'the molten hate of the Hun and his works'.[64] After the *Lusitania* incident in 1915, Durban mobs burned and looted German-owned buildings and demanded the confiscation of German businesses.[65]

South Africa's sacrifices at Delville Wood during the Battle of the Somme in July 1916 and on other battle fronts made a profound impression on

---

[60] Thompson, *Natalians First*, 16–18.

[61] Ibid. 18.

[62] *S. Michael's Chronicle*, 3/9 (Oct. 1914), 1.

[63] See Lambert, 'Munition Factories' and 'Britishness, South Africanness and the First World War', 285–304.

[64] *The Nongqai*, 8/2 (Aug. 1917), 72.

[65] *Natal Mercury* (18 May 1915); Thomas Boydell, *'My Luck Was In'* (Cape Town, 1948), 107.

Natalians and after 1918 they made concerted efforts to maintain their wartime camaraderie. Monuments were unveiled, memorial services were held and ex-servicemens' associations were formed, most noticeably the South African Legion of the British Empire Service League, and the Memorable Order of Tin Hats, the MOTHS, founded in Durban in 1927. Ex-servicemen also founded the great road race, the Comrades Marathon.

Although pride in their wartime achievements stimulated South Africanist sentiments amongst some Natalians, the growth of Afrikaner nationalism in the 1920s which directly threatened Natal's British character and South Africa's position in the empire, further strengthened their British and provincial loyalties. In the 1924 general election the National Party won a majority of seats and, in a pact with the Labour Party, including three Natal members, formed the government. The province's working class only reluctantly supported this pact with the Nationalists and from 1925 they joined with Natalians of all classes in vehemently rejecting a bill to replace the Union Jack with a national flag. The flag controversy aroused a storm of virulently anti-Afrikaner sentiment in Natal, rallying SAP and Labour supporters, Caledonian societies and Sons of England, men and women, in defence of the Union Jack. The flag symbolized the Natalians' position as British subjects and the province's separate status and they were determined to maintain it. Their success in retaining it as one of two national flags was largely due to the fact that English-speakers throughout the Union joined forces and used the SAP as a vehicle for their campaign.[66] The support that the SAP leader, Jan Smuts, gave the campaign strengthened Natalian support for the party even if their MPs always acted as a separate 'Natal Party' faction within the party. Used by politicians like George Heaton Nicholls to assert Natal interests and stimulate Natal patriotism, the flag campaign paved the way for later separatist movements.

Although the Natal faction was large enough to make its voice heard, its contribution to the party was generally negative. Natal continued to return mediocre MPs who were generally regarded with contempt by both English- and Afrikaans-speaking South Africans. Even the province's most influential interwar politician, Heaton Nicholls, was a political lightweight. Consistent with the province's aggressive masculinity, there were very few female members of Parliament or the Provincial Council. The Natalians' main

---

[66] Thompson, *Natalians First*, ch. 3.

contribution was to strengthen the SAP's conservative, racist, wing. By the 1920s, they were advocating strengthening Zulu tribal authorities as instruments to control Africans[67] and, in response to intensified African migration to urban areas following wartime industrialization, began instituting a segregation system that gathered momentum during the following decades and was extended to include Indians. The so-called 'Durban System' influenced segregation policies elsewhere in the Union, foreshadowing post-1948 apartheid policies.

The war had stimulated economic growth in Natal, particularly in Durban which witnessed rapidly increased industrialization and the consolidation of its position as the subcontinent's premier port; by the 1930s it handled 80 per cent of the Union's maritime cargo.[68] Sugar farming expanded rapidly on the coast as did wattle and sheep farming in the midlands. This steady capitalization of white agriculture enabled white farmers to tighten their control further over African and Indian tenants.[69] The 1929–33 Depression years, however, destabilized white society. Farmers slid heavily into debt and both whites and Africans moved to the cities, particularly to Durban. Social destabilization led to political instability, manifested in the emergence of a number of small separatist or federalist parties. Although economic discontent was an important factor in this development, the government's proposal to balance the national budget by abolishing provincial councils gave it impetus. By the 1930s the provincial council was seen as the strongest safeguard of the Natalians' way of life[70] and, in 1932, the Devolution League was formed to safeguard it. Federalism remained a constant theme in Natal politics, particularly in Durban, for the rest of the century. Although successive federal parties enjoyed only minority support among Natalians, they did have short-term successes. In the 1933 general election, a Home Rule coalition won two Durban seats while the provincial elections of August 1933 saw seven of their number returned in Durban seats.[71]

[67] Paul Maylam, 'The Changing Political Economy of the Region, 1920–1950', in Morrell (ed.), *Political Economy*, 97–118.

[68] D. W. M. Edley, 'Population, Poverty and Politics: A Study of Some Aspects of the Depression in Greater Durban, 1929–1933', MA thesis (Natal, 1983), 19.

[69] Maylam, 'Changing Political Economy', 97–118.

[70] George Heaton Nicholls, *South Africa in my Time* (London, 1961), 206.

[71] Thompson, *Natalians First*, 102–7; Edley, 'Population, Poverty and Politics', 94–106.

Ideally the Natalians during these years would have liked to be in the position of the southern African British community they most resembled, the Rhodesians. There was, indeed, a steady if small emigration of Natalians to Southern Rhodesia which combined the Natalian ideal of being both a British and a white man's country. In the best of all worlds, Natal would have remained a responsibly-governed colony but with the economic and strategic benefits of Union intact. In many ways the province was comparable to Ulster. In 1899, Milner had referred to Natal as 'a secure outpost of England, loyal in the fashion of Ulster'[72] and the comparison remained valid for the remainder of the imperial period.[73] At a time when most South African English-speakers, sometimes reluctantly, accepted constitutional change, Natalians were as determined as Ulstermen to protect their cultural and provincial identity and drew on Ulster prototypes when expressing their determination to remain British.[74] Increasingly they became defined as much by what they were against as what they were. In the process, like Ulster's Unionists, their interests became localized and provincialized and they developed into an idiosyncratic, separatist, and impotent community.

Although the threat to the provincial councils passed, 1933 saw South Africa's imperial links called into question. In that year the Depression forced the Nationalists to ally with the SAP, leading to the formation of the United Party. As part of the negotiations Smuts agreed to support the Nationalists' proposed Status Acts which, consistent with the 1931 Statute of Westminster, proclaimed the Union Parliament the country's sovereign legislative body. The Natalians reacted with considerable bitterness, many seeing this as the first step towards severing the Union's imperial ties. While a tiny minority, mainly ex-servicemen, formed neo-fascist movements such as the New Guard, with links to British and Australian groups,[75] most opponents of the Acts used parliamentary means. Eight SAP MPs from throughout the Union, including Natal's Sidney Marwick, broke away to form the Dominion Party whose agenda was to 'embrace all that is dear to British tradition' and repeal the Status Acts.[76] The party's stronghold was

---

[72] G. H. L. le May, *British Supremacy in South Africa, 1899–1907* (London, 1967), 77.

[73] See George H. Calpin, *There are No South Africans* (London, 1941), 205.

[74] In 1955 e.g. the Anti-Republican League based their Natal Convention on the earlier Ulster Convention. See Donal Lowry, 'Ulster Resistence and Loyalist Rebellion in the Empire', in Keith Jeffery (ed.), *'An Irish Empire'? Aspects of Ireland and the British Empire* (Manchester, 1996), 200.

[75] Thompson, *Natalians First*, 108–18.

[76] Wilks, *For the Love of Natal*, 191.

Durban and the south coast, where in the 1938 general election it secured seven seats.[77]

The outbreak of the Second World War in September 1939, rallied both the Dominion and the Labour Party behind Smuts, who became Prime Minister after Hertzog was defeated on a vote of neutrality. The support given Smuts by the two parties reflects the unanimity with which Natalians entered the war, many agreeing with Heaton Nicholls during the neutrality debate that 'We are at war in the eyes of every British subject and if we are not at war, we cannot be British subjects.'[78] Even more so than in 1914, they were united with English-speakers elsewhere in a common and whole-hearted commitment to the imperial cause. There are no figures for the number of English-speaking South Africans who volunteered but every indication suggests that their numbers were greater than between 1914 and 1918. Natal's regiments distinguished themselves in North Africa and Natal-ians won three of South Africa's four VCs. The great majority believed they were fighting for a just cause, particularly from June 1940 when Britain and the Commonwealth stood alone. In addition to those bearing arms, many were involved in home defence while women volunteered to serve as nurses or in the South African Women's Auxiliary Services. Durban became a major wartime port, revictualling and repairing allied shipping and providing quarters for allied servicemen in transit, resulting in ties of friendship that often lasted long after the war.[79]

Thompson suggests that the Natalians experienced the imperial connection more strongly during the war than at any other time.[80] Their whole-hearted commitment to the war effort brought out their best characteristics and by mid-1945 they felt immense pride in what Natal, South Africa, and the Empire/Commonwealth had achieved. In the following years they found it difficult to accept Britain's diminished power and found British withdrawal from India particularly hard to stomach. But, as the extent of Britain's economic crisis sank in, there was widespread agreement on the need to provide aid to British people. Between 1945 and 1948 the Natalians

[77] See Schoeman, *Parliamentêre Verkiesings*, 236–7.
[78] Hansard, 36, 3rd session, 8th Parliament, Heaton Nicholls, p. 34.
[79] D. R. Fuchs, *Durban During the Second World War, c1939–1945*, MA thesis (Natal, 1990), pp. viii, 48–9, 118, 180. See also John Lambert, '"Their Finest Hour?" English-Speaking South Africans and World War II', *South African Historical Journal*, 60/1 (2008), 60–84, and Jennifer Crwys-Williams, *A Country at War, 1939–1945* (Rivonia, 1992).
[80] Thompson, *Civic Culture*, 64.

contributed generously to fund-raising schemes. Street collections, concerts, fetes, and auctions were held and, to personalize the appeals, individual British towns were identified as 'blitzed areas' in need of assistance.

The royal visit to South Africa in 1947 reaffirmed the Natalians' loyalty to the Crown and reinforced their sense of pride in the British and imperial connection. The Nationalists' victory in the 1948 general election, however, returned a government committed to republicanism. Over sixty years after the event, elderly Natalians still reflect on the shock of the unexpected result and their own horror, dismay, and devastation.[81]

Until the early 1950s, however, the new government downplayed its republican agenda while many Natalians approved of its racist policies to Indians and Africans. Despite more enlightened racial attitudes among returning servicemen, attitudes that were reflected in Natal's schools and university, and were to lead to the formation in the 1950s of the Union-wide Liberal and Progressive Parties, most Natalians were hostile to the growth of African militancy after 1945 and to Indian and United Nations' support for the Union's Indians. They welcomed the government's removal of Indians from the common voters' roll in 1949, while the Durban corporation readily cooperated in enforcing the government's 1950 Group Areas Act.[82] The extent of Natalian support for anti-Indian policies led the Commonwealth Relations Office to describe Natal as 'politically the rogue province' which could not be relied on to oppose apartheid policies.[83] Few Natalians were, however, prepared to vote National Party and after 1948 the province became a United Party enclave. In 1952, a revival of separatist sentiments among groups like the Defenders of the Constitution and the War Veterans' Torch Commando failed to shake the UP hold on Natal and these groups were only able to make a political impact by forming a Natal Stand with the UP and Labour in the 1953 general election on a platform of protecting the Constitution's entrenched clauses.[84] When the NP was returned with an

---

[81] Personal information received from elderly Natalians.

[82] Paul Maylam, 'The Struggle for Space in Twentieth-Century Durban', in Paul Maylam and Iain Edwards (eds.), *The People's City: African Life in Twentieth-Century Durban* (Pietermaritzburg, 1996), 22.

[83] Ronald Hyam and Peter Henshaw, *The Lion and the Springbok: Britain and South Africa since the Boer War* (Cambridge, 2003), 31.

[84] The NP government was trying to amend the Constitution to remove the franchise rights of Coloureds in the Union. The Natalians feared that, if successful, the government would introduce legislation to dismantle the provincial system.

increased majority, the Natal Stand disintegrated and, despite Heaton Nicholls's establishment of the Union Federal Party,[85] the UP was able to consolidate its provincial position.

As the 1950s drew to a close the government came out openly in favour of a republic. In 1957 the Union Jack and 'God save the Queen' were abolished and at the beginning of 1960 a whites-only republican referendum was announced for October. In defence of what they continued to believe defined their distinctive identity, the Natalians presented a united front. In the months leading up to the referendum, large, rowdy anti-republican meetings were held and republican meetings were broken up. The press warned against breaking 'the links that bind your future to a great past'.[86] Freedom Radio, broadcast by the semi-secret Horticulturalist organization, rallied opposition.[87] There was unprecedented enthusiasm on polling day. Natal had the highest percentage turn-out in the Union: 93 per cent of the voters turned out, of whom 75.9 per cent voted against the republic. Country-wide, the referendum saw a small vote in favour of the republic, with Natal the only province opposed. Natalians reacted with emotional demands for secession but the UP leadership in the Provincial Council followed the party's national stand in accepting the decision. Finally the Provincial Council compromised by calling for stronger provincial powers, a call that was ignored.[88] On 31 May 1961 Natal reluctantly and with considerable foreboding became a province of the Republic of South Africa, outside the Commonwealth.

The question asked then and even now is, why did the Natalians capitulate in 1961 and why in the following years did they, apparently easily, accept republican rule? For a few years there was increased emigration but most Natalians accepted the inevitable. In the last resort, as in 1909, economics and security rather than culture and identity dictated their actions. Despite overwhelmingly rejecting the republic, the realization that they could not go it alone in an increasingly hostile world saw the Natalians move towards a *modus vivendi* with the apartheid government. Had Britain been prepared to support a secessionist Natal, the situation might have been different. But

[85] Heaton Nicholls, *South Africa in my Time*, 460–8; M. Facchini, 'The Union Federal Party and Secession, 1953–1956', *Journal of Natal and Zulu History*, 19 (1999–2001), 73–94.

[86] *Natal Mercury* (5 Oct. 1960).

[87] Thompson, *Natalians First*, 163–6.

[88] W. J. Stewart, 'Natal and the 1960 Republican Referendum', MA thesis (Natal, 1990), 153, 162–4, appendix C.

successive British governments had reacted warily after the Nationalist government had warned in 1953 against encouraging a Natal Ulster.[89] Despite the Natalians' strident insistence that they would resist the republic, British officials realized there was more sound than substance to their protestations. In 1954, the British high commissioner told London that 'in many ways they present an unflattering picture of Britons gone soft and flabby...lacking the punch required of successful rebels'.[90] In 1960, Natal's UP leader, Douglas Mitchell concurred, referring to the Natalians as 'lethargic, too damn lazy'.[91]

More importantly, the Natalians reluctantly accepted that Britain had little desire to help them. As already noted, they had often felt betrayed by British governments. In the 1950s many, seeking a scapegoat for their own impotence, blamed their predicament on Britain's failure to support them.[92] By 1960 the Natalians could no longer close their eyes to the fact that time was running out for the British settlers in Central and East Africa and in February Macmillan's 'Winds of Change' speech brought home the message that Britain would no longer support white South Africans against Africans. For Mitchell the writing was on the wall: 'One thing is certain. Britain is getting out of Africa...Macmillan said in effect: "Good-bye...You are on your own." '[93] That the Natalians could no longer depend on British support was reinforced once South Africa became a republic, when Britain began criticizing South Africa's treatment of Indians.[94] Because of this, many Natalians became vociferous opponents of British policies. As a small white minority, reinforced by a steady influx of British settlers from East and Central Africa from the 1960s, they were aware of the threat Britain's decolonization of Africa posed to their position. Most enthusiastically supported Ian Smith's Rhodesia and by the late 1960s the *Natal Mercury*, ten years earlier the most jingoistically British newspaper, had become a strident opponent of the British government.

Such attitudes made acceptance of the republic easier. Despite this, the Natalians continued to regard themselves as different from the rest of

[89] TNA, DO 35/6716, 'Current Events in Natal'; Facchini, 'Union Federal Party', 81–90.
[90] TNA, DO 35/5036, UK High Commissioners' visits to Natal, 1952–1954, confidential, 22 Sept. 1954, p. 2.
[91] Stewart, 'Natal and the 1960 Republican Referendum', 120.
[92] TNA, DO 35/5095, Current events in Natal, report 33 for Mar. and Apr. 1955.
[93] Stewart, 'Natal and the 1960 Republican Referendum', 29.
[94] Hyam and Henshaw, *Lion and Springbok*, 165.

the country. As English-speakers elsewhere moved slowly towards accepting the more liberal Progressive Party, the Natalians stuck resolutely to the UP and its successor, the New Republic Party. Even in the 1981 elections, when the Natalians finally abandoned the New Republic Party at national level, it won the majority of provincial council seats on the slogan 'Natal Stay Free—Vote NRP'.[95] Yet despite their attitudes to blacks, Natalians had difficulty accepting the ideological justifications given for apartheid and straight-jacketing all South Africans in a common system and they resented the Nationalist government's steady reduction of provincial rights. Impotent to prevent change, the Natalians withdrew into a cocoon of nostalgia for a lost past. The day before South Africa became a republic, at the request of the Natal Executive Council the Royal College of Arms had promulgated the provincial coat-of-arms, surmounted by a crown, as the province's official device. The Union Jack continued to fly on historic days on Pietermaritz-burg's and Durban's city halls while the colonial red ensign enjoyed a popular revival. As late as the 1977 Silver Jubilee, Natal audiences applauded the Queen when she appeared on cinema screens. After Tommy Bedford's 1970 outburst, 'Natal—the last outpost' became a popular slogan. But all these were now irrelevant to the province's position. Nostalgia had replaced action.

Nostalgia helped the Natalians ignore present realities, which included the unwelcome fact that the demise of Britishness had also undermined whiteness. In South Africa at large the ANC was winning the battle against Afrikaner nationalism and Durban was rocked by a growing militancy and widespread strikes.[96] A new aggressive Zulu movement, Chief Mangosuthu Buthelezi's Inkatha Freedom Party, challenged the Natalians' position and offered a radically different ideology for the province. Yet paradoxically, the revival of Zulu traditionalism seemed to offer the Natalians a radically new scenario, that of moving towards a *modus vivendi* with the Zulu in a federated Natal-Zulu province in a federal relationship with the rest of South Africa.

The advent of democracy in 1994 saw the end of much the Natalians held dear. A new province, KwaZulu-Natal, arose, in whose provincial parlia-ment whites were an insignificant minority. Power also passed into African hands in both Pietermaritzburg and Durban, while in the countryside white

---

[95] *Sunday Tribune* (29 Mar. 1981).
[96] Maylam, 'Struggle for Space', 24–6.

farmers became a beleaguered community. Today, the Natalians are very different from what they were during the imperial period. Culturally they remain inherently British while their educational system continues to reflect a British ethos and to extend that ethos to Africans and Indians. With their business leaders scrambling to embrace change after 1994, they retain considerable economic power in the new province. But in a post-apartheid South Africa they have lost political control of the province and this has robbed them of their identity. Yet, unlike the other British communities in this volume, and despite the growing fear of crime, most Natalians have accepted black rule rather than go into exile, reflecting the deep roots most have sunk in Natal's soil. They, have, however, like other English-speaking South Africans, withdrawn 'into a private world of business and home and sunlit leisure. Politically they have atrophied . . . they have no vision of South Africa's future or their role in it.'[97]

Select Bibliography

Jo Beall, 'Class, Race and Gender: The Political Economy of Women in Colonial Natal', MA thesis (Natal, 1982).

Edgar H. Brookes and Colin de B. Webb, A History of Natal (Pietermaritzburg, 1965).

Andrew Duminy and Charles Ballard (eds.), The Anglo-Zulu War: New Perspectives (Pietermaritzburg, 1981).

——and Bill Guest (eds.), Natal and Zululand from Earliest Times to 1910: A New History (Pietermaritzburg, 1989).

Bill Guest and John M. Sellers (eds.), Enterprise and Exploitation in a Victorian Colony: Aspects of the Economic and Social History of Colonial Natal (Pietermaritzburg, 1985).

Jeff Guy, The Heretic: A Study of the Life of John William Colenso, 1814–1883 (Johannesburg, 1983).

Alan F. Hattersley, Portrait of a Colony (Cambridge, 1940).

—— The British Settlement of Natal: A Study in Imperial Migration (Cambridge, 1950).

Ronald Hyam and Peter Henshaw, The Lion and the Springbok: Britain and South Africa since the Boer War (Cambridge, 2003).

John Laband and Robert Haswell (eds.), Pietermaritzburg, 1838–1988: A New Portrait of an African City (Pietermaritzburg, 1988).

John Lambert, Betrayed Trust: Africans and the State in Colonial Natal (Pietermaritzburg, 1995).

[97] Allister Sparks, The Mind of South Africa (London, 1990), 47.

SHULA MARKS, *Reluctant Rebellion: The 1906–1908 Disturbances in Natal* (Oxford, 1970).

ROBERT MORRELL (ed.), *Political Economy and Identities in KwaZulu-Natal: Historical and Social Perspectives* (Durban, 1996).

——*From Boys to Gentlemen: Settler Masculinity in Colonial Natal, 1880–1920* (Pretoria, 2001).

GEORGE HEATON NICHOLLS, *South Africa in my Time* (London, 1961).

SIR JOHN ROBINSON, *A Lifetime in South Africa: Being the Recollections of the First Premier of Natal* (London, 1900).

SHELAGH O'BYRNE SPENCER, *British Settlers in Natal, 1824–1857: A Biographical Register*, Vol. 1– (Pietermaritzburg, 1981–).

P. S. THOMPSON, *Natalians First: Separatism in South Africa, 1909–1961* (Johannesburg, 1990).

——*The British Civic Culture of Natal, South Africa, 1902–1961* (Howick, 1999).

Twentieth Century Impressions of Natal: Its People, Commerce, Industries, and Resources (London, 1906).

7

Avatars of Identity
The British Community in India

David Washbrook

A Colony of Transience

According to the imperial historical record, the first 'Englishman' arrived in India with the ships of Captain William Hawkins's East India Company fleet on 24 August 1608, and the last 'Briton' left with the hauling down of the Union Jack at midnight on 14 August 1947—although, of course, a few had come 'unrecorded' before and some were to stay on afterwards. But, in the three and a half centuries between, the whole world was to pass through multiple changes, not least those constructing 'Britons' out of the erstwhile English, Scots, Irish, and Welsh.[1] It has to be asked, amidst the various comings and goings and the many, changing relationships with the British Isles, how far a historical 'British community' can be represented in India—rather than many communities, with different habits and mores, at different times.

It also can be asked whether the concept of 'community' fits particularly well with the kinds of relationship which each and every one of these 'gatherings of English/Britons' developed both with the Indians surrounding them and even with each other. 'Community' implies a form of permanence. But, if there were a consistency in English/British attitudes, it was that India was never, by intention, 'home': its (various) colonies were always ones of transience, places of opportunity to be exploited to achieve fortune or to raise station back in Britain. Of course, some aspirations were never fulfilled and India became *de facto* a living place to many from the British Isles, who never managed to return. Most noticeably, it became a graveyard for British bones: where a mixture of hostile climate and dubious diet made

---

[1] Linda Colley, *Britons: Forging the Nation 1707–1837* (New Haven, 1992).

it a permanent resting place for perhaps two-thirds of those who ever visited it before the later nineteenth century.[2] But transience and early death make poor qualities on which to build 'community'.

And so, too, do sparseness of numbers and opportunities for (socially approved forms of) procreation. There seems little doubt that, at all times, people from the British Isles preferred their own company to that of anybody else and would set up forms of exclusion against the outside world whenever and wherever they could. Even by the mid-eighteenth century, Calcutta—the principal locus of British residence—was showing signs of 'ghetto-ization'.[3] But Calcutta was very unusual before the nineteenth century in supplying a critical mass, albeit only a few hundreds strong, out of which to forge a self-regarding 'community'. Elsewhere, the English/British were very thin on the ground, making it essential, if they were to participate in a community at all, that they make it with other people. Sometimes, especially in port cities, this might be with other Europeans—French, Dutch, Portuguese—where barriers of religious difference, insurmountable in Europe, were temporarily lowered. But, not infrequently, it was also with sections (usually elite) of Indian society where quasi-Nawabi or Brahmanic lifestyles came to embrace both.

Of course, as British power and physical numbers in India built up over the course of the nineteenth century, the exclusionary principle came increasingly to the fore. To be tolerated, other Europeans had to follow 'British' ways and, by Kipling's time, 'going native' was permissible only for the purposes of spying. Nonetheless, even Kipling recognized the continuing dilemma and the pain that it brought. The choice for many was to live in lonely isolation or to 'succumb' to the vibrant, pulsating Indian culture to be seen from their verandas.[4] More than a few Britons, at all times, 'succumbed' not only to the pleasures promised, but also to the alternative life-principles expressed. Kipling may have seen such cases, where 'civilization' was deserted, as leading inevitably to the opium-pipe; but, at least by the 1930s, the path could also lead a Verrier Elwin to desert

[2] Famously, the death rate among British regiments in India in 1859–63 was 6.9% a year. Florence Nightingale, *Observations on the Evidence Contained in the Stational Reports Submitted to the Royal Commission on the Sanitary State of the Army in India* (London, 1863).

[3] P. J. Marshall, 'The White Town of Calcutta under the Rule of the East India Company', *Modern Asian Studies*, 34/2 (2000), 307–33.

[4] Rudyard Kipling, *Plain Tales from the Hills* (Calcutta and London, 1888); Rudyard Kipling, *Kim* (London, 1908).

the Indian Civil Service (ICS) in order to become a 'tribal' and Gandhian social reformer.[5]

Moreover, to reproduce themselves, communities need members of both sexes and the British community in India was always deficient in one. Until the transport revolution of the mid-nineteenth century, there were very few women of 'British Isles-origin' in India. Thereafter, increasing numbers arrived, many in the notorious 'fishing fleet', which sailed in annually for the Calcutta season to catch and marry young military officers and government officials. Some historians have argued that this change, of itself, hardened the self-conscious boundaries of community. With the opening up at the same time of the hill stations, it permitted Britons to transfer a purely British lifestyle to the tropics and to segregate themselves from all things beyond.[6] However, the solution can only have been partial and the problem very much remained. The gender imbalance in the 'European' community was always striking—as late as 1921, it was still 3:1.[7] Equally, the 'fishing fleet' was only interested in, and the hill stations only accessible to, the upper levels of British-Indian society, which comprised only a small part of it.[8] Also, both upper-class and later Victorian conventions dictated that the children and sometimes the wives of British residents spend long periods back in Britain without their fathers and husbands.[9] Family life of any kind was constrained and British India always possessed a very masculine face.

As a result, perhaps, it was always heavily involved in liaisons with non-British women and, as Ann Stoler has argued of colonialism more generally, lines of race and of gender could cross-cut in complex ways.[10] In his *White Mughals*, William Dalrymple has sought to contrast a time, before the mid-nineteenth century, when these liaisons were open, acceptable, and mutually honoured, with a later time when they became highly unrespectable and were denied. He also sees this reflecting a wider shift in cultural attitudes

[5] Ramachandra Guha, *Savaging the Civilized: Verrier Elwin, his Tribals and India* (Chicago, 1999).

[6] Thomas R. Metcalf, *The Aftermath of Revolt: India 1857–1870* (Princeton, 1965).

[7] Judith M. Brown, 'India', in Judith M. Brown and Wm Roger Louis (eds.), *The Oxford History of the British Empire*, iv. *The Twentieth Century* (Oxford, 1999), 421 46.

[8] David Arnold, 'European Orphans and Vagrants in India in the Nineteenth Century', *Journal of Imperial and Commonwealth History*, 2/7 (1979), 109–27.

[9] Rosemary Marangoly George, 'Homes in the Empire, Empires in the Home', *Cultural Critique*, 26 (winter 1993–4), 95–129.

[10] Ann Laura Stoler, *Carnal Knowledge and Imperial Power: Race and the Intimate in Colonial Rule* (Berkeley, Calif., 2000).

towards India across the period, from sympathy and engagement to hostility and distance.[11] And, certainly, there were differences between the late eighteenth and late nineteenth centuries. However, the historical record may suggest the need for some degree of shading.

Even before the nineteenth century, liaisons with Indian women were not unproblematic, for religious as much as for racial reasons. It was difficult to contract valid forms of cross-religious marriage and contracts with *bibis* (non-European concubines) although enforceable at law did not carry the same prestige.[12] Also, such relationships, although more open than later, were never entirely respectable and what they say about the cultural attitudes of their times is complex. Job Charnock, the seventeenth-century founder of Calcutta, may have rescued and married an Indian princess from the funeral pyre of her previous husband, but he was denounced by several of his contemporaries for his 'heathen' ways.[13] In the late eighteenth century, James Kirkpatrick may have married a Hyderabadi princess and himself have converted to Islam. But he was heavily criticized by the then-Governor General and sent his children back to England to be educated as Protestants.[14] Equally, later on, relations with Indian women may have become unrespectable and been more closely concealed. But this was always more so in certain places, such as Calcutta, than in others, such as Madras and Bombay, where inter-racial marriages were not unknown into the late nineteenth century. Moreover, the penalties of 'disapproval' never stopped cross-racial liaisons actually taking place nor proving long-lasting nor involving patriarchal forms of patrimony and protection.

How far non-British female 'partners' were or were not part of any British 'community' was always a delicate matter. In his diaries of early nineteenth-century Calcutta, the architect Richard Blechynden records in vivid detail the prevailing etiquette of his day. Like many of his peers, he lived with a succession of *bibis*, several of whom he cherished and by whom he had children who were acknowledged, endowed, and even sent to England for education. Moreover, by convention, he would 'step out' with them publicly

---

[11] William Dalrymple, *White Mughals: Love and Betrayal in Eighteenth-Century India* (London, 2002).

[12] Durba Ghosh, *Sex and the Family in Colonial India: The Making of Empire* (Cambridge, 2006).

[13] P. Thankappa Nair, *Job Charnock: The Founder of Calcutta in Facts and Fiction* (Calcutta, 1977).

[14] Dalrymple, *White Mughals*.

whenever visiting fellow British *men*. But he would never bring them to company where any 'true' British *woman* was to be present.[15] Here, the proper boundaries of British 'community' would seem to have been oscillating, inflected by the gender of whoever was and was not physically present at any given time.

And this was no less true of the converse relationship between British women and Indian men. At least until the early decades of the nineteenth century, class appears to have held the superior hand over race and European women might move in the company of at least upper-class Indian men—princes and members of the Company's own Indian officer corps.[16] However, by mid-century (and with the disappearance of the Indian officer corps), such relationships had become very problematic. They were rendered even more difficult by the shadow of the 1857 Mutiny, which was seen in some quarters as driven by the lust of Indian men for white women.[17] The need to protect British women from Indian males became a sub-theme of later Victorian imperialism and, for a time, drew the races farther apart. Its motif coloured many incidents in British Indian history—not least the fear that Indian judges would have power over British women 'prisoners', which informed 'white' agitation against the notorious Ilbert Bill.[18]

But it is possible to wonder how far these sexual fears were felt more in the far-away metropolis than the local colony, and by men rather than women themselves. While the penny-press in London may have called for a bloody retribution against rapist-mutineers, post-Mutiny policies in India featured more an exercise in conciliation conducted under the viceroyalty of 'Clemency' Canning.[19] Also, as Indira Ghose has noted, the only two Mutiny diaries written by British women were marked by ambiguous attitudes towards the mutineers and a degree of compassion towards their families.[20] Repeated judicial investigations into the circumstances of the

---

[15] Peter Robb, *Clash of Cultures? An Englishman in Calcutta in the 1790s* (London, 1998).

[16] James Wathen, *Journal of a Voyage in 1811 and 1812 to Madras and China* (London, 1814).

[17] Nancy L. Paxton, *Writing under Raj: Gender, Race and Rape in the British Colonial Imagination* (New Brunswick, NJ, 1999).

[18] Mrinalini Sinha, 'Chathams, Pitts and Gladstones in Petticoats: The Politics of Gender and Race in the Ilbert Bill Controversy, 1882–1884', in N. Chaudhuri and M. Strobel (eds.), *Western Women and Imperialism: Complicity and Resistance* (Bloomington, Ind., 1992), 98–116.

[19] Michael Maclagan, *'Clemency' Canning: Charles John, 1st Earl Canning, Governor-General and Viceroy of India, 1856–62* (London, 1962).

[20] Indira Ghose, *Women Travellers in India: The Power of the Female Gaze* (Delhi, 1998), ch. 5.

Mutiny found little evidence of sexual molestation. Certainly, fears of sexual danger did not stop British women from coming to India after 1857, which they did in increasing numbers, nor from exposing themselves to it in 'fearless' ways. Women figured strongly among missionaries and education-ists bringing 'civilization' to the 'native', often in remote locales. Indeed, the ferocious figure of the Victorian 'memsahib', dominating all the males surrounding her—white and brown alike—was essentially a post-Mutiny construction and scarcely bespeaks a context of sexual fear, at least on the part of women.[21]

Moreover, by the twentieth century, consensual sexual unions had begun to creep back into fashion—at least with the proper class of Indian men. Much to the discomfort of the Government of India's Political Department (which was wedded to the idea of the 'traditional' Maharaja), several Indian princes acquired 'white' wives;[22] and at least a few among the growing numbers of Indians going to Britain for education married English women while they were there. The frontiers of gender and race were by no means always congruent, not least when that of class crossed them both.

And class which, as David Canadine has shown, exercised a pervasive influence over imperial attitudes[23] also inflected relations between 'true Brits' themselves, who did not abandon deeply engrained, metropolitan prejudices when they stepped aboard an East India ship. The community of the East India Company was sharply divided between 'writers' and 'cadets', between 'officers' and 'men'—with the latter treated hardly better than 'natives', and sometimes worse. For several periods in its history, the Bengal army permitted the flogging of European enlisted men, but not Indian sepoys.[24] Later in the nineteenth century, as the British population expanded and diversified, class hierarchies became ever more elaborate. They were strongly sustained by the institution of 'the club', intended for social association but actually used to practise social exclusion. The different classes of British-Indian society gathered in their separate clubs and

[21] Indrani Sen, *Women and Empire: Representations in the Writing of British India, 1858–1900* (Delhi, 2002).

[22] Most notably, the Raja of Pudukkottai and successive Maharajas of Indore.

[23] David Cannadine, *Ornamentalism: How the British saw their Empire* (London, 2001).

[24] Douglas M. Peers, *Between Mars and Mammon: Colonial Armies and the Garrison State in India, 1819–35* (London, 1995).

turned their backs on each other.[25] At the apex of this hierarchy stood the Bengal Club in Calcutta, patronized by senior members of the ICS and the managing partners of the major banks and agency houses. A contemporary noted it as: 'one of the most cliquey places in India. They dislike the society of foreigners, adventurers, upstarts and natives. You must convince Calcutta society that you belong to none of those undesirable classes ... before you can cross the threshold of the Bengal Club even as a guest.'[26] Beneath the 'heaven-born' in the Bengal Club came a congeries of tradesmen, business-men, and petty professionals: 'All these latter groups of Europeans were to be found in the more easy-going clubs and gymkhanas. The one thing that they all had in common was that they were not Eurasians.'[27]

The British in India very much did not come all-of-a-piece. They stretched virtually from the aristocracy, represented betimes by the likes of Lord Curzon, through the middle and professional classes to 'common' artisans and retired soldiers and sailors. The various 'estates' did not mix easily and, once the mantle of imperial authority had been assumed, a major concern for the upper echelons was whether the 'lower orders' ought to be allowed to live in India at all—where their very presence risked bringing 'the mystique of the white race' into disrepute. British India possessed strict deportation laws, permitting the forced removal of European 'undesirables' and 'vagrants'.[28]

Equally, internal disputes rankled over the qualities of culture and eth-nicity defining 'Britishness'. The early Company consisted of London-based merchants. But, as its organization expanded to embrace empire, it was invaded by the Celtic fringe whose 'union' with England it helped to cement.[29] Scots and Irish soldiers, administrators, and technicians came to the fore—often to the irritation of people from the English home counties. However, as the nineteenth century wore on, a more 'proper' balance was restored. The establishment of the ICS and the introduction of appointment by examination, rather than patronage, brought the uni-

---

[25] Mrinalini Sinha, 'Britishness, Clubbability and the Colonial Public Sphere: The Genealogy of an Imperial Institution in Colonial India', *Journal of British Studies*, 40/4 (2001), 491–521.

[26] H. Hobbs, *John Barleycorn in the East: Old Time Taverners in India* (London, 1944), 19.

[27] N. Carrington, unpublished memoir cited in Maria Misra, *Business, Race and Politics in Colonial Calcutta, c.1860–1950* (Oxford, 1999), 22.

[28] David Arnold, 'European Orphans'.

[29] C. A. Bayly, *Imperial Meridian: The British Empire and the World, 1780–1830* (London, 1989).

versities of Oxford and Cambridge into prominence and pushed Edinburgh and Dublin into the background. Indeed, by the early twentieth century, the Celtic fringe was as much represented in India by Dundee and Glasgow, whose 'mechanics' ran one of the rare modern industries brought to India under British rule, that of jute textiles. But tensions between Celts and 'Anglos' existed on many planes and were given many forms of expression. The Company's old, patronage-based 'covenanted' servants derided the new Oxbridge-educated ICS as effete 'competition-wallahs' without the hardy qualities necessary to ruling; and the latter, in turn, derided the industrious Scots as mere 'box-wallahs', without education or grace.[30]

Religion, no less, provoked conflict. The Company was a self-avowedly Protestant organization, which discriminated against Roman Catholics even more forcefully than Hindus or Muslims. No Roman Catholic could be the member of a Company artillery regiment. By the mid-nineteenth century, such tensions had eased. But problems arose in relations between different Protestant sects. Many in the very Anglican hierarchy of the Company government were suspicious of the activities of evangelicals, whose proselytizing activities disturbed indigenous religious tradition and were inclined to give low-caste groups ideas above their social station. British-Indian statesmen imputed the major share of blame to them for stirring up the Indian Mutiny and moved, afterwards, to separate their role in education from their practice of religion.[31] Low-church British missionaries were not necessarily welcome within the community of high-church British rulers.

And 'mixed race' Britons were progressively less welcome anywhere. Miscegenation, especially between low-class British men and Indian women, spawned a substantial 'Eurasian' or 'Anglo-Indian' population. It merged into a broader population of low-class people, who might very well have been racially 'white', but whose poverty prevented them from following an acceptable imperial lifestyle. In the eighteenth century, they had not constituted much of a problem—except for the cost of orphanages—and some Company officials even regarded their existence as advantageous, in that it created a natural client group.[32] However, during the nineteenth century, they became seen as a rising menace.

---

[30] Misra, *Business*, ch. 1.
[31] Metcalf, *Aftermath of Revolt*.
[32] Christopher J. Hawes, *Poor Relations: The Making of a Eurasian Community in British India, 1773–1833* (Richmond, 1996).

Eurasians/Anglo-Indians/poor whites looked like, dressed, and adopted the manners of 'the ruling race'. They attended the same churches, read the same books, and had aspirations to do the same jobs. But they were, emphatically, not accepted as members of the same 'community'. Ever more complex rules were elaborated in order to distinguish them. Columns appeared in bureaucratic forms demanding information on places of birth, education, and 'habitual residence'; the census added to its category of 'European' a second and refining reference: 'born outside Asia'. In effect, another 'British' community started to be defined in Indian social space: one which was 'not-quite-white', was 'domiciled' in India, and, specifically, was to be excluded from prestigious government employment and association with its progenitors.[33]

It is not only the span of 350 years that makes it difficult to write the continuous history of a British community in India. It is also the character of the social relations which 'people from the British Isles' developed there. They interacted with Indian society in different ways at different times and in different places. They fought with and despised each other often as fiercely as they did other 'nations' and 'races'. And, from the mid-nineteenth century, many of them were vitally concerned to repudiate connection with a substantial population who, by most legal, cultural, and social criteria, had as much right to be called 'British' as they themselves and who were unmistakably products of the connection between India and the British Isles. There was less a British community in India than there were multiple social arenas in which people who came (at some point) from the British Isles variously participated.

Arrivals and Departures

The English initially came to India as traders and set up residence in a small number of enclaves dotted along the coasts. Madras came first; then Calcutta (which proved the pearl); and finally Bombay. In sharp contrast to Asian merchants, the Europeans—beginning with the Portuguese—had always seen trade as intimately connected to power and demanded concessions from local India governments for monopoly privileges and rights to self-governance. Their society developed around specific 'forts' within

---

[33] Satoshi Mizutani, 'The British in India and their Domiciled Brethren: Race and Class in the Colonial Context, 1858–1930', D.Phil. thesis (Oxford, 2004).

which they introduced their own procedures of justice and religion. Correspondingly, their society was always to a degree segregated from that of the surrounding Indian population: even in the seventeenth century, 'White Towns' tended to grow up adjacent to 'Black Towns'. However, the lines of segregation were not very clearly marked. The Company's own formal establishments were extraordinarily few in numbers. As late as the 1720s, the number of 'writers' (the senior mercantile position) at the leading station of Calcutta was still confined to just twenty-eight, the better to keep up the value of each. Moreover, the prospect of trade with the Europeans attracted large numbers of Indian merchants and artisans to their vicinity with whom they often formed business partnerships. Into the mid-eighteenth century, wealthy Indian merchants continued to live in Madras's White Town and some Europeans ventured outside, and beyond even Black Town, to enjoy the gardens in neighbouring villages.[34] Also, lines of putative segregation broke down in matters of governance. The 'mayoral' law courts set up under the Company were intended only for the business of its own merchants and other Europeans living under its jurisdiction. But Indian merchants found them convenient for their own purposes and pressed to have their disputes included under 'mayoral' remit, blurring ethnic distinctions once again.[35]

In addition to official members of the Company's own establishment, a motley collection of other people from the British Isles and parts of Europe were also drawn into its habitat. From the later seventeenth century, European ships carried an increasing proportion of the Indian Ocean's commerce. Sailors frequently jumped ship to spend time enjoying the casual pleasures of the port cities. More purposefully, ships' artisans found a ready market for their skills and stayed on to build the imposing bungalows of the mercantile elite, both European and Indian. Also, increasing numbers of 'free merchants' bought rights to practise business in the Company's shadow. Some of these came from England, but many were of broader 'Euro-

---

[34] Holden Furber, *Private Fortunes and Company Profits in the India Trade in the 18th Century* (Aldershot, 1997); Holden Furber, *John Company at Work: A Study of European Expansion in India in the Late Eighteenth Century* (Cambridge, Mass., 1948); Susan Neild Basu, 'Colonial Urbanism: The Development of Madras City in the Eighteenth and Nineteenth Centuries', *Modern Asian Studies*, 13/2 (1979), 217–46.

[35] Niels Brimnes, 'Beyond Colonial Law: Indigenous Litigation and the Contestation of Property in the Mayor's Court in Later Eighteenth-Century Madras', *Modern Asian Studies*, 37/3 (2003), 513–50.

pean' origin. The fact that their respective 'nations' might also have their own coastal forts and enclaves did not mean that they would not do business, and live, with each other, even (albeit surreptitiously) during times of inter-European war. Business was business and gold was gold.[36]

However, the Company's relations with 'free merchants' could sometimes be tense: not only when it was at war with their 'nations', but even more when their activities were seen to cut into its profits and, perhaps more importantly, the profits which its 'writers' made in their own private trading capacities. At these moments, there was never any doubt that the Company was English and Protestant. But such moments were few and inclined to pass. For the most part, the society developing around the Company's forts was a polyglot mixture of races, cultures, and religions, which intermingled closely on a daily (and very commercial) basis, but also never entirely forgot its different origins, Indian as much as European—where patterns of caste, religious, and linguistic difference no less informed tendencies towards social segregation.

The first build-up of the English/British presence in India took place during the middle decades of the eighteenth century. India's position in European trade shifted as it ceased to be merely a supplier of textiles and spices to home markets and became the pivot both of a triangular trade, connected to China, and of a series of multilateral trades reaching south-east Asia, Africa, and even Latin America. Its new and expanding role sucked in men and capital, especially from Scotland and Ireland. The number of 'writers' at the Company's forts expanded steadily, as did the population of 'free merchants', shippers, traders, and artisans supporting its establishments.[37]

But the build-up was also facilitated by the new political roles inside India, as military power and emergent state, which the Company came steadily to adopt: notionally, to overcome conflicts with other European 'nations', but as much to take advantage of the decline of the Mughal empire. From the time of Robert Clive, the Company began to recruit an army. For the most part, this consisted of British (and initially Indian) officers leading Indian sepoys. But, as early as the 1760s, attempts were made to transport British 'enlisted' soldiers—6,500 being recruited for the purpose. However, the death rate among them was atrocious and, thereafter, the

---

[36] Holden Furber, *Rival Empires of Trade in the Orient, 1600–1800* (Minneapolis, 1976).
[37] P. J. Marshall, *Bengal: The British Bridgehead, Eastern India 1740–1828* (Cambridge, 1987).

Company largely left troop recruitment from Britain to the British government, concentrating its own efforts on its sepoy forces. Once war was joined with Revolutionary and Napoleonic France, the government took up the challenge in earnest and, thereafter, supplied a regular force of British line regiments to help sustain the Company's growing power.[38]

By the later eighteenth century, the expansion of trade and military force was also beginning to create imperatives for more formal institutions of government. The Company's appointments procedures, although always patronage-based, were brought under more open parliamentary scrutiny and 'professionalized' with the establishment of training colleges, both in Britain and in India. The bureaucracy steadily expanded and, with it, the courts of law, which brought the scions of another 'honourable' profession flocking to India as they scented rich new pickings. As the Company turned into an Indian government (and was progressively, if informally, absorbed into the British imperial state), it lost many of its monopoly privileges on trade and the licensing of 'outsiders'. From the 1810s, India was opened to whichever British subject wished to go there: which notably included Christian missionaries (whom the Company had tried to keep out before), as well as 'private' merchants, men of business, and adventurers.

In the 1830s, the British discovered the Indian hills, which offered cool periods of respite from the heat of the plains and were seen to be 'empty' (except for a few tribal groups) and thus available for plantation agriculture and the development of British lifestyles.[39] Moreover, the period coincided with improvements in shipping and navigation, which facilitated easier connections with 'home'. Larger numbers of British (and European) women started to come to India, fleshing out deeper possibilities of building a community.

Lack of adequate census-taking, together with the Company's loss of its rights to control entry, make it difficult to provide accurate statistics on the number of Britons (even if that were not a controversial category) resident at any time in Company India. But, up to the 1760s, it can have been little more than 10,000. Thereafter, it grew quickly—reaching an estimated 31,000 by 1805.[40] Further growth followed: we know that, by the 1830s, the Com-

[38] Peers, *Mars and Mammon.*

[39] Paul Hockings (ed.), *Blue Mountains Revisited: Cultural Studies on the Nilgiri Hills* (Delhi, 1997).

[40] D. A. B. Bhattacharya, 'Report on the Population Estimates of India (1820–1830)', *Census of India, 1961* (Delhi, 1963).

pany's elite covenanted service consisted of about a thousand bureaucrats; that, by the 1840s, Calcutta's European population was approaching 5,000; that, on the eve of the 1857 Mutiny, the number of European officers and enlisted men available to the Bengal Army was 20,000. Overall, the total 'British' population by the mid-1850s may have been in the region of 70,000: far more than only half-a-century before, but still infinitesimally small in comparison to a total population of India (Company and 'Princely') which by then must have been in excess of 200 millions.[41]

Lack of numbers, and hence potential vulnerability, was always a major concern of British rule. Even at the turn of the nineteenth century, it gave rise to calls for more purposive efforts to attract immigration and settlement. But these calls were noticeably louder at home than in India itself. The Company remained suspicious of 'free merchants' and all people outside its direct control. It doubted that land could be made available from an already-dense peasantry; and viewed the hills as places in need of capital-intensive plantation industries not small-scale European farms. It emphasized the hostility of the climate and its own experience of heavy death-tolls. Perhaps most of all, as its new governing role informed its views of social etiquette, it disliked the idea of large numbers of 'poor whites' arriving to disturb relations with 'the natives' and to challenge its own despotic authority with claims to the rights of 'free-born Englishmen'.[42] It already faced such challenges in the major port cities from the plebeian lower orders and 'mixed-race' British gathered at the bottom of society. It wanted no more of these.

Indeed, on many occasions it acted as if it wanted even fewer of them— unless in army uniform and under strict military discipline. As noted above, one of the first casualties of the rise of British dominion in India was a large class of the 'British' themselves. Calcutta contained a notable 'submerged' society, of plebeian Britons, other Europeans, mixed races, and various 'Indians': the product, already, of 150 years of random residence and history. Some of these people had played important roles in the Company's rise to power, not least the brilliant military commander, James Skinner, of the

[41] P. J. Marshall, 'British Immigration into India in the Nineteenth Century', in P. Emmer and M. Morner (eds.), *European Expansion and Migration: Essays on the Intercontinental Migration from Africa, Asia and Europe* (Oxford, 1992), 179–96; P. J. Marshall, 'British Society in India under the East India Company', *Modern Asian Studies*, 31/1 (1997), 82–108.

[42] P. J. Marshall, 'The Whites of British India: A Failed Colonial Society', *International History Review*, 12/1 (1990), 26–44.

legendary 'Skinner's Horse'.[43] However, the social imperatives created by new forms of authority led to a sharp change in perspective.

In seeking to establish new rules of governance in the 1790s, Lord Cornwallis immediately singled out 'Eurasians' as symptomatic of the 'old' corruption, which he had been sent out to reform. Henceforth, they were to be banned from the covenanted service. He was soon joined by the Church militant, or at least evangelical, which saw in their very existence the stain of sin. And also by Company accountants, who pointed out how much, in a context of early death, maintaining their orphans and support-ing their 'widows' was costing in potential Company profits.[44]

Less commonly spoken, but arguably more important in practice, was development of the ruling strategy which was to keep the British in power in India for the next 150 years. This centred on 'collaboration' and on recruit-ing upper-caste Indian groups into the middle-to-lower levels of the bur-eaucracy and army to sustain the institutions of the Raj. They carried more influence in Indian society and, often, were cheaper than Eurasians and 'quasi-Britons'.[45] The day of the Eurasian/Anglo-Indian in British India was already nearly done, even as the nineteenth century dawned. He was excluded from 'place'; treated as the symptom of a social disease; and, in various schemes, ordered to be passed from institution to institution (preferably, orphanage to army) or else consigned to the outer margins of the empire, where, for all his urban origins, he might 'usefully' farm and not get in the way.[46]

Moreover, this problem never went away although, over time, it did take on other, more complex forms. It was partially exacerbated by several of the forces expanding British 'colonization' in India from the second half of the nineteenth century. The bureaucracy and army remained the principal agents of recruitment of personnel from Britain but, post-Mutiny, they increased their levels of activity. Military strategy now dictated that a larger number of British regiments be stationed in India: to counter not only threats from across the North-West Frontier, but potential insurgency in the Indian army itself.[47] The bureaucracy expanded to take on new tasks, but

[43] J. Baillie Fraser, *Military Memoir of Lieut-Colonel James Skinner* (London, 1851).

[44] Hawes, *Poor Relations*.

[45] This was the principal argument made against Eurasian recruitment by Sir Thomas Munro. Burton Stein, *Thomas Munro: The Origins of the Colonial State and his Vision of Empire* (Delhi, 1989).

[46] Mizutani, 'British in India'.

[47] Metcalf, *Aftermath of Revolt*.

also to become more 'British' at its lower levels. Not only the Mutiny but, even more, the rise of Indian nationalism among the ranks of Western-educated Indians started to give British rulers pause for thought. Their previous strategy of 'collaboration' began to appear a two-edged weapon. To blunt at least one of its blades, they introduced new forms of discrimination to keep Western-educated Indians from ascending to higher offices; and also looked to expand recruitment from home. While the ICS never rose much above a serving strength of one thousand, new services—in Forests, Police, Public Works, Health, and Education—developed to draw in Britons in supervisory and managerial roles of a lesser kind. 'Recruitment from home' became the watchword for schemes meant to raise the quality of administration in all areas.[48]

And the dynamics supplied by militarism and bureaucracy now were also joined by those deriving from economic development and industrialization. With the building of the Suez Canal and the arrival of steam-shipping, India opened out as a primary product supplier to the world and a major market for British goods—attracting larger numbers of merchants and traders. This was facilitated by the development of the railways, which again brought British engineers and mechanics to the subcontinent. From the 1860s, modern forms of industry began to emerge: creating in Calcutta an extraordinary enclave jute industry, largely owned and managed by the Dundee Scots. Even in the era of the census, it is difficult to be precise about numbers because contemporary procedures counted 'Europeans' and even 'European and Allied Races' and not, singularly, 'Britons'. But, by 1911 at the height of the British Raj, the European population had reached 164,000 in relation to a total Indian population then approaching 300 million.[49]

However, expansion was not without its problems for senses of British 'community'. Immediately after the 1857 Mutiny, the issue of encouraging mass immigration had been raised again by Parliament for security reasons. Ultimately, it was disposed of without consequence. But some of the evidence brought before Parliament raised a particular frisson of horror with a British public made more race-conscious by the experience of the Mutiny. To overcome the continuing hazards of climate and disease, one Dr John Crawfurd insisted that it would be essential to encourage British immigrants to interbreed with 'natives' in order to raise their

[48] Mizutani, 'British in India'.
[49] E. A. Gait, *Census of India, 1911*, i/2, pt xiii (Calcutta, 1913).

resistance and strengthen their physical stock.[50] On such conditions, middle-class Britons of the post-Mutiny era were hardly likely to countenance anybody emigrating anywhere at all.

But working-class Britons were less socially constrained. The building of the railways in India represents a subject which, until recently, has attracted the attention more of novelists than social historians. However, it offers a fascinating counter-history to that usually recorded of the British in India. Railway construction necessarily brought an influx of working-class Britons, albeit of the more 'respectable' sort (engineers and skilled mechanics), who were not initially under the institutional discipline of the army or bureaucracy. Many of them promptly found Indian wives and settled down to a 'mixed-race' family life in jobs which their progeny still largely occupy.[51] This was very much not what the authorities in the later Victorian Raj expected or wanted to happen and these 'railway children' added increasingly to the Eurasian/Anglo-Indian problem.

Moreover, their example intensified pressures to see that other plebeian contacts between Britain and India did not go in the same direction. The army tightened its rules about intermarriage (and any marriage) for enlisted British soldiers. To compensate, it made arrangements with Indian brothels and also turned an institutional blind-eye to various malpractices.[52] Famously in 1903, the Viceroy Lord Curzon charged Lord Kitchener's army with imposing only the most trivial penalties on British soldiers who molested and raped 'native' women. But his protests were ineffective and eventually cost him his job.[53]

Attempts to cut off the ordinary British population from legitimate social contacts with Indians (other than servants) proliferated through the institutions of government, economy, and society. Agency houses and banks increasingly insisted that their new recruits from Britain sign contracts requiring 'permission' for them to marry, and instantly dismissed any who broke the rules. In the Calcutta jute mills, Scottish mechanics and under-managers were confined to living in compounds adjacent to the factories, which were outside the main part of the city. Many were only

[50] Mizutani, 'British in India', ch. 2.

[51] Laura Bear, 'Public Genealogies: Documents, Bodies and Nations in Anglo-Indian Railway Families', *Contributions to Indian Sociology*, 3/35 (2002), 356–88.

[52] Kenneth Ballhatchet, *Race, Sex and Class under the Raj: Imperial Attitudes and Policies and their Critics, 1793–1905* (London, 1980).

[53] David Dilks, *Curzon in India*, ii (London, 1970), chs. 7–9.

'allowed out' on Sundays when they would be driven to church, to sit in assigned rows under the managing partners' eyes, and then driven back again straight afterwards.[54] Viewed from the top–down, 'British India' came to consist of an elaborate effort to prevent Britons and Indians from meeting except under the closest institutional supervision. But the obsessive character of the effort may suggest, also, that it did not always work.

And, after the First World War, even the effort began to run down. Psychologically, the British Raj moved into retreat mode. The ICS lost much of its prestige during the interwar years, not only because its pay deteriorated (which had been happening since the 1880s), but because many of its members were now expected to serve 'Indian' ministers, as political concessions to Indian nationalism slowly changed the character of the state.[55] By repute, it survived only by recruiting a lower class of Briton— many educated at grammar schools open to 'common' people. Also, the apparatus of the old colonial economy began to creak. Even before the Great Depression, British capital started to leave the colonial trades and many businesses were sold to Indians.[56] Post-war fiscal problems, too, led to the slashing of the British Indian army to the bone.[57]

Nonetheless, in numerical terms, the 'European' population sustained itself: there continued to be about 165,000 Europeans in India throughout the 1920s and 1930s.[58] However, they were becoming of a rather different kind. In a belated effort to satisfy an Indian public opinion, increasingly informed by ideas of nationalism, that it served their interests, government expanded in new directions. It took on development and welfare functions which involved the recruitment of yet larger numbers of British technicians, again often from plebeian backgrounds. Colonial mercantile capital may have withdrawn from India, but British industrial capital certainly did not. However, its new function was to manufacture for Indian consumers with the support of Indian managers and share-holders, rather than to sell British-made goods and extract commodities and raw materials for sale overseas. Also, the number of 'Allied Races' proliferated, making the category of

[54] Misra, *Enterprise and Empire*, chs. 1, 2.
[55] David Potter, *India's Political Administrators 1919–1983* (Oxford, 1986).
[56] B. R. Tomlinson, *The Political Economy of the Raj 1914–47: The Economics of Decolonization in India* (London, 1979).
[57] David Omissi, *The Sepoy and the Raj: The Indian Army 1860–1940* (Basingstoke, 1994).
[58] J. L. Marten, *Census of India*, 1921, i/2, pt xiii (Delhi, 1923); J. H. Hutton, *Census of India*, 1931, i/2, pt xi (Delhi, 1933).

'European' less 'British': as foreign business agencies—Japanese, American, Greek, Belgian, Dutch—moved into the spaces left by Britain's economic disengagement from India during the war and the post-war recessions.[59]

In effect, the First World War broke the century-long stranglehold which the British upper classes had possessed on India's external relations, and forced the remaining Britons-in-India to live in a much more plural social context, including even some Indians. There remained a place for them until after the Second World War, but it was not the same place as in the heyday of the Victorian Raj. And, eventually, even that place disappeared— although not without a final flourish. Ironically, the greatest concentration of people of 'British Isles-origin' in India gathered just before the great majority of them entirely 'quit'. Between 1939 and 1945, the European population grew to 250,000, with an expanded 'white' army lying at its core. Although recruited ostensibly to fight the Japanese, this army carried implications also for the governance of India. It enabled the British to face down rising nationalist opposition, especially after 1942, and to rule more directly, as an army of occupation, than at any time in the past.

But the corollary was that, if the British intended to stay on after 1945, they would also have to do so as an army of occupation, which served few post-war strategic calculations. The flag came down and with it went the great bulk of the British population who had been tied to army and government. A few did 'stay on': to help the new national government; to continue in business; to service churches, hospitals, and schools; to preserve a lifestyle which they could never have afforded at home. But most of the 'community' had melted away by the early 1950s—and many parts that were left behind, no doubt, would have liked to go too. Large numbers of the 'not-quite' Britons tried finally to reach a home they had never seen and were, yet again, rebuffed or diverted towards other colonies.[60] Even at the death of empire, the aspirations which they possessed to be 'true' Britons were frustrated.

Cultures of Community

'Peoples from the British Isles' had many different experiences of India and formed and participated in many different kinds of society. Received

[59] Tomlinson, *Political Economy of the Raj.*
[60] Lionel Caplan, *Children of Colonialism: Anglo-Indians in a Post-Colonial World* (Oxford, 2001).

historiography, unsurprisingly, has focused on the British elites and has constructed a particular set of stereotypes. As noted with regard to relations of race and gender, a popular perspective of the 'post-colonial' twenty-first century has been of a multicultural, open-ended community to the end of the eighteenth century, as engaged with Indian society and as interested in Indian arts and religions as it was in Indian women. But, as British power became consolidated, this gave way to increasing discrimination and segregation.

Senses of British superiority and 'difference' grew and Indian culture became regarded as 'inferior', its society inherently barbarous. There is a broad truth to this characterization. However, its time-frame may need to be modified by elements of space. What may have been acceptable in the 1790s at the Nizam's court in distant Hyderabad was already, and certainly, not acceptable in the 'whiter' society of Calcutta. But, even more, it may need to be modified, and complicated, by other factors.

If the heroic 'Age of the Nabobs' was more multicultural than later, it was also far more venal and corrupt. The Company's men came to India to make money and were never very particular about how they did it. The first history of India written by a Briton, Alexander Dow, accused them directly of looting Bengal and bringing it to a ruinous famine.[61] The fortune which Robert Clive expended, on buying half of Shropshire and building castles in Wales, was gained at the cost of countless lives. By contrast, the ICS of the later nineteenth century, while more distanced from Indian society and, perhaps, more arrogant in their attitudes towards Indian culture, were a source of disinterested justice and near-paragons of financial integrity.

Given the enormous powers that its members wielded, and the scale of private wealth over which they presided, cases of peculation and extortion among them were remarkably few. Moreover, judging by the mounds of paper they left behind, they worked extraordinarily hard—for progressively depreciating pay—and lived in circumstances marked by considerable hardship. Unless they achieved rare and highly paid senior positions (which only a few did), ICS officers were expected to spend much of their time 'on tour', living out of tents, arbitrating disputes and 'settling' revenue across districts of thousands of square miles.[62] Their dedication to imperial 'service' bore

---

[61] Alexander Dow, 'An Enquiry into the State of Bengal', prefixed to Muhammad Kasim Hindu Shah Frishta, *A History of Hindostan . . . to the . . . Settlement of the Empire under Aurungzebe*, ed. A. Dow (London, 1768).

[62] David Gilmour, *The Ruling Caste: Imperial Lives in the Victorian Raj* (London, 2005).

much in common with that of the missionary: not a coincidence, as the most prominent other occupation among their families was that of clergyman.[63] Kipling's tales bring out the discomfort and isolation of the ICS's lifestyle—as well, perhaps, as hinting at their tragedy. By the end of the nineteenth century, it was becoming increasingly unclear what end their 'mission' was meant to serve and what precisely they hoped to achieve. Kipling saw it increasingly as 'the white man's burden', a thankless task imposed on Western civilization by virtue of its superiority, but bringing no tangible reward to those who had to undertake it.

The world of the ICS was tightly bound by institutional rules and discipline. And this became increasingly true of many of the other 'worlds' inhabited by the British in India. The army, the missionary society, the railways, even the jute factory sought to be 'total' institutions, supplying all their members' needs and separating them off from an alien society outside. The irony, that these procedures also separated them from other Britons and even replicated, within British-Indian society, the cellular structures of the Indian caste system, seems largely to have been missed. But many of these institutions (at least those where women were available) quickly showed tendencies to become in-bred and to provide the bases for almost dynastic connections. Army officers, to a remarkable degree, married the daughters of other army officers; after the first encounter, 'mixed-race' railwaymen generally married the daughters of other railwaymen; ICS officials by and large married the daughters of their seniors.[64] For the ICS, the Macnabb family may represent the paradigm case, but their history was partially shared by many others. Between 1757 and 1947, the family sent successive generations of sons to serve, first, in the Company's covenanted service and, then, in the ICS—leaving behind, at the India Office Library in London, one of the most remarkable and continuous 'family' correspondences ever to find archive space.[65]

Yet even these forces of dynastic continuity and institutional segregation never entirely prevented some Britons from a fascinated engagement with a surrounding Indian society and culture. The study of 'Oriental' religions and philosophies deepened and embedded itself in the British universities.

---

[63] Clive Dewey, *Anglo-Indian Attitudes: The Mind of the Indian Civil Service* (London, 1993).

[64] Elizabeth Buettner, *Empire Families: Britons and Late Imperial India* (Oxford, 2004).

[65] Macnabb Collection, MSS, EUR 206/223–37. Oriental and India Office Collection, British Library.

Nor was it only a 'distanced' species of study, as of museum curiosities. India offered the possibilities of alternative philosophies and lifestyles, which became increasingly attractive as late nineteenth-century Britain launched its own 'revolt against reason' and came to question the values of progress. It was not a pure fantasy that, in his Sherlock Holmes story 'The Sign of Four', Conan Doyle should have created an 'Indic' household, presided over by an Englishman, in Victorian South London.[66] And it is fact that a group spanning metropolitan, colonial, and Indian elites gathered together around the Theosophical Society in Madras to project (a romanticized version of) Hinduism as a new world religion for the twentieth century, to take the place of a discredited Christianity.[67] As mid-Victorian optimism gave way to *fin-de-siècle* pessimism, India offered an 'Other' civilization, which could (re)command respect.

Moreover, sometimes the British broke out of their separate institutions to meet, and have society, even with each other. These occasions have tended to be typified by Calcutta which, from the late eighteenth century, was not only the capital of British India (albeit officially only until 1911), but also possessed by far the largest concentration of 'Europeans'—over 15,000 by the early twentieth century. And, at least from a British perspective and providing that the other 99 per cent of the population living there are overlooked, Calcutta was always and emphatically a British city. It was built in classical style to bring constant reminders of the more elegant parts of London. Its exclusive clubs, invitation-only balls and dinner parties, and peculiar leisured past-times (horse-racing, golf, cricket) were meant to convey the impression that it was a continuous part of middle-class British society. Indeed, 'British-ness' and the cultivation of connections with Britain were pursued obsessively.[68] With the coming of steamships, English magazines circulated readily and Calcutta fashions were never more than three weeks behind those of Knightsbridge; wives visited England on extended vacations, as an alternative to going to the hills; children were packed off to British boarding schools at the end of the holidays. Calcutta indulged in extreme forms of 'Anglicism', which frequently surprised even the 'native' British when they first arrived.

---

[66] Sir Arthur Conan Doyle, *The Sign of Four* (London, repr. 1987; orig, 1890).

[67] Bruce F. Campbell, *Ancient Wisdoms Revived: A History of the Theosophical Movement* (Berkeley, Calif., 1980).

[68] Misra, *Enterprise and Empire*, ch. 1.

In part, as Elizabeth Buettner has argued, this may have reflected the fear, shared by many 'colonials', that they would be looked down upon at home, if they did not keep their manners hyper-refined.[69] But, in Calcutta, it also and undoubtedly reflected the presence of the Eurasian and 'not-quite-white' population, whose aspirations to be considered British had to be kept at distance by constantly stretching social goals beyond their reach, specifically back to Britain.[70] After the abolition of the Company and the establishment of Crown government, all were equally 'British subjects' at law: only a constant emphasis on density of 'home' connections could separate the 'true' British from the 'domiciled' herd. But a further consequence of this was that relations with Indian society, even beyond, also became progressively distanced and eventually strained. At least until the 1840s, British businessmen had maintained commercial (if more rarely social) contacts with Indian merchants.[71] But, thereafter, even these disappeared. British Calcutta lived in a hermetically sealed bell-jar: even its industries were replicates from home.

However, Calcutta was never the only 'British' India although it did exercise a hegemonic influence over the rest. In many ways, every city presented a slightly different British India and the most noticeably different were Madras and Bombay. By the late nineteenth century, they were even beginning to look different: built in new 'Indo-Saracenic' architectural styles, which hinted at multiculturalism and 'hybridity'.[72] Moreover, attempts at cultural hybridity also characterized some of their wider associations and activities. Britons were heavily involved in the revival of local vernacular traditions; in the discovery and preservation of historical sites and artefacts; even, as with Theosophy, in the formulation of Indian religions.[73] Economically and politically, too, there were more open interactions. In Madras, Parry and Company's principal agent and financier into the twentieth century was Raja Sir Savalai Ramaswami Mudaliar; and successive generations of the 'Norton' family of British lawyers were involved not only in presenting Parliament in 1853 with a petition, on behalf

[69] Buettner, *Empire Families.*

[70] Mizutani, 'British in India'.

[71] Blair B. Kling, *Partner in Empire: Dwarkanath Tagore and the Age of Enterprise in Eastern India* (Berkeley, Calif., 1976).

[72] Shanti Jayawardene-Pillai, *Imperial Conversations: Indo-Britons and the Architecture of South India* (Delhi, 2007).

[73] Jyoti Chandra, *Annie Besant: From Theosophy to Nationalism* (Delhi, 2001).

of the Indian citizens of Madras, calling for the abolition of the East India Company, but also, in 1885, in helping to found the Indian National Congress.[74] The Congress's foundation followed 'white' protests against the Ilbert Bill, which threatened to remove race privileges from the practices of the law courts. It was highly contentious in Calcutta and its related out-stations.[75] But, in Bombay and Madras, the protests were distinctly muted and even led the latter's Eurasian and Anglo-Indian Association to break with its Calcutta confrères—whose desires to sustain 'white' privilege it did not so readily share.[76]

The reasons for the differences are many. Not least may have been jealousies among the Bombay and Madras services at Calcutta's belated (1786) positioning as the capital of India. This long rankled in the old, previously independent, presidencies and had serious practical implications too. The covenanted service and ICS in Madras and Bombay produced institutions just as 'total' and inclined to be in-bred as in Calcutta and adjacent North India. But, having lost access to the capital, the resulting genealogical lines became broken, preventing later cadet-branches from ever recovering it. Very few Madras or Bombay men were invited to join the Government of India's Secretariat and the Viceroy's Council. In reflection, their attitudes to Calcutta tended to be hostile and they delighted in point-ing out its ignorance of their 'local' conditions and inability to rule them. But if Calcutta were to be held 'ignorant', to press their own claims Madras and Bombay must needs 'know' the local cultures and societies of their respective presidencies. Close dialogues developed between Madras and Bombay officials and (some) local Indians to construct this knowledge;[77] and the rhetoric of government came to echo with a curious kind of regional patriotism, binding Indians and Britons together against the common enemy in Calcutta (and, betimes, London too).[78]

---

[74] R. Suntharalingam, *Politics and Nationalist Awakening in South India, 1852–1891* (Tucson, Ariz., 1974).

[75] Sinha, 'Chathams, Pitts and Gladstones in Petticoats'.

[76] Alexander Morrison, 'White Todas, the Politics of Race and Class among European Settlers on the Nilgiri Hills, c.1860–1900', *Journal of Imperial and Commonwealth History*, 32/2 (2004), 54–85; Mizutani, 'British in India'.

[77] Eugene F. Irschick, *Dialogue and History: Constructing South India, 1795–1895* (Berkeley, Calif., 1994); Thomas R. Trautmann, *Languages and Nations: The Dravidian Proof in Colonial Madras* (Delhi, 2006).

[78] David Washbrook, 'South India 1770–1840: The Colonial Transition', *Modern Asian Studies*, 38/3 (2004), 479–516.

Also, there were far fewer Britons in Madras and Bombay; and those that there were possessed a less tight a grip on the privileges of power and wealth. In Bombay, which underwent prodigious commercial and industrial development in the later nineteenth century, the key entrepreneurs were Indian (or even Middle Eastern); and there, and even more in Madras, major Indian princely states touted at least the symbols of independent authority and more than symbolic hoards of cash. The Nizam of Hyderabad was widely rated to be the richest man in the world. In both cities, it was by no means unusual for the race hierarchy, as perceived from Calcutta, to be inverted, with Indian princes and businessmen 'employing' white men—albeit never in very menial capacities. Another feature was the long presence of European communities other than the British—Portuguese, French, Dutch—who had stayed on even after the English Company's conquest. In 1871, 28 per cent of the 'Europeans' in Madras Presidency were Roman Catholics.[79] This made a generic 'European' identity more salient than an exclusive British one.

In the case of the Portuguese and French, who had extensively intermarried with the Indian population, it also blurred the category of 'European' into 'Eurasian' in subtle ways. There was something of a Portuguese-French/ Roman Catholic-based 'Creole' culture at the middle levels of society in these two cities into which 'Anglo-Eurasians' and 'poor Brits' might blend without wholly losing status. Further, this Catholic/Creole culture stretched out to embrace Indian Christians, who were especially numerous in the south. In effect, race relations were deflected across a broader spectrum and the harsh binaries, so basic to Victorian Calcutta, remained considerably softened.[80] The concept of 'cosmopolitanism' has recently come in for criticism and, certainly, it would be inappropriate if the term were meant to suggest a complete lack of racial, ethnic, and cultural boundaries.[81] But Madras and Bombay were cities in which the hierarchies of class, race, and ethnicity were not perfectly aligned and were capable of twisting one another into curious shapes. In that sense, they were cosmopolitan.

Their flavour, perhaps, can be caught in the now-forgotten 'Madras' novels of Mrs B. M. Croker, which were popular at the turn of the century.[82]

[79] W. R. Cornish, *Census of the Madras Presidency, 1871*, i (Madras, 1874), 31–5.
[80] Washbrook, 'South India'.
[81] Carol A. Breckenridge (ed.), *Cosmopolitanism* (Durham, NC, 2002).
[82] Shuchi Kapila, 'The Domestic Novel Goes Native: Bithia Mary Croker's Anglo-India', *Nineteenth-Century Contexts*, 26/3 (2004), 215–35.

Her *The Company's Servant: A Romance of Southern India* sets out a cast of
characters who never would have been assembled in a 'Calcutta' novel.[83]
Her hero, Vernon Talbot, is a pure-bred 'Brit', but one who works as a
humble guard on the Madras Railway, based in the small town of 'Tanu-Kul'.
He moves within a community consisting of: Colonel Lennox, the head of
the local army regiment; the handsome adventurer Charlie Booth, who is
the discarded orphan of a British army sergeant brought up at the Lawrence
Asylum in 'Ootie'; Madame Tanzy, the French-Eurasian wife of an English
railway fitter, who holds 'tea dances' and soirées where much intercourse,
ostensibly of a social kind, takes place; her niece, Rosita Fontaine, who is of
lustrous beauty and charm; Mr Coelho and Mr and Mrs Pereira who are
sturdy local merchants; Beatrice Arminger who is the runaway daughter of
an English Archdeacon and risks falling into Madame Tanzy's clutches; the
'devil' Pilchai-Moothoo-Pillai who lends money to all, pressing them ever
deeper into penury; and Gojar who is an Indian watchman with a philosophical bent of mind and Vernon's closest confidant.

In the story, Vernon is torn between the Eurasian orchid, Rosita, and the
English rose, Beatrice; and, to boot, is falsely accused of a robbery. Identities
begin to unravel: Colonel Lennox, the upholder of Pax Britannica, turns out
really to be Carlo Moccato, a notorious international spy; Gojar turns
out really to be an Englishman, who has freely chosen the lifestyle of a
poor Indian in preference to that of his 'own kind' and who comes to
Vernon's rescue with an act of great self-sacrifice when the rest of the empire
appears to have abandoned him.

At this point, no doubt, Kipling's indomitable Mrs Hawksbee would have
thrown the novel into the wastepaper basket: appalled, alike, at the plebeian
nature of its characters and the way that the etiquette of 'civilization' was
being violated on every page. This was not the 'British India' to which she
was used in the ballrooms of Calcutta and Simla. However, had she perse-
vered, she might at least have found that her own class prejudices would not
go unflattered. Vernon Talbot, it transpires, is actually the Honourable John
Herbrand Patrick Vernon Sacheverall-Talbot, nephew to Lord Rotherham
from whom he was separated, and dismissed to the colonies, as the result
of a misunderstanding. The two are rapturously reunited. Gojar confesses
that he did not elect to live like an Indian because of deep philosophical

---

[83] B. M. Croker, *The Company's Servant: A Romance of Southern India* (London, 1907).

conviction, but because of an addiction to *ganja* and polygamy. Nor is he a mere Englishman, but no less than the Honourable Algernon Craven, heir to Lord Parland, and he transfers his unneeded fortune of £130,000 to Vernon so that the latter can live like a gentleman in his stead. Whereupon Vernon picks the rose over the orchid; and Rosita, herself, turns her back on handsome-but-penurious Charlie Booth to go off and become a celebrated night-club *chanteuse* in Paris. In the end, the proprieties of class—perhaps the core value of British imperial society—are fully validated. Calcutta and Madras did not belong to completely different worlds. But their textures and colours also stand out as extremely distinct.

India offered people from the British Isles an extraordinary and rich tapestry on which to stitch 350 years of social history. They made their societies in many ways, with a variety of other peoples in diverse situations at different times. They always brought something distinctive from home to these mixtures. But perhaps only in Calcutta were they able to make a 'British India', which excluded everything and everybody else.

Select Bibliography

DAVID ARNOLD, 'European Orphans and Vagrants in India in the Nineteenth Century', *Journal of Imperial and Commonwealth History*, 2/7 (1979), 109–27.

KENNETH BALLHATCHET, *Race, Sex and Class under the Raj: Imperial Attitudes and Policies and their Critics, 1793–1905* (London, 1980).

LAURA BEAR, *Lines of the Nation: Indian Railway Workers, Bureaucracy and the Intimate Historical Self* (New York, 2007).

ELIZABETH BUETTNER, *Empire Families: Britons and Late Imperial India* (Oxford, 2004).

DAVID CANNADINE, *Ornamentalism: How the British Saw their Empire* (London, 2001).

B. M. CROKER, *The Company's Servant: A Romance of Southern India* (London, 1907).

WILLIAM DALRYMPLE, *White Mughals: Love and Betrayal in Eighteenth-Century India* (London, 2002).

INDIRA GHOSE, *Women Travellers in India: The Power of the Female Gaze* (Delhi, 1998).

DURBA GHOSH, *Sex and the Family in Colonial India: The Making of Empire* (Cambridge, 2006).

DAVID GILMOUR, *The Ruling Caste: Imperial Lives in the Victorian Raj* (London, 2005).

CHRISTOPHER J. HAWES, *Poor Relations: The Making of a Eurasian Community in British India, 1773–1833* (Richmond, 1996).

P. J. MARSHALL, *East India Fortunes: The British in Bengal in the Eighteenth Century* (Oxford, 1976).

——'The Whites of British India: A Failed Colonial Society', *International History Review*, 12/1 (1990), 26–44.

P. J. MARSHALL, 'British Society in India under the East India Company', *Modern Asian Studies*, 31/1 (1997), 82–108.

——'The White Town of Calcutta under the Rule of the East India Company', *Modern Asian Studies*, 34/2 (2000), 307–33.

MARIA MISRA, *Business, Race and Politics in British India, c.1860–1960* (Oxford, 1999).

DOUGLAS M. PEERS, *Between Mars and Mammon: Colonial Armies and the Garrison State in India, 1819–35* (London, 1995).

DAVID POTTER, *India's Political Administrators 1919–1983* (Oxford, 1986).

MRINALINI SINHA, 'Britishness, Clubbability and the Colonial Public Sphere: The Genealogy of an Imperial Institution in Colonial India', *Journal of British Studies*, 40/4 (2001), 491–521.

ANN LAURA STOLER, *Carnal Knowledge and Imperial Power: Race and the Intimate in Colonial Rule* (Berkeley, Calif., 2000).

8

'Permanent Boarders'
The British in Ceylon, 1815–1960

Margaret Jones

> Although I was born in an atmoshere of rigid British ideas: ideas that
> made me feel, as thorough a Briton as if I had never been out of
> England, yet I lived in a climate that was tropical: surrounded with all
> the contracting influences, that unconsciously, or subconsciously,
> become Colonial.[1]

This observation was made in 1923 by Frederick Lewis in the opening pages
of a memoir of his sixty-four years in the island. Born in Ceylon, Lewis
spent his working life there as a coffee, tea, and cinchona planter, and then
as a forester in government service; but he always regarded Britain as his
home. However, he, at least, understood the anomalies of his position. He
was British but he was also colonial. It is the purpose of this chapter to
examine what this conjunction meant through the experiences of a variety
of Britons who came to administer, to heal, to 'civilize', to speculate, and/or
to make their fortunes in the 'Tom Tiddler's ground' that was the colony of
Ceylon.[2]

Ceylon was long regarded as Britain's model colony and is therefore a
pertinent example in any analysis of British communities. The East India
Company acquired the coastal regions of Ceylon from the Dutch during the

---

[1] Frederick Lewis, *Sixty Four Years in Ceylon: Reminiscences of Life and Adventure* (New Delhi, 1993), preface.

[2] The phrase 'Tom Tiddler's Ground' is taken from a children's game, and meant a place where it was easy to make a fortune. Ceylon was so described by Frederick Lewis, ibid. 84.

Napoleonic Wars. They were transformed into a Crown Colony in 1802, and the whole of the island into a colony with the incorporation of the ancient Kandyan kingdom in 1815. A unified system of government was implemented with the 1833 Colebrook-Cameron reforms which imposed the superstructure of a *laissez-faire* state. Ceylon was first termed a model colony because it set the pattern of Crown Colony governance. This epithet was reinforced in 1931 when the Donoughmore Constitution granted virtual responsible self-government to the Ceylonese. Under this constitution the colony was governed by a legislative body, the State Council (elected under universal suffrage, only some four years after it had been conceded in the UK); and an executive, the Board of Ministers (chosen from the State Council representatives). In 1948 it again provided a model by achieving independence relatively free from conflict.

At least at an elite level, continual European occupation from the sixteenth century onwards created a highly Westernized society although it was only under British rule that Western penetration extended into the interior of the island. A constant influx of Britons after 1805 provided a predominating presence although their actual numbers were always small in relation to the total population, as demonstrated in Table 8.1. Most of the British-born were English, followed by Scots, in the low hundreds, and a sprinkling of Welsh and Irish. Despite the constancy of their presence this varied group of colonisers had one thing in common. They were not settlers, that is, they did not consider themselves to be settled, as did white Australians or South Africans, but this did not preclude generations of the same families from owning coffee and tea estates. Usually, like their compatriots in India, they alternated years of work with periods of leave back in Britain. They established families in Ceylon, but sent their children back to Britain for schooling, if they could afford to, and on retirement they also returned there to live

Table 8.1 British Born Population for Census Years 1871–1946

	1871	1891	1901	1911	1921	1946
British born	1,653	2,481	5,098	6,093	7,649	2,936
Total population	2.4m	3.0m	3.6m	4.1m	4.5m	6.6m

Source: *Census Reports* for relevant years and *Census Report 1946*, p. 220, table 155. The relevant figures were not collected in the 1881 and 1931 reports. The category 'British-born' excludes Ceylon-born Britons.

Table 8.2 European Male Population by Age for Selected Years

	1901	1911	1921
0–4	350	262	397
5–9	220	194	229
10–14	138	116	106
15–19	179	149	145
20–24	508	590	344
25–29	678	808	570
30–34	522	687	711
35–39	365	568	599
40–44	303	452	513
45–49	252	273	402
50–54	136	212	263
55–59	97	140	147
60 and over	102	193	209
Total	3850	4644	4635

Source: *Census Reports* for 1901, 1911, and 1921 after which these figures were not recorded.

Table 8.3 European Female Population by Age for Selected Years

	1901	1911	1921
0–4	332	296	395
5–9	206	229	248
10–14	148	146	128
15–19	178	160	144
20–24	324	251	260
25–29	357	433	447
30–34	282	422	471
35–39	206	334	421
40–44	127	234	291
45–49	103	141	236
50–54	55	96	144
55–59	64	76	111
60 and over	60	128	184
Total	2442	2946	3483

Source: *Census Reports* for 1901, 1911, and 1921 after which these figures were not recorded.

with other ex-colonials like themselves.[3] This pattern is illustrated by the breakdown of the European community by age for selected years as presented in Tables 8.2 and 8.3. The peak age for both men and women in the colony was between 20 and 40.

As Elizabeth Buettner has recently shown, this life-cycle pattern 'created specific forms of racial, class and geographical identity', which separated the British colonizer not only from the indigenous population but also from his or her own countrymen and women at home.[4] Her comments were anticipated by a Ceylon planter in the 1950s when he described the British community as 'permanent boarders', at ease neither in the place of their birth nor in their adopted country.[5]

The British colonizer in Ceylon entered a society which had a rich and diverse cultural heritage, albeit already fractured along ethnic, religious, and caste lines. The majority Sinhalese population was Buddhist with the next largest ethnic group, the Hindu Tamils. There were also smaller groups of Muslims and the Christian descendants of the Portuguese and Dutch—the Burghers. British colonization added a further horizontal division by creating a highly Westernized elite (Sinhalese, Christian, and Tamil) who were separated both from their compatriots and fellow religionists by their acquisition of British norms and values but also separated from the British by their race.[6] Interwoven in any analysis must be the interaction of the colonists with this indigenous population. The construction of the 'other' is a necessary part of the process of forming a cultural identity and for British colonists in Ceylon, as elsewhere, the creating and/or sustaining of differences between themselves and the indigenous population provided cohesion to a life which at times could be atomistic and anomic. However, it is important to remember that the resulting identities were also shifting and various, according to both time and circumstance.

This chapter is divided into four sections. The first part focuses on the two main shapers of British influence in the island, the planters and the British administrators, and explores the conflict inherent in their differing roles. The second focuses on the construction of a 'British' identity in the

---

[3] Frederick Lewis e.g. explained that he met his wife in Bedford on a visit to retired Ceylon friends: Lewis, *Sixty Four Years in Ceylon*, 301.

[4] Elizabeth Buettner, *Empire Families: Britons and Late Imperial India* (Oxford, 2004), 2.

[5] Harry Williams, *Ceylon: Pearl of the East* (London, 1953), 328.

[6] See Kumari Jayawardena, *Nobodies to Somebodies: The Rise of the Colonial Bourgeoisie in Sri Lanka* (London, 2000).

colony, whilst the third examines British women colonists in this context. The final section looks at the effects of the long decolonization after 1931.[7]

Official and Unofficial Colonists

Table 8.4 is designed to serve as an illustrative snapshot of the occupations of the British colonists. It suggests that their two major occupational areas were agriculture and government. In these two census years, the planters outnumbered the government administrators by a ratio of about 2:1. Table 8.4 also illustrates that the planters were, as might be expected, overwhelmingly male. Not all planters were owners, of course. Many Britons on estates were employees and there was a clear career path from the lowliest position of 'creeper', for the newly arrived, to becoming a manager of a large estate. 'Planter' is used in this chapter to cover all those positions.

Table 8.4 Numbers of Europeans Engaged in Selected Occupations in 1901 and 1921

	1901		1921	
	Male	Female	Male	Female
Tea, coffee, coconut, rubber plantations	1228	51	1613	177
Public administration	516	29	865	664*
Missionaries	147	34	188	53
Teachers	25	78	50	197
Civil engineers	81	–	1107	–
Tailors, dressmakers	24	14	28	18
Brokers	20	–	43	–

Source: *Census Reports* for 1901, Table LXVIII and 1921, Table VII. These figures are not definitive. (1) Only the generic category of European is included in these particular tables, but most of these were British. (2) Although the categories look similar on the reports they may have changed in content.

* This figure for women in public administration is explained by the inclusion of nurses and teachers employed by the government. Such 'working' women were always outnumbered by the 'non-working' wives and daughters: e.g. in 1921 they accounted for one third of the total of 3,483 in the colony: 1921 *Census Report*, table LXVIII, 1901, table XXIX, 1911, and table VII, 1921.

[7] This chapter makes no more than a passing reference to Ceylon during the Second World War when the British community was greatly inflated by the influx of army and naval personnel. After the fall of Singapore and Hong Kong, Ceylon was strategically important (it suffered two Japanese air raids in Apr. 1942) and in Oct. 1943 the headquarters of South East Asia Command under Lord Mountbatten was established at Kandy. Space does not permit an analysis of this atypical period.

In the first three decades of the colony's existence, the boundaries between planter and administrator were substantially blurred. Until 1844–5, when it was prohibited, members of the administration and the British establishment were among the prime speculators in land and coffee in order to supplement their inadequate official salaries.[8] After these civil service reforms, there developed regular conflicts between administrator and planter, which reflected their different interests and perspectives. This exposed the multi-faceted nature of being a Briton in Ceylon. Who made up these groups and how were their attitudes formed?

THE BRITISH ADMINISTRATORS

The Colebrook-Cameron reforms established a unified administration and judicial system theoretically based on British liberal principles. Civil servants for Ceylon were recruited, alongside those for Hong Kong and Malaya, into what was known as the Eastern Cadet Service.[9] From 1904 all candidates for these cadetships had to be of 'pure' European descent on both sides of the family, except in Ceylon, where recruitment of Ceylonese remained the intention. For example, between 1870 and 1880 the entrance exam, with identical papers to the UK, was held in Colombo. However, as this was based on a British university education it was still difficult for Ceylonese to compete, and few initially entered the service. One notable exception was Sir Ponnambalam Arunchalem (the first Ceylonese to be elected to the Legislative Council in 1912), who passed the exam in 1875.[10] But overall the numbers of Ceylonese in the Ceylon Civil Service (CCS) indeed remained low until the 1920s.[11]

From the mid-nineteenth century the colonial civil service as a whole began to acquire its own professional ethos, a process which was accelerated in the twentieth with the establishment of training schemes, the Warren Fisher reforms (which set up recruitment by interview), and the unification

[8] H. A. J. Hulugalle, *British Governors of Ceylon* (Colombo, 2002), 68–9, 80; Asoka Bandarage, *Colonialism in Sri Lanka: The Political Economy of the Kandyan Highlands, 1833–1886* (Berlin, 1983), 274.

[9] Charles Jeffries, *Ceylon: The Path to Independence* (London, 1962), 30.

[10] C. Collins, 'Ceylon: The Imperial Heritage', in R. Braibanti (ed.), *Asian Bureaucratic Systems Emergent from the British Imperial Tradition* (Durham, NC, 1966), 464.

[11] Ibid. 465. In 1896 out of a total of 79 officers in the CCS the number of 'Ceylonese' were 13, of whom four were Sinhalese, three were Tamil, and the remainder other British subjects including Europeans who were born in Ceylon.

of the service.[12] These latter two initiatives, however, came too late to influence the CCS directly so its ethos derived more from the common educational and family backgrounds of those who joined. The system of recruitment favoured applicants of a particular background, that is, usually public school-educated, Oxbridge graduates, who were the sons of clergy-men, army officers, or civil servants.[13]

The experiences of many of these colonial civil servants have been recorded in biographies, memoirs, and interviews. They joined the colonial service for a variety of reasons from a 'wish to help those less fortunate', a yen for adventure, or because of family connections.[14] They received little or no formal training but 'learnt the ropes' through what amounted to an apprenticeship system; shadowing the work of those above and learning from practical experience.[15] In Ceylon, as government agents in conjunc-tion with indigenous leaders (the *Mudaliyars* and village headmen), they provided the basic provincial administrative and judicial structure, under the auspices of the colonial secretariat (the Governor's office) based in Colombo. The system of training did not encourage innovation or individ-uality but it did establish continuity of practice and fostered a common group identity. However, there were clearly varying levels of perceptiveness about their role. For Leonard Woolf, his experience at the beginning of the century as a district agent turned him into a convinced anti-imperialist. He recorded his enjoyment of his position, the 'flattery of being the great man and the father of the people' but, whilst 'he loved the peoples and their way of life', he also knew 'how evil the system was, beneath the surface, for ordinary men and women'.[16] Similarly, R. B. Naish, who had come with an open mind on the people he had to govern, wrote to his mother that 'I sometimes think that "civilisation" and "Western culture" and the rest of it aren't everything'. Others who served in the island appear less introspective

---

[12] Anthony Kirke-Greene, *On Crown Service: A History of HM Colonial and Overseas Civil Services, 1837–1997* (London, 1999), 27; Ralph Furse, *Acuparius: Recollections of a Returning Officer* (London, 1962), 219–40.

[13] Kirke-Greene, *On Crown Service*, 94; I. F. Nicolson and Colin A. Hughes, 'A Provenance of Proconsuls: British Colonial Governors 1900–1960', *Journal of Imperial and Commonwealth History*, 1/4 (1975), 75–95.

[14] Kirke-Greene, *On Crown Service*, 96.

[15] Cambridge South Asian Archive (CSAA), Naish papers, letters of R. B. Naish, 24 Jan. 1915.

[16] Leonard Woolf, *Growing: An Autobiography of the Years 1904–1911* (London, 1964), 92, 158–9. See also C. Ondaatje, *Woolf in Ceylon: An Imperial Journey in the Shadow of Leonard Woolf, 1904–1911* (Toronto, 2005).

and questioning. W. T. Stace, for example (CCS, 1910–32), confidently claimed that his public school and Oxford had given him a 'humanistic education to fit a man for ruling human beings'.[17] Nevertheless, whatever the particular individual responses of civil servants in Ceylon, it is possible to identify an 'official' perspective in their interactions with the other predominant group of British colonists, the planters.

THE PLANTERS

The Colebrook-Cameron reforms also ushered in a period of rapid economic development on capitalist lines. From 1833 a policy of land sales was introduced which was greatly accelerated in 1840 by the Crown Land Encroachment Ordinance. This laid down that all land not proved to have been granted previously was the property of the Crown and could be sold. A land market was duly created and from the 1840s 'the entire economy of the island was transformed by the rise of coffee plantations'.[18] The opening up of the highlands came at an opportune moment for some with experience of plantation agriculture. The disruption of plantation activities in the British West Indies after the abolition of slavery 'forced planters there to reconsider their options', and some chose to bring their know-how and their capital to Ceylon where the costs were lower. The capital inflow in turn encouraged the land market.[19] This example of capital and skills transfer across the empire was to be replicated right at the end of the period when prescient British planters in Ceylon set out to establish tea growing in what seemed at the time (the 1950s) the more secure environment of East Africa.[20]

Another group of early planters were Scots, often from neighbouring villages. This group included James Taylor the pioneer tea grower and also the influential Ferguson family. In general the early planters were a mixed group from varied backgrounds.[21] It is also apparent from the existing memoirs that family connections persisted as a significant factor

---

[17] Rhodes House Collection MSS IND OCN S174, 'Transcript of Taped Interviews by M. W. Roberts with 47 former Ceylon Administrators, 1902–1961', W. T. Stace, Dec. 1965.

[18] Chandra de Silva, *Sri Lanka: A History* (New Delhi, 1994), 161.

[19] James L. A. Webb, *Tropical Pioneers: Human Agency and Ecological Change in the Highlands of Sri Lanka, 1800–1900* (Athens, Ohio, 2002), 77.

[20] See e.g. Oral History Archive, British Empire and Commonwealth Museum, no. 210, Interview with Mrs Islay Kitson, 6 Sept. 1995.

[21] Maxwell Fernando, *The Story of Ceylon Tea* (Colombo, 2000), 54, 63; D. M. Forrest, *A Hundred Years of Ceylon Tea, 1867–1967* (London, 1967), 194–6.

in attracting young men to the colony. However, if the administrators' shared culture was created from their common background, education, and training, the planters, coming from disparate social groups, needed formal linkages to protect their political and economic interests and to foster their cultural identity. The most significant of these was the Planters' Association (PA) established in Kandy on 17 February 1854 by the business partnership of George Wall and Captain Keith Jolly.[22] Its objective was to 'promote, foster and protect the Planting Industry of Ceylon and the interests of the Planting Community'. Clause V of its constitution stated that 'property' was the 'chief basis of membership'. It was open to owners of estates (an estate being defined as comprising more than 50 acres); and to 'Gentlemen not owners of estates' on the payment of the subscription (Clause VII).[23] The planting interest also gained their own representation on the colony's Legislative Council (LC) in the 1850s; but their power to influence government decisions was first circumscribed by the official majority on the LC and after 1931 by an elected government.

The PA was supplemented in 1894 by the Planters' Benevolent Fund established to commemorate Queen Victoria's Jubilee. The question of how to use the money generated much debate. Some planters wanted a permanent memorial in the form of a statue in order to 'put the population of Ceylon in mind of our splendid Queen'.[24] Amongst other, more practically minded suggestions were a convalescent ward for planters at the General Hospital Colombo, an aquarium, and, in tribute to Queen Victoria's 'womanliness', the provision of an experienced midwife for every government hospital.[25] In the event, the planters settled on protecting their own interests with the establishment of the Benevolent Fund 'for the relief of necessitous persons of European birth who are or have been members of

[22] Forrest, *Hundred Years of Ceylon Tea*, 191, 176.

[23] Sri Lankan National Archives (SLNA) Library, Colombo, Year Book of the Planters' Association of Ceylon, 1874.

[24] *Times of Ceylon* (18 Apr. 1890), 'Monument of the Jubilee of Her Majesty Queen Victoria, 1837–1887. Proceedings of Meeting of Subscribers at Kandy to decide disposal of the fund', W. D. Gibson, p. 10. The *Times of Ceylon* was the mouthpiece of the planters.

[25] SLNA Library, Proceedings of Meeting of Subscribers, Correspondence, letter, A. G. K. Borrow, 21 Mar. 1890, James Westland, 4 Apr. 1890, T. N. Christie, 9 Oct. 1889, James Ryan, 26 Mar. 1890.

the planting community and of the wives, widows and children of such persons'.[26]

The fund gave pensions, special grants, loans, educational grants, help with medical expenses, and, if necessary, passages home to those unable to work. However, these were only available to the 'deserving'. In order to receive a benefit the recipient had to be 'entirely free from any suspicion that their distress is the result of their own lack of wisdom or control'.[27] This kind of conditional charity was a common feature in colonial societies where the presence of impoverished Europeans threatened to undermine the hierarchies of colonial society.[28] Europeans who were jobless were commonly termed 'loafers'.[29] Lewis recounted that he would almost prefer to starve than be deemed a 'loafer' such was the shame.[30] Such conditionality lagged behind changing metropolitan attitudes by the 1930s.

CAPITALISTS VERSUS 'PATERNALISTIC PREFECTS'[31]

The planters' need for an organization to protect their interests arose directly from conflicts with the colonial government. Frederick Lewis's move from the world of the planter to that of the professional gave him unique insights into both. He understood that the European planters' way of life rendered them 'little kings within their own limited kingdoms' and they naturally found any 'interference with their systems of control...repugnant'. There was a 'considerable gap', he noted, 'between the sympathies of the planter...and of the local administrators, whose ideas...were completely out of keeping with planting methods and ways' and this produced a 'barrier between the white community and the administration'.[32] The resulting disputes, invariably based around questions of money, were frequently couched in terms of rights and liberties. Two of the

---

[26] SLNA Library, Year Book of the Planters' Association of Ceylon, 1930, s. 44.

[27] Ibid.

[28] See e.g. Ann Laura Stoler, 'Rethinking Colonial Categories: European Communities and the Boundaries of Rule', *Comparative Studies in Society and History*, 31/1 (1989), 134–61.

[29] Lake House Library Archive, *The Island*: 'Midweek Review', V. Basnayake, 'The Colonists and Others in Ceylon in 1900', 16, 8 Aug. 2002.

[30] Lewis, *Sixty Four Years in Ceylon*, 107. This was not an idle boast. At the time he was in charge of a coffee estate that had completely failed and he was going hungry.

[31] The phrase is borrowed from Bernard Porter, 'An Awfully Big Colonial Adventure', *Times Literary Supplement* (14 Jan. 2000), 4–5.

[32] Lewis, *Sixty Four Years in Ceylon*, 6–7.

most important issues were the size of the military contribution and the condition of the Tamil estate worker.[33]

The military contribution and the question of financing medical aid for the estate workers were, in the mind of at least one planter, J. L. Shand, perfect examples of the oppressiveness of their colonial government. On becoming a colonist, he argued in 1884, 'you lose all the privileges of a British subject, and you are ranked, not even equal with, but positively subordinate to the native'. There are two things, he went on, that 'rule the colonies: greed and sentiment'. The greed was, in his view, to be found totally on the government's side. The evidence was the £2.5 million taken out of the colony since 1864 by the government for the military contribution; and the Medical Bill, where the planters 'were expected to contribute about six times as much for the medical attendance of the coolies as the Government think it proper to give to the natives'. He likened their situation to that of the American colonists over the stamp duty, no doubt intending to pose a similar threat.[34]

This second grievance, medical aid, emerged as an issue almost as soon as the Indian workers started to work on the coffee estates in the 1840s. It was the most open manifestation of a continuing conflict, because it centred on the planters' right to conduct their economic enterprises free from interference and the administrators' right to claim good government as the basis of their right to rule. The 'coolies' came first as seasonal workers, driven by poverty in India. The substitution of tea from the late 1870s changed this itinerant labour force into a settled one in response to the year-long demands of tea growing. These workers endured such privations that their resulting high morbidity and mortality provoked a continuing crisis between planter and administrator. It began in the 1840s when, for example, one magistrate, J. S. Colepepper, had 'no hesitation' in stating that 'this class of population is in much worse condition in the Central Province than the Negro slave was described to be in the West Indies in former days'.[35]

As the planters argued in an 1846 petition, the 'distress' of the 'coolies' was of 'such magnitude' that it was 'quite beyond the control of the voluntary exertions of any class'. In addition, it was 'self-evident that the prosperity' of

---

[33] Forrest, *Hundred Years of Ceylon Tea*, 177–80.

[34] Proceedings of the Planters' Association of Ceylon, J. L. Shand, 21 Sept. 1884.

[35] The National Archives (Kew) (TNA), CO 57/235, J. S. Colepepper, Police Superintendent, Central Province, 18 Jan. 1847.

the colony depended 'upon its agricultural operations, and that the introduction of labour must contribute in every way to the public Revenue and
benefit all classes, and not the Planters in particular'.[36] Furthermore, government attempts at enforcing legislation were perceived as an attack on
planters' fundamental rights. R. B. Tytler's passionate appeal in 1872 to his
fellow planters not to be 'mealy-mouthed' but to 'manfully speak out in
plain Anglo-Saxon common sense: Let us, and our coolies, alone', stands
testament to a strand of thinking in protest discourse which had found
expression in the English and then the American revolutions.[37] As Shand's
1884 comment illustrates, the planters were not averse to threatening open
disobedience. Another such threat in a petition from the planters to Queen
Victoria against the 1880 Medical Wants Ordinance evinced a horrified
response from Sir Charles Lucas at the Colonial Office that it was 'a serious
matter when a class of English, for whom a great deal has been done by the
government openly declare that they will do their best to defy the law'.[38]

For the administrators it was the planters who benefited from the Tamil
worker and it was they who should pay to ensure their living and working
conditions were humane. As C. H. D. Sarum, a magistrate from the planting
districts, saw it in the 1840s, 'the deaths on the bog road, bye paths and at the
hospital, as well as the great number of helpless beings seen daily lingering
out a life of wretchedness and starvation' resulted entirely from 'a want of
the due care and attention on the part of the planter'.[39] Moreover, as the
then colonial secretary, Emerson Tennent, added, 'the whole body of the
inhabitants of Ceylon are not dependent on the successful cultivation of
one grand staple... on the contrary the vast mass of the population are
supported by totally different pursuits'. It would therefore 'be a manifest
injustice', he concluded, for the 'revenue raised by contributions from the
entire community' to be used to support one sector alone.[40]

Legislation in the ensuing decades, compelling planters to finance improvements in the living and working conditions on their estates, gradually

---

[36] TNA, CO 54/227, Memorial of the Planters, 9 Sept. 1846.
[37] TNA, CO 54/478, Medical Treatment of Coolies, R. B. Tytler to H. Byrde, 15 Feb. 1872.
Tytler had been a planter in the West Indies. Webb, *Tropical Pioneers*, 80.
[38] TNA, CO 54/537, Petition to Her Most Glorious Majesty Victoria, included in the despatch
of Feb. 1882, and signed by the Chairmen of the Planters' Association and the Ceylon Chamber
of Commerce; TNA, CO 54/537, Minute, Charles Lucas, 5 Apr. 1882.
[39] TNA, CO 57/235 C. H. D. Sarum, Police Magistrate, Gampola, 8 Feb. 1847.
[40] TNA, CO 54/235, Tennent, 21 Apr. 1847.

eroded their capacity to be 'little kings'. In the case of the Indian worker colonial administrators did indeed play the part of the 'paternalistic prefect' in their efforts to mitigate the worst effects of unconstrained capitalism. Such conflicts were not peculiar to the colony of Ceylon: nor were they peculiarly colonial. All European governments, including Britain's, faced similar quandaries and these in turn generated similar divisions between the entrepreneurial and the professional classes.[41] What is different about the context in Ceylon was that these workers were even more powerless than the industrial working class in nineteenth-century Britain. Their economic position rendered them totally weak, and moreover they were foreign workers so would not generate the kind of support from a paternalist aristocracy that was instrumental in nineteenth-century British protective legislation. The pressure to mitigate the worst excesses of unrestrained capitalism in Ceylon (until the expansion of the suffrage and the granting of some form of self-government towards the end of the colonial period) could only come from those in the administration. The direct confrontations over these workers' conditions played a large part in defining the formal relationship between the official and the unofficial British colonist in Ceylon.

The Construction of Identity

The collective conflict between planters and officials was not necessarily transferred to their individual interactions. As one colonial secretary explained: 'I was told that I should find the planters of Ceylon to be first rate fellows when you meet them singly, but whenever they get together, they are the most unreasonable set of men you can meet. And I am bound to say that experience here confirms those impressions.'[42] The fact of being British and 'white' obviously created strong ties of unity. Being a 'Briton' in Ceylon, however, was an ever-changing experience varying over time, place, and class.

The pioneer colonists experienced very different conditions from those which confronted their successors. In opening up the land for planting it was possible to be extremely isolated from fellow Britons. It was therefore difficult to maintain the values of the home culture. Living conditions could also be very primitive. One of Lewis's early homes, for example, as late as the

---

[41] See Harold Perkin, *Origins of Modern English Society* (London, 1986), 257–61.
[42] Quoted in 'Monument of the Jubilee of Her Majesty Queen Victoria', p. xxii.

1870s consisted of a 'log hut, comprising one room 12 by 8 feet...with an opening at one end for a door, over which hung a mat. The floor was bare ground...and the roof consisted of talipot leaves.' This hut was furnished with 'a table made of planks', a stool, and a bed consisting of 'some sticks covered with a little grass'.[43] Even in 1924 when Ronald Weeks arrived at his first bungalow he found it had no electricity or water laid on, the lighting was by oil-lamp or candle and sanitation was a dry earth closet.[44] The usual social restraints on behaviour could also be lacking. Whilst for some this would mean being even more careful to uphold 'civilized' values, for others it was an opportunity to 'run wild'. Men could forget 'themselves as regards propriety' to the extent that at least one Cambridge undergraduate 'had quickly parted with his claims to be even regarded as a gentleman'.[45] This ill discipline in some planters was reputedly fuelled by a culture of drinking. However, Williams, for example, has denied that the Ceylon tea planters' reputation for heavy drinking was entirely fair, and justified the drinking that did go on with reference to the lack of alternative entertainments and of course the temperature, which led to a 'sapping of energy' and the need for a 'stimulant'.[46] Nevertheless, the amount of alcohol that could be consumed still 'amazed' at least one newcomer to the colony in the 1940s.[47] And the stories of some of the drunken pranks such as 'picking up the entire bar of the Galle Face Hotel and dropping it on Galle Face Green' were part of the 'folk' memory of the community. One planter's wife was told this story forty years after it happened. Her verdict was that 'they did what they liked, of course, they were a terrible crowd'.[48]

The opening up of the island with rail and road networks towards the latter half of the nineteenth century and the development of steamship companies who stopped off at Colombo accelerated a shift in the way of life for the British colonists. Their isolation both within the colony itself and between the colony and Britain was reduced and even more significantly it brought many more women to the colony. As Stoler and others have

---

[43] Lewis, *Sixty Four Years in Ceylon*, 41.

[44] Oral History Archive, British Empire and Commonwealth Museum, no. 246, Ronald Weeks, 13 Feb. 1996.

[45] Lewis, *Sixty Four Years in Ceylon*, 88.

[46] Williams, *Pearl of the East*, 270.

[47] South and East Asia Archive, University of Cambridge, Ruth Randall, 'Serendipity of Three Happy Years in Ceylon. Memoir of the Wife of a Rubber Planter, 1946–1948', 110, 113.

[48] Kitson, 6 Sept. 1995.

suggested, the advent of women into a previously male society could have a radical effect.[49] The 'wild west' aspects of life in Ceylon began to concede ground to a more formalized 'colonial' life, where the home culture was more self-consciously reproduced and the gap between the colonizer and the colonized became more pronounced. As one old planter mused: 'Our simple ways suddenly changed in many places such as dressing for dinner and that sort of thing, never heard of in the jungle before the 60s.'[50]

The absence of women meant that many planters took Sinhalese women as partners. For some this was the result, as Harry Williams contended, of a lack of 'morals' and 'moderation'. However, marriage in the first five years of a contract for the newly arrived employee on a tea estate was frowned upon, if not actually forbidden. As a result even the 'ordinary, conscientious and thoroughly decent boy' could succumb to temptation and take a Sinhalese girl to live with. The 'two often have real happiness together', it was conceded, but the birth of a child was the 'payment', and this often meant that the planter took on the care of the whole family, providing them with a house and land.[51] While this was more common in the early years it did not cease altogether with the arrival of European women in greater numbers. Ronald Weeks, for example, remembered that it was common knowledge in his time (from 1920s onwards) that 'many planters had local concubines'.[52] Although the Sinhalese fully accepted the children of these mixed-race unions into their community, the same could not be said for the British. The existing Eurasian community, the Burghers, being the most Westernized group, were welcomed as collaborators in British rule but they were not accepted as social or racial equals. R. B. Naish commented in 1916 that the career of the government agent in Kurunegala had been 'hampered' a 'great deal' by his marriage to a Burgher, although she was, he added, 'the least Burgherish Burgher I have ever met as she was brought up in France'.[53]

A far greater 'threat' to community identity was presented by Ceylonese who were educated in European culture. In this case it was crucial to

---

[49] Stoler, 'Rethinking Colonial Categories', 134–61, 146–9.

[50] Quoted in Roy Moxham, *Tea Addiction, Exploitation and Empire* (London, 2003), 168.

[51] Williams, *Pearl of the East*, 268; John Weatherstone, *The Pioneers, 1825–1900: The Early British Tea and Coffee Planters and their Way of Life* (London, 1986), 180.

[52] Ronald Weeks, 13 Feb. 1996.

[53] CSAA, Letters of R. B. Naish to his Mother, 12 Dec. 1916.

maintain a space between the races through 'housing, dress codes, trans-port, food, clubs, recreation'.[54] However, the indigenous bourgeoisie in Ceylon were adept at assimilating the dress, education, architecture, and lifestyle of their colonizers.[55] The institutionalization of difference was therefore crucial and this was achieved through that most ubiquitous of colonial establishments, the club. Established from the latter part of the nineteenth century in Ceylon, these clubs formed the focal point for the social and cultural life of the British community. It was at the club that the British bonded and played, both metaphorically and literally. Ronald Weeks considered that 'without games you were a lost soul' and that once it became known that you were good at games unasked for promotions came your way, to an estate, for example, which 'badly needed a loose scrum half'.[56] In Colombo, the clubs included the eponymous Colombo Club. In the 'old days', Mirabel Hawkes noted in her memoir, it was 'entirely for men, mostly well-off heads of firms ... and kept its old-fashioned outlook for as long as it could'. There was also, she added, the Yacht Club; the Princes Club which had a 'racecourse, stables, tennis courts, ballroom etc'; the Garden Club; the Ceylon Hockey and Football Club (rugby football) where the up-country versus low-country match was played (the central event of August week), and where the main races took place; and the Swimming Club. This had a 'beautiful swimming pool, good restaurant and a few bedrooms where we found too many rats and cockroaches for our taste'. The clubs dotted around the rest of the island had similar sports amenities with clubhouses and large rooms for dances.[57]

The clubs in Colombo at least, were exclusively reserved for Europeans. Harry Williams, who was in Ceylon both before and after independence, was 'impenitent' about their exclusiveness. 'I mixed freely with both Tamils and Sinhalese in my time on the island, and considered them men in precisely the same mould as myself. But I wanted and needed a club in which I could meet my own kind and only my own kind.'[58] However, there is evidence that the rule of exclusiveness was not adhered to stringently

---

[54] See Stoler, 'Rethinking Colonial Categories', 147.

[55] Jayawardena, *Nobodies to Somebodies*, 248–62.

[56] Weeks, 13 Feb. 1996.

[57] South and East Asia Archive, University of Cambridge, Hawkes Papers, Mirabel Hawkes, 'Pearls, Palms and Riots, Clubs: Some Unfinished Notes' (1984). This memoir concentrates mainly on the interwar period.

[58] Williams, *Pearl of the East*, 263.

everywhere. When asked by his mother how he had 'managed to converse with Mr Pieris' (a Burgher district judge) 'on equal terms' Naish replied that 'it wasn't very difficult' as Pieris had been allowed into the 'otherwise exclusively European Tennis Club' in Galle. He further anticipated that the same would happen for Pieris in Jaffna where the judge had recently been posted.[59] Attendance at church also entailed a mixing of all races, albeit then united by their Christianity.[60]

Another means to maintain difference was through food. The British attempted to establish a 'sense of normalcy' by paying 'particular attention to the "regularisation" of their diet'. This entailed attempts at naturalizing, with mixed success, the flora and fauna of home so that familiar meat and vegetables could be available.[61] It also meant that wherever possible a British diet was adhered to, no matter how unsuitable: curry and rice was for the 'natives'. In particular, the British, Webb has argued, 'were able to distinguish themselves from the Sri Lankan population by their commitment to eating red meat'.[62] Even those living upcountry relied on their weekly 'boxes' from the nearest town to provide it. This often meant a considerable journey and contents could arrive in a dubious condition. The Hawkes family weekly box in the years immediately after the First World War contained '8 lbs of sirloin beef, 2lbs of rump steak, 2 lbs of soup meat, onions, potatoes, ham, tongue etc'.[63] Ruth Randall was somewhat horrified at the excessive meals she was served on arrival at her first home in Ceylon: 'it was well cooked and served but rather excessive . . . eggs, bacon, tea and toast for breakfast, and three course lunch and a five course dinner'. It was only after three months that she dared to try a curry but she only 'managed to take small helpings of all the dishes offered with iced water in between'. After a few months, however, she was 'beginning to enjoy' curries and deeming English dinners 'wishy-washy' by comparison.[64]

Lastly the British in Ceylon had their hill station: Nuwara Eliya in the heart of the tea country. Built alongside a lake 600 feet above sea level, it was to Ceylon what Simla was to India, a centre of rest and recreation and a health resort. Harry Williams described it as 'akin to a Scottish highland

[59] CSAA, Letters of R. B. Naish, 1 Oct. 1916.
[60] Ibid., 29 Dec. 1915.
[61] Webb, *Tropical Pioneers*, 53.
[62] Ibid. 55.
[63] Hawkes, 'Pearls, Palms and Riots', 2.
[64] Randall, 'Serendipity of Three Happy Years, 32, 63, 99.

resort' with many hotels, 'conventional English amusements, an enchanting golf course and a race-course' and here the British reproduced their gardens with 'brilliant beds of flowers, hydrangeas, phlox, roses, michaelmas daisies ... scarlet rhododendrons and golden broom'.[65] Kandy was where the British of all stations in life, including missionaries, estate employees, and civil servants of all grades, spent their leave but everyone who was anybody tried to spend April in Nuwara Eliya when the Governor and his wife repaired to the Queen's Cottage to avoid the heat of Colombo. The greatest social cachet accrued from an invitation to one of the Governor's select parties there but failing that there was always the Governor's ball. There were also amateur theatricals, and the Kandy Volunteer band played in the afternoons on the esplanade.[66]

This analysis has been suggestive rather than comprehensive. Increased formalization of colonial life was the most notable change over time but the extent to which this happened varied. The 'niceties' of British life could always be best observed in those centres of British culture, Colombo and Nuwara Eliya, but elsewhere they were more vulnerable to negotiation. Even within this increased formalization, however, there were significant variations in experience for different groups of colonists. The following section identifies one of these more fully by examining what it meant to be white, British, and female.

Wives and Workers

The study of the role of women within the empire came into colonial studies relatively late.[67] Nevertheless, gender, as Clare Midgley has argued, is among the 'crucial shapers and differentiators of colonial experience', and in this it interacts with race and class. This section will explore the experiences of a varied group of women who came to the colony either as workers in their own right or as wives.

The wives of administrators participated in the colonial project by supporting and supplementing their husbands' official work, thus incorporating

---

[65] Williams, *Pearl of the East*, 278.

[66] Lakehouse Library Archive, Colombo, *The Island*, V. Basnayake, 'Midweek Review: The Colonist and Others in Ceylon in 1900', 9 Aug. 2002, p. 16.

[67] See Helen Callaway, *Gender, Culture and Empire: European Women in Colonial Nigeria* (London, 1987); Mary A. Procida, *Married to the Raj: Gender, Politics and Imperialism in India* (Manchester, 2002); Clare Midgley (ed.), *Gender and Imperialism* (Manchester, 1998).

their role within their husbands'. For example, Lady Ann Havelock (wife of the Governor, 1890–5), following the example of Lady Dufferin in India, pursued her 'special hobby', as one Colonial Office official described it, and was instrumental in the establishment of both the first women's hospital and female medical education in the island.[68] Later, in the catastrophic malaria epidemic of 1934–5 which resulted in the loss of as many 100,000 lives, Mrs Newnham accompanied her husband on one of his tours as Commissioner for Relief in 1935 (which meant travelling over 1,400 miles in difficult terrain) specifically to advise him on the condition of women and children. Mrs Gimson, the wife of a government agent, organized child welfare clinics and personally delivered milk and food supplies to them in that same epidemic.[69]

Others, however, went to the colony to work in their own right. Notable among this group are the British nurses, recruited through the Overseas Nursing Association (ONA). They came out from the 1880s onwards to train Ceylonese women in Western nursing, to work in the colony's major hospitals, or to nurse the Europeans, at home and in the private Hatton and Fraser nursing homes.[70] From their individual files it is apparent that these women came from similar class backgrounds, that is, skilled working-class or from middle-class families who had fallen on hard times. Those who worked at the Hatton and Fraser homes and/or nursed privately had, however, a very different experience from those who were based in government hospitals. The homes were funded by and served only Europeans (in Kandy and Colombo respectively) and nurses employed by the Ceylon Nursing Association (CAN) were only required to nurse European patients, although they were warned that they might have to work with indigenous doctors in home cases.[71] For these women, contact with the indigenous population, apart from servants, was therefore negligible, but their job gave them instant access into the British community, and for some of course access to husbands. They were expected to fit into that society. The advantage of being good at games has already been noted. The comment in

[68] TNA, CO 54/618, minute, Lucas to Fairfield, 13 Dec. 1894.

[69] Such glimpses of the lives of the wives of colonial administrators can be gleaned from the official records of the colonial government.

[70] See Margaret Jones, 'Heroines of Lonely Outposts or Tools of the Empire? British Nurses in Britain's Model Colony: Ceylon, 1878–1948', *Nursing Inquiry*, 11/3 (2004), 149–60.

[71] Rhodes House Library, Overseas Nursing Association Archive (ONA), 134/1 Ceylon Nursing Association, General Rules.

reports back to the ONA from the CAN that a nurse was 'socially unsuitable' occurs on more than one occasion; and the refusal of the matron of Hatton to have a Miss Walters back after her leave in 1928 because she was 'too much the "nurse-maid" type' is telling.[72]

The women who worked in the government hospitals led very different professional lives, which also impacted on their social life. For one thing they had close contact with the indigenous population as patients, nurses, and doctors. This encounter was a vital aspect of their experience. Kathie Brown described her first 'night duty' immediately after arriving at the Kandy Hospital in 1925 as 'weird'. 'The still tropical night, the buzzing of insects, the black faces of the patients, the unfamiliar accent of the nurses, the visit of the native HS [house surgeons] . . . altogether it was a strange and wonderful experience.' She was clearly open to adventure but her understanding of what she encountered was circumscribed by her sense of difference and superiority. 'It is quite a fascinating study to try and get into the minds of the people and although they differ in colour the human nature is something akin to ours albeit the veneer is lacking.'[73] Another British nurse clearly had a problem in perceiving her patients as individuals and not just as a racial type; 'I thought that I should never be able to distinguish one patient from another, they all appeared so much alike.'[74] They also worked in often quite difficult conditions. Hospitals were over-crowded and ill-equipped, and they had to adapt to the vagaries of a tropical climate and strange food.

However, work in the colony gave both sets of women opportunities for excitement, adventure, and a social life, which would have been denied them, given their backgrounds, in Britain. This may not have been true in the early decades when the difficulty of keeping nurses was attributed to their isolation. Dr Perry the Principal Medical Officer commented to the ONA in 1908 that the nurses in Ceylon were 'left very much to themselves and the ladies of Colombo practically take no notice of them—they (the nurses) are consequently left very much on their own resources'.[75] This social isolation clearly diminished over time as the nurses became more integrated into the British community.

[72] ONA 120/4b, Ceylon Nursing Association, May 1927, July 1928.
[73] ONA, 137/4, Kathie Brown to Miss Adams (undated, internal evidence suggests late 1925).
[74] ONA, 132/4, Nursing Notes (undated, internal evidence suggests 1920s).
[75] TNA, CO 54/718, A. Perry, 11 Sept. 1908.

The other and more numerous group of women, the tea planters' wives and daughters, had no clearly defined role. Harry Williams in the 1950s claimed that they were therefore forced to 'fall back upon sport; golf, swimming, tennis and riding' as 'the main activities, with bridge, dancing and gossip as indoor occupations' and with 'club life' forming 'a large part of their existence'.[76] Memoirs confirm that this was largely the reality for the interwar period but again it cannot be applied throughout the period. Certainly before communications improved planters' wives could endure hardship and isolation. Frederick Lewis's mother in the 1860s, for example, was the only white woman in the district. Stranded, in their 'little bungalow' (a 'four-roomed building, with straw roof, mud walls and sand floor') her nearest white neighbour was thirty miles away, 'an impassable gulf' at the time.[77] She had to deal with the vagaries of ordinary life, including serious illness, with only the help of servants, and therefore needed considerable inner reserves.

This life was a far cry from the parties, games, and dances which almost entirely encompassed Mirabel Hawkes's daily life on her upcountry tea estate in the interwar period. The Hawkes bungalow had six bedrooms, three bathrooms, dining room, two drawing rooms and a paved courtyard into the garden. 'No day went by without tennis and dancing.' Every Friday was an 'at home day when the district came to tea and tennis' and 'special people' for dinner. 'Saturdays and rugger matches' were the 'high spot of the week' and the August week in Colombo the highlight of the year. She thought it was 'splendid starting married life with my own retinue of servants'. This lifestyle was expensive but at the club it was 'easy to sign a chit for everything and the bazaar keepers didn't mind us running up vast bills to pay off in dribs and drabs'.[78] Similarly tradesmen in the UK extended such credit to enable the upper classes to live beyond their means. This planter lifestyle was clearly unsustainable in the long term.

Mirabel Hawkes was born into this society. Ruth Randall, who came out with her husband in 1946 had a very different perspective. Used to working for her living, having been a nurse before her marriage, she felt uncomfortable with her new status. She found the 'domestic staff were bewildering' as she 'had always done her own housework'. 'I seemed to have changed

[76] Williams, *Pearl of the East*, 329.
[77] Lewis, *Sixty Four Years in Ceylon*, 11.
[78] Hawkes, 'Pearls, Palms and Riots', 11, 12, 22, 24.

overnight', she concluded, 'from an English housewife clutching ration books and shopping bag to a Victorian memsahib'. She chose to manage with the minimum of household servants and to look after her young son, Andrew, herself. On visits to other British families she had been worried to see some children 'shout Ayah in an imperious fashion to summon their nannies and to see the obsequious way' the *ayahs* 'let their charges dominate them'. She noted that she was regarded as 'odd' for not having an *ayah* but 'we had no intention of allowing a young dictator in our family'. This did not mean that Andrew had no interaction with the servants. He quickly picked up Sinhalese and also 'caused great amusement at the planters' tea party' with the Tamil swear words he had been taught by the 'bathroom man'.[79]

All these women, however, whatever their class or cultural background, had 'racial privileges'.[80] They all participated to a greater or lesser extent in the benefits of being white in a racially unequal society. However, beneath that overarching context there were evident differences in experiences and perceptions. For some indeed, like the nurses, this status provided access to a life they could only aspire to at home; a fact they seemed to fully appreciate. For others who were born into that lifestyle, it was accepted as the natural order of things. For the outsider who came to the colony on the eve of its independence, when attitudes towards empire and colonization were undergoing fundamental revision, it engendered disquiet and an awareness of the passing of an era.

The Long Decolonization 1931–1960

The position of the British community in Ceylon underwent a fundamental change in 1931 with the granting of responsible self-government. For the civil servants, the change was felt almost immediately. Their privileged official position came increasingly under threat. In 1920, the proportion of Ceylonese to British officers was fixed at one third, rising in 1923 to one half. In 1931, however, recruitment of Europeans to the civil service ceased. It resumed briefly in 1935 but the last British cadets were appointed in 1937. In 1920 the ratio of European to Ceylonese had been 79 to 11. By 1940 it was 49 to 81. British civil servants had to adjust to being under the authority of, and

[79] Randall, 'Serendipity of Three Happy Years', 28, 39, 67, 35.
[80] Clare Midgley, 'Introduction', in Midgley (ed.), *Gender and Imperialism*, 7.

being accountable to, indigenous politicians who now controlled most of the functions of government.[81]

For other official members of the British community the same picture is apparent. The medical services after 1936, for example, were run by a Ceylonese. For British nurses this meant that they increasingly found themselves working under Ceylonese doctors. This inverted the usual racial hierarchy through the imposition of the gender-biased medical hierarchy. In addition, they might find themselves subordinate to a Ceylonese matron and furthermore, their privileged conditions of service *vis-à-vis* their Ceylonese colleagues were increasingly threatened. They lost their higher pay, superior allowances, and their right to separate quarters. By the 1940s the deteriorating conditions really began to bite and there was a flurry of complaints from British nurses to the ONA. In November 1944, for example, Ellen Crow reported the refusal by the Ceylon government of an appeal by the British nurses for more diet allowance, 'while local staff feeding in the same Mess and drawing the same diet allowance were allowed Rs 42 per month cost of living allowance'. Also an 'increased scale of salary has been paid to local staff; a 53% increase on initial salary but none, so far, to us'.[82]

For some losing their privileges was too much. In 1945 Miss Reid complained that she found working with the Ceylonese very difficult: she was 'the only European in the mess, they like different foods, oily hot curries. Had different habits in the bathrooms, strong scented hair.'[83] The last British nurse left Ceylon in early 1949.

Following such changes the 'official' colonists had virtually no role to play once full independence was won in 1948 and they left. For the 'unofficials' there was no such abrupt end to their role. The planters clung onto their economic influence (a Briton, for example, remained head of the Ceylon Chamber of Commerce until 1964), but their privileged lives came increasingly under threat. The nationalization of estates did not materialize immediately. Instead the government embarked on a gradual policy of takeover. Nevertheless, the industry was taxed rigorously to finance development; restraints on the export of capital were imposed; regulations put in place to

---

[81] E. F. C. Ludowyk, *A Modern History of Ceylon* (London, 1966), 180; K. M. De Silva, *A History of Sri Lanka* (London, 1981), 433.

[82] ONA, 140/3, Crow to Secretary, 23 Nov. 1944.

[83] ONA, 129, Notes of a conversation with Reid, nursing sister at the General Hospital Colombo, 13 Sept. 1945.

ensure the employment of Ceylonese management and staff on the estates; and attempts were made to broaden the basis of the tea industry by encouraging smallholdings and establishing state-owned plantations.[84] Only after the assassination of S. W. D. Bandaranaike in 1959 did the prospect of outright nationalization come onto the agenda.

The exodus from Ceylon began in the mid-1950s. Those who were employees of the big planting companies began to leave first. Ironically they were in a better position to do so. If they were young they had the possibility of employment elsewhere or, if older, they had pensions.[85] Proprietary planters, however, were less mobile. Compensation was offered for estates, which were ultimately nationalized in the 1960s, but only for 'a fraction of the real value'. According to Mrs Kitson, the £65,000 they received for their '1,000 acres, two houses and a factory' was a quarter of what it was worth.[86] Moreover, increasingly stringent regulations on the export of capital made it almost impossible for them to take any of their wealth out of the country. It took the Islay family until the early 1980s to get the last of their capital out and the Hawkes family were still in dispute with the Sri Lankan government in 1984 about family money held in Sri Lanka.[87] There is evidence that the planting community felt betrayed by the lack of support they received from the UK. Harry Williams, for example, accused British 'officialdom' and the British public generally of 'indifference', and lacking in 'loyalty and support', and he defended his class. 'Wrong motives' may have driven the pioneer planters, he accepted, 'many mistakes were made, many wrongs committed, much damage done'. However, 'Ceylon is the second largest producer of tea', he argued, and without the colony the 'Cup of Tea', that was 'supposedly a vital part of the English way of life' would be under threat.[88] According to this perception the British in Ceylon did not only reconstruct an outpost of Britishness in a tropical island, they also directly helped to define what it meant to be British in its heartland.

The political and economic changes of the post-independence era resulted in great changes in the social and cultural life of the British community.

[84] Forrest, *Hundred Years of Ceylon Tea*, 238–9.
[85] Kitson, 6 Sept. 1995; Weatherstone, *Pioneers, 1825–1900*, 219.
[86] Kitson, 6 Sept. 1995.
[87] Britons born in Ceylon had to register at the British High Commission after independence if they wanted to remain a British citizen rather than be deemed Ceylonese. Mrs Kitson recounted that she 'registered immediately' to ensure her British citizenship.
[88] Williams, *Pearl of the East*, 193–4.

The mechanisms for ensuring the separateness of the British were, for example, eroded. Most obviously this can be seen in the admission of Sinhalese and Tamils to the clubs. For some this new racial mixing came as something of a pleasant surprise. When Jo Weeks first went out to Ceylon in 1942, there was no social contact with the locals. A meeting with a 'well educated and rich Tamil boy' at a club prompted a radical change of attitude for her as she realized that 'they are people who have ideas and they are interesting to talk to' and she began to 'think this business of not mixing with them very silly'. The increasing employment of Ceylonese at a managerial level on the estates also ensured their integration into the British social scene as they joined the upcountry clubs, 'played tennis, badminton and bridge even'. However, this new interaction between the races was often superficial. Weeks could not 'honestly say that [she] had any friends who were Sinhalese', feeling that this was often also due to the 'lack of confidence' of the Ceylonese because they 'didn't feel that they were socially accepted by the English. It was a barrier', she felt, 'which both sides should have overcome earlier.'[89]

Like Ruth Randall, Jo Weeks was a relative newcomer to the colony and hence was less entrenched in her attitudes. For those who had been born in the colony, or who had been there from the interwar period, these changes was far more difficult to accept. Mirabel Hawkes returned to Ceylon in 1945 to find 'that everything seemed to have altered. The Galle Face Hotel looked shoddy, so many familiar faces were gone' and she and her husband 'rented a horrible little bungalow in Colombo, very suburban'.[90] That symbol of British life, the club, was in decline. Randall thought the Galle club in 1946 'had an air of past and faded glory...The walls had pictures of the Royal family, some faded group photos of cricket teams and "meets"' (gatherings of planters for special events) and 'moth eaten heads of animals'.[91] In one important respect at least there was a significant advantage to the ending of the white-only rule for these clubs. As more and more Britons began to leave it was increasingly difficult to maintain those most vital activities of British cultural life: sport and drinking. Ralph Banks argued that as the 'whole social life revolved around rugby and cricket': no team meant no social life.

[89] Oral History Archive, British Empire and Commonwealth Museum, no. 260, Mrs Jo Weeks, 25 Mar. 1996.
[90] Hawkes, 'Pearls, Palms and Riots', 53–4.
[91] Randall, 'Serendipity of Three Happy Years', 53, 56.

Ceylonese began to make up the numbers (and even in rugby some were 'bloody good', he noted) and they kept the 'bar profits up'.[92]

Conclusion

This survey has only been able to touch upon some aspects of the multi-faceted experience of being British in Ceylon. Over time, across classes and gender there were obvious nuances of variation in that experience but one aspect above all bridged such divisions. Being 'white' and a member of the colonizing race, whatever other identities could be claimed, endowed the colonizer with a sense of racial and cultural superiority. On the one hand, this could translate into an interest in and paternalistic concern for the welfare of the colonized; on the other hand it could result in an arrogant disregard for basic rights and human needs. Some colonists undoubtedly led the purposeless life of parties, games, and socializing, which has become such a cliché in representations of colonial life. Others, however, while enjoying some of these pastimes, did not lead a life of privilege and ease. These included, for example, the women who nursed indigenous patients in the overcrowded and ill-equipped hospitals of the island. Whatever judgements can be made about the planting industry as a whole, many Britons employed on the estates worked long hours, in difficult conditions. Administrators could also find themselves, as young men, assuming enormous responsibilities with very little training or support. As has been seen, these experiences induced some to question the whole basis of their enterprise and the claims which underpinned it.

Nevertheless, what is indisputable is that in their entirety Britons in Ceylon tried to reproduce what they at least considered to be the defining characteristics of their culture. To succeed it was necessary to establish a group identity centred around such things as manners, clothes, food, and leisure activities, plus separation from the local population. In the manner of immigrant groups then and now what they were preserving in Ceylon, to borrow Benedict Anderson's phrase, was indeed an 'imagined community' but one which derived from a particular time. It was based on a nostalgic and moreover a static understanding of their homeland. Frederick Lewis provides an example of this reimagining. He was what was disparagingly termed in colonial circles as 'country-bottled'. The relative poverty of his

---

[92] Oral History Archive, British Empire and Commonwealth Museum, no. 413, Ralph Banks.

parents had meant that he had not been educated in the UK.[93] Yet as he passionately explained, 'all my life I had looked on England as my home', and the thought of being 'only English by profession' had been 'a life-long agony'. The knowledge he had of the 'land of my forefathers, the land of my countrymen; the land from which came all that made the Empire', was gained solely from books until he visited the UK in 1893.

His account of this trip is littered with disappointments and disillusion. The whole country, with its contrasts of wealth, misery, and poverty, shocked him. The man with 'sunken cheeks' and 'death-like eyes' who was selling matches, pipe cleaners, and boot laces presented to him a more 'wretched' sight than any 'sick cooly in Ceylon'. Likewise, he considered that the children in the slums were in a far worse position than the children on the tea estates. He makes constant reference to the general ignorance and poor education of all classes of people that he met. He was bemused by the manifestations of working-class culture he encountered: the music hall, football matches, and by the ever-present class discord on all sides. In short, the reality of the 'England' he experienced was nothing like the country he had 'imagined'. The one aspect, which did match up to his ideal, was the royal family. A visit to Sandringham with its atmosphere of 'quiet dignity and perfect taste' and a chance but silent encounter there with the Princess of Wales left him thoroughly imbued with an intense sense of loyalty to the Crown.[94] His disappointment is echoed in the experiences of many ex-colonials on their retirement to the UK. The England which had been preserved in their minds and which was such a focus for their identity no longer existed. As Ralph Banks mused, 'England is not my home. I don't know where it is. I am a citizen of the world.'[95]

What remains of the 150 years of British presence in Sri Lanka in the early twenty-first century? English continued to be the official language until 1961 when it was replaced by Sinhalese. An English-speaking education nevertheless has once more become an objective of the elites, receiving new impetus in latter years as part of a resurging globalization of skills based on the English language. Parliamentary democracy has survived, despite

---

[93] Nor had he been sent to school in Ceylon; his parents considered that option 'undesirable'. Lewis, *Sixty Four Years in Ceylon*, 32, 20. See Buettner, *Empire Families*, 74, for the importance of an English education for the children of the Raj.

[94] Lewis, *Sixty Four Years in Ceylon*, 260–303, 248, 262, 274, 287.

[95] Oral History Archive, British Empire and Commonwealth Museum, no. 413, Ralph Banks.

twenty-five years of a terrible civil conflict. By the 1940s there was an 'embryo welfare state' in existence, the major component of which was a system of free health care for the whole population.[96] Lastly of course, and appropriately given the significance of sport to British colonial life, Sri Lankans play cricket on every bit of level ground. Consequently in common with their fellow ex-colonized nations, they can and frequently do emerge victorious from their cricketing encounters with their old imperial masters, at least some small revenge.

Select Bibliography

ASOKA BANDARAGE, *Colonialism in Sri Lanka: The Political Economy of the Kandyan Highlands, 1833–1886* (Berlin, 1983).

R. BRAIBANTI (ed.), *Asian Bureaucratic Systems Emergent from the British Imperial Tradition* (Durham, NC, 1966).

HELEN CALLAWAY, *Gender, Culture and Empire: European Women in Colonial Nigeria* (London, 1987).

CHANDRA DE SILVA, *Sri Lanka: A History* (New Delhi, 1994).

H. A. J. HULUGALLE, *British Governors of Ceylon* (Colombo, 2002).

KUMARI JAYAWARDENA, *Nobodies to Somebodies: The Rise of the Colonial Bourgeoisie in Sri Lanka* (London, 2000).

CHARLES JEFFRIES, *Ceylon: The Path to Independence* (London, 1962).

MARGARET JONES, *Health Policy in Britain's Model Colony: Ceylon 1900–1948* (New Delhi, 2004).

—— 'Heroines of Lonely Outposts or Tools of the Empire? British Nurses in Britain's Model Colony: Ceylon, 1878–1948', *Nursing Inquiry*, 11/3 (2004), 149–60.

FREDERICK LEWIS, *Sixty Four Years in Ceylon: Reminiscences of Life and Adventure* (New Delhi, 1993).

CLARE MIDGLEY (ed.), *Gender and Imperialism* (Manchester, 1998).

C. ONDAATJE, *Woolf in Ceylon: An Imperial Journey in the Shadow of Leonard Woolf, 1904–1911* (Toronto, 2005).

MARY A. PROCIDA, *Married to the Raj: Gender, Politics and Imperialism in India* (Manchester, 2002).

LEONARD WOOLF, *Growing: An Autobiography of the Years 1904–1911* (London, 1964).

[96] K. M. De Silva, 'Introduction', in K. M. De Silva (ed.), *Sri Lanka*, part 1. *The Second World War and the Soulbury Commission, 1939–45: British Documents on the End of Empire* (London, 1997), p. xxxii; for an account of this healthcare system see Margaret Jones, *Health Policy in Britain's Model Colony: Ceylon 1900–1948* (New Delhi, 2004).

9

The British 'Malayans'

Tim Harper

In 1954 a retired civil servant, Victor Purcell, reviewed the British experience in Malaya. 'All golden ages are legendary', he wrote, 'and some are entirely mythical, but Malaya's "golden age" of between the wars has a firm foundation in fact.'[1] Purcell was writing at the height of the Communist Emergency (1948–60), and he had become an astringent critic of Britain's legacy to the soon-to-be-independent state. But his own memoirs are shot through with nostalgia for a lost world, a mourning for that which colonialism had itself changed or destroyed. This nostalgia was embedded in imperial mentalities everywhere.[2] But it seems particularly acute in the case in Malaya, and foundational to the British community's sense of its identity. From the late nineteenth century, the literature of empire fashioned a luminous Malaya of the imagination. It was most vividly captured in the writings of outsiders: of the Ukrainian-born Joseph Conrad, the French rubber planters Henri Fauconnier and Pierre Boulle, and latterly, more acerbically, by the Mancunian-Irish Anthony Burgess, and Han Suyin, who was of Flemish-Chinese descent. From the 1920s, the colony was a principal staging post on the new imperial grand tour. Celebrity visitors mocked the pretensions of colonial society. 'After meeting your best people', Noel Coward announced at Singapore's prestigious Tanglin Club, 'now I know why there is such a shortage of servants in London.'[3] The writer who did most to fix Malaya on the world map was Somerset Maugham. He spent only six months in Southeast Asia in 1921 (of which three were spent in a sanatorium in Java), and another four months in 1925. But, as Victor Purcell reported, his 'passage was marked by a trail of angry people'. In 1938, the *Straits Times*

---

[1] Victor Purcell, *Malaya: Communist or Free?* (Stanford, Calif., 1954), 11.

[2] Renato Rosaldo, 'Imperialist Nostalgia', *Representations*, 26 (1989), 107–22.

[3] Quoted in John Bastin (ed.), *Travellers' Singapore: An Anthology* (Singapore, 1994), 241.

was still complaining that his stories drew out 'the worst and least representative aspects of the European life in Malaya—murder, cowardice, drink,
seduction, adultery...always the same cynical emphasising of the same
unpleasant things. No wonder that white men and women who are living
normal lives in Malaya wish that Mr Maugham would look for local colour
elsewhere.'[4]

But long-term residents had only themselves to blame. While they protested their 'normality' they also displayed a distinct capacity for self-
mythology and, to outsiders, self-regard. At the height of the idyll, in
1928, the man charged with recruiting Britons to the higher cadre of colonial
service, Sir Ralph Furse, accompanied his colonial secretary to the colony.
To its residents, he observed, Malaya was 'the navel of the universe'. But their
complacency, Furse believed, belied a degree of insecurity: in the greater
scheme of empire, it was widely agreed that a career in Malaya ranked lower
than one in India, or even the Sudan, and this was a sore point with officials
in Malaya.[5] But, by this time, life for Britons in the colony was compensated
with a personal luxury and outward tranquillity that was to be enjoyed in
few other postings. Residents embellished the myth of Malaya in their own
profuse writings: local legends and imagery were constantly recycled, so that
their private recollections—of elephant rides, eccentrics, and excess—all
percolated through what they had read about themselves, until, as one old
hand described his first arrival in Singapore in 1902, life became a 'chapter
by Walpole inserted in a novel by Conrad'.[6]

This mythology is very important to understanding the collective experience of the British community in Malaya, for it came to crystallize around
the nemesis of the community in 1942. The military and civil collapse of
British Malaya in the face of Japanese invasion was broadcast to the world as
the folly of Blimpish officials and 'whisky-swilling planters', who had 'no
roots in the life of the country'. This image, originating in the despatches
of The Times's correspondent, Ian Morrison, became seared into British

---

[4] Victor Purcell, *Memoirs of a Malayan Official* (London, 1965), 271; Ted Morgan, *Somerset Maugham* (London, 1982), 257.

[5] A. J. Stockwell, 'The White Man's Burden and Brown Humanity: Colonialism and Ethnicity in British Malaya', *Southeast Asian Journal of Social Science*, 10/1 (1982), 51; Ralph Furse, *Aucuparius: Recollections of a Recruiting Officer* (London, 1962), 206–8.

[6] Richard Winstedt, *Start from Alif: Count from One. An Autobiographical Mémoire* (Kuala Lumpur, 1969), 35.

memories of the surrender of Singapore on 15 February 1942. This was bitterly resented by residents of Malaya, who pleaded that it did not reflect their reality or their commitment to the country, not least the sacrifices of those who had fought courageously as volunteer soldiers and who experienced three and half years of internment by the Japanese. This too, was a rather unique facet of the British experience in Malaya: rarely in modern history has an entire ruling class been incarcerated for so long. Rarer still has it emerged to continue to lead where it left off. Recollected through the horrors of war, the 'golden age' seemed ever-more dreamlike. But both inside and outside internment, during and beyond the war years, in words and deeds, the community strove to repair its reputation. This led to an attempt to refashion the British presence in Malaya after 1945, on a scale few colonial communities attempted elsewhere. It carried with it a claim to speak for Malaya, and even to dictate the content of a 'Malayan' nationalism. In many ways, this project of rehabilitation continues in the work of memory.

Yet it is far from clear who the British 'Malayans' actually were. 'Malaya' itself was a vague geographical expression. The origins of the British community lay in a much wider diaspora of traders and adventurers, the 'abundance of rogues' who, from the early eighteenth century, fanned out from British India along the seaboard of Sumatra (the 'West-coasters') and eastwards to Banten, Batavia, and beyond. In the nineteenth and twentieth centuries, British family networks continued to stretch across the western archipelago, to Sarawak, North Borneo, Bangkok, and the China coast.[7] This chapter focuses on 'British Malaya' as Sir Frank Swettenham defined it by the end of the nineteenth century: the Straits Settlements of Penang, Malacca, and Singapore, and the Malay States of the peninsula, where by the 1900s there were families who had seen three or four generations of service. They tended to stand apart from more recent arrivals, and on such distinctions the public debates of the community increasingly centred. But throughout the colonial period, careers continued to made on a much wider canvas and some of the most important contributions to the making

[7] For this prehistory see Carris Jones, 'The Tensions of Imperial Rule on the Periphery: The East India Company's Settlements in West Sumatra 1700–1780', M.Phil. thesis (Cambridge, 2004); Jeya Kathirithamby-Wells, *The British West Sumatran Presidency, 1760–1785: Problems of Early Colonial Enterprise* (Kuala Lumpur, 1977); D. K. Bassett, 'British "Country" Trade and Local Trade Networks in the Thai and Malay States, c. 1680–1770', *Modern Asian Studies*, 23/1 (1989), 625–43.

of the community came from those whose sojourns in the region were relatively brief.

In terms of self-definition it is hard to tell where the 'European' population ended and the 'British' population began. The presence of large numbers of people from other imperial nations encouraged 'colonial society' to refer to itself habitually as 'European' rather than 'British'. For example, by 1901, a German 'invasion' of Singapore had created a wealthy community of 236 people; its flagship enterprise, Behn, Meyer & Company, was one of the largest shipping firms in the region. In times of imperial crisis, a more exclusive 'Britishness' asserted itself. In 1914, German assets were seized and many German nationals interned.[8] But by 1931, the census counted a total of 17,708 'Europeans' in Malaya, of which only 10,523 were English; 2,464 Scottish, 901 Irish, 194 Welsh, 793 Australian, 168 New Zealanders, 38 Canadians, and 235 'Other British'. That is, 80 per cent from the home islands (a disproportionate 17 per cent of them Scots); 7 per cent from the dominions or elsewhere in the British empire, and 13 per cent from other nations, the largest contingent of these (825) being the Dutch.[9] At its pre-war height, in 1941, the 'European' population of Malaya was around 31,000; but after 1939, and again after 1945 the picture is further complicated by the large inflow of military personnel. More Britons were perhaps living and working in Malaya and Singapore after their independence in 1957 and 1963, than at any time under colonial rule. These late imperial settlers were rarely in the country long enough to put down deep roots. Yet the experience marked them deeply. In the afterlife of the community, the memory of national servicemen and service children has become very important, although few service families had intimate dealings with longer term expatriate residents, and still less with Asians.

This chapter examines the several lives of the British 'Malayans'. Recent studies of Britons overseas have highlighted the diversity of experience and identities that emerged in the empire. They trace the interactions between Britons at home and abroad, and the ways each supported and shaped the other. They now see the empire as a system of transnational networks that

---

[8] Sharon Siddique, 'Early German Commercial Relations to Singapore: Behn-Meyer and Co., Singapore-Arnold Otto Meyer, Hamburg', in *Southeast Asia and the Germans* (Augsburg, 1977), 166–81.

[9] C. A. Vlieland, *British Malaya: A Report on the 1931 Census and on Certain Problems of Vital Statistics* (London, 1932), 165–6.

sometimes bypassed 'home' altogether.[10] This has been a fruitful way of re-examining Britain's imperial experience. But this focus on the lives of 'Britons', and on the category of the expatriate, can sit uneasily with the broader histories of the regions in which they sojourned. It often obscures, excludes, or relegates to the margins other communities, not least a creole experience in which the British, whoever they were, were intimately implicated. It can miss much of the ambivalence in the idea of 'Britishness' within colonial society.[11] In Malaya, it is important to remember at every turn that the 'British' were part of a cosmopolitan and kaleidoscopic world, in which many other people claimed—by affinity, identity, or citizenship—'Britishness'.[12] This was why, as British rule came under more pressure, those who managed colonial society became so obsessed with who was 'inside' and 'outside' the community. Malaya was at once one of the most plural, yet one of the most insidiously hierarchical of British colonial societies. For all its vivid life, 'British Malaya' was a strangely elusive and ephemeral affair, and now few traces of the imperial community remain. And, once again, it is perhaps in fashioning its own memory that the idea of the 'Malayan' community comes more clearly, if fleetingly, into view.

The Making of 'British Malaya'

The self-perception of the British in Malaya rested on a simple foundation myth: that Britons had pioneered the settlement and development of the Malay peninsula. A commemorative history of the centennial of the founding of Singapore in 1819 was inscribed to 'the race of trader-statesmen and the clan of trade-fighters' who 'built' the colony.[13] Many of the central themes of Victorian and Edwardian empire were expressed in this idea, and given a distinctive local meaning. There was the liberal fantasy of free

---

[10] For a review, see Catharine Hall and Sonya Rose, 'Introduction: Being at Home with the Empire', in Hall and Rose (eds.), *At Home with the Empire: Metropolitan Culture and the Imperial World* (Cambridge, 2006), 1–31.

[11] Ann Laura Stoler and Karen Strassler, 'Castings for the Colonial: Memory Work in "New Order" Java', *Comparative Studies in Society and History*, 42/1 (2000), 4–48.

[12] This point has been well made by Lynn Hollen Lees, 'Being British in Malaya, 1890–1940', *Journal of British Studies*, 48/1 (2009), 76–101.

[13] From the Dedication, by 'J. A. N.' to Walter Makepeace, Gilbert E. Brooke and Roland St J. Braddell, *One Hundred Years of Singapore: Being Some Account of the Capital of the Straits Settlements from its Foundation by Sir Stamford Raffles on the 6th February 1819 to the 6th February 1919*, i (Singapore, 1991 [1921]).

trade and enterprise, in which, in the words of the founder of Singapore, Thomas Stamford Raffles, 'while with one hand we carry to their shores the capital of our merchants, the other should be stretched forth to offer them the means of intellectual improvement'.[14] This was tempered from the outset by the conviction that Enlightened rule and commercial security necessitated strong, even authoritarian government. By the later nineteenth century, there was a growing insistence on the prerogatives of science and race. The mines and plantations of Malaya became a showcase for Britons' conviction that an advanced civilization measured by its technological advantage had a right and a duty to develop the tropical world.[15] The conquest of nature also embodied the biological determinism of popular racial theory; writings of planters emphasized the Anglo-Saxon's physical mastery of the 'subtle magic of the hot sunshine'.[16] Malaya's intricate systems for the management of migrant workers pursued the imperial ideal of an efficient global and racial division of labour. Victorian notions of liberalism, race, and science combined in varying proportions to constitute colonial Malaya's civil religion. For British residents, they were self-evident truths, never a systematic philosophy. However, from time to time, from Raffles's own writings to the work of bodies such as the Straits Philosophical Society (1893–1915)—an unusual colloquium of officials, missionaries, scientists, and Chinese educators—we see attempts to articulate one.[17] The liberal ideal resurfaces in many later histories of Britons in Malaya, and traces of it can be found in the narratives of modernity of the post-colonial state.[18]

---

[14] Minute by Sir T. S. Raffles on the establishment of a Malay College at Singapore (n.pl., 1819), 3.

[15] For this see Michael Adas, Machines as the Measure of Men: Science, Technology and Ideologies of Western Dominance (Ithaca, NY, 1989).

[16] e.g. C. Ward-Jackson, Rubber Planting: A Book for the Prospective Estate Assistant in British Malaya (Kuala Lumpur, 1920) and E. M. Collingham, Imperial Bodies: The Physical Experience of the Raj, c. 1800–1947 (Oxford, 2001).

[17] For the Straits philosophes see T. N. Harper, 'Globalism and the Pursuit of Authenticity: The Making of a Diasporic Public Sphere in Singapore', Sojourn: Journal of Social Issues in Southeast Asia, 12/2 (1997), 261–92.

[18] For the former, Pat Barr, Taming the Jungle: The Men Who Made Malaya (London, 1977); Margaret Shennan, Out in the Midday Sun: The British in Malaya, 1880–1960 (London, 2000). For a critical discussion of the latter, see C. J. Wee Wan-Ling, 'Mediating "Progress": The National Narrative of Economic Development and Liberalism in Singapore', Communal/Plural: Journal of Transnational and Cross-Cultural Studies, 9/2 (2001), 223–42.

This pioneer status was an expatriate delusion. Malaya in the nineteenth century was one of the most contested frontiers of the earth, which the British—although they might possess primacy in trade and arms—never succeeded in dominating entirely. Throughout the brief seventy or so years of British rule, colonial enterprise in Malaya had to contend with waves of Asian entrepreneurs: Chinese miners and merchants, South Asian financiers, Arab and Jewish traders. The man who created 'British Malaya'—in print at least—Sir Frank Swettenham, admitted that it was 'due to the enterprise and labour of the Chinese' that the peninsula was opened up to mining and plantation agriculture.[19] In their settlements, the British enjoined family formation on the Chinese long before they attempted it on any scale themselves.[20] The first great works of the Straits Settlements were undertaken by slaves and convicts: Singapore was the 'Botany Bay of India'.[21] The epidemiological burden of the opening of Malaya's forest interior was also borne by Asians; Indian plantation labour in particular experienced some of the highest mortality rates anywhere in the late nineteenth- and early twentieth-century empire, for which, fifty years after independence, Malaysian Indian activists sought £2 trillion compensation from the British government.[22] It is against this background that the claims of 'the men who made Malaya' must be read.

The founding myth also glossed over the division and disunity among the early British residents in the Malay world. At the forefront in the eighteenth century were freewheeling 'country' traders operating out of Calcutta and Madras. The first permanent settlement, George Town, on Penang island, was ceded by the Sultan of Kedah to the private trader, Francis Light, in 1786. A more formal East India Company administration was slow to wrest control of property, the marketplaces, and official positions from the prin-

---

[19] Frank Swettenham, *British Malaya* (London, 1948), 351. See also Carl A. Trocki, *Opium and Empire: Chinese Society in Colonial Singapore, 1800–1910* (Ithaca, NY, 1990); Rajeswary Ampalavanar Brown, *Capital and Entrepreneurship in South-East Asia* (London, 1994).

[20] C. M. Turnbull, *The Straits Settlements, 1826–67: Indian Presidency to Crown Colony* (London, 1971), 52–3. This classic study is a mine of social data.

[21] Clare Anderson, '"The Ferringees are Flying—the Ship is Ours!": The Convict Middle Passage in Colonial South and Southeast Asia, 1790–1860', *Indian Economic and Social History Review*, 41/3 (2005), 143–86; Anand A. Yang, 'Indian Convict Workers in Southeast Asia in the Late Eighteenth and Early Nineteenth Centuries', *Journal of World History*, 2/2 (2003), 179–208.

[22] Ralph Shlomowitz and Lance Brennan, 'Mortality and Indian Labour in Malaya, 1877–1933', *Indian Social and Economic History Review*, 29/1 (1992), 57–75; 'Malaysian Police Break up Rally', 25 Nov. 2007, URL: <http://news.bbc.co.uk/2/hi/asia-pacific/7111646.stm>.

cipal merchants and to impose taxes on them. Until 1867, the British
settlements were governed from Calcutta, but in 1864 they were connected
by only one steamer a month. The British were always a small minority in
their own settlements. The 400 Europeans recorded in George Town in 1822
were only 2.9 per cent of a total population of 13,781. Despite the much-
vaunted rule of law and commercial probity of the British settlements, they
were volatile, often violent places. The early history of Penang is dominated
by the struggle to control disease and the scourge of fire which nearly
destroyed George Town in 1798, 1812, and 1814. In these years, the average
life expectancy of Europeans was around 28 and a half years.[23] Grief for lost
infants is a prominent theme of early colonial memoir. Isolation shaped the
British community in crucial ways. The first settlers formed attachments
with local women: Light's own wife was an Indo-Portuguese from Siam, but
she and others like her, from a variety of Asian backgrounds, were part of
the 'European community'. These women exercised considerable influence
through the home; and family life—as evinced in patterns of child care, for
instance—was culturally hybrid.[24] But by George Town's second decade, a
perceived need for cohesion within the European community led to a drive
for 'respectability' and hierarchy. In Penang, 'Rules of Precedence' were
promulgated in 1814 'in order to prevent disputes'. They set 'the principal
people' above the motley: the 'printers, tavern-keepers, fiddlers, hair-dressers,
coach-makers, watchmakers, coopers and shipwrights'. Colonial society
became steadily divided into what one visitor to the region in the 1830s
termed the 'mechanical and the aristocratical party', and this kind of social
distinction endured.[25] There was growing intermarriage among the elite of
the settlements, and long-term attachments outside the British community
became less public. Thomas Stamford Raffles brought two sisters with him
to Penang who were soon married off, and he himself found a wife there.
While the food habits of Europeans remained Asianized during the nineteenth century, patterns of sociability—banquets, concert parties, and excursions—tended to follow metropolitan norms and residential patterns

---

[23] The best study is Nordin Hussin, *Trade and Society in the Straits of Melaka: Dutch Melaka and English Penang, 1780–1830* (Singapore, 2007). The population is discussed on pp. 184–92. See also E. G. Cullin and W. F. Zehnder, *The Early History of Penang, 1592–1827* (Penang, 1905), 32.

[24] Christine Doran, '"Oddly Hybrid": Childbearing and Childrearing Practices in Colonial Penang, 1850–1875', *Women's History Review*, 6/1 (1992), 29–46.

[25] George Bennet, in *Wanderings in New South Wales, Batavia, Pedir Coast, Singapore, and China* (London, 1834), excerpted in Bastin (ed.), *Travellers' Singapore*, 35.

became more segregated. The founding of Singapore in 1819, and the acquisition of the old Dutch settlement of Malacca, boosted the British presence in the region; by this time, there were around twenty European arrivals and departures a month and the East India Company's family networks stretched across the Indian Ocean to Sumatra, South China, and Australia.

In the course of the nineteenth century two patterns of expatriate life emerged in Malaya, each with its own ethos. The establishment of the Straits Settlements in 1826 created a colonial urban tradition which over time became increasingly centred on Singapore. The oldest British possession, Penang, remained a vibrant port town, but its strategic and commercial status receded. Malacca, which in its early sixteenth-century heyday had been one of the largest cities in the world, declined to become 'the Brighton of the Chinese', and many of its Straits Chinese families resettled in Singapore, whose population grew dramatically: between 1824 and 1860 from 10,683 to 80,792. In the same period, Singapore's European contingent rose from 74 to 466 people, and new kinds of settler arrived, not least an influx of missionaries after the lifting of many of the East India Company's restrictions on their activities. The London Missionary Society, the Church Missionary Society, the American Baptist Board, and American Board of Missionaries, in their patronage of education and public works, shaped society in ways that went far beyond proselytization.[26] A more purposeful colonial government attempted to discipline urban space on the model of the military cantonment. Town-planning gave Singapore's European quarters a spacious Regency character. On the waterfront 'Mayfair of Singapore', the Irish architect G. D. Coleman deployed a distinctive tropicalized Anglo-Indian style in the construction of the principal public edifices, such as the first St Andrew's and Armenian churches (1836), and the court house (1839). The elegant verandas of European bungalows also borrowed from Malay domestic architecture. For the colonial elite, the good life was to be found on a small wooded estate in the vicinity of the town, especially in the plantation villas of the exclusive Tanglin area. By 1862, there were seventy plantations within a two-to-three mile radius of the central public space, the Padang.

---

[26] Turnbull, *The Straits Settlements*, 22. For a fresh interpretation of this, Su-Lyn Seah, 'Vicars, Tarts and Old Farts? New Ways at Looking at the Colonial Anglican Church in Singapore', in Derek Heng Thiam Soon (ed.), *New Perspectives and Sources on the History of Singapore: A Multi-Disciplinary Approach* (Singapore, 2006), 87–99.

This residential style was also adopted by the wealthier Asians, and from the mid-century vacant intervening plots and smaller lots on hilltop sites were filled. This second wave of settlement created new enclaves of European settlement in the countryside in ever-diminishing circles of prestige; 'messes' for single men in places such as Balestier Road could overlap with Asian residential areas. Everywhere, the house names—Glyndhurst, Malvern, and Mapledurham—conjured up images of home.[27] The British experience in Singapore was a succession of increasingly elaborate suburban fantasies.

An intensely cultivated sociability brought the British community into closer definition. By 1865, John Cameron, in his famous survey of the colony, noted 'the very formidable barrier which confines "society" in its usual acceptation to a rather limited section'.[28] As elsewhere in the empire, the key institution was the 'club'. The first, the Teutonia, was founded by the German community in Singapore in 1856, and the British followed with the Tanglin Club in 1865. By the end of the century, few British communities of any consequence in Malaya lacked their own clubhouse. Loneliness, transience, and high mortality encouraged a culture of conspicuous consumption and lavish civic display which endured until the interwar slump and, notoriously, revived on the eve of the fall of Singapore. As Bruce Lockhart remarked of his days as a junior estate manager: 'the hospitality of the Malaya of those golden, prosperous days of 1908 was for a youngster almost overwhelming, and few there were that survived it unscathed'.[29] The social web was at its most elaborate in Singapore. At its centre was sport: a Billiard Club was founded as early as 1829, then a Cricket Club, a Swimming Club, a Yacht Club, a Fives Club, and a growing number of golf clubs. This signalled the growing prominence of Scots in trade and plantations, institutionalized in a St Andrew's Club (1908), with its 'Pipers of Malaya'. There was also a debating society, a general fetish for amateur dramatics, and a rich tradition of philanthropic activity. One of the most ubiquitous institutions was the Masonic lodge. The first was founded in Penang in 1819, and Masonic rituals

[27] For this see Norman Edwards, *The Singapore House and Residential Life, 1819–1939* (Singapore, 1990).

[28] John Cameron, *Our Tropical Possessions in Malayan India: Being a Descriptive Account of Singapore, Penang, Province Wellesley, and Malacca: Their Peoples, Products, Commerce, and Government* (London, 1865), 285.

[29] R. H. Bruce Lockhart, *Memoirs of a British Agent: Being an Account of the Author's Early Life in Many Lands and of his Official Mission to Moscow in 1918* (London, 1932), 9.

accompanied many key civic events, such as the completion of the Horse-
burgh and Raffles Lighthouses in the 1850s. Between 1888 and 1922 ten
lodges were founded in peninsular towns and a further two in Singapore.
Secret societies ingrained a sense of electness amongst empire-builders.
Public sociability buttressed the mystique and prestige of Europeans in
the eyes of others. It found expression in a small but vigorous colonial
public sphere. Campaigning newspapers such as the *Straits Times* and
Singapore Free Press could on occasion hold the imperial executive to
account; especially on issues regarding the sanctity of the person and of
property. They led a long campaign to free the Straits Settlements from the
control of British India, and to defend civic institutions such the Grand
Jury, which survived in the Straits Settlements long after it had died out in
England. Faith in sociability as a road to stability, order, and progress
underpinned the nascent settler identity. In debates on the future of municipal administration in 1873, it was argued that leisure was the indispensable
qualification for public service. This was the principal argument for debar-
ring otherwise qualified Asians. As settler identity asserted itself, so too did
its exclusivity.[30]

But this is not the complete picture. Not all Europeans lived their lives
solely within the confines of the expatriate community. Some of the most
prestigious colonial institutions were inclusive of others in a partial way. In
a crucial sense, the overarching edifice of colonial rule needed the limited
participation and acculturation of Asians to appear 'imperial' in a universal
and progressive sense. This was another way of affirming the overarching
privilege of imperial belonging. Even redoubts such as the Masonic lodges
showed a capacity to involve Asians. Lodge Singapore was the only lodge in
the empire known to have all of the eight holy books that were available to
Freemasons for swearing oaths. The powerful Sultan of Johore established
his own Lodge Johore Royal in 1922, and its charter juxtaposed Quranic and
Masonic injunctions.[31] There was a sphere of sociability, a middle ground,
between the colonial elite and wider Malayan society. Britons and Malayans
met socially in other forums, whether Christian, philanthropic, and or other
secular bodies like Rotary, which was adopted early on in Malaya as a

[30] This paragraph and the next are based principally on Harper, 'Globalism and the Pursuit
of Authenticity', 261–92.
[31] A. J. S. T. [A. J. Shelley-Thompson], *Bye-Laws and History of the Lodge Johore Royal
No. 3946 E.C.* (Johore Bahru, 1922).

conscious attempt to build links across 'the colour line'; by 1939 there were
eight Rotary branches.[32] Wealthy Asians created parallel clubs and societies,
and these carried with them similar claims of imperial citizenship and even
of 'Britishness'.[33] Up until the early 1920s the wealthiest communities in
Singapore in terms of property ownership were the Jewish and Arab merchant families. The influence of Singapore's mostly Sephardic Jews—a
population of around 1,500 by the Second World War—was extensive, but
their precise status within the colonial hierarchy was ambiguous. The
Hadrami Arabs drew additional prestige from their role as honorary consuls
for the Ottoman empire, and the most colourful of the Chinese merchants
of early Singapore, Hoo Ah Kay—known as Whampoa after his town of
origin in China—acted as deputy consul for Tsar Alexander III of Russia.[34]
The colonial 'core' of society was perforated by the wealth, influence, and
ambivalent position of many other communities.

Away from the larger port towns, a rather different tradition of expatriate
life evolved. There was, of course, much interconnectedness between the
Straits Settlements and the Malay States. But for the 'outstation', the central
reference points lay—in the title of Sir Hugh Clifford's classic stories—'In
court and kampong'. British rule and legitimacy rested on treaties with the
Malay sultans, and a complex patchwork of indirect rule evolved between
1874 and 1914 in the shape of the Federated and Unfederated Malay States.
The workings of power were underpinned by the governing fiction of an
Anglo-Malay special relationship. Again, this can be traced back to the
writings of Raffles, who saw the founding of Singapore as the revival of a
lost golden age of Malay civilization.[35] This idea was elaborated by a long
line of scholar-administrators within the Malayan Civil Service. Senior
officials such as Hugh Clifford and Sir Frank Swettenham wove tales of
Malay life and defended 'the Real Malay' against the encroachments of
modernity. This had a political intent: the logic of 'protection' was that
the Malays could not survive by themselves. But this was not solely an
ornamental conceit to bind the Malay rulers to British patronage.[36] Many

---

[32] *Service Above Self: 30 Years of the Rotary Club of Petaling Jaya* (Petaling Jaya, 1992), 10.

[33] Su Lin Lewis, 'Echoes of Cosmopolitanism: Colonial Penang's "Indigenous" English Press'
in Chandrika Kaul (ed.), *Media and the Empire* (Basingstoke, 2006), 233–49.

[34] Turnbull, *Straits Settlements*, 34.

[35] Christina Granroth, 'European Knowledge of South East Asia: Travel and Scholarship in
the Early Modern Era', Ph.D. thesis (Cambridge, 2003), ch. 5.

[36] *Pace* David Cannadine, *Ornamentalism: How the British Saw their Empire* (London, 2001).

British officials found many of their own values reflected in what they saw as the leisured, aristocratic culture of the Malays, and allowed themselves to be enmeshed in the world of the Malay courts. The relationship was encapsulated in Kuala Kangsar in 1894, when the district magistrate was observed playing the Tengku Temenggong at chess with Malay retainers as chessmen.[37] The British invested a great deal in 'knowing' Malay language and customs; in so doing, they fixed Malay tradition and found it wanting. It was said of Sir Richard Winstedt that 'God gave the Malays a language; Winstedt gave them a grammar.'[38] He built a picture of himself fighting the loneliness of outstation life by collecting lore from Malay informants in the evening and turning the veranda of his bungalow into a 'Malay Athenaeum'.[39] The journals and monographs of the Malaysian Branch of the Royal Asiatic Society are a monument to the scale of his and others' achievement. The canon of colonial knowledge endured for several generations, and some of its assumptions continued to underpin Malay social criticism into the post-colonial era. But to later Malay scholars, such as the poet and critic, Mohammad Haji Salleh, scholarship in the colonies was 'a free-for-all-affair', amateur and arbitrary, and it distorted Malay culture.[40] Above all, it did not reflect the new reality of peninsular society. As late as 1914, there were only eight British officials trained in the languages of the Chinese, who by 1921 accounted for 30 per cent of the population of the Malay States. But, nevertheless, the 'Royal Road' of the scholar-administrators was central to the self-image of the British in Malaya.[41]

By the 1910s, the frontier began to close. Improved communications brought isolated communities closer together. The rapid growth of the rubber industry created a substantial plantocracy. The long gaps between home leave, and the ability of civil servants to refuse other postings, encouraged family formation.[42] Outside the main towns of the Federated

[37] William R. Roff, 'Colonial Pursuits', *Journal of the Historical Society of the University of Malaya*, 6 (1967/8), 52.
[38] C. Blake to Robert Heussler, 5 Sept. 1979, Heussler Papers, Rhodes House Oxford.
[39] Winstedt, *Start from Alif*, p. ix.
[40] Muhammad Haji Salleh, *Romance and Laughter in the Archipelago: Essays on Classical and Contemporary Poetics of the Malay World* (Pulau Penang, 2006), 248. See also A. B. Shamsul, 'A History of an Identity, an Identity of a History: The Idea and Practice of "Malayness" in Malaysia Reconsidered', *Journal of Southeast Asian Studies*, 32/3 (2001), 355–66. For later echoes, Syed Hussein Alatas, *The Myth of the Lazy Native* (London, 1977), 147–81.
[41] Purcell, *Memoirs of a Malayan Official*, 97.
[42] Stockwell, 'White Man's Burden', 50–3.

Malay States, the ratio of European women to men rose from 17 women per
100 men in 1911 to 38 in 1921. Sexuality was a barometer of change. In his
memoirs, Victor Purcell stated publicly what most privately knew, that it
was 'common practice' for European men to keep Asian mistresses.[43] The
intimate history of the British in Malaya has yet to be fully written, and the
scale of the liaisons across European and Asian communities remains
unclear. The practice was never so institutionalized as in the 'temporary
wives' of the Dutch in the neighbouring East Indies. But it appears—from
memoirs and oral testimonies—to have been ubiquitous. Some relationships were highly predatory; estate managers might take a mistress from a
neighbouring estate or village, if not, following the unwritten code, from
their own workforce. Other liaisons—perhaps more often than has been
credited in existing studies—ended in marriage. But from around 1910, it is
clear that these relationships became less open, if only very slowly less
common. In 1909, the secretary of state for the colonies, Lord Crewe, issued
his famous 'concubinage circular' that officially condemned the practice. It
was not issued in the Federated Malay States, but it was certainly an issue in
the Straits Settlements.[44] Crewe acted less on grounds of morality than on
those of prestige. The circular was part of a wider drive for a more efficient
and caste-bound administration across the empire, in which the Malayan
Civil Service was captured by a 'Public School Oxbridge Class' recruited in
London by examination. The bureaucracy grew at a striking rate after the
creation of the Federated Malay States in 1896. By 1915, 257 new men had
arrived; by contrast, the larger Ceylonese civil service grew by only 123 men
between 1885 and 1919.[45] An austere gentlemanly ethos surrounded government, in which the assumptions of 'race' became more militant, and
through which Europeans asserted their claims as pioneers.

These changes can be traced in the rise of the new federal capital, Kuala
Lumpur. A centre of European administration since 1880, in 1891, 'KL' had
only 154 European inhabitants (there were only 190 in the entire state of
Selangor), that is, 0.35 per cent of the district's population. But by 1911 this
had risen to 1,396 people. In its early days, state revenues were entirely

---

[43] John Butcher, *The British in Malaya, 1880–1941* (Kuala Lumpur, 1983), 208–10.

[44] Ronald Hyam, 'Concubinage and the Colonial Service: The Crewe Circular (1909)', *Journal of Imperial and Commonwealth History*, 14/1 (1986), 170–86.

[45] James de Vere Allen, 'Malayan Civil Service, 1874–1941: Colonial Bureaucracy/Malayan Elite', *Comparative Studies in Society and History*, 12/2 (1970), 149–78. Butcher, *British in Malaya*, 31.

reliant on duty from Chinese tin mining, Chinese revenue farmers, and railway receipts. At one point the Selangor State Railway was leased to the leading Chinese citizen, Yap Ah Loy, in order to keep it running. The Europeans mixed in their own clubs—the Selangor Club (1884) and the Lake Club (1890)—but the Chinese merchant princes gave the finest dinners, where Britons and Chinese conversed in rudimentary Malay. However, by the turn of the century, Chinese were dislodged from key administrative roles; their leaders were consulted less. The rise of rubber capital made European businesses more assertive and competitive. The Chinese merchants were no less wealthy and resourceful than the British; they responded by diversifying their portfolios, employing European business methods and even European managers. But the earlier ease of contact and mutual dependency had disappeared. Social mixing was reserved to the more formal events. And while the Europeans had always settled on the elevated west bank of the Klang river, their housing now became more formally segregated.[46] The extent of this barrier was exposed by a series of ugly disputes over the sharing of social space. In 1904, the Federated Malay States Railway put two first-class carriages on its lines, one of them labelled 'For Chinese'. There was an outburst of protest, and not only from the Chinese. The 'obnoxious' signs were removed, but a system of 'A' carriages and 'B' carriages, which were exclusively for Europeans, was retained. The fact that non-British Europeans were allowed to sit where they pleased exposed the racism and emptiness behind claims of imperial belonging. The restriction hit hardest the wealthiest Chinese, who had the means to travel first class and were used to mixing with Europeans. Incidents involving Eurasians revived the question of who the 'Europeans' actually were. Wives were separated from husbands. Formal discrimination was, after a struggle, abandoned and a system of self-segregation was devised in carriages with multiple small compartments. This set a pattern for the policing of the boundaries of colonial society throughout Malaya: that of iron convention rather than bureaucratic fiat; conventions which 'respectable' Asians, by tacit agreement, were on occasion able to flout. The success of the campaign

---

[46] This account is drawn from J. M. Gullick, *A History of Kuala Lumpur, 1856–1939* (Kuala Lumpur, 2000); J. G. Butcher, 'Towards the History of Malayan Society: Kuala Lumpur District, 1885–1912', *Journal of Southeast Asian Studies*, 10/1 (1978), 104–18; Chong Seck-Chim, 'The Development of Kuala Lumpur District', *Malayan Journal of Tropical Geography*, 3/1 (1954), 48–50.

against segregation on the railways—which mobilized not only the Chinese reform movement, but also the Chinese Chamber of Commerce—showed the limits of British ability to enforce segregation. It also marked the end of the era when 'public opinion' was coterminous with expatriate opinion. But the underlying tensions were not resolved. When, in 1911, a public fancy-dress ball was announced, the question was still asked: who was the 'public'? With heavy irony, an Asian correspondent to the town journal, the *Malay Mail*, demanded an answer of the organizers. 'You will be earning the gratitude of many who would be spared the painful humiliation of being told again that they are not the public.'[47] These anxieties would come to the fore during and after the First World War, in what was later seen as the high noon of the community.

The Empire of the Jazz Age

In February 1919, the British of Singapore celebrated their centennial with a two-volume memorial, *One Hundred Years of Singapore*. It was edited by Walter Makepeace, the proprietor of one of the colony's oldest journals, the *Singapore Free Press*, Gilbert Brooke, an expert on tropical medicine, and Roland St. J. Braddell, a noted lawyer. Braddell's grandfather had first come to Penang as a sugar planter in 1844, and by 1919 his family was one of several which could claim Malayan lives over four generations. Makepeace was a leading figure in the pre-eminent citizen's organization of Malaya, the Straits Settlements Association, which had recently scourged the administration over issues such as income tax and the colony's contribution to London's military expenditure. In the 1920s, a powerful lobby of commercial and plantation interests, together with retired officials who often sat on their boards, was able to make its voice heard by coordinated pressure on both the local government and Whitehall. It played an important role in the debates on the future constitutional shape of Malaya that dominated these years.[48] Braddell contributed a chapter to the memorial on 'The Good Old Days'. It was an attempt 'to tell the little things' that defined Singapore for the 'Singaporean'. 'That is the keynote of Singapore; never mind the swarming masses in the streets, yellow, black and brown, or the chattering Babel of

---

[47] Butcher, *British in Malaya*, 97–107. This is a classic study of a colonial society.

[48] For this see Yeo Kim Wah, *The Politics of Decentralization: Colonial Controversy in Malaya, 1920–29* (Kuala Lumpur, 1983).

their many tongues—the place is British, stolid, prosperous, conservative, resentful of change, distrustful of enthusiasm, and commercial—about all, behind all, beyond all, commercial.'[49] *One Hundred Years of Singapore* was a testament to the solidity of municipal achievement and a celebration of British community life. There were as many pages to the chapter on 'Amateur Theatricals and Music' as on the other 'Peoples of Singapore'. Yet the shrill emphasis on 'Britishness' was something new. The centennial came in the wake of traumatic events that brought the community into closer definition. The First World War shook commercial confidence and exposed the vulnerability of the colonial order. Malaya in its 'golden age' was already a changed world and steeped in nostalgia.

A defining moment came on 15 February 1915, when a unit of mostly Muslim Indian soldiers in Singapore, the 5th Light Infantry, mutinied. Fourteen Britons were attacked and killed, along with five Chinese and Malays. Early reports fanned hysteria over what *The Times* called 'unspeakable things in the range of possibility' that might befall European women. In fact, women were not molested, and the one young British woman who died seems to have been killed by accident, by throwing herself in front of her husband. But the event evoked memories of the hysteria in India in 1857. The British all but lost control of the island, and, embarrassingly, the revolt had to be put down by a makeshift militia of French, Russian, and Japanese sailors, and the private army of the Sultan of Johore.[50] The British exacted a bloody retribution: a summary general court martial was held and thirty-seven men were executed. The mutiny exposed deep fault lines in the colonial structure. The war had provoked outward displays of empire loyalty: as well as war taxation, Malaya contributed $5,172,174 to voluntary war funds and charities; it provided fifty-three aeroplanes and coolie labour for the East African and Mesopotamian campaigns.[51] Much of the financial contributions came from Asians; the Sultan of Johore alone provided sixteen of the planes. But with the declaration of war against the Ottoman Caliphate, the assumed allegiance of local Muslims to empire—which

[49] Walter Makepeace, Gilbert E. Brooke, and Roland St. J. Braddell (eds.), *One Hundred Years of Singapore*, 2 vols. (Singapore, 1991 [1919]): see the introduction by C. M. Turnbull, pp. v–xiii, and 466.

[50] R. W. E. Harper and Harry Miller, *Singapore Mutiny* (Singapore, 1985); Nicholas Tarling, 'The Singapore Mutiny of 1915', *Journal of the Malaysian Branch of the Royal Asiatic Society*, 55/2 (1982), 26–59; Christine Doran, 'Gender matters in the Singapore mutiny', *Sojourn*, 17/1 (2002), 76–93.

[51] Sir Charles Lucas (ed.), *The Empire at War* (London, 1926), 389–401.

underpinned the Anglo-Malay condominium—could no longer be taken for granted. There was rebellion in 1915 in the state of Kelantan, and both its leaders, and the mutineers in Singapore, seemed to connect their struggles to a wider world of Islamic protest. Colonial enterprise was hit by shipping shortages; strategic resources were in short supply and there were food riots in the towns. The local administration was overextended as young officials and planters volunteered for the Western Front. War took away 20 per cent of the MCS, that is, forty-five officers; in total 700 European men left the Federated Malay States during the war and 200 of them were killed.[52] Those who remained were denied leave, and the personnel records of these years are littered with cases of men going 'troppo', or breaking under the strain, of alcoholism, hallucinations, and madness. There was a minor epidemic of suicides.[53] These men, the governor, Arthur Young, remarked, were all victims of the war. A post-war report on salaries warned of the low morale of officials and the spectre of weakened prestige. The rhetoric that accompanied the conflict against Germany reaffirmed ties of blood. Since the late nineteenth century the idea of 'race' was asserted in various bureaucratic processes, such as the hardening of census categories.[54] But war gave this a new urgency. Men who were 'noticeably Eurasian' were weeded out of government service because, Young informed London, it might interfere with 'that spirit of harmonious co-operation which is secured by unity of race and social feeling'.[55] In response to the mutiny, a 'Reserve Force and Civil Guard Ordinance' passed in August 1915 was the first law passed in any British colony that imposed compulsory local military service. But the expansion of the local militia was hampered by the refusal of Europeans to serve alongside Eurasians.

Racial boundaries were policed more directly than ever before. In early 1916, a Briton was disciplined under the terms of the Crewe Circular. The case provides a rare documentary account of the private space of empire. The case was taken very seriously at the time as the man, A. W. Hamilton,

---

[52] Robert Heussler, *British Rule in Malaya: The Malayan Civil Service and its Predecessors, 1867–1942* (Westport, Conn., 1981), 135.

[53] Gullick, *History of Kuala Lumpur*, 237–8.

[54] Charles Hirschman, 'The Meaning and Measurement of Ethnicity in Malaysia: An Analysis of Census Classifications', *Journal of Asian Studies*, 46/3 (1987), 552–82; Charles Hirschman, 'The Making of Race in Colonial Malaya: Political Economy and Racial Ideology', *Sociological Forum*, 1/2 (1986), 330–62.

[55] Arthur Young to Harcourt, 19 Aug. 1914, GD/C 18, Singapore National Archives.

was a police officer and this placed it at the heart of security concerns, as most of the police rank and file were Muslim. The incident was provoked by an anonymous letter to the governor, written by a Malay, which claimed that Hamilton had pretended friendship to the Malay family of one Tengku Omar in the Telok Blangah area of Singapore, where they 'associate together in his house like brothers'. But Hamilton, the letter-writer claimed, had lured a married niece of Tengku Omar to his own house, where they now lived together 'as husband and wife'. The Malay girl, Teuku Alimah, was of aristocratic family. Besides this 'nasty trick', it was alleged that Hamilton was also harbouring a Japanese woman, and 'keeping his house like one of the fairies of the Arabian nights'. Very often', the letter claimed, 'he will indulge in all sorts of amusements, "Gambus" "Dancing", etc... so that through his flaunting display he will be able to induce and kidnap some more young ladies to be his concubines.' The petitioner spoke ominously of 'a great sensational feeling among the Kampong people'.[56] Hamilton denied the charges. He pleaded the impossibility of sexual impropriety due to chronic gonorrhoea (a major scourge of European men at the time). An investigation ensued, and witnesses were summoned before a special three-man tribunal. But this was far from being a straightforward case of 'concubinage', as the initial charges against Hamilton had suggested.

A complex world of Anglo-Malay intimacy unfolded. At the root of his friendship with the Malay family was the fact that Hamilton had converted to Islam in 1912 when on local leave in Kuala Lumpur. This revelation identified the author of the anonymous letter as his 'Boy', or Malay servant, also called Omar, who was one of the few people who knew of Hamilton's conversion. They had been close, and on his visit to Kuala Lumpur Omar had accompanied him, and witnessed his circumcision there. It had been Omar who had encouraged him to offer sanctuary to Alimah who was separated from her own husband, and unhappy in her uncle's house. The 'Boy', Omar, had a wife, a Japanese woman convert to Islam; she was stricken with beri-beri, and Alimah was engaged to care for her. But the relationship between Hamilton and Omar soured when Omar had abandoned her and taken a second wife. Hamilton would not accept the new woman in his house, and Omar was dismissed, Hamilton continuing to care for his sick Japanese first wife. Hamilton did not deny that the women were

---

[56] Sir Arthur Young's despatch to Andrew Bonar Law, 1 June, 1916, GD/C 21, Singapore National Archives.

in his house. He said that Alimah had been given shelter on leaving her home, and a small allowance for domestic service. The estranged husband of the Malay girl was summoned, and he confirmed that the girl had not been compelled and that they were now divorced. The women had their own rooms and took their meals separately. But, stated Hamilton, 'being free agents to do as they choose, and not servants, I do not treat them as such'.[57] And this was the heart of the case. Omar's complaint was provoked by losing his position; but also, and not least, as the transcript of the proceedings shows, by being displaced in Hamilton's affections. On returning from his office, Omar testifed, Hamilton would dress in Malay *sarong* and *baju*. 'We were friends...I could walk with him and could talk with him.' Hamilton would visit Omar's room and play cards with him. There were many other Malay visitors, some were people of rank. The *gambus* mentioned in the petition was a Malay form of the lute, used in Arabic-influenced music such as the *ghazal*; an unusual choice, perhaps, for a European home. But Omar was offended that Hamilton now spent the evenings walking and talking with Alimah, although, he admitted, Hamilton did not visit her room. 'I do not say that you are wrong', he said. But on examination it appeared that in Omar's eyes, it was not Malay protocol that was breached, but the European's own: 'I know the customs of the Malay Royal Family. They can mix up with the common people and do not lose prestige. It does not look nice, though, for a European to mix up with a lower class European, It does not look nice for a European to keep company with his punkah or another European's punkah.'[58]

The charge of keeping a concubine was not upheld. But the tribunal agreed with Omar's moral reading of the situation. Hamilton was found guilty of a secondary charge of living with his servants 'in such circumstances as to cause scandal and grave discredit to the public service'. He kept his job: he went on to serve in the political intelligence branch, and in posts across the peninsula until his retirement in the early 1930s. But he lived with the consequences of this affair for a long time afterwards. His salary was frozen for two years and he also was fined £500 (around two years' salary) over the next fourteen years.[59] The case shows all the complexities of attempting to 'fix' 'British' identity in Malaya. It shows how interwoven

---

[57] Hamilton to Chief Secretary, Straits Settlements, 16 Mar. 1916, GD/C 21, Singapore National Archives.

[58] 'Report of Committee of 11 April 1916', ibid.

[59] Young to Bonar Law, 1 June, 1916, ibid.

British and local social practice could become, and the complexities and ambivalence of attachment that could emerge within the overarching inequalities of the colonial system.

The system stabilized somewhat in the 1920s. The European population swelled with new arrivals. By 1921 nearly half the Europeans in Malaya were employed in the rubber industry, and many of them were war veterans. Older Malaya hands claimed a special status, on the grounds that the newcomers did not 'know the country' as they did. In the words of one traveller in 1926, it was now 'possible for the Europeans to live a life almost on their own, knowing little of the customs of the country and seeming to care less'.[60] The major change was the new prominence given to 'home life'. Before the Great War, the orthodoxy on the part of the government and large employers was that younger men should not marry, as they could not support wives at a European standard of living. But after the war it was now accepted that the stability and respectability of colonial society depended on Europeans marrying younger and forming families. These new communities retreated deeper into imperial suburbia. In Singapore, families were corralled by their rank and profession on new housing estates. For officials there were the 'black-and-white' houses, the kampong mock Tudor, of Malcolm Road and Mount Pleasant; there were the sparer army estates of Alexandra Park and Portsdown Road; and private company estates—such as the Firestone Estate of the rubber company, with its sixteen-hole golf course.[61] The opening of new hill stations symbolized the domestication of the Malay peninsula and the imperial body's mastery of its environment. These playgrounds bore the names of Scottish pioneers: Maxwell's Hill, the Cameron Highlands, and Frazer's Hill, with its village pub, post office, and its streets named after officials' wives. They were, along with the other great engineering works of the 1920s—the Perak River hydroelectric scheme, the east coast railway, and the navy's infamous dry dock at 'Fortress Singapore'—some of the most enduring physical monuments of the Malayan Raj. The provision of road and water up to the Cameron Highland cost $973,905 and the lives of eighty-four labourers.[62]

In all of this there was a sense of keeping the world at bay. The jazz age of empire was also a time of rising nationalism, street demonstrations, and

[60] R. J. H. Sydney, *Malay Land: "Tanah Melayu"* (London, 1926), 81.
[61] Edwards, *Singapore House*, 96–100.
[62] Federated Malay States, *Report for 1930* (London, 1931), 10–11.

strikes. The quiet rhythm of life in Kuala Lumpur was shattered in January 1925, when a sober and smartly dressed young Chinese woman entered a government office and detonated a bomb, hidden in a suitcase, nearly killing two British officials. It was Malaya's first experience of political terror. In 1930 alone there were 352 murders, and a rising tide of gang robberies. Singapore was known as 'the Chicago of the East'. Malaya was screwed down by 4,384 police officers.[63] In the face of all this, colonial society continued to close ranks. Definitions of 'European', the boundaries of who was 'in' and who was 'out', tightened. But in doing this, British society in Malaya placed an unsustainable burden on itself. Although employers agreed to meet to some degree the enhanced costs of family life, a 1919 official committee on salaries laid down a cardinal principle: 'Malaya is not a suitable country for the "poor white"; unless a European can earn his wage on which he is able to live as a European should, he merely brings discredit and contempt upon the British community.'[64] The costs of this were crippling. The depressions of the immediate post-war years and early 1930s squeezed salaries, particularly those of the growing number of 'unofficials'. 'Poor whites' were the objects of relief and soon began to be shipped home. At the same time, it was becoming hard to define what living 'as a European should' might mean. How was it different from the lives of a growing middle class of Anglophone Asians, whose wealth and education often outstripped that of Europeans, and with whom they shared a booming new consumer culture?[65] From as early as the 1860s, European life in Malaya had rested on imports—brandy and Schweppes, Sydney beef, Nagasaki umbrellas, ice from the United States—but now being 'European' placed ever more emphasis on maintaining a diet from the temperate world. Imports of Australian butter, New Zealand meat, and international cocktails all added to costs. So too did the demand for servants, whose presence in the home was indispensable to prestige, but also—as the Hamilton case showed—created all kinds of opportunities for its erosion.[66]

This febrile obsession with white prestige and purity, the efforts to keep in line any Europeans who threatened to blur the margin, all placed women

[63] Federated Malay States, *Report for 1930* and *Annual Report on the Social and Economic Progress of the People of the Federated Malay States, 1931* (Kuala Lumpur, 1932).

[64] Quoted Ward-Jackson, *Rubber Planting*, 35.

[65] For this see Chua Ai Lin, 'Anglophone Asians, Modernity and Urban Culture in Colonial Singapore, 1920–40', Ph.D. thesis (Cambridge, 2008).

[66] For this, see Collingham, *Imperial Bodies*.

and the home at the heart of policy concerns. This dynamic has been explored in other colonial contexts.[67] But in Malaya, the stereotypes surrounding European women seem to have been uniformly vicious and the anxieties particularly acute. It was argued that the arrival of women in larger numbers had broken the free and easy intercourse between Britons and Asians and reinforced social hierarchy. At the same time their presence undermined prestige. In the words of one official: 'all the *mems* did in Malaya was play bridge and fornicate'. The misogyny of Edwardian empire was strongly evident in Malaya, in both the bluff masculinity of the frontier and in a homoerotic ascetic within the Malayan Civil Service.[68] Upcountry wives were a particular target: the segregated women's area of one club near Kuala Lumpur was termed 'The Cowshed'. By contrast, research on the experience of women in Malaya has emphasized the diversity of roles and types, from the maternal imperialism of 'incorporated wives' to the independent spirit and empathic eye of many memoirs of Malaya by women. Katherine Sim's *Malayan Landscape* (1946), for example, a chronicle of life in a Malay village by the artist wife of a customs official, is one of the most distinctive portraits of Malaya by any European writer of the 1930s, wholly lacking the condescension and ennui of much of the genre.[69] But crucial to the shaping of the experience of the British in Malaya was a concerted attempt in official circles to mobilize women to shore up colonial prestige. This took a variety of forms. Some involved putting women to good works, and in this sphere some women could at times challenge racial boundaries and gender roles.[70] But most inescapably, it

[67] Helen Calloway, 'Purity and Exotica in Legitimating the Empire: Cultural Constructions of Gender, Sexuality and Race', in Terence Ranger and Olufemi Vaughan (eds.), *Legitimacy and the State in Twentieth-Century Africa: Essays in Honour of A. H. M. Kirk-Greene* (London, 1993), 31–61. For the polarization, see esp. Ann Laura Stoler, 'Sexual Affronts and Racial Frontiers: European Identities and the Cultural Politics of Exclusion in Colonial Southeast Asia', in Frederick Cooper and Ann Laura Stoler (eds.), *Tensions of Empire: Colonial Cultures in a Bourgeois World* (Berkeley, Calif., 1997), 198–237.

[68] For the former, *passim*; for the latter, see Purcell, *Memoirs of a Malayan Official*, 293.

[69] See Janice N. Brownfoot's ground-breaking 'Memsahibs in Colonial Malaya: A Study of European Wives in a British Colony and Protectorate', in Hilary Callan and Shirley Ardener (eds.), *The Incorporated Wife* (London, 1984), 190. Also, Katherine Sim, *Malayan Landscape* (London, 1942).

[70] Janice N. Brownfoot, 'Sisters Under the Skin: Imperialism and the Emancipation of Women in Malaya, c. 1891–1941', in J. A. Mangan (ed.), *Making Imperial Mentalities: Socialization and British Imperialism* (Manchester, 1990), 46–73.

placed an oppressive burden on women to 'maintain form'. Travellers observed that rituals such as 'calling' survived in Malayan society long after they had been abandoned at home. A new arrival in a colonial outpost would be compelled to make a round of the homes of the senior wives merely to deposit a visiting card; it was a formal obeisance to the hierarchy and to women's role in it. The 'pecking order' was even carried into the Japanese internment camps in 1942. The governor's confidential reports on officers for promotion routinely hinged on his assessments of their women: in the case of the 1935 candidates, 'wife delicate', 'has gone off with another', 'a merry, happy Amazon', 'a bit of a shrew'.[71] But the picture was complicated before the war by the arrival of independent professional women in growing numbers, particularly working in health care and education. Malaya was a major recipient of nurses recruited by Colonial Nursing Association, and for these women it was an opportunity for travel, some autonomy, but also betterment by marriage in a colony where unattached European women were still in short supply.[72] For this reason, officials went to great lengths to ensure that only women 'of the right type' remained in Malaya. A veiled reference, say, in a report on two assistant headmistresses that they lacked the 'exceptional degree of understanding sympathy' and 'personality' required, was enough to send them home.[73] By such informal mechanisms the colonial community in Malaya was policed; but equally, women without men posed a real danger to their effectiveness.

'The unseen book of rules' was targeted, above all, at the Eurasian community, and the ever-present shadow of 'degeneration'. By 1931, in Singapore, those designated 'Eurasian' in the census were only slightly smaller in number, 6,134 people, than the European community of 6,518 people. In studies of the British in Malaya, the Eurasians are largely absent. But, as we have seen, 'British' and 'Eurasian' were unfixed, arbitrary categories, and they signal histories that are inseparable. In the interwar years, it was increasingly in relation to the Eurasians that British society defined itself. And as census categories and the politics of 'race' hardened, 'Eurasians' themselves—a population of very diverse ancestry—began to

---

[71] Thomas Shenton Thomas, minute, 10 Oct. 1935, The National Archives, Kew (TNA), CO 273/603.2.

[72] Anne Marie Rafferty, 'The Seductions of History and the Nursing Diaspora', *Health and History*, 7/2 (2005), 2–16.

[73] Sir Lawrence Guillemard to Leo Amery, 27 Jan. 1925, TNA, CO 717/14.

explore their 'Eurasianism' and see themselves as one community.[74] This
boundary was not marked by statute; it was drawn by social convention and
insinuation. It was policed by the manipulation of salaries and status. As an
Australian journalist in pre-war Singapore put it: 'Employment of the
Eurasian is the main method used to keep him "in his place".' Mere
suspicion of Eurasian blood was enough to set the ceiling of a man's
promotion or to blight a woman's marriage prospects. In Malaya, it was
not possible to 'pass' for a European. For Europeans, it was not so much
dalliance, as its legitimation in marriage, that acted as an 'unseen rope
which binds the renegade and drags him away from the society of his own
colour and kind'.[75] The ultimate challenge to order came when European
women married Eurasian or Asian men. This, as one account of Penang
in the 1930s put it, was an act that 'resulted in almost complete segregation
from everybody'.[76] Yet, it is important not to see these relationships principally through the eyes of colonial writing, that is, solely in terms of trans-
gression or marginalization. They were another important 'middle ground'
that perhaps stretched further than many writers have acknowledged. These
were not lives at the 'margin'. The most successful writer to come out of
Malaya in these years was Leslie Charles Bowyer Yin, *alias* Leslie Charteris,
creator of 'The Saint', born in 1907, the son of Dr Suat Chuan Yin, the Straits
Chinese surgeon and reformer, and his English wife.[77] Malay princes,
educated in England, often returned with British wives, including the future
first prime minister of Malaya. The Colonial Office was greatly alarmed
when, in 1940, a son of the Sultan of Kelantan, eloped to Gretna Green
with a young woman 'of the small shopkeeper class', from Bournemouth,
'common but not blatantly vulgar'.[78] With the characteristic quirkiness of
Malayan administration, this issue was a direct stimulus to the development

[74] Kirsty Walker, 'Eurasian Communities and the Boundaries of "Race" in Malaya and
Singapore, 1919–1945', MA thesis (Universiti Sains Malaysia, 2008), opens up rich new perspectives on this. I am grateful to her for her comments on a draft of this chapter. For a particularly
robust expression of 'Eurasianism', see C. H. Crabb, *Malaya's Eurasians: An Opinion* (Singapore,
1960).
[75] R. C. H. McKie, *This was Singapore* (London, 1951), 74.
[76] George Blainkin, *Hail Penang! Being the Narrative of Comedies and Tragedies in a Tropical
Outpost, among Europeans, Chinese, Malays and Indians* (London, 1932), 102.
[77] Andrew Lycett, 'Ian, Leslie Charles Bowyer Charteris (1907–1993)', *Oxford Dictionary
of National Biography* (Oxford, 2004); online edn., URL: <http://www.oxforddnb.com/view/
article/51562>, accessed Oct. 2007.
[78] J. R. Innes to Director of Colonial Scholars, 4 Mar. 1940, TNA, CO 717/144/10.

of education for Malay women, by which the British sought to provide more suitable consorts for these worldly young men.[79] The marriage of Sultan Ibrahim of Johore in 1930 to a Scottish lady, Mrs Wilson, led to a vexed debate as to whether she could be received at Buckingham Palace as her royal status entitled her, and whether her attendance at the 1937 Coronation would be seen to 'glorify a mixed marriage'. This controversy ignored the fact that the Sultan himself had Danish ancestry.[80] In the Dutch Indies by the late 1930s, 28.5 per cent of marriages involving a European partner were mixed.[81] In Malaya these were never so many, but, equally, behind the façade of colonial society there lay a deep-set creole experience.

War, Memory, and the 'New Malaya'

All of these tensions came to the surface with the outbreak of war with Japan. The sudden arrival of thousands of British and particularly Australian servicemen who had nothing but contempt for colonial society, placed its codes further under strain. The squalid evacuation of Europeans from Penang on the night of 16 December 1941, when senior Asian civil servants were turned away at the quayside, and of the European women and children from Singapore in the following weeks, exposed the racial foundation of rule in its most elemental form. The fall of Singapore was an unequalled humiliation for British power and prestige. It also fragmented the British community in Malaya. The civilian survivors were interned together *en masse* in Changi prison. By late March 1942 there were 2,585 of them, but many more were dispersed in camps throughout the archipelago, detained in the flight from Singapore. There also were hundreds of volunteer soldiers in the prisoner-of-war camps. The civilian camps were swelled by later arrivals of Eurasian and Jewish internees. The camps became a peculiar microcosm of colonial society on the outside. Hierarchies were, on the whole maintained; for some, formality was necessary for unity and survival. But the tensions of race and class were sometimes enacted with acute intensity, particularly with regard to the Eurasian inmates. Some of the distinctive

---

[79] G. E. Gent, minute, 1 May 1940, TNA, CO 717/144/10.

[80] Sir John Maffey to Lord Wigram, 10 Mar. 1937, TNA, CO 323/1478/3. 'Darah Kacukan', 'Elite Malays and Mixed Marriage', *Asia Sentinel* (27 July 2007), URL: <http://www.asiasentinel.com/index.php?Itemid=34&id=600&option=com_content&task=view>, accessed 12 Dec. 2009.

[81] Ulbe Bosma and Remco Raben, *Being 'Dutch' in the Indies: A History of Creolisation and Empire, 1500–1920* (Singapore, 2008), 343.

patterns of sociability that defined the British Malayans also revived—sport, theatricals, scout troops, and golf clubs. At Changi there was even a clandestine Masonic lodge. There was a late flowering of amateur scholarship on Malayan themes, a mood of introspection, and a shared suffering that became important to the continued identity of the community.[82] A parallel process occurred on the outside. There is a sense in which the experience of being 'Malayans in exile', and in public disgrace, created a firmer sense of a British 'Malayan' identity. As one official wrote, dispersal to India, South Africa, and Australia, as well as the home islands, fortified a sense of belonging: 'The British in Fiji do not call themselves Fijians nor do the British in Burma call themselves Burmese but people of many races, including British, from Malaya do call themselves Malayans.'[83] In exile and in retirement Britons claimed to speak for Malaya and took a lead in preparing for the reconquest of the colony. They made the bold claim, in the words of the voice of the Malaya lobby in the House of Commons, Captain L. D. Gammans: 'For all intents and purposes we are Malaya'.[84]

By the reoccupation of Malaya in August and September 1945, the British did not regain the world they had lost. Japan was defeated by the American atomic bombs at Hiroshima and Nagasaki, and not by the British through right of arms on Malaya's soil. The initial British military administration was remembered locally for its demoralization, corruption, and repression. As civilian government returned in 1946, it was confronted by the new forces of nationalism, communism, and by rising ethnic tensions. Many long-term British residents never recovered from the harrowing experience of defeat and internment. When the camps were liberated, most internees were repatriated, and many old residents did not return. Those who did often found it hard to readjust to the new dispensation of life, not least the lack of deference, even indifference, on the part of Asians. A new community arrived in Singapore with its rapid growth as a garrison colony and centre of an expanded regional administration between 1945 and 1957: the European population of KL grew from 1,800 to 6,600. The outbreak of the Emergency in 1948 and the manpower needed to fight it further changed the

<hr />

[82] Christopher Bayly and Tim Harper, *Forgotten Armies: The Fall of British Asia, 1941–45* (London, 2004). For a new study see, F.M.L. Yap, 'Reassessing the civilian internment experience in Japanese-occupied British Asia 1942–45', PhD Thesis (Cambridge, 2013).
[83] O. W. Gilmour, *With Freedom to Singapore* (London, 1947), 18.
[84] Capt. L. D. Gammans, 'Post-War Planning in South-East Asia', *British Malaya* (Nov. 1942).

complexion of peninsular society. British Malaya was now a more divided community. The industrial unrest prior to the Emergency pitted planters against liberal-minded officials. Men of the old order attacked the new arrivals for their 'uncertainty of mind'.[85] The old hands were themselves divided between those who had been detained, and those, for whatever reason, who had not. The military largely formed their own circles. But there was a late flowering of British family life in Malaya. The new generation of colonial servants and the military families in the cantonments could not always afford to send their children home for schooling, as had been the norm before the war. For the first time, European schools were founded: in Kuala Lumpur, the Alice Smith School (1946) and the Garden School (1951), founded by the wife of a fireman, and the Uplands School in Penang (1955). But even more so than in the past, this was no longer a 'British' community.

In the 1947 census, the 'European' category was broken down into 'White British', that is 16,625 people: including 10,819 English, 2,529 Scottish (with a 69 per cent preponderance in peninsular Malaya), 255 Welsh, 685 Irish, 796 Australian, 200 New Zealander, 100 Canadian, and 2,026 'other British white'. There was also a growing mélange of other 'European' communities: 359 Americans, 135 Danes, 790 Dutch, 423 French, 94 Italians, 94 Portuguese, 86 Swiss, and 861 'Others'.[86] In the late colonial period, a wider European identity reasserted itself. As one new arrival at the new University of Malaya in Singapore, Patrick Anderson, put it: 'People who have never lived anywhere more glamorous than Surbiton, never been abroad . . . suddenly find themselves regarded as *Europeans* . . . Even Empire Builders prefer not to call themselves British; they are Europeans . . .'[87] Colonial culture was increasingly shaped by American influences, which grew markedly in the 1950s, through consumerism, popular entertainment, and as an arm of United States cold war policy. This was a fresh source of anxiety to those charged with shoring up British prestige in the region.[88]

Pre-war social boundaries began to dissolve, but slowly and principally at an elite level. The cosmopolitan commissioner-general in Southeast Asia, Malcolm MacDonald, used his time in Singapore between 1946 and 1955 to

[85] René Onraet, 'Crime and Communism in Malaya', *British Malaya* (Sept. 1948).
[86] M. V. Del Tufo, *Malaya, Comprising the Federation of Malaya and the Colony of Singapore: A Report on the 1947 Census of Population* (London, 1949).
[87] Patrick Anderson, *Snake Wine: A Singapore Episode* (Kuala Lumpur, 1980 [1955]), 158.
[88] Joey Long Shi Ruey, 'Containment and Decolonization: The United States, Great Britain and Singapore, 1953–61', Ph.D. thesis (Cambridge, 2006).

promote sociability across communities, not least through golf, which became the pastime of choice for the new Asian managerial class, and by abandoning the oppression of the necktie. But old attitudes died hard; a continuing measure of this was the treatment of Eurasians. Intellectuals from the community—such as the Harrovian radical John Eber and the communist Gerard de Cruz—took the lead in the early nationalist movement in Singapore, and this provoked the ire of many Europeans. In 1952, when Han Suyin came to Malaya as the wife of a British policeman, she was already an international celebrity with the publication of her novel, *A Many Splendored Thing* (1952), and was befriended by Malcolm MacDonald, who wrote a preface to the English edition. MacDonald, as she told him, 'could even make even neo-colonialism palatable', but colonial society was less generous. The book's barely disguised account of her affair with *The Times* correspondent, Ian Morrison, caused outrage in Malaya, and brought out old stereotypes of Eurasian women in which Han Suyin was seen as 'a loose nymphomaniac' and her husband as a 'security risk'.[89] Thirty years later a former governor of Singapore would still describe her as 'bristling with propaganda and [the] latent inferiority of the Eurasian who is not fully accepted by either race'.[90] But those who wished to defend old exclusions now found it harder to do so. The Emergency brought a new floating population of 'poor whites' to Malaya: the 'Virgin Soldiers' on National Service who did not observe the protocols of a colonial society which did little to welcome them. A new generation of service wives could not afford keep the 'form' laid down by the 'high born' elite. In 1955 there were stories in the Malayan press that up to fifty service wives were engaged in a prostitution racket. A Singapore *Sunday Standard* journalist reported a rendezvous with one of them in a Singapore hotel: 'I've got to live, haven't I', was her explanation. The senior officer on the island declared the allegations to be fabricated and defended the honour of his men: 'they and their women folk have been grossly slandered'.[91] But the following year, the commander-in-chief in the Far East voiced concerns about the scale of 'illicit relations' in Kuala Lumpur; he observed that the men were away for

---

[89] Han Suyin, *My House has Two Doors* (London, 1980), 88–9.

[90] Sir William Goode to Robert Heussler, 16 Apr. 1982, Mss. Brit. Emp. S. 480/13/1, Rhodes House Library, Oxford.

[91] *The People* (28 Aug. 1955); Maj.-General D. D. C. Tulloch to Commander-in-Chief, Far Eastern Land Forces, 2 Sept. 1955, TNA, CO 859/550.

long periods, and their wives' scattered lodgings in Asian areas, together
with easy credit and debt, 'combine and produce unusual temptation and
unusual opportunity'.[92] There were attempts to hold the 'colour line' by
building new cantonments and by other cruder means. In 1952, there was a
public scandal when members of the Lake Club attempted to bar the Sultan
of Selangor from a St George's Society Dinner in his own state. The high
commissioner, Sir Gerald Templer, ran the club committee out of the
colony. This said, the Tanglin Club in Singapore went fully mixed only in
1961, two years after the colony had achieved internal self-government.[93]

If the British community acquired a common purpose, it was to redeem a
reputation lost at the fall of Singapore, and to stake a claim to in some way
belong to the new nation that was coming into being. Although imperial
policy moved away from the idea of Anglo-Malay condominium and
towards citizenship for Malaya's other communities, the Malayan Civil
Service sought to revive its Brahminical traditions. Armed rubber planters
on the frontline of the Emergency made a last appeal to an image of the
heroic pioneer. But the Emergency also signalled the end of the influence of
the settler lobby. It brought the intervention of Whitehall and powerful pro-
consuls such as Templer. It created a new kind of colonial state. But it also
brought a final mission for the British in Malaya. To recover their moral
authority, Britons attempted to take a lead in the definition of a new
'Malayan' nationalism. Its watchwords were 'multi-racialism' and 'integration' and Britons saw themselves as uniquely equipped to lead its formation,
by envisaging a 'Malaya' united by its attachment to British institutions and
the English language. The policy was one arm of the counter-insurgency
against the Malayan Communist Party and so an unusual amount of
resources were given to it. It animated many official initiatives such as the
expansion of education, the foundation of the University of Malaya in
Singapore, 'public information', and 'community development'. It brought
in new specialists, who were often different kinds of men and woman to
those who had served in Malaya before the war: the products of grammar
schools, red-brick universities, and the post-war Labour government. Many
of them were deeply ambivalent about imperialism. But what was also
unusual about this work was the extent to which it encompassed private

[92] Commander-in-Chief, Far Eastern Land Forces to Adjutant General, 11 June 1957, TNA, CO 859/548.
[93] T. N. Harper, *The End of Empire and the Making of Malaya* (Cambridge, 1999), 221–3.

initiative: the fashioning of a 'Malayan' culture through an arts council, print and broadcast media, architecture, and even in stock colonial pursuits such as amateur dramatics—all of which began to elaborate 'local colour'. The fiction of Anthony Burgess portrays an alcohol-sodden decline of empire, but his fictional alter ego, Victor Crabbe, captures well the desire to leave behind a durable cultural inheritance, albeit an Anglophone, Europhile, and modernist high culture. As a schoolteacher, Burgess would write a history of English literature for Malayans, 'from an angle of tropical heat', and attempt (unsuccessfully) to translate Pound's *Cantos* and Eliot's *The Waste Land* into Malay. A recurring motif of the memoir and fiction of the end of empire is of Western sojourners attempting, often without success, to find freedom and self-expression by submerging themselves in an exotic and kaleidoscopic Asia.[94] This gave a different sensibility to 'going native'; for many it was short-lived, but it led some expatriates to reject colonial society and its constrictions and to seek to embrace fully a Malayan life. As another schoolteacher, Francis Thomas, the son of a country vicar, wrote: 'For the first time, I felt fully part of a living human community'. Thomas would spend the rest of his life in Singapore and play an important role in its schools, church, and labour movement.[95]

The colonial vision of the 'Malayan' stood uneasily alongside the nations-of-intent of the people of Malaya, and was in many ways irrelevant to them. The British were responding to, and competing with, an intellectual renaissance within Asian society. When Anglophone Asians had taken up the term 'Malayan' in the 1920s and 1930s, it had been from the outset a challenge to exclusion and a claim for citizenship, and one which had been continually frustrated.[96] When the idea was resurrected after 1945, it was articulated most forcibly by the radical left—not least by the Eurasian leaders of the Malayan Democratic Union—with whom British officials would have no truck, on grounds of ideology—the taint of 'communism'—and through personal animus. Both movements tried to provide an alternative to the rise of ethnic politics. A tragic irony of the end of empire in Malaya was that the

---

[94] Anthony Burgess, *Little Wilson and Big God* (London, 1987), 403; Clive J. Christie, *A Preliminary Survey of British Literature on South-East Asia in the Era of Colonial Decline and Decolonisation* (University of Hull, Centre for South-East Asian Studies, 3; 1986).

[95] Francis Thomas, *Memoirs of a Migrant* (Singapore, 1972).

[96] Chua Ai Lin, 'Imperial Subjects, Straits Citizens: Anglophone Asians and the Struggle for Political Rights in Inter-War Singapore', in Michael D. Barr and Carl A, Trocki (eds.), *Paths Not Taken: Political Pluralism in Post-War Singapore* (Singapore, 2008), 16–36.

British rebuffed the movement that was closest to the kind of nationalism they had sought to foster, and that, for all the talk of 'integration', it was to an alliance of ethnic-based political movements that they devolved power.[97]

For all its intensity, the late imperial life of the British 'Malayans' was strangely ephemeral. One reason for this was the speed of 'Malayanization', which was accelerated to rally the Malay elite who led the alliance around the counter-insurgency campaign. As Malaya approached decolonization in 1955, the government estimated that it needed to replace some 1,650 senior civil service posts from an establishment of 3,000, as well as fill 500 more vacancies created by the Emergency. It was envisioned that Britons would stay in large numbers until 1965.[98] In the event, 80 per cent of entitled officers retired by 1962 and only 200 remained for a short period after that.[99] British business also moved quickly to adjust to the changing reality, and to appoint Malayans to the boards of their local subsidiaries.[100] The continuities were strongest in the security forces, where key personnel stayed to serve the new governments of Malaya and Singapore. One of the most senior of those who stayed on was Mervyn ffranck Sheppard who, escaping a tyrannical father at home, reinvented himself in Malaya in a career that began in 1928 and was broken only by his internment by the Japanese. He renounced his estate in Ireland, and in the course of a long post-colonial career, founded the Malaysian National Archives and Museum, involved himself in heritage work, and, after his conversion, in Islamic charities. Showered with Malaysian honours, Tan Sri Dato' Mubin Sheppard lived and died as a Malay; his passing in 1994 marking, perhaps, the end of the 'Royal Road'.[101] There were other, similar cases and a number of planting families remained rooted in Malaya. But they left little imprint on the demographics or politics of the new nation. When the British community in the region began to grow again in the 1990s it was a branch of a new British diaspora in Asia, and had

[97] Christopher Bayly and Tim Harper, *Forgotten Wars: The End of Britain's Asian Empire* (London, 2007), 261–71.

[98] Federation of Malaya, *Malayanisation of the Public Service: A Statement of Policy* (Kuala Lumpur, 1955); Federation of Malaya, *Report of the Committee on Malayanisation of the Public Service* (Kuala Lumpur, 1956).

[99] Robert O. Tilman, *Bureaucratic Transition in Malaya* (Durham, NC, 1964), 63–76.

[100] For this process, see Nicholas J. White, *Business, Government and the End of Empire: Malaya, 1942–57* (Kuala Lumpur, 1996) and *British Business in Post-Colonial Malaysia, 1957–70* (London, 2004).

[101] Mubin Sheppard, *Taman Budiman: Memoirs of an Unorthodox Civil Servant* (Kuala Lumpur, 1979).

little connection with the first. By 2006, Singapore had 56,000 full- and part-time British residents, including 309 retirees. In Malaysia, there were 16,000 full- and part-time British residents, 493 of them retirees, many attracted quite recently by the government's 'Malaysia, My Second Home' scheme.[102] Many belonged to the cosmopolitan corporate worlds of Singapore and Kuala Lumpur. As one geographer has described them, they were 'hyper-mobile and engage in micro-networks which are both global and local in scope, embedded in the working environment, yet disembedded from the local social sphere'.[103] Translated from its contemporary jargon, there is a faint echo here of travellers' accounts of Britons in Singapore in the 1920s and 1930s.

The story of Britons' return from Malaya has yet to be written. It was a protracted affair, and for many old residents it did not end in the United Kingdom, but much further afield. 'Haji' Hamilton's life after Malaya indicates a lifelong attachment to the region, although he never returned to live there. Unable to settle in England, it seems, he lived in Canada, South Africa, Kenya, before establishing himself in Australia where he produced some of the best English translations of Malay proverbs and *pantuns*, the richly allusive verse form of the western archipelago. He also was responsible for the first translation of the *Rubaiyat of Omar Khayyam* into Malay. In Australia, he was a largely unsung pioneer of Malay language teaching at Sydney University in the 1940s, and one of the first people to lobby Australia's politicians to invest in a deeper intellectual engagement with their closest neighbour, Indonesia. His popular Malay primers remained in print until the 1990s.[104] For many others who did return to the UK, the Malayan experience remained the most vivid of their lives, and they kept connections alive through the British Association of Malay[si]a, and its journal which continued until 1973, and the Malaysian Branch of the Royal Asiatic Society. The afterlife of the community shows a similar pattern to that of British

---

[102] 'Brits Abroad: Country by Country', 11 Dec. 2006, URL: <http://www.bbc.co.uk/1/hi/uk/6161705.stm>.

[103] Jonathan V. Beaverstock, 'Transnational Elites in Global Cities: British Expatriates in Singapore's Financial District', *Geoforum*, 33/4 (2002), 536; cf. Katie Willis and Brenda Yeoh, 'Gendering Transnational Communities: A Comparison of Singaporean and British Migrants in China', *Geoforum*, 33/4 (2002), 553–65.

[104] See Jennifer Brewster and Anthony Reid, 'A. W. Hamilton and the Origins of Indonesian Studies in Australia', in R. J. May and William J. O'Malley (eds.), *Observing Change in Asia: Essays in Honour of J. A. C. Mackie* (Bathurst, 1989), 22–32.

India.[105] From the 1960s, a campaign began to better memorialize and to recognize the achievements of colonial Malaya in the face of unsympathetic public opinion. From the 1960s, spearheaded by a retired official, H. P. Bryson, there was a concerted attempt to encourage British Malayans to write down their recollections and to collect their papers. It led to two semi-official histories of the Malayan Civil Service: their theme was redemptive, of 'the completion of a stewardship'. The lingering anguish of the fall of Singapore gave a particular intensity to this work of memory. It resurfaced in campaigns for reparations for victims of the Japanese, and for the right for veterans to wear the medal given to them by the Malaysian government, the *Pingat Jasa Malaysia*, for their role in post-war conflicts in which 519 British soldiers were killed, a right denied by the British government. Cemeteries in Malaysia, and in particular the Emergency memorial at 'God's Little Acre' in Perak, erected privately by the Perak Planters' Association in 1989, became sites of pilgrimage.[106] After 2001, there was renewed public interest in the Malayan Emergency, as it seemed to offer a 'textbook' case of counter-insurgency, and a fresh wave of military and police memoirs appeared. In this way, the British 'Malayans' became one of the best-documented imperial communities, and perhaps most clearly seen in retrospective and through the construction of memory.

But memory flows in many different directions. By the late 1990s, it was taking new forms and building new communities. Much of the life of associations of veterans, prisoners of war, and internees shifted online, and the custodians of it were increasingly the children and grandchildren of former residents of Malaya. As the older British Malayans began pass away, there was a new emphasis on the experience of childhood, of the self-styled 'Britbrats' who spent at most two years in Singapore when their parents were posted there in the 1950s or early 1960s. One early website attracted 150,000 visitors in its first six months. Another commercial website claimed, in 2006, over 2,000 subscribed ex-pupils from the Alexandra Grammar and the Royal Naval School in Sembawang, Singapore. These sites brought together written testimonies across vast distances that focused on the vivid minutiae and reflected the innocence of childhood experience.

---

[105] Elizabeth Buettner, 'Cemeteries, Public Memory and Raj Nostalgia in Postcolonial Britain and India', *History and Memory*, 18/1 (2006), 5–42.

[106] R. Thambipillay, *God's Little Acre, Batu Gajah: A Commemorative Book on the 50 Anniversary of the Malayan Emergency, 1948–60* (Ipoh, 1998).

Ironically, as one Singapore history blogger remarked, they attempted to build a cultural bridge 'which close physical proximity could not do all those long years ago'.[107] To some extent these were collaborative projects—pooling the recollections of Britons and Singaporeans who may or may not have met as children—but they remained very one-sided. This began to be redressed by a wave of public recollection from Singapore and Malaysia, not least from those who were on the other side of Britain's colonial wars. A dialogue between these traditions of memory was slow to develop. Among the first Malaysian voices to register in British public debate were the new testimonies of ageing survivors of the Batang Kali massacre of 1948, in which twenty-four Chinese villagers were killed by the Scots Guards in circumstances that have never been the subject of an open public inquiry. It was only in early 2009 that a Malaysian campaign forced the British government to revisit the issue, but by 2010 the last adult eyewitness had died.[108] The episode showed how far Britain's imperial reckoning has yet to run. Yet histories of 'memory' alone cannot adequately encapsulate the experience of empire. By 2001, 89,387 Britons had been born in Malaysia or Singapore. To understand the multiple cross-cutting connections that this figure signifies demands something more. It requires a careful retracing of the family networks that crossed communities and borders over several generations. It demands thinking outside the boundaries of colonial and colonized that the politics of memory can sometimes re-enforce. Above all, it involves dissolving the categories that the very idea of the British 'Malayan' was devised to entrench.

Select Bibliography

JAMES DE VERE ALLEN, 'Malayan Civil Service, 1874–1941: Colonial Bureaucracy/Malayan Elite', *Comparative Studies in Society and History*, 12/2 (1970), 149–78.
CHRISTOPHER BAYLY and TIM HARPER, *Forgotten Armies: The Fall of British Asia, 1941–45* (London, 2004).
—— and —— *Forgotten Wars: The End of Britain's Asian Empire* (London, 2007).
JANICE N. BROWNFOOT, 'Memsahibs in Colonial Malaya: A Study of European Wives in a British Colony and Protectorate', in Hilary Callan and Shirley Ardener (eds.), *The Incorporated Wife* (London, 1984), 186–210.

---

[107] Respectively, <www.yesterday.sg> and <www.Alexandragrammar.org>, Juliana June Razul, 'To Singapore with Love', *Weekend Today* (Singapore, 16–17 Sept. 2006).

[108] For this see, Bayly and Harper, *Forgotten Wars*, 449–56.

JOHN BUTCHER, *The British in Malaya. 1880–1941* (Kuala Lumpur, 1983).

T. N. HARPER, 'Globalism and the Pursuit of Authenticity: The Making of a Diasporic Public Sphere in Singapore', *Sojourn*, 12/2 (1997), 261–92.

LYNN HOLLEN LEES, 'Being British in Malaya, 1890–1940', *Journal of British Studies*, 48/1 (2009), 76–101.

NORDIN HUSSIN, *Trade and Society in the Straits of Melaka: Dutch Melaka and English Penang, 1780–1830* (Singapore, 2007).

A. J. STOCKWELL, 'The White Man's Burden and Brown Humanity: Colonialism and Ethnicity in British Malaya', *Southeast Asian Journal of Social Science*, 10/1 (1982), 44–68.

C. M. TURNBULL, *The Straits Settlements, 1826–67: Indian Presidency to Crown Colony* (London, 1971).

NICHOLAS J. WHITE, *Business, Government and the End of Empire: Malaya, 1942–57* (Kuala Lumpur, 1996).

10

Shanghailanders and Others
British Communities in China, 1843–1957

Robert Bickers

In any cost-benefit analysis of British empire, the manpower contribution that was vital to the British war effort in 1914–18 needs to be included.[1] The loyalties that impelled the individual rush to the colours across the empire were a tangential but tangible return on British investment, and a clear demonstration of pan-imperial community, and pan-empire British identity. At the same time they were strongly infused by colonial nationalisms, and by local patriotisms. 'I put one or two in for Shanghai', wrote Alfred Grimble, stoutly, of his bayonet, in a 1916 letter to his former commanding officer in the Shanghai Municipal Police (SMP). Grimble left Shanghai, as he put it, 'to fight for my King and country and the cause of freedom'.[2] At least 200 Shanghai Britons died in the First World War. Grimble lost his legs but had satisfied Shanghai honour, as he saw it, before doing so. 'Three cheers for Shanghai' called the leader of the first contingent of volunteers to leave for Britain, as their ship pulled away from the jetty in October 1914.[3] Three weeks later 7,000 people crowded the riverside bund (embankment) to send off 110 men who had answered a call for a 'Shanghai contingent'. In the preceding days there had been a special service at the Holy Trinity Cathedral, a farewell football match (the volunteers losing by six goals), and a reception at the ritzy Palace Hotel. 'The men of Shanghai', ventured one senior resident in his address, 'when they put their hearts and

---

[1] Avner Offer, 'Costs and Benefits, Prosperity and Security, 1870–1914', in Andrew N. Porter (ed.), *The Oxford History of the British Empire*, iii. *The Nineteenth Century* (Oxford, 1999), 708.

[2] Shanghai Municipal Archives, U 102-5-23, A. F. Grimble to K. J. McEuen, 1 and 6 Apr. 1916.

[3] *North China Herald* (*NCH*, 3 Oct. 1914), 70.

minds to a thing, will do it well'.[4] The rousing Shanghai send-off, noted the *North China Herald*, offered an 'individual touch of colour to the future historian's picture of Britons abroad rallying to the standard of the old country'.[5] It certainly does that, but it also offers a way in to understanding the multi-layered identities of the China coast communities, and to trying to grasp what this 'Shanghai' was on whose behalf Grimble wielded his bayonet to such effect, and at such personal cost, on a French battlefield.

The Shanghai British formed the most numerous of the British communities in the settlements that developed after Chinese cities beyond Macao and Canton were formally opened to British residence under the 1842 Treaty of Nanjing. The British population in the city peaked in 1935 at around 10,000, living across the city's three administrative zones.[6] There were more Britons normally resident in Shanghai than in Hong Kong—counting only the civil population.[7] They formed a bigger community than the Ceylon British ever comprised in peacetime, and were half the numbers of the Kenya British in 1939. The 'Shanghailander', a monicker they developed for themselves early on, also held the most stridently articulated of local China coast identities, and they controlled the heart of twentieth-century China's most vibrant city. Self-government underpinned their attitudes, their mistakes, and their impact on Shanghai politics at moments which came to have national importance, such as the 1925 May Thirtieth movement, and at the apex of the 1926–7 national revolution.[8] These Shanghai Britons operated on complex legal foundations—extraterritoriality, which tied them individually to the jurisdiction of their consuls, and a locally agreed and delineated zone of settlement—but also with such a vague line of consular authority over the municipal administration that they operated, the Shanghai Municipal Council (SMC), that they were able to develop the

---

[4] The women of Shanghai too: see the China entry in *Queen Mary's Needlework Guild, its work during the Great War: St. James's Palace 1914–1919* (London, 1919).

[5] *NCH* (24 Oct. 1914), 255–8.

[6] The International Settlement, the French Concession, and the (Chinese) Municipality of Greater Shanghai.

[7] *Sessional Papers laid before the Legislative Council of Hong Kong 1931*, no. 5, 1931, 'Report on the Census of the Colony of Hong Kong 1931', p. 111.

[8] R. W. Rigby, *The May 30 Movement: Events and Themes* (Canberra, 1980); Nicholas R. Clifford, *Spoilt Children of Empire: Westerners in Shanghai and the Chinese Revolution of the 1920s* (Hanover, NH, 1991); Jürgen Osterhammel, *Shanghai, 30. Mai 1925: Die Chinesische Revolution* (Munich, 1997); Robert Bickers, *Empire Made Me: An Englishman Adrift in Shanghai* (London, 2003).

most prominent and seemingly intractable of autonomous identities and ambitions.[9] From being a solution to the difficulties of trade with China encountered before 1842—by running a British safe haven on Chinese soil ('safe' thereby from the perceived vagaries and cruelties of Chinese jurisdiction)—they became for a while the British state's biggest China problem. All of this developed, it needs to be remembered, while they were settled in an independent, sovereign country.

Hong Kong, Shanghai, and the Chinese treaty ports occasioned a volume in Arnold Wright's series on the overseas Britons. And while, as the preface to the 1908 edition noted, the Chinese treaty ports formed 'a congeries of separate but distinct units', they also formed on a different level a clear 'homogeneous whole'.[10] The British in China developed a 'China coast' identity and culture.[11] There was a recognizable common pattern of spatial settlement and development, a clear architectural style, and a common repertoire of administrative and governmental practice.[12] A familiar pattern developed. As a port opened to foreign trade and residence on river or coast, a consul or customs official took up residence, a waterside zone of settlement was demarcated, and construction of a bund commenced.[13] The bund-side lawns were often marked out as a Europeans-only leisure area. Established trading firms such as Butterfield & Swire, or Jardine, Matheson & Co., opened branch offices and built new 'hongs' (company offices and messes) and 'godowns' (warehouses) by the bund. Their shipping lines, Swire's China Navigation Company, Jardine's Indo-China Steam Navigation

---

[9] On the China and Shanghai British see: Jürgen Osterhammel, 'Britain and China 1842–1914', in Porter (ed.), *Oxford History of the British Empire*, iii. 146–69; Robert Bickers, *Britain in China: Community, Culture and Colonialism, 1900–49* (Manchester, 1999); Jürgen Osterhammel, 'China', in Judith Brown and Wm Roger Louis (eds.), *The Oxford History of the British Empire*, iv. *The Twentieth Century* (Oxford, 1999), 643–66; Robert Bickers, 'Shanghailanders: The Formation and Identity of the British Settler Community in Shanghai 1843–1937', *Past and Present*, 159 (1998), 161–211; and Bickers, *Empire Made Me*.

[10] Arnold Wright (ed.), *Twentieth Century Impressions of Hong Kong, Shanghai, and Other Treaty Ports of China: Their History, People, Commerce, Industries and Resources* (London, 1908), preface.

[11] China coast is the most adequate term, but it includes the riverine and interior settlements.

[12] On architecture: Edward Denison and Guang Yu Ren, *Building Shanghai: The Story of China's Gateway* (London, 2006); Jon W. Huebner, 'Architecture of the Shanghai Bund', *Papers on Far Eastern History*, 39 (1989), 127–65; Peter Hibbard, *The Bund Shanghai: China Faces West* (Hong Kong, 2007).

[13] See Jeremy Taylor, 'The Bund: Littoral Space of Empire in the Treaty Ports of East Asia', *Social History*, 27/2 (2002) 125–42.

Company, would establish new schedules calling at the port. The maritime customs station formally opened to administer foreign trade. A club or two was established, freemasons opened a lodge branch, a race course was usually marked out, and a cemetery was always needed very shortly after the first foreign residents arrived.

In larger ports a volunteer corps might be formed, and it would sooner or later be blooded (and afterwards the men would pose for photographs with their guns).[14] There might or might not be a permanent British consul (in most locations with British concessions there was). A mission station might already be present, but would certainly be developed further, and new outposts of other societies might take advantage of the new ease of access. A summer resort was identified in nearby hills; property there was some-times purchased and communal facilities developed. Prospectors arrived rapidly at the port, eager to establish a niche or corner a market. Journalism was one such fleet-footed profession. A larger port might generate its own newspaper in time, Fuzhou's *Foochow Daily Echo* (1873–), Hankou's *Hankow Times* (1866–8), *Hankow Daily News* (1906–), *Central China Post* (1904–), Tianjin's *Peking and Tientsin Times* (1894–1941), but from smaller ones 'outport' correspondents would pen regular news round-ups to the *North China Herald* in Shanghai.[15] In these various ways the new outports quickly incorporated themselves into the existing web of China coast com-munities. Any new British arrival from elsewhere in China would know where he was once he stepped off the boat (and it was usually a boat), and what to look for. It was a British Chinese world, a Britain in China which evolved and expanded, siting its familiar practices and appurtenances on and in Chinese soil—its clubs, lawns, flower gardens, race courses—some-times with Chinese characteristics, but more often than not with British Indian ones, but either way usually bluntly foreign, familiar, and clearly British. Histories or guidebooks would be published, and in time the early memorials or cemeteries would become sites of communal memorialization or sightseeing interest. Unusually for a British community, however, they faced the abrupt dislocation of communist victory in 1949. This story and those histories have a beginning and an end.

---

[14] Putnam Weale, *Why China Sees Red* (New York, 1925), opposite p. 243.

[15] To date there exists only a preliminary account of the extent of activity: Frank H. H. King and Prescott Clark (eds.), *A Research Guide to China Coast Newspapers, 1822–1911* (Cambridge, Mass., 1965).

This chapter explores what can be learnt from this China century. The passages to Asia of the China Britons were varied. They came directly from Britain, recruited through the London agents, offices, or headquarters of businesses, municipal administrations (John Pook and Co., for the SMC), or the Chinese Maritime Customs (on Great Queen Street, Westminster). Those recruiting competed in the classifieds and professional journals with the agents of formal empire service, and informal empire opportunity. The China Briton might easily have become a Natalian, taken a post in Ceylon, or found a billet in Buenos Aires. They joined on the spot as well, having made their way under their own steam in search of openings, or liking what they saw of life as they arrived with the British military or as merchant seamen. They also came from elsewhere in the British world. A file of applications to the customs in the second half of the 1930s includes letters from men in Southern Rhodesia (eight years in the British India Steam Navigation Company, then two in the British South Africa Police), Hong Kong (seven years prior service in the Straits Settlements and Federated Malay States Agriculture Department for one man, another had purchased his army discharge in the colony), from Ulster (trading, as many did, on 'the late Sir Robert Hart's connection with Portadown'), from London and from elsewhere in China, from 21-year-old P. J. Evans, in Tianjin, who hoped there might be 'good prospects for a young man who will diligently apply himself to his duties'. There were letters from Shanghai too, from Nancy Bentley, 18 years old, of 'British descent', 'borne [sic] in Shanghai, but obtained my education in Canada' (such as she evidently had), from A. C. Harmer (three times made redundant now in under four years), and from H. C. Pelling, 'a Britisher, age 40 of good social standing', 'absolutely destitute', who had been in China over twenty years.[16] Foreign recruitment to the customs, contract work aside, had formally ended in 1929, but the Irish ties were still useful ones. All the others were to be disappointed. The British came to China in good numbers, from all over the British world, and they moved on too, back into that world. China was a staging post, but it was also by the 1930s a routine terminus, for professional and private migrations.

---

[16] Second Historical Archives of China, Chinese Maritime Customs Service records, 679(1), 17242, 'Applications for appointment in the Customs: Foreign, 1936-48'.

One way of mapping the pattern of British settlement in China is to lay out the concessions and treaty ports that were identifiably British, and whose acquisition, management or retrocession was a matter for treaty (either before or after the fact of retrocession—the latter was the case for Hankow and Kiukiang). Table 10.1 identifies the British concessions in

Table 10.1 Settlements in China under British, or part-British jurisdiction

	Status	Year opened	Year retroceded	
Kulangsu, Amoy (Gulangyu, Xiamen)	Internat. settlement	1902	1943	
Amoy (Xiamen)	British concession	1843	1930	
Chinkiang (Zhenjiang)	British concession	1861	1929	
Hankow (Hankou)	British concession		1927	Became a Special Admin. District
Hong Kong	British Crown Colony	1842	1997	Became a Special Admin. Region
Kowloon New territories	Leased territory (British)	1898	1997	Incorporated in above
Kiukiang (Jiujiang)	British concession	1961	1927	Became a Special Admin. District
Peking Legation Quarter	Internat. jurisdiction	1901	1943	
Shanghai	Internat. settlement	1843	1943	
Shameen (Shamian, Canton)	British concession	1859	1943	
Tientsin (Tianjin)	British concession	1860	1943	
Weihaiwei	Leased territory (British)	1898	1930	Royal Naval summer station retained

China.[17] The flag flew most prominently at these sites. They were spread along the coast, and the Yangzi river. Other nominal concessions, dominated by Britons, had less if any basis in treaty, such as the hill station at Guling, a private land-development initiative, which was eventually run by an 'Estate Council', but which was returned to Chinese jurisdiction in 1936.[18] Most Britons lived and worked entirely within such geographically scattered settlements and concessions. They might make local excursions, jaunting to Hangzhou from Shanghai, or taking slow house-boat shooting trips into the waterways west of the city. They vacationed at the summer resorts of Qingdao (the former German naval colony), or Beidaihe, or at Guling, but they mostly did not travel for pleasure in China. On long leaves they mostly went to Britain or the dominions; on short leaves they often went to Japan, single men often as sex tourists. These British concessions, however, also served as nodes in a number of other, overlapping, networks. British residence was not restricted to British or international concessions, and there were another three dozen ports formally opened in one way or another to foreign residence. An informal 'most favoured nation' practice (which built on some formally agreed most favoured nation clauses in mid-nineteenth-century treaties) meant that subjects of one nation often assumed the residency rights of others in newly opened ports. Trading firms such as Butterfield & Swire, Jardine Matheson, the Asiatic Petroleum Company, Imperial Chemicals Industries, and British American Tobacco all maintained networks through towns and cities well beyond the treaty port map. Missions operated within the treaty settlements, and deeper inside the Chinese hinterlands, well past the last railway station and steamer stops. Their engagement with local society and culture was of a different order to that of most other facets of the foreign presence.[19]

---

[17] There is no distinction in Chinese in discussions of the treaty ports between 'concession' and 'settlement', both are rendered as 'zujie' (literally 'rented land'). In practice the distinction helps highlight the difference between zones acquired by single foreign states (concessions), and those which were internationally administered (settlements).

[18] Jeanie Woodrow Woodbridge, *Glimpses of Kuling: A Souvenir of Lushan* (Shanghai, 1904), 14–16. On Guling's founder, E. S. Little, see Maureen L. Rustichelli, 'Edward Selby Little: The Forgotten Victorian, 1864–1939', unpublished MS, 2003.

[19] A comprehensive geographical survey is provided by Milton T. Stauffer *et al.* (eds.), *The Christian Occupation of China; A General Survey of the Numerical Strength and Geographical Distribution of the Christian Forces in China, Made by the Special Committee on Survey and Occupation, China Continuation Committee, 1918–1921* (Shanghai, 1922).

Business and mission also operated well beyond China as well of course. Trading or banking firms were linked into their own international networks, and staff might move away from China itself. The world of the Hongkong and Shanghai Bank, as represented in the murals on the ceiling of the entrance hall to its 1923 Shanghai bund headquarters, encompassed that city, Hong Kong, Tokyo, London, Calcutta, Paris, New York, and Bangkok. Mission councils ran operations across continents, circulating ideas, practices, and, to a lesser extent, personnel, between them. Another network comprised Britons in the formal or *ad hoc* employ of the Chinese state. Over 5,000 British men worked for the Chinese Maritime Customs Service at some point between 1854 and 1949, and they were often rotated through different postings at maritime, riverine, and land customs stations, or in the lighthouse network built by the customs, although some had long periods of service in just one port. Less formally, numbers of men, some of them former customs employees, worked as advisers for central or provincial administrations, or their enemies.[20] Extraterritoriality's greatest benefit, however, was that it extended foreign privileges—of consular instead of Chinese jurisdiction—wherever a Briton actually went, as it was invested in his or her person (and was often and aggressively extended by firms to British-owned property or goods). In effect, practical considerations aside, wherever a British subject set up shop or residence, the flag followed.

Other flags always flew there too. While they developed communal associations and institutions that demonstrated their Britishness, treaty port residents were also mostly living and working in broader, multinational, communities, and in cities sometimes parcelled up by neighbourhood in minute, almost mocking, replica of the African land grab. A single walk crossed empires. Hankou was home to German, French, Russian, and Japanese concessions. There were seven other foreign concessions in Tianjin. Britons in Shanghai worked with European, American, and Japanese partners in the running of the International Settlement. They often chose to live in the French concession, and some Britons also served on the council of the concession itself. Britons in Tianjin often preferred to live in the German concession.[21] In the customs, Germans and Austrians in 1914 formed the

---

[20] See e.g. Eiko Woodhouse, *The Chinese Hsinhai Revolution: G. E. Morrison and Anglo-Japanese Relations, 1897–1920* (London, 2003); Daniel S. Levy, *Two-Gun Cohen: A Biography* (New York, 1997); C. W. Mason, *The Chinese Confessions of Charles Welsh Mason* (London, 1924).

[21] H. G. W. Woodhead, *A Journalist in China* (London, 1934), 63.

second largest foreign contingent (219, against 753 Britons), and all were employees of the Chinese state, regardless of nationality. As inspector-general of the service, Sir Francis Aglen, wrote letters of condolence to the widow of at least one of his men, an Austrian officer killed in December 1914.[22] China did not enter the war until 1917, and the international settlements in particular were therefore neutral zones throughout most of the conflict. The German Club Concordia, and the British Shanghai Club, both graced the Shanghai bund (and the Germans had hosted the British while their new club building—opened in 1912—was being constructed), and although wartime legislation served to prohibit trading with the enemy, disentangling Anglo-German ties proved extremely difficult, if not, for some, unpopular. They could at least cut each other on the street, as one American observed, as they made their way to their respective clubs to discuss the news from Europe over lunch.[23]

The cosmopolitan intimacy of the treaty ports went beyond the fact of proximity, and collaboration in local government. Anglo-German business links were particularly strong, and in some cases vital. It proved impossible for British directors of the Anglo-German Brewery Company to wholly remove the German element from their Qingdao-based firm. How, they asked, could they make their Tsingtao Beer without their German brewmaster?[24] Don't let's be beastly to the local Germans, counselled the *North China Daily News* in August 1914, eager to avoid unpleasantness on Shanghai's streets, which might not have done much good to 'white' prestige in Chinese eyes, and which might—and this danger was explicitly signalled—have provided an opportunity for 'unruly elements' to imperil 'Great Britain's heritage in Shanghai'. Imperialist disunity offered potential anti-imperialist opportunities for disrupting what was vaguely termed 'the common good', that is, the common imperialist good, the International Settlement itself.[25] A fitful peace then followed in the treaty ports, with British and German companies of the Shanghai Volunteer Corps, for example, sensibly conducting military manœuvres in different parts of the settlement. Beastliness of a sort was postponed until victory, when the British

[22] See 'Maximilian Hey', URL: <http://www.austro-hungarian-army.co.uk/biog/hey.htm>, accessed 3 July 2006. Hey had served in the Customs since 1898.
[23] John B. Powell, *My Twenty-Five Years in China* (New York, 1945), 55.
[24] TNA, PRO, FO 371/2310, F152722, Peking No. 243, 21 Sept. 1915, enclosures and file.
[25] *NCH* (8 Aug. 1914), 406.

aided the Chinese in the systematic expulsion of all former enemy subjects from China. The Germans had the last laugh. The new post-war recruits to German enterprise worked very effectively without the mental or legal baggage of treaty and imperialism that weighed down the British in the fast evolving politics of the 1920s and 1930s.[26]

British and German interests intertwined, but Chinese collaboration underpinned entirely the British presence in China. From the opening of the treaty ports onwards, when Cantonese traders (and prostitutes) moved north with the British, Chinese collaboration facilitated British activity at all levels. 'The system itself being adapted to Canton and founded on principles only understood at that place renders the assistance of a Canton man, in the first instance, indispensable', noted Fuzhou Consul G. T. Lay of his Cantonese staff in 1845.[27] Jardines needed its compradors, the London Missionary Society its Bible-women, the 'missee' her 'boy', the single man his 'China girl'. At all levels, even as bodies of information and cadres of expertise (the consuls, the Hong Kong cadets[28]) were developed—as produce and product names were translated and systematized by the customs, or Chinese news translated or recorded in the treaty port press—the British presence, masked as such, actually had a Chinese face. Furthermore, the deterritorialized zones offered opportunity for Chinese commercial, political, or cultural entrepreneurship, which found British agents ready to offer the extraterritorial privileges for considerations ranging at one extreme from the useful stipend and flowing liquor (for a semi-vagrant possessing nothing of value beyond his nationality), to sophisticated front companies.[29] One such common arrangement, by which the Chinese vessel the *Arrow* was British-flagged, prompted a series of unfolding events which provided the occasion for war in 1856.[30] Concessions offered opportunities for Chinese land investment, negotiated through British land renters; treaty port business welcomed Chinese capital, if it did not in many instances rely on it.

[26] W. C. Kirby, *Germany and Republican China* (Stanford, Calif., 1984), 24.

[27] TNA, PRO, FO 228/52, Fuzhou No. 10, 18 Mar. 1845.

[28] H. J. Lethbridge, 'Hong Kong Cadets, 1862–1941', *Journal of the Hong Kong Branch of the Royal Asiatic Society*, 10 (1970), 36–56.

[29] Case of Charles H. Nail, *NCH* (18 Nov. 1885), 584–5; Eiichi Motono, *Conflict and Cooperation in Sino-British Business, 1860–1911: The Impact of the Pro-British Commercial Network in Shanghai* (Basingstoke, 2000), 167–8.

[30] John Wong, *Deadly Dreams: Opium, Imperialism, and the 'Arrow' War (1856–1860) in China* (Cambridge, 1998).

On a smaller scale, some Chinese families allied themselves to British interests, to the Anglo-Chinese School, to the Anglo-Chinese College, to work in the British-owned Shanghai Waterworks for example, sometimes extending their Anglophile leanings to service in the volunteer militia, the Shanghai Volunteer Corps (SVC).[31] Language skills and contacts were obviously of value and used by such families, but extending activity into participation in the SVC indicates a more engaged alliance with British interests in particular. Other groups made less legitimate use of their alliance, such as the Cantonese traders, servants, and followers who moved with the British into the early treaty ports, and who provided a steady flow of difficult work for consuls, as they claimed extraterritorial rights through their British connection.[32] Conversely, some British entrepreneurs worked adeptly across cultures with Chinese collaborators, most strikingly perhaps Southampton native Ernest Major (1841–1908), who launched various Chinese-language publishing ventures in Shanghai, most notably the *Shenbao* newspaper in 1872. This supplanted other more opportunistic titles, which were founded to capitalize on relaying property and shipping information to Chinese businessmen, and *Shenbao* became the most widely read and influential Chinese newspaper, sometimes at the cost of consular anxiety and hostility. Major's achievement was to work fluently within and with Chinese circles in the city in a way that remained unusual outside parts of the missionary world. His own ability to speak Chinese was also critical, and equally unusual well into the early twentieth century.[33]

On the whole, reliance mingled with insularity bred contempt. Treaty port administrators aspired to a harmonious community of interest. Elite and official Chinese were incorporated into the ritual life of the settlements (but sometimes at cross purposes, as has been shown of the different discourses around the 1893 Shanghai jubilee). But even elite Chinese were excluded from formal political life until the 1920s, and

---

[31] e.g. Zee Way Zung (Xu Huishun), his sons and son-in-law T. T. Chen: Wright, *Twentieth Century Impressions*, 548; I. I. Kounin (ed.), *Eighty-Five Years of the SVC* (Shanghai, 1938), 184–6; personal information from T. T. Chen.

[32] A running theme at Fuzhou in 1846–7 e.g.: see TNA, PRO, FO 228/62, and FO 228/74, *passim*.

[33] Rudolf G. Wagner, 'The *Shenbao* in Crisis: The International Environment and the Conflict between Guo Songtao and the Shenbao', *Late Imperial China*, 20/1 (1999), 107–43; Barbara Mittler, *A Newspaper for China? Power, Identity, and Change in Shanghai's News Media, 1872–1912* (Cambridge, Mass., 2004).

exclusionary practices were widespread in private associational life, and in
the provision of public and municipal facilities.[34] Outside work, and aside
from their servants, and their wives, or regular or irregular sexual contacts,
Britons did not know or meet Chinese. They did not taste Chinese food. They
did not like or comprehend Chinese music. They detested the sounds of the
living streets. They did not like China, and they did not see themselves as
living in China as such. They were white. Nothing in their education, or in
popular or elite culture, much taught them humility. There were always
exceptions. Missionaries worked within and with Chinese communities, but
patterns of exclusion were also common in missionary life well into the 1920s.
Evidence of friendship in any sector is in short supply, although memory—
inflected by the common experience of fighting Japan after Pearl Harbor—
tends to record another story. Early consular regulations aimed to head off
conflict by regulating the movement of British subjects, requiring at Ningbo
for example, applications for licences to hunt, travel further than three miles
from the city, enter other towns and villages, and enjoining Britons to 'do no
positive injury to the people, [and] always to guard against doing anything
that may shock their prejudices'.[35] Evidence from magistrate court accounts,
and from the press, suggests that daily interaction on the streets even eighty
years later could be fraught with tension, and with the potential for sullen
violence. Argument, itself exacerbated by mutual incomprehensibility, often
led to physical remonstrance, and conflict—the rickshaw puller was kicked,
the man obstructing passage was shoved aside. Assault was punished in the
consular courts, but only where it was brought to their notice and successfully
prosecuted. A culture of suspicion seems to have developed, and such daily
minor violence probably far exceeded the number of cases ever brought to
consular attention.

Shanghai

We can map a specifically British story in internationalized Shanghai, and it
serves to tell us much about the China coast Britons generally. British

---

[34] Bryna Goodman, 'Improvisations on a Semi-Colonial Theme, or, How to Read a Celebration of Transnational Urban Community', *Journal of Asian Studies*, 59/4 (2000), 889–926; Robert Bickers and Jeffrey N. Wasserstrom, 'Shanghai's "Chinese and Dogs Not Admitted" Sign: Legend, History and Contemporary Symbol', *China Quarterly*, 142 (1995), 423–43.

[35] TNA, PRO, FO 228/31, Ningbo No. 4, 20 Jan. 1844, enclosure 1, 'Regulations to be Observed by All British Subjects; Residing at, or Resorting to Ningpo'.

residence formally began on 14 November 1843 when Consul George Balfour, who had arrived six days earlier, declared the port open to foreign
trade. A British, later the International, Settlement, developed thereafter.
The new foreign residents were allowed to rent land in a strip alongside the
Huangpu river outside the walled city. Regulations governing land use in
this settlement were first drawn up by the Chinese authorities in 1845, and
later versions (1854, 1869, 1898) provided the basis on which the mainly
British land renters elected a committee to maintain order and construct
roads and jetties; in 1854 this became the Shanghai Municipal Council
elected thereafter annually on a property-based franchise by foreign rate-
payers (and after 1928 including Chinese representation).[36] In 1854 these
Land Renters established a Shanghai Municipal Police Force (SMP) and
also, in response to the seizure of the Chinese city of Shanghai by rebels in
1853, the SVC.[37] British settlers dominated the treaty port's culture, and
language, inflecting the language of their German neighbours, and the
accents of the Americans, while pidgin English was resorted to by Chinese
sojourners and immigrants who did not understand each others' languages
and dialects.[38] The British, however, with suitable due deference to the
requirements of local *realpolitik*, in the form of their US or German partners, controlled the SMC, and generally they did things their way.

In the first seventy years of the development of the International Settlement the British presence grew steadily. The institutions established
evolved, and arrogated to themselves more territory, and more power—
and more autonomous power—and although the British state through
the consul general kept its eyes on events, there was no need for diplomats
to think seriously about the impact of this settlement until the 1920s.
There were local incidents of conflict with the local Chinese state and/or
populace, such the 1897 Wheelbarrow Riots, or the 1905 Mixed Court
Incident, but even though blood flowed these were confined, circumscribed

---

[36] Robert Bickers, 'Citizenship by Correspondence in the Shanghai International Settlement,
1919–43', in Yves Chevrier, Alain Roux, and Xiaohong Xiao-Planes (eds.), *Citadins et citoyens
dans la Chine du XXe siècle* (Paris, 2010).

[37] *NCH* (2 July 1854), 203; (2 Sept. 1854), 18; (11 Nov. 1854), 58–9. See also Kounin, *Eighty-Five
Years of the SVC*.

[38] See e.g. Françoise Kreissler, *L'Action culturelle allemande en Chine: De la fin du XIXe siècle à
la Seconde Guerre mondiale* (Paris, 1989), and James Huskey, 'Americans in Shanghai: Community Formation and Response to Revolution, 1919–1928', Ph.D. thesis (University of North
Carolina, 1985).

Table 10.2 Numbers of British Residents in Shanghai, Hong Kong, and China, 1851–1951

	Internat. settlement	French concession	Chinese jurisdiction	Total British in China (excl. Hong Kong)	Brit. residents Hong Kong (civil)	Brit. military personnel Hong Kong	Total Brit. population Hong Kong
1851	256						
1865	1,372*	19					
1871	894				869	1,739	2,608
1876	872						
1880	1,057						
1881					785	3,756	4,541
1885	1,453						
1890	1,574						
1891					1,448	2,900	4,348
1895	1,936						
1900	2,691						
1901					3,007	13,237	3,007
1903	3,713			5,662			
1905							
1906				9,256			
1910	4,465	314		10,140			
1911					3,761		
1915	4,822	681		8,641			
1920	5,341	1,044		11,082			
1921					7,889		
1925	5,879	2,312		15,247			
1930	6,221	2,219	891	13,015			
1931				13,344°	6,684	7,682	14,366
1934		2,630	1,153				
1935	6,595						
1936		2,648					

Year		
1940		172
1941		
1942	5,865*	
1943		133
1945§	635*	
1946	3,103*	
1947	4,424*	
1948	4,608*	
1949#	3,228*	
1950 (Feb)	1,850	
1951 (Jan)	1,311	2,284
1951 (Oct)	697	997

*Number once army, navy and seamen excluded. ° After this date the Chinese Maritime Customs Service ceased to publish estimates of foreign population statistics in its *Annual Return of Trade* from where these figures are taken. # Population in December 1949, after takeover. § Dec 1945 figure: initially, most former internees were required by the British authorities to leave Shanghai, and most did so in order to recuperate.

Sources: NCH, 3 May 1851, p. 159, 1 Apr. 1865, pp. 50–1, and SMC, *Annual Reports*, 1871–1935; H. G. W. Woodhead (ed.), *The China Year Book 1931* (London, 1931), 694; Zou Yiren, *Jiu Shanghai renkou bianqian de yanjiu* (Research on population change in old Shanghai) (Shanghai, 1980), 145–7.

emergencies.[39] Shanghailanders heralded their fiftieth anniversary with a triumphant jubilee celebration in November 1893; processions, parades, and fireworks marked the event, and hymns to the city's cosmopolitanism were sung. 'Where in the world', asked one banner, 'is not Shanghai known?' Another warned: 'Shanghai guards its own'.[40]

Family life and cultural life, of a sort, developed. The familiar colonial imbalance in the ratio between British men and women eased over the decades, especially after the turn of the twentieth century, as developments in refrigeration, communications, and public health, encouraged more men to have their families with them in China. Many more men, of course, found local solutions to their individual predicaments, although the informality of such arrangements, and changing social mores make this hard to quantify. For J. O. P. Bland, writing in his memoirs, Chinese mistresses played 'an inconspicuous but by no means unimportant part in the life of the [Hankow] Concession' in the mid-1880s. Bland was tempted, but claimed that his wallet decided against a companion.[41] The Shanghai British led mostly insular lives. They had come to Britain in China, and to Shanghai, not to China, although this did not stop them sounding off in letters to the local press about what they saw as Chinese inadequacies, be they social, 'racial', or political. But they were as eager to debate parochial issues and events, to read *Sport and Gossip* (1897–), buy Mrs Mina Shorrock's magazine *Social Shanghai* (1906–c.1914), with its photographs of their sporting events, or to participate gamely in the Shanghai Amateur Circus.[42] In common with other Europeans, the Shanghai British bought with them the culture of amateur musical life, and then used their local governing power to direct municipal rates to the upkeep after 1881 of a town band which entertained

[39] Samuel Couling, *The History of Shanghai*, part 2 (Shanghai, 1923), 322–3; Bryna Goodman, *Native Place, City, and Nation: Regional Networks and Identities in Shanghai, 1853–1937* (Berkeley, Calif., 1995), 187–95.
[40] *The Jubilee of Shanghai 1843–1893, Shanghai: Past and Present, and a full account of the proceedings on the 17th and 18th November, 1893* (Shanghai, 1893); on the jubilee see Jeffrey N. Wasserstrom, 'Imagining Community in the International Settlement: The Shanghai Jubilee as an Invented Tradition', paper presented at the University of California, Berkeley, Centre for Chinese Studies, 2 Dec. 1994; Goodman, 'Improvisations on a Semi-Colonial Theme'.
[41] Bland memoir, ch. 2, pp. 6–8, box 27, Papers of J. O. P. Bland, Thomas Fisher Rare Book Library, University of Toronto.
[42] Wright, *Twentieth Century Impressions*, 363–4; *Shanghai Race Club Amateur Circus*, programmes 1894, 1895, private collection; J. Em. Lemière (comp.), *The Amateur Circus of 1901* (Shanghai, 1901).

them as they sat in the bund's public gardens, and which evolved into a fine and influential Shanghai Symphony Orchestra.[43] They lived and worked, and died in China, then. By 1941 there had been just under 4,000 grants of probate through the British Supreme Court at Shanghai and its predecessors; hundreds more records of the intestate dead also survive. By 1939, there had been almost 16,000 burials in Shanghai's foreign cemeteries. A significant proportion of these were Britons.[44]

Visitors often reported them philistine and vulgar. This was not entirely fair. A North China Branch of the Royal Asiatic Society was established in 1857. Papers were read, debated, and published in its journal (1858–1948), and its large library became a public resource by the 1930s.[45] Kelly & Walsh developed into the most formidable local publisher, producing works of scholarship, phrasebooks and guidebooks, translations and commentary. Its operations grew across East and Southeast Asia. But scholarship remained a minority pursuit, and Sinology even more so. A popular literature was generated—parochial light prose from the likes of J. O. P. Bland, and exotic and usually formulaic thrillers, but there is no Kipling, and British China never prompted an E. M. Forster. Graham Greene resigned from British American Tobacco just before his China posting was due. There were later and more oblique responses in the work of the China-born J. G. Ballard and Mervyn Peake, but the more direct and lasting sketches come from the visiting Somerset Maugham, who lampooned his hosts to devastating effect in *The Painted Veil* (1925) and *On a Chinese Screen* (1922).[46]

They made themselves at home. Lea & Perrins placed advertisements in the *North China Herald* urging them to avoid counterfeit bottles of its ubiquitous sauce. They were followed to China by consignments of 'London made jewellery', Holloway's Pills, 'elegant household furniture', and J. C. White's pale sherries and brandies. The Shanghai Library's new arrivals in

[43] Robert Bickers, '"The Greatest Cultural Asset East of Suez": The History and Politics of the Shanghai Municipal Orchestra and Public Band, 1881–1946', in Chi-hsiung Chang (ed.), *Ershi shiji de Zhongguo yu shijie* (China and the World in the Twentieth Century) (Taipei, 2001), 835–75.

[44] China probates are in TNA, PRO, FO 917, and intestate files for Shanghai: FO 1092/260–9; *Annual Report of the Shanghai Municipal Council, 1939* (Shanghai, 1940), 177.

[45] Harold Otness, 'Nurturing the Roots for Oriental Studies: The Development of the Libraries of the Royal Asiatic Society's Branches and Affiliates in Asia in the Nineteenth Century', *International Association of Orientalist Librarians Bulletin*, 43 (1998), 9–17.

[46] In this they were not unique of course. See A. Riposte (a pseudonymous Elinor Mordaunt), *Gin and Bitters* (New York, 1931) for an attack on Maugham, which he had suppressed.

February 1860 included *Australian Facts and Figures*, *The West Indies*, Samuel Smiles's *Self Help*, and *Punch's 1860 Pocket Book*.[47] They could surround themselves with such familiar stuff, warding off China in small parts of their lives, and keeping the wider world of empire and empire opportunity on their horizon. What began as conspicuous bachelor consumption in the early days, became the material of the full-scale domestic recreation of home as family life developed, and as communications improved.[48] Outside the home, the cabaret and the recreation club, the hotel bar or the cinema, and not the library, were in fact the more likely off-duty haunts of the community. Social life was public, and exaggerated. It was a 'regular mish-mash of free and easy living', reported one Scot who arrived in 1926, and rather than scholarship, Britons in Shanghai put their off-duty energies into living out what was even then a mythologized nightlife.[49] 'There exists in Shanghai', reported a Municipal Salaries Commission three years earlier:

a standard of living which is extravagant beyond all necessity and beyond all reason, and this false standard of extravagance reacts unfavourably on the life of the whole Community but most unfavourably on new arrivals who perhaps less through the fault of themselves than of their surroundings are tempted to maintain a standard beyond both their needs and their means.[50]

It is sometimes difficult to see through the 'Happy Valley' mist. The lurid social life which is romanticized in memoir was the subject of overseas newspaper tittle-tattle at the time, and in the twenty-first century is recreated as tourist chic in a reglobalizing city. Sometimes the Shanghai British provided good meat for the yellow press feast—'Suspicious events in China' ran one newspaper account of the Shanghai prehistory of a broker at the centre of a sensationally lurid criminal sex case heard at the Sussex Assizes in 1925.[51] There was 'just sufficient truth to make the complacent resident of this port a little uneasy' noted an otherwise bemused newspaper

[47] *NCH* (29 Mar. 1862), 50; (27 Aug. 1853), 16; (21 June 1862), 98; (25 Feb. 1860), 31.

[48] Although it deals with North American missionary women, Jane Hunter, *The Gospel of Gentility: American Women Missionaries in Turn-of-the-Century China* (New Haven, 1984), suggests much about European home making in China more broadly.

[49] Bickers, *Empire Made Me*; Andrew Field, 'A Night in Shanghai: Nightlife and Modernity in Semicolonical China, 1919–1937', Ph.D. thesis (Columbia University, 2001).

[50] 'Report of the Municipal Salaries Commission', *Municipal Gazette* (9 Apr. 1921), 113.

[51] Reprinted in *The Times* (10 May 1932), 5.

review of Henry Champly's salacious exposé of the 'white slave trade', *The Road to Shanghai* (1935), when it touched on the White Russian predicament. But it was the same predicament in Paris, Berlin, London, he concluded, there was nothing unique to Shanghai about it.[52] It needs to be remembered that daily life mostly followed familiar patterns, recreated as far and as exactly as possible. And boredom followed the flag too, 'the same faces every day at the same tennis courts and whist tables, and the same dull topers at the Club bar' remembered Bland of his months in Canton in 1887.[53] Perhaps boredom loomed heavier where men and women were so far from kith, kin, and their home networks. Still, opportunities were provided for extravagance and enjoyment not to be met with in the English and Scottish towns from which young men came. They embraced them, and often fell as a result.[54] Browsing the newspapers suggests, further, that alienation and failure, compounded by distance, perhaps led more easily to suicide.

They were a long way from the familiar, however well they could recreate it in China. The fastest clipper in 1851 made the journey in 107 days. Travelling got speedier, and towards the end of the treaty port century, in 1937, Imperial Airways inaugurated an expensive Hong Kong run of just eight and a half days (Pan American had extended its San Francisco to Manila service to the colony in the same year).[55] But distance was never truly conquered, and it meant separation. People were parted: young men going east from their families, and sometimes from fiancées, children heading from China to schools, from their parents. Letters travelled only as fast as people could, and 'With what greediness we devour the contents' wrote one chazee (tea trader) in 1851, as the mails arrived.[56] As elsewhere in the worlds of empire, separation was a norm, and as elsewhere high mortality rates often made separation final. The cost of China postings,

---

[52] *North China Daily News* (24 Mar. 1935). On this genre of work, see Michael B. Miller, *Shanghai on the Metro: Spies, Intrigue and the French between the Wars* (Berkeley, Calif., 1995).

[53] Bland memoir, ch. 4, p. 1, box 27, Papers of J. O. P. Bland, Thomas Fisher Rare Book Library, University of Toronto.

[54] Bickers, *Empire Made Me*, 144–5, 156–7; consular wrecks are sketched in P. D. Coates, *The China Consuls: British Consular Officers, 1843–1943* (Hong Kong, 1988), 357–62.

[55] James Dow, 'Journal of a voyage to China, etc., 1851–1864', entry 13 Oct. 1851, private collection; *The Times* (18 Dec. 1937), 9; (29 Apr. 1937), 15).

[56] James Dow, 'Journal of a voyage to China, etc., 1851–1864', entry 31 Oct. 1851, private collection.

Table 10.3 Number of British residents, Tianjin, 1913–1951

	Tianjin British concession	Tianjin
1913	388	634
1925	682	1,300
1927*	650	200
1929	755	
1934	1,451	
1938	1,372	
1951 Jan		175
1951 Oct		107

Sources: 1913, 1925, 1929, 1934, 1938: *Report of the Tientsin British Municipal Council 1938*; 1927: TNA, FO 228/3836, Tianjin No.5, 20 Jan. 1928, Enclosure 1. In the entire consular district there were another 1,287 British residents; 1951: Bickers, *Britain in China*, p. 242.

especially on infants, was very high. In its early decades Shanghai became notorious as an unhealthy station for the military, much more so than Hong Kong. Political turmoil in the mid-nineteenth century prompted waves of refugees to enter the settlements, bringing with them, and falling victim to, contagious disease. The worst single year for foreign mortality, in raw numbers, was 1863, when 1,600 military personnel died.[57] Dealing with this seemingly structural crisis was a key factor in the development of the institutions and practices of the municipal administration in Shanghai. There was no alternative, even if the financial cost was resented. The logic of settlement drove the creation of the public health departments, sanitation projects, licensing and inspection regimes which made it feasible, and made a settlement out of sojourners.

All of this—life, work, death—took place elsewhere in British China of course. Tianjin housed the second biggest settlement (Table 10.3), but there was a different feel to its local politics and identity. Tientsiners prided themselves on being less belligerent than the Shanghai die-hards in what Arthur Ransome labelled the 'Ulster of the East'.[58] There were seven other foreign concessions in the city, and theirs was a British concession, not an international settlement, and was thereby much more under effective

---

[57] Kerrie L. MacPherson, *A Wilderness of Marshes: The Origins of Public Health in Shanghai, 1843–1893* (Hong Kong, 1987).

[58] In his *The Chinese Puzzle* (London, 1927).

consular control, with a council also much more under the heel of the oligarchs. There was a strong local business interest—notably Kailan Mining—but their community overall lacked the cohesiveness, confidence, and distinctiveness of Shanghai.[59] They wrote less about themselves at the time, and in retrospect, and a distinctive Tianjin identity was much less easy to outline than the Shanghai world that could be packaged for children in Patricia Allen's *Shanghai Picture-Verse* (1939). Treaty port life elsewhere, amongst for example the 180 Amoy Britons in 1910 (augmented by 181 'registered Chinese') out of 2,525 registered foreigners, was of a muchness, small in scale, and in significance, and best portrayed in Maugham's *On a Chinese Screen*.[60] The sometimes extreme isolation of the 'outport' British has a limited contribution to make to understanding the broader picture of settlement and identity, except in its often faithful mimicry, in miniature, of the patterns and practices of concession life.

A shared identity at one level, as Britons in China, was generated and maintained by a number of factors. Shared nationality, and so a shared relationship with the British consular system in China, which was formalized in the annual registration process required of Britons, was one factor. This underpinned their access to the benefits of extraterritoriality. Sport provided another vehicle. 'Interport' cricket and rugby fixtures were arranged between the major ports, and even with British teams from communities in Japan and the Straits Settlements. (Only two members of the Hong Kong team survived their 1892 visit to Shanghai, as their steamer foundered on the journey south.)[61] The key to a sense of 'national' identity lay in the press. Although it had a strong Shanghai focus, the weekly edition of the *North China Herald* was critical. This was as close to a national newspaper that the China coast British developed, and gave the British in China their clearest sense of forming at one level a single, cohesive community. From Nanning to Harbin, they could read the same paper, which talked

---

[59] On the Tianjin British see e.g. William McLeish, *Life in a China Outport* (Tianjin, *c*.1917); O. D. Rasmussen, *Tientsin: An Illustrated Outline History* (Tianjin, 1925); Tianjin Municipal Archives *et al.* (comps.), *Tianjin zujie dang'an xuanbian* (Selected Archives of the Tianjin Concessions) (Tianjin, 1992).

[60] Revd Philip Wilson Pitcher, *In and about Amoy: Some Historical and Other Facts Connected with One of the First Open Ports in China* (Shanghai and Foochow, 1912), 216. On other outports see e.g. 'S. H. S.', *Diary of Events and the Progress of Shameen 1859–1938* (Hong Kong, 1939).

[61] Wright, *Twentieth Century Impressions*, 253–4; *Shanghai by Night and Day*, i (Shanghai, *c*.1902), 113–27.

to their shared concerns and interests, and which circulated their news. Letters 'from the outports' were relayed to the Shanghai offices, and then recirculated through the pages of the *Herald*. News from Chefoo was deemed to be newsworthy for Hankow. China Britons going on long leave overseas sometimes had their copies sent on so as to keep up. The *Herald*, and its quotidian version, the *North China Daily News*, also of course relayed British, imperial, and international news. The letters pages allowed them to vent spleen, and dismay also joined them together—dismay at their portrayal in the press overseas, and what they saw as the failure of those 'at home' to understand their situation, especially in the face of the nationalist upsurge in the 1920s.

Memorialization was also telling. Shanghai streets were named mostly after Shanghailanders' great men—municipal grandees, or philanthropists—but their public monuments were indicative of their aspiration for membership of a wider China and imperial community, as well of the seductions of empire celebrity.[62] Sir Robert Hart, who had few Shanghai connections, graced the bund (in a statue shaped by H. A. Pegram, a sculptor with impeccable imperial credentials), alongside Sir Harry Parkes, one of the most bellicose of the China diplomats, and a memorial to the dead officers of the anti-Taiping 'Ever Victorious Army'. The latter linked Shanghai to Charles Gordon, of Khartoum fame, who had commanded this mercenary force in 1862–4. The municipal offices of Tianjin's British concession were housed in Gordon Hall.[63] The importance they attached to such physical symbolism was also shown in 1918. On the night of 11 November British residents in Tianjin pulled down a statue commemorating German military actions during the 1900 Boxer war, dragged it to the Tientsin Club and decapitated it. In Shanghai, persons unknown pulled down the bund-side memorial to the sailors on the German gunboat SMS *Iltis*, which had foundered off the Shandong coast in 1896. The memorial stood on land owned by Jardines.[64] The Shanghai British used their own memorials—and some abused their enemies in this way—in order to mark their participation in the wider British China story, and the global world of British empire. Grimble's less fortunate colleagues were remembered in 1924 by an impressive Anglo-French war memorial on the bund, while Holy

[62] A guide to these is A. H. Gordon, *Streets of Shanghai: A History in itself* (Shanghai, 1941).
[63] Wright, *Twentieth Century Impressions*, 724–6.
[64] Woodhead, *Journalist in China*, 80–1; *NCH* (7 Dec. 1918), 604.

Trinity Cathedral installed a memorial window, and the SMC, private firms, and clubs all created their own memorials. The Shanghai British then located themselves in the wide world of empire, rather than merely in China. At the end of the Asia Pacific War they searched for the remains of their statues, all of which had been removed by the collaborationist city government in 1943, and they even attempted to persuade the Chinese authorities to agree to reinstall the war memorial on a bund now fronting a Chinese-controlled city.[65]

Hong Kong

Hong Kong was different, and yet it was not entirely so, it was not cut off from the China coast world, but it stood obliquely outside this imagining of the geographic shape and memorialized identity of British China. The colony was originally designed as the capital city of the British China enterprise. Until the 1856–60 *Arrow* war, the British Minister was concurrently governor (as representation in Beijing itself was not permitted by the Qing). However, although the colony developed as a port city, and although the population steadily grew, the centre of gravity of the British community in China steadily moved north, and following the opening of new treaty ports in North China and on the Yangzi in 1861, Hong Kong's pre-eminence had been greatly eroded by the mid-1860s (as it had similarly already sucked away Canton's trade and British firms).[66] Thereafter Hong Kong and Shanghai were on a par in any schematized hierarchy of British activity in China, although Hong Kong was the quieter, more formal—because more formally colonial—of the two. The British Minister was based in Peking from 1860 onwards, and China matters properly fell to his jurisdiction, and that of the Foreign Office. British populations grew at a roughly similar pace in each city.[67] But Shanghai became more important as modern industry developed there after 1895, and it developed further as a financial centre, as the home of new Chinese educational institutions, publishing ventures, and cultural innovations. Its administrative interstices meant it provided havens

---

[65] *North China Daily News* (22 Jan. 1947), 1; (19 Mar. 1947), 3.

[66] This argument is developed at fuller length in my 'The Shifting Roles of the Colony in the British Informal Empire in China', in Judith M. Brown and Rosemary Foot (eds.), *Hong Kong's Transitions* (London, 1997), 33–61.

[67] For surveys of Hong Kong's non-Chinese communities see the papers in Cindy Yik-yi Chu (ed.), *Foreign Communities in Hong Kong, 1840s–1950s* (New York, 2005).

(up to a point) for Chinese political activists. Hong Kong certainly provided a model for its geographically closer twin city, Canton, but in other ways it looked systematically away from China, to the world of British empire of which it was formally a part. Governors came to it from postings in Southeast Asia, Fiji, New Zealand, Australia, West Africa, or the Caribbean (or worse, in Sir John Pope-Hennessy's case, from controversy in a combination of these), and they went off to such posts after serving their Hong Kong time. Chinese convicts were sent from the colony to India, Van Diemen's Land, Singapore, or Penang.[68] Tied in as it was to a network of circulating ideas and practices, governance in Hong Kong was more open and progressive in some ways than the more parochial Shanghai Municipal Council, which could find itself wrongfooted as a result. It assumed, for example, that public gardens in the colony would mirror its own in restricting Chinese access. This proved not to be the case (although of course residence on the Peak, and on Cheung Chau island, was restricted until

Table 10.4 Number of British residents in Hong Kong, 1871–1931

	British residents (civil)	British military personnel	Total British	Total non-Chinese	Total population
1871	869	1,739	2,608	8,754	124,198
1881	785	3,756	4,541	9,712	160,402
1891	1,448	2,900	4,348	10,446	221,441
1901	3,007	13,237*		9,148	283,975
1911	3,761			11,225	450,098
1921	7,889		7,889	12,856	625,166
1931	6,684	7,682	14,366	28,322	849,751

Source: Hong Kong census reports, 1871–1931.

* Inflated by the presence of the Boxer war China Campaign force.

These figures must serve as a guide, and this table does not accord exactly with others. The category of 'British' mutated over the decades, but as far as possible given, further, the inconsistencies in the range of data collected, these figures refer to Britons, rather than to other British-protected subjects (Southeast Asians, Indians, Eurasians, Macanese).

[68] Kate Lowe and E. McLaughlin, 'Sir John Pope Hennessy and the "Native Race Craze": Colonial Government in Hong Kong, 1877–1882', *Journal of Imperial and Commonwealth History*, 20/2 (1992), 223–47; Christopher Munn, *Anglo-China: Chinese People and British Rule in Hong Kong, 1841–1880* (Richmond, 2001), 221–6.

1946.[69] Hong Kong shirts seemed more stuffed and the gubernatorial rituals of place and precedence seemed to contrast sharply with the self-proclaimed meritocracy of the Shanghailander. Paradoxically, however, anxieties and performances of status and place were probably as prominent in Shanghailander living, as in Hong Kong society, as the self-(re)made devised their own rules and rituals on the bund. As Wright's volume put it when discussing Shanghai social mores, 'anomalies have been established'.[70]

The similarities and differences between the two cities need noting. The China British had their subsets, and Shanghai highlights these most closely, although the tiny outpost which housed two clubs, one for the customs 'indoor' staff, and business assistants, and the other for the outdoor staff and British supervisors, might also demonstrate how class naturally continued to matter, and in fact to matter even more where most in danger of being subsumed as a reality. Class aside, the social landscape broadly encompassed settlers and expatriates. The former were more prominent in Shanghai, because more powerful and autonomous, than in Hong Kong, but it is clear that the self-regarding flashiness of Hong Kong elite society— which attracted the attention of Maugham amongst others—has obscured the presence of other British social groups. While use of the term 'settler' requires nuance, it is needed if the composition and the politics of the treaty port societies are to be understood. These were the people who had everything to lose if they lost the treaty ports.

'Middle class sojourners' was how Henry Lethbridge described Hong Kong's European population, 'not one of whom thought of bringing up his children to regard Hong Kong as a permanent home'.[71] And indeed, as late as the 1921 census, it was estimated that the non-Chinese population of Hong Kong was probably renewed almost entirely every five years. A comparison between 1911 and 1921 city directories identified only 197 non-government employees who were listed in both. A fifth of these worked for

---

[69] John M. Carroll, *Edge of Empires: Chinese Elites and British Colonials in Hong Kong* (Cambridge, Mass., 2005), 90–6; Peter Wesley-Smith, 'Anti-Chinese Legislation in Hong Kong', in Ming K. Chan (ed.), *Precarious Balance: Hong Kong between China and Britain, 1842–1992* (Armonk, NY, 1994), 100–1.

[70] Wright, *Twentieth Century Impressions*, 342.

[71] Henry Lethbridge, 'Condition of the European Working Class in Nineteenth Century Hong Kong', in *Hong Kong: Stability and Change. A Collection of Essays* (Hong Kong, 1978), 189–90.

the dockyards.[72] As Lethbridge also pointed out, the socially prominent (and the official) left more visible traces in their memoirs, in the press and public life—in street names—and, as a result, in the histories, than the numerous 'low status Europeans' on whom they relied. These he identified as the policemen (598 in 1921), dockyard staff (over 250 that year), the military, the men in the Chinese Maritime Customs, to which broad category he also added a scattering of prostitutes, crooks, or drifters. Lethbridge also included with these those in service trades, shop-owners and so on, and proposed that up to a third of the European population (and the Europeans are mostly British) fell into this category.[73] Clearly, in the cold light of day, the shop-owner and the prostitute might object to such a catch-all category of analysis. But these groups, if anybody, together with the administrative personnel—the lower grade government employees—comprised the Hong Kong equivalent of the Shanghailander.

Unlike their Shanghai counterparts they had no access to a vote, and little by way of a voice. Shanghailanders could derail reform, if not managed properly (with appeals to their broader British loyalty), as they did in 1930 when they vetoed an increase in Chinese representation on the SMC. Shepherded days later back into an emergency meeting, and after much micro-management from a panicked consul general and his allies, they delivered the right result at a second vote.[74] The political reality of the difference was missing in Hong Kong, where the unofficial British had no effective say in local politics. They were appointed to the governor's legislative and executive councils, but were always outnumbered by the governor and his senior administrators.[75] The 'unofficial' British could informally make things uncomfortable for a governor they found fault with, such as Hennessy, but there was on the whole little by way of unofficial opposition over the decades. Hong Kong was a much more tightly run ship.

With a governor to cluck around as well, the expatriate and administrative elite created a more theatrical ritual world up and down the Peak than was devised for the minister in Peking, or consul generals elsewhere. This was also tied in with the 'refanement' author and resident Stella Benson sneered at in 1930, and the 'desire for exclusiveness' commented on by

---

[72] *Sessional Papers*, 15/1921, 'Report on the Census of the Colony of Hong Kong 1921', p. 159.
[73] Lethbridge, 'Condition of the European Working Class', 199.
[74] Bickers, *Britain in China*, 143–4.
[75] Norman Miners, *Hong Kong under Imperial Rule, 1912–1941* (Hong Kong, 1987), 43–78.

Wright in 1908.[76] The particular local shapes status consciousness took provided one salient difference between the two communities. A second was that, although Hong Kong expatriate networks certainly overlapped with or involved China coast ones, there were clear differences. Expatriate businessmen might move within wider East and Southeast Asian networks of employment, while colonial administrative, technical, and other professional staff (in education, health, etc.) circulated within the more international colonial professional networks. As Margaret Jones has noted, for example, British nurses dismayed by Ceylonization in the 1930s transferred to jobs in Hong Kong.

The British drew other boundaries around and between themselves. Terms of service in most sectors usually included restrictions on marriage or access to marriage benefits (quarters, pay allowances) for early career recruits. But there were in addition, and building on such common practices, taboos—and sometimes formal bars—on regularized public relationships between British men and Chinese women, for example.[77] A ban operated within the SMP until 1927. Expatriates added taboos of their own—a marriage with a Shanghailander was not necessarily in an ambitious young man's best interests. The conventions which did exist were raced, but other local factors were also added: Russians, for example, lost their 'European' status in treaty port eyes after 1917. Marriage with a Russian woman was as taboo in some circles as marriage with a Chinese. Issues of nationality clearly intersected with issues of class. Lower ranking Britons in the Maritime Customs, for example, were more likely to marry Chinese, Japanese, or Eurasian women. This pattern was replicated across all sectors of the British presence. After 1917 such men were also more likely to marry Russian women. The marriage/public relationship bar declined throughout the 1930s, and Chinese women became public objects of European desire—a change perhaps best exemplified by the developing successful career of Hollywood film actress Anna May Wong—and slowly became more acceptable as marriage partners.[78] Relationships between Chinese men and British women remained a mostly unvoiced topic, but did sometimes surface as an

---

[76] Stella Benson diaries, 26 Oct. 1930, University of Cambridge, Add. 6799, Stella Benson Diaries; Wright, *Twentieth Century Impressions*, 340.

[77] A fuller discussion of this issue is in Bickers, *Britain in China, passim*, and e.g. 97–102.

[78] Anthony B. Chan, *Perpetually Cool: The Many Lives of Anna May Wong (1905–1961)* (Lanham, Md., 2003).

issue for anxiety, usually in the context of British women who had come to China having married Chinese diplomats or students in the United Kingdom, although the marriage of Norwegian missionary Anna Sofie Jakobsen to a Chinese evangelist in 1898 was the occasion for intemperate comment in the treaty port press. She was expelled from the China Inland Mission, having, in the eyes of more than one commentator, 'imperilled scores of single ladies in the interior' through her action.[79]

Cutting across these basic community distinctions were others. These overseas Britons were indeed British, not merely English. They were disproportionately born in Scotland or Ireland, and they paraded their Scottishness and Irishness in settlement life, through the kilted Scottish Company of the SVC, and a busy St Patrick's Society.[80] There were at times murmurs and jealousies over the alleged favouritism of senior Scots in the Shanghai Municipal Police, or Hart's Ulster favouritism in the customs, but nothing to match the vitriol unleashed in Hong Kong against the Irish, Catholic governor, Sir John Pope Hennessy, and his alleged 'Chinomania'.[81] Other groups with British passports or under British protection were excluded in varying degrees from this community, from its formal and informal gatherings, and from its self-ascription, from its public discourse and from its memoirs and commentaries. There were the Sephardi Jews, who came from Baghdad via Bombay and Hong Kong, and for that part of the Eurasian community which had British protection, the same applied.[82] There was a relatively large Indian community, varied in origin, mostly, but not only, subaltern and almost entirely excluded.[83] Hong Kong Chinese, who were also British protégés, were not pukka. Unlike the Japanese in China the British did not cultivate a policy of creating proxy-subjects—and so expand

[79] 'British Girls in Peril', NCH (14 Jan. 1898), 37–8, and (21 Jan. 1898), 89; see letters on the 'mixed missionary marriage' in NCH (15 Aug. 1898), 304 (5 Sept. 1898), 443 (quoted), (12 Sept. 1898), 494–5.

[80] Elizabeth Buettner, 'Haggis in the Raj: Private and Public Celebrations of Scottishness in Late Imperial India', Scottish Historical Review, 81/2: no. 212 (2002), 212–39.

[81] Lowe and McLaughlin, 'Sir John Pope Hennessy', esp. 241–2.

[82] Chiara Betta, 'From Orientals to Imagined Britons: Baghdadi Jews in Shanghai', Modern Asian Studies, 37/4 (2003), 999–1023. See also Maisie J. Meyer, From the Rivers of Babylon to the Whangpoo: A Century of Sephardi Life in Shanghai (Lanham, Md., 2003).

[83] Claude Markovits, 'Indian Communities in China c. 1842–1949', in Robert Bickers and Christian Henriot (eds.), New Frontiers: Imperialism's New Communities in East Asia, 1842–1953 (Manchester, 2000), 55–74; Caroline Plüss, 'Constructing Globalized Ethnicity: Migrants from India in Hong Kong', International Sociology, 20/2 (2005), 201–24.

their interests—through encouraging Chinese or others to claim British protection.[84] It cannot be said, however, that they always policed with zeal the boundaries between what was claimed and what was legally justified, though this did get tougher after the later 1920s, when British protection was stripped from some Eurasians who had previously enjoyed it.

As a model, and as a distinction understood by contemporaries, the categorization of 'settler' and 'expatriate' presents a problem which lies at the heart of the communities studied in this volume. It is clear that the overseas Britons in many cases were both settlers and expatriates, sometimes serially in one place, or serially across different parts of the world of work and residence opened through British empire. Alan Lester and others have highlighted the importance of 'horizontal' movement within British empire, which went far beyond the world of the colonial service career.[85] A man might, like Basil Duke, move to a dominion, then to Shanghai, then to a second dominion or to a position in a colonial service. An expatriate trader might settle down. Political transition could eventually make continuing residence uncomfortable, or quickly—or more creepingly—impossible. A settler might therefore lose the ability to stay on, and be forced to move on within the British empire or dominions, or back to Britain. All of this is true for China, although the retention of Hong Kong did provide an offshore base to which some mainland China residents and institutions resorted after 1949 in particular. But while the distinction ultimately needs nuance in the Shanghai case it had a political reality, and accords with the shape—and self-perceptions—of the contrasting political interests which dominated British settlement politics in the years down to 1941. In their settler politics and allegiance lay the beating heart of their settler identity. Once that was shattered, with the implementation of the 1943 Sino-British Friendship Treaty—which abolished extraterritoriality and the treaty ports—after the end of the Asia Pacific War, many more moved on from China. In this they were not alone, as work elsewhere in this volume demonstrates, but the further dislocation caused by the communist victory in 1949 provided a definitive break. They were not welcome to pursue their dreams of settlement in the People's Republic.

---

[84] Barbara J. Brooks, 'Japanese Colonial Citizenship in Treaty Port China: The Location of Koreans and Taiwanese in the Imperial Order', in Bickers and Henriot, New Frontiers, 109–24.

[85] Alan Lester and David Lambert (eds.), Colonial Lives across the British Empire: Imperial Careering in the Long Nineteenth Century (Cambridge, 2006).

Conclusion

Did any of this matter? The China coast British had nearly all left by 1954,
only Hong Kong remaining as a bastion, for them as it was for much larger
numbers of Chinese refugees.[86] Their monuments had mostly been pulled
down and their streets renamed three times over in the space of a few years
by the early 1950s. Even the dead were disturbed. Cemeteries which had
survived urban redevelopment in the 1950s—Shanghai's Bubbling Well was
turned into a park—usually failed to survive the Cultural Revolution's
assault after 1966 on the 'four olds' (customs, ideas, habits, and beliefs).
Shanghai gravestones lie scattered still throughout the western suburbs of
the city where many were pragmatically recycled by farmers. The cosmopolitan architecture of their city, with its distinctive stock of art deco
buildings, was degraded in the face of the galloping urban redevelopment
of the turn of the twenty-first century. Less survives elsewhere.

Moreover, Shanghai was a city, while, for example, Kenya was a country.
It need always to be remembered that China was not significant for British
trade. In Asia, India was more important. Globally, trade with Europe
mattered more.[87] But Shanghai was China's capital city in all but name,
and British settlers dominated aspects of it from 1843 to 1941. This picture
needs nuancing, but after taking into account the resilience of Chinese
society in the city in the face of the foreign presence, it is clear that the
Shanghai British, more than any other China coast community, had a
national impact. Moreover, Shanghailanders in particular and their actions
had come by 1925 to represent in Chinese eyes British policy and concerns,
at the expense of a slowly liberalizing official British China policy. They did
not much help British China policy in the age of robust popular and state
nationalism.[88]

When expatriates and settlers alike emerged from the internment camps
in Shanghai and north China they found that the settlements, their councils,
and their extraterritorial status had all been abolished. A steady dispersal

---

[86] Siu-lun Wong, *Emigrant Entrepreneurs: Shanghai Industrialists in Hong Kong* (Hong Kong,
1988).

[87] David R. Meyer, *Hong Kong as a Global Metropolis* (Cambridge, 2000), 77.

[88] The point is made in E. S. K. Fung, *The Diplomacy of Imperial Retreat: Britain's South
China Policy, 1924–1931* (Hong Kong, 1991); Clifford, *Spoilt Children of Empire*; Bickers, *Britain in
China*.

from China which had begun after the onset of the Sino-Japanese War, resumed, and affected more than just the municipal employees who were as redundant in Chinese eyes as their municipal employer. The day communist forces occupied Shanghai, 25 May 1949, heralded the start of a rapid, terminal decline. Within two years the British population there had been reduced by three-quarters. The British had been driven out of their clubs which were requisitioned by the new authorities, and indeed all that was left of the elite British Shanghai Club was its drink stocks, which lay impounded in a warehouse, and its chairman, who was refused permission to resign his post and was under threat of detention for non-payment by the club of 'back taxes'.[89]

Within another year or so there was nothing remaining of the Shanghai British community. Some of those who left Shanghai in and after 1945 for good had moved back to the UK, but they also went to Australia, Canada, New Zealand, and elsewhere. Of the about 400 British members of the SMP emerging from the camps in 1945, at least fifty went permanently to Australia, and ten to New Zealand. The only SMP veterans society that seems to have been active anywhere after 1945 was based in Sydney.[90] Some men moved on down south to Hong Kong. Shanghailanders leaving after 1949 were similarly dispersed. Outside Hong Kong there was very little 'staying on' for them to do, although a tiny number of the politically committed, and a small number of the chronically rootless, did stay, but the politics of anti-imperialism, and the daily changing grind of violent socio-economic transformation in early communist China forced them out.[91]

Dispersal shuffled the China pack. Where they met as groups they often met in full cosmopolitan formation, reality replaced rhetoric in some instances for the first time. At the SVC centenary dinner in Hong Kong in 1854, Sir John Kinloch, Bt., Shanghai Scottish, sat down with nine da Silvas from the Portuguese Company and twenty Chinese former volunteers. The Shanghai Police veterans society in Sydney included Russians in its membership. Settler social fracture certainly persisted—one former policeman who had attended an SMC employees dinner in London complained that

[89] On these travails see: TNA, PRO, FO 371/99345, Shanghai No. 179, 6 June 1952, FO 371/108089, Peking No. 54, 30 Jan. 1953, enclosing Shanghai No. 30, 16 Jan. 1953.

[90] Correspondence from Jack Albon to members, 1955–7, private collection.

[91] Thomas N. Thompson, *China's Nationalization of Foreign Firms: The Politics of Hostage Capitalism, 1949–57* (Baltimore, Md., 1979).

those organizing it 'never did much have time for the police'. And, more-over, the beer was too expensive.[92] But even the very term 'Shanghailander' has undergone a mutation. At the biannual 'Old China Hands' meetings held in the United States it is used by Jewish refugees who found security in the city after late 1938 to refer to themselves. Dispersal effectively destroyed the community, although the arrival of the internet, and the family history movement which has worked through it, has led to the re-establishment of many old ties. The internet has proved an important vehicle and location for the perpetuation of more recent post-colonial identities—Rhodesians, for example—and it has also played a key role in re-establishing older connections.

Britons in Shanghai and China generally were not unusual in their development of a repertoire of identities, in which the professional, the particular, the national, and the supranational overlapped. They were 'foreigners', Britons, Shanghailanders, loyal subjects of empire. They might be missionaries or members of the Shanghai Race Club. What is clearly distinctive is the internationalized locale in which they lived, influenced by American culture and by Japan, by Germany and by international communism, and by a dynamically evolving China. Empire lives were elsewhere, of course, open to other influences, but the world on show in open city Shanghai, of Japanese inns and imported American cars, was wider than most by far. Faced with this some retreated into Britishness, but others slipped themselves into the life on offer. The China coast settlements also remind us of the ongoing fact of transience and the speed of socialization and the willingness of new recruits to assimilate to local 'anomalies'. The 'old China hand' certainly existed, and there was a static and steadily increasing China coast population, but more common nearly always was the five-year turnaround identified by the Hong Kong Census in 1921. For the greater number of China coast Britons, even before the great dispersal of the mid-twentieth century, China was a staging post on a cross-British world journey. As well as the practices and predilections of settlement, we might consider further how fundamental transience and movement was to the British experience, and to the British experience of empire in the nineteenth and twentieth centuries.

[92] Jack Albon to Jock Smith, 30 Nov. 1957, correspondence from Jack Albon to members, 1955–7, private collection.

Select Bibliography

ROBERT BICKERS, 'Shanghailanders: The Formation and Identity of the British Settler Community in Shanghai 1843–1937', *Past and Present*, 159 (1998), 161–211.

—— *Britain in China: Community, Culture and Colonialism, 1900–49* (Manchester, 1999).

—— *Empire Made Me: An Englishman Adrift in Shanghai* (London, 2003).

—— *The Scramble for China: Foreign Devils in the Qing Empire, 1832–1914* (London, 2011).

JOHN M. CARROLL, *Edge of Empires: Chinese Elites and British Colonials in Hong Kong* (Cambridge, Mass., 2005).

NICHOLAS R. CLIFFORD, *Spoilt Children of Empire: Westerners in Shanghai and the Chinese Revolution of the 1920s* (Hanover, NH, 1991).

BRYNA GOODMAN, 'Improvisations on a Semi-Colonial Theme, or, How to Read a Celebration of Transnational Urban Community', *Journal of Asian Studies*, 59/4 (2000), 889–926.

HENRY LETHBRIDGE, *Hong Kong: Stability and Change: A Collection of Essays* (Hong Kong, 1978).

KERRIE L. MACPHERSON, *A Wilderness of Marshes: The Origins of Public Health in Shanghai, 1843–1893* (Hong Kong, 1987).

NORMAN MINERS, *Hong Kong under Imperial Rule, 1912–1941* (Hong Kong, 1987).

EIICHI MOTONO, *Conflict and Cooperation in Sino-British Business, 1860–1911: The Impact of the Pro-British Commercial Network in Shanghai* (Basingstoke, 2000).

CHRISTOPHER MUNN, *Anglo-China: Chinese People and British Rule in Hong Kong, 1841–1880* (Richmond, 2001).

JÜRGEN OSTERHAMMEL, 'Britain and China 1842–1914', in Andrew Porter (ed.), *The Oxford History of the British Empire*, iii. *The Nineteenth Century* (Oxford, 1999), 146–69.

——'China', in Judith Brown and Wm Roger Louis (eds.), *The Oxford History of the British Empire*, iv. *The Twentieth Century* (Oxford, 1999), 643–66.

ARNOLD WRIGHT (ed.), *Twentieth Century Impressions of Hong Kong, Shanghai, and Other Treaty Ports of China: Their History, People, Commerce, Industries and Resources* (London, 1908).

11

'We Don't Grow Coffee and Bananas in Clapham Junction You Know!'
Imperial Britons Back Home

Elizabeth Buettner

In her 1964 novel *A Man from Nowhere*, Elspeth Huxley portrayed a white settler's first visit to Britain after a life lived in an unnamed African colony that had just achieved independence under African majority rule. As the subject of much curiosity about his little-known background, his landlady observed that 'Mr Heron didn't quite fit into any of the niches, he didn't belong and yet he must belong to something.' Recalling what her local MP, the Cabinet Minister Peter Buckle, had said, she pondered her tenant's identity that lay outside her comprehension:

Colonial. Colonials were English and yet they weren't. They were loyal to the Queen and fought for England when needed, for which they got little thanks. She'd only once been to a meeting of Mr Buckle's and she remembered that he'd said we should never forget the debt we owed to them but they were not colonials now, they had turned into something else—the Commonwealth. But the Commonwealth had mainly black men, black and brown, who didn't feel the same way, naturally. It was all too confusing.[1]

Huxley's thinly veiled portrait of the white settler community of Kenya, the land of her own upbringing, examined how men like the fictional Dick Heron came to believe they had been betrayed by the colonial authorities. Writing against stereotypes of colonials' privileged lifestyle— an act of rebuttal that in itself became a common trope in colonizers'

[1] Elspeth Huxley, *A Man from Nowhere* (London, 1964), 18, 21.

representations—Huxley recounted how the Heron family had 'no money, barely enough to develop the farm his father had bought very cheaply thirty years before, although they'd ploughed back into it everything they'd ever earned'.[2] Anti-colonial violence caused the value of their land to plummet and many of their white neighbours to leave; Heron's brother had been brutally murdered by insurgents and his wife, a third-generation settler, committed suicide in despair. His arrival in England did not signal an attempt to start life anew but rather to take revenge on the politician responsible. As Peter Buckle had been sent to implement constitutional change and devolve power to the African leader who supposedly had orchestrated his brother's killing, it was Peter Buckle who symbolized Britain's failure to protect everything he held dear and who now became the target of Heron's wrath. Throughout the novel, Heron's sole objective while on British soil is to kill Buckle to avenge his own multiple losses.

Huxley's account touches on many themes that are central to the history of overseas Britons in the late imperial era and its post-colonial aftermath. Whether rendered as fiction or taking a more explicitly autobiographical form, stories of white settlers' arrival in the metropole differ considerably from narratives about the returns of Britons who had lived overseas but had never intended to do so permanently. Dick Heron had been born in Africa and never known a lifestyle other than that of a farmer in a colony where a white minority community had power over the African majority, and he made his journey in his thirties when this existence had collapsed upon decolonization. Going back to Britain after several years away or even an entire career spent in the empire as an official, in the army, or as part of the commercial sector diverged sharply from travels undertaken by those who had never lived outside a colony, even if 'coming home' was often how both forms of arrival were described. British returns home took shape on the basis of the roles individuals had played overseas, where they lived, and the timing of their journey: had repatriates lived in the empire as sojourners or settlers; officials or non-officials; as men or women? Did they arrive in Britain as children, adults, or retirees? Had they come in the late nineteenth century during a time of 'high' imperialism and ongoing confidence in the nation's overseas role, or done so at the end of empire upon the transfer of power to the formerly colonized?

[2] Ibid. 130.

This chapter addresses this range of experiences upon entering, or re-entering, Britain for those whose identities were inseparable from the imperial contexts that had long shaped their lives. It asks how timing affected their reintegration and responses to British domestic life and the ways they adapted—or failed to adapt—to it, and how wider British society in turn responded to them. Despite their vastly different backgrounds, what many repatriated Britons shared was a sense of being at once insiders and outsiders within the nation meant to be 'home'. To reiterate Huxley's words, 'they were English and yet they weren't'. British ancestry—full or partial—was central to colonials' ability call the metropole 'home' even after several generations' absence, and even as separate national identities developed in some instances.[3] Racial identity was integral to the question of belonging: as Angela Woollacott asserts with reference to Australian women travelling to London in the late nineteenth and early twentieth centuries, they were 'insiders in the empire because of their whiteness while simultaneously outsiders in England due to their colonial origins and subordinated because of their sex'.[4] Whiteness in combination with nationality had always been

---

[3] A South African resident writing in 1916 described the tendency of both British-born colonials and their children to persist in describing the British Isles as 'Home' whether or not they had ever set foot there. In the second generation, 'naturally the love of that country is instilled into them by their parents. It is also the ambition of the majority of Colonials to make at least one visit "Home", and learn for themselves the greatness of England at first hand.' F. A. Morris, 'British Isles as "Home"', Overseas: The Monthly Journal of the Overseas Club and Patriotic League of Britons Overseas (hereafter Overseas), 9 (1916), 38. It was also common for persons of 'mixed' ancestry—e.g. Anglo-Indians—to refer to Britain as 'Home' although few had actually visited. See Alison Blunt, '"Land of Our Mothers": Home, Identity, and Nationality for Anglo-Indians in British India, 1919–1947', History Workshop Journal, 54 (2002), 49–72. Although the later imperial era witnessed the increased tendency for many white colonials to assert a separate national identity and for Anglo-Indians to more readily view India as their motherland, this did not necessarily preclude an ongoing sentimental tie with Britain that stemmed from ancestral connections.

[4] Angela Woollacott, To Try Her Fortune in London: Australian Women, Colonialism, and Modernity (New York, 2001), 34. For a broader discussion of 'insiders' and 'outsiders', see Paul Gilroy, The Black Atlantic: Modernity and Double Consciousness (Cambridge, Mass., 1993), 4, 11. Key studies of whiteness in a variety of contexts include Catherine Hall, White, Male, and Middle Class: Explorations in Feminism and History (New York, 1992); Ruth Frankenberg (ed.), Displacing Whiteness: Essays in Social and Cultural Criticism (Durham, NC, 1997); Ann Laura Stoler, Race and the Education of Desire: Foucault's History of Sexuality and the Colonial Order of Things (Durham, NC, 1995); Ann Laura Stoler, Carnal Knowledge and Imperial Power: Race and the Intimate in Colonial Rule (Berkeley, Calif., 2002); David Roediger, The Wages of Whiteness: Race and the Making of the American Working Class (London, 1991); Richard Dyer, White (London, 1997).

critical, but arguably became most salient in augmenting repatriates' 'Brit-ishness' after the Second World War when the empire was rapidly replaced by the Commonwealth—which, as Huxley's fictional landlady noted, 'had mainly black men, black and brown'. Increased 'coloured' immigration from countries including Jamaica, Pakistan, and India caused considerable con-cern about who should count as British regardless of what privileges of entry 'New Commonwealth' citizenship may have bestowed.

While frequently not feeling as though they belonged, repatriates none-theless personified imperial Britishness, and all its positive or negative connotations, for the majority of those in metropolitan society who them-selves lacked direct exposure to colonial life.[5] Their resettlement experiences shed light on the contrasts between life lived as a Briton overseas and life back home and suggest the reasons why time spent in Britain was just as important to understanding their identity as time spent overseas. Equally important, their evaluations of how mainstream British society viewed and treated them raises the question of how much Britain's attitude to former colonial representatives corresponds to the value, or lack thereof, the nation placed upon its imperial activities more generally until (and indeed beyond) the era of decolonization.

Transient Imperial Life Courses

Although many adults born into British communities in settler colonies and in the dominions only made their first journeys home later in life, others had come and gone at regular intervals since childhood.[6] In parts of the

---

[5] Since the 1980s, historians, literary critics, and anthropologists convincingly have contested the image of a Britain disconnected from its empire and charted the manifold ways imperialism pervaded popular as well as elite culture in the metropole. The Manchester University Press 'Studies in Imperialism' series edited by John MacKenzie has been at the forefront of this engagement, while Edward Said's work has decisively shaped the interdisciplinary agenda (see e.g. *Culture and Imperialism* (New York, 1993)). On bringing together Britain's histories 'at home' and 'away', see esp. Catherine Hall and Sonya O. Rose (eds.), *At Home with the Empire: Metropolitan Culture and the Imperial World* (Cambridge, 2006); Catherine Hall (ed.), *Cultures of Empire: A Reader. Colonizers in Britain and the Empire in the Nineteenth and Twentieth Centuries* (Manchester, 2000); Ann Laura Stoler and Frederick Cooper (eds.), *Tensions of Empire: Colonial Cultures in a Bourgeois World* (Berkeley, Calif., 1997); Andrew Thompson, *The Empire Strikes Back? The Impact of Imperialism on Britain from the Mid-Nineteenth Century* (Harlow, 2005).

[6] These topics receive more extensive coverage with respect to India-connected families in Elizabeth Buettner, *Empire Families: Britons and Late Imperial India* (Oxford, 2004).

empire that were not considered appropriate for white settlement, British lives were meant to alternate between metropole and colony. Unhealthy climates, small white minorities, and a lack of desirable schooling opportunities for white children ranked high among the reasons why certain parts of the empire counted as sojourner as opposed to settler colonies. India and West African colonies were only some of the many regions where Britons were not intended to remain permanently: rather, colonizers ideally took periodic home leaves, educated their children in Britain, and ultimately retired there. White non-settler colonial communities effectively were divided between those living overseas and those in Britain—often temporarily before returning for another stay in the empire.

Transport facilities proved central to expatriate Britons' circulation between home and away. For those in India and further east from the mid-nineteenth century on, the overland route through the Middle East and subsequently the Suez Canal replaced months-long voyages around the Cape, reducing journeys to Bombay to three weeks. As a result, men took home leave more readily than before, often returning for several months every five years. Many wives returned more frequently to see children sent back for their schooling, or alternatively stayed in Britain with the children and left overseas life to their husbands. Years of separation characterized relationships between Britons based in the empire and their friends and family back home, with parent–child separations becoming a particular cause of regret and repeatedly singled out as the biggest drawback of men's imperial careers. Between the Second World War and decolonization, air travel provided some expatriates with opportunities to visit both their homeland and absent family members more regularly.[7] Children attending school in Britain during and after the 1950s also might spend their summer holidays with their parents, whereas pre-war families commonly had to wait years for a reunion. Yet travelling home by air remained prohibitively expensive for many families until the end of empire, and separations more often than not continued to span years rather than months.

Educating children in Britain proved a financial drain as well as an emotional one. Writing in 1950, a colonial administrator's wife long based in Africa described circumstances that would have appeared as familiar to

---

[7] See advertisement for BOAC, *Corona: Journal of His Majesty's Colonial Service*, 2/4 (Apr. 1950).

late Victorian families as to those after the Second World War. When children were away,

there will be times when their mother is with them in England and there are two homes to keep up. School fees and provision for holidays in post-war England may take as much as a third of their pay for one child and over half if there are two. Theirs is the real poverty and sacrifice, often for children they rarely see, and who are being brought up by dubious strangers.[8]

Whatever their regrets about divided families, however, most who could afford to send children home did so because of the benefits it brought. Most considered painful separations to be a price worth paying in light of the socio-economic, and indeed racial, costs resulting from the inability to provide children with metropolitan cultural capital. Until the end of empire, going home was a marker of social status that separated middle- and upper-middle-class Britons able to pay for periodic visits from poorer settlers and lower-ranking expatriates who could ill afford repeated voyages or education upon arrival. This was particularly marked in regions where Europeans were meant to be temporary residents rather than permanent settlers. Indeed, in a sojourner society such as India, failing to remain transient and becoming a 'domiciled European' suggested an inferior socio-economic and cultural status on par with that of the poorer, mixed-race Anglo-Indian community shunned by middle-class Britons. Whether or not domiciled Europeans—or 'poor whites'—were partly of Indian ancestry, they were widely suspected of having 'mixed blood' because of their social and occupational similarity to Anglo-Indians.[9] European children who attended schools in India catering for those 'of European descent' faced the same social and career limitations as their predominantly Anglo-Indian peers, whereas those 'sent home to school' attained valued metropolitan

---

[8] Emily Bradley, *Dearest Priscilla: Letters to the Wife of a Colonial Civil Servant* (London, 1950), 140.

[9] On domiciled Europeans in India, see esp. Satoshi Mizutani, 'The British in India and their Domiciled Brethren: Race and Class in the Colonial Context, 1858–1930', D.Phil. thesis (Oxford, 2004); on 'poor whites', see David Arnold, 'European Orphans and Vagrants in India in the Nineteenth Century', *Journal of Imperial and Commonwealth History*, 7/2 (1979), 104–27; David Arnold, 'White Colonization and Labour in Nineteenth-Century India', *Journal of Imperial and Commonwealth History*, 11/2 (1983), 133–58; Harald Fischer-Tiné, 'Britain's Other Civilising Mission: Class Prejudice, European "Loaferism" and the Workhouse-System in Colonial India', *Indian Economic and Social History Review*, 42/3 (2005), 295–338; Stoler, *Race and the Education of Desire*; Stoler, *Carnal Knowledge*.

credentials. For boys, a British schooling opened doors to higher-level careers and higher incomes than Indian alternatives, and after their education many returned either to India or another part of the empire to enjoy occupational prospects that otherwise would have eluded them. Time spent in Britain, most crucially for education, was just as important as ancestry in creating a white racial and middle-class imperial identity in the next generation.

The stigma attached to educating children overseas, however, decreased somewhat in certain colonies in the twentieth century. In East and Central African colonies where European settlement was advocated, more schools opened locally (especially after the First World War) where white children could study among their social equals without associating with a largely mixed-race peer group as their counterparts would have done in late imperial India. By the 1950s more parents questioned the deeply entrenched imperial practice of sending their children home when they began school or wondered whether to postpone their trip until adolescence. African administrators' wives contributed a series of articles to *Corona*, the monthly journal of the Colonial Service, arguing whether it was more important for younger children to remain with their parents instead of being raised by 'dubious strangers' or reluctant relatives in Britain. One woman invoked Rudyard Kipling's well-known writings about the bullying meted out by his guardians after he was sent away from India as a 5-year-old in the 1870s when recalling her own early years, concluding that 'the worry and suffering caused to ourselves and our families had not been compensated by the English education'.[10]

Others continued to condemn those who kept their children in East Africa. 'The colonial child of to-day is not growing up to regard England as home', one woman regretted. Children

are denied visits to theatres, concerts, picture galleries—they grow up with only a secondhand knowledge of the culture of Europe which is their heritage. They are also cut off from that factor which more than anything goes to make the Englishman the Empire builder, explorer, sailor that he has been in the past: the English climate. There is no doubt that the endurance called for to live

---

[10] Elizabeth June Knowles, 'Don't Send Them Home', *Corona*, 3/3 (March 1951), 108; see also Ursula Minns, 'Colonial Education: Making the Best of it', *Corona*, 3/10 (Oct. 1951), 390–1; Helen Griffiths, 'Educating our Children', *Corona*, 3/4 (Apr. 1951), 151–2.

through our particular variety of damp cold is the factor which has made us tough enough to stand up to the vicissitudes of our history.[11]

Yet England's advantages for colonials had ceased to be the subject of consensus. One writer adamantly insisted that children suffered from learning about 'the English attitude to colonials, and of colonial inferiority':

'This is my little niece, her parents are in Kenya,' says the gossipy aunt over the dull tea-table, and looks are exchanged…And always she overhears such gems as:

'What a pity she should be tone-deaf.'
'Yes, but after all she is a colonial.'

Whereas the 'It's very good she should captain the tennis VI,' is invariably greeted by: 'Yes, certainly England is doing her all the good in the world.' So the colonial child learns that all her failings are because she is a colonial, and her abilities—if any—are due to her English blood and the splendid opportunity she has to enjoy the English Way of Life.[12]

Despite these commonly voiced reservations, most families continued to prioritize metropolitan education during adolescence if not before, and many who could ill afford British school fees for more protracted periods may have made a sentimental virtue out of financial necessity by keeping them overseas longer. Whatever the real and imagined social advantages of going home when young, however, memories of Britons' condescendingly superior attitude towards colonials rankled in many accounts. Adults and children alike who returned to Britain after time in the empire long resented what they viewed as contemptuous and ignorant metropolitan responses to the imperial world responsible for shaping their identity.

   'Coming home' to Britain was repeatedly said to feel anything but.[13] Periods of metropolitan residence suggested and secured a higher status in the empire than less affluent colonials could expect, yet they caused many repatriates to become disenchanted with the lifestyle available to them when they ceased to reside within a British community overseas. In large part, this

---

[11] Cecily Evans, 'The Problem of our Children', *Corona*, 2/11 (Nov. 1950), 412–13.

[12] Knowles, 'Don't Send Them Home', 109.

[13] Brief discussions of the difficulties Britons returning from India found in readjusting to metropolitan life include B. G. Moore-Gilbert, *Kipling and 'Orientalism'* (London, 1986), 42–7; Benita Parry, *Delusions and Discoveries: India in the British Imagination, 1880–1930* (2nd edn. London, 1998), 50–3. For a longer analysis, see Buettner, *Empire Families*, 188–251.

stemmed from a loss of status in comparison with what many had become accustomed to enjoying within a colonial community where racial 'superiority' combined with middle-class incomes paved the road to social elevation. As Francis Hutchins once argued, the British in India formed a 'middle-class aristocracy' as they, like many colonizers elsewhere in the empire, became able to live 'in a manner well above the station from which they had sprung in England'.[14] Edward Waring, writing *The Tropical Resident at Home* in 1866 after his own service in the West Indies and India, suggested that dislike for England's dreary weather was only the tip of the iceberg of disenchantment upon return:

Another source of disappointment arises from a feeling, which is more or less experienced by all, but especially by those who have held high and important positions in India and other portions of our colonial empire, of their comparative insignificance as individuals in the busy world of England, and of London in particular. For years, perhaps, in their distant homes, they have been held in high and deserved respect, have exercised a wide and powerful influence, have been leaders in the society in which their lot has been cast... They come to London, and find that they are nobodies... they are speedily lost in the crowd.[15]

Moreover, men who opted for imperial careers were advised not to delude themselves that similarly powerful and well-paid positions would have been open to them at home. As another commentator stressed in his 1875 book *At Home on Furlough*, 'there is no small temptation for a man who has discovered that he is a somebody in India, to think that had he remained at home, he would have been recognised as a somebody in England, and been rewarded in proportion to his present estimate of his merits'. Instead, 'lapsing into lifelong genteel poverty' was his more likely alternative.[16] In short, if repatriates resented their British circumstances, they nonetheless had cause to be thankful that a working life in the empire had at least enabled a protracted escape from precarious middle-class mediocrity.

Mid- to late-Victorian complaints about loss of standing at home continued unabated throughout the imperial era, indeed intensifying in

---

[14] Francis G. Hutchins, *The Illusion of Permanence: British Imperialism in India* (Princeton, NJ, 1967), 107–8.

[15] Edward J. Waring, *The Tropical Resident at Home: Letters Addressed to Europeans Returning from India and the Colonies on Subjects Connected to their Health and General Welfare* (London, 1866), 5–6.

[16] Charles A. Lawson, *At Home on Furlough*, 2nd ser. (Madras, 1875), 465–6.

the twentieth century. As will be discussed further below, during and after the interwar years the increased cost of living along with rapid social and cultural change were facts of British life that repatriates found particularly distasteful. Nostalgia and longing for the homeland that they left behind found common expression among expatriates overseas, only to be followed by rude awakenings when confronted with the ways the metropole and the people they knew had altered irrevocably in their absence. The most jarring forms of change were seen in London and other cities, but even the timeless English rural idyll of colonial fantasy proved unable to withstand the onslaught of modernity—particularly in the wake of the Second World War. In her poem reflecting on letdowns that followed 'The Return', the wife of a Uganda Public Works Department official reflected on how at odds with post-war life many repatriates felt. The village to which they returned was largely unrecognizable, with 'changeling council houses' now dominating the landscape and

> The homely chutter of hens is stifled under the deep litter,
> All noises now are modern, road traffic and the B.B.C.
>
> .   .   .
>
> Wistful and out of date 'them people from abroad'
> Walk the green lonnin [lane] in the dusk,
> Away from the television aerials, potato crisps, hire purchase,
>
> .   .   .
>
> Here can we try to slake the long years of homesickness
> Which now we have come home can never be appeased.[17]

Ironically, even those whose livelihoods stemmed from careers in fields like public works that were meant to modernize and 'improve' the colonies resented the metropolitan variants of modernity they found awaiting them upon return.[18] Time and again, colonials appeared—to themselves, and often to others as well—as behind the times and anachronistic when they re-entered a Britain in the throes of its own dynamic evolution.[19]

---

[17] Ruth Bulman, 'The Return', *Corona*, 7/11 (Nov. 1955), 411.

[18] Elizabeth Buettner, 'From Somebodies to Nobodies: Britons Coming Home from India', in Martin Daunton and Bernhard Rieger (eds.), *Meanings of Modernity: Britain from the Late-Victorian Era to the Second World War* (Oxford, 2001), 221–40.

[19] Brief suggestions of empire-based Britons as archaic include George Orwell, *Coming Up for Air* ([1939]; London, 2000), 138; E. M. Collingham, *Imperial Bodies: The Physical Experience of the Raj, c.1800–1947* (Cambridge, 2001), 150–3, 161, 165.

Repatriates' discontent most frequently centred on the contours of metropolitan social relationships, which had been a main reason why many had
opted for colonial life in the first place. Dane Kennedy's study of the
development of settler societies in Kenya and Southern Rhodesia aptly
stresses how the former region in particular attracted Britons raised to
value the lifestyle of the 'traditional gentleman' but who proved unable
to attain or perpetuate it at home, particularly in the interwar era. 'The
rising and progressive rate of income taxes and death duties, the declining
number and increasing expense of servants, the spreading influence of
technocratic and meritocratic values, the growing power of the working
class as evidenced by the Labour party's bettered fortunes and the general
strike' combined to clinch the appeal of African settler colonies. Colonial
life for this social sector was 'free from the pollution of modernity', he
concludes.[20] When invoking the distinctions between African and English
conditions decades later, Elspeth Huxley's Dick Heron still felt able to
encapsulate these as 'more sun and less democracy'.[21]

Domestic service was repeatedly used as a yardstick against which Britain's and the empire's living conditions for white society were measured,
with those in the metropole habitually falling short. As the pages of Punch
attested, the 'servant problem' preoccupied middle-class Britons whether or
not they had colonial experiences to draw upon, but for those who had lived
overseas metropolitan households suffered even more when compared with
colonial counterparts. By the 1920s, middle-class families in the colonies
able to employ between ten and thirty household servants—a key signifier
of an empowerment resting on racial and class foundations—commonly
returned home to find they could afford, at best, one live-in servant or
possibly a 'daily' maid or other part-time help. Frustrated ex-colonials
frequently honed in on the inadequacies of the 'modern maid' who, when
she featured in their lives at all, was criticized for demanding an inordinately
high wage and being overly particular about her conditions of work. At a
time when working-class women could choose many other occupations,
those seeking servants needed to make sacrifices. As one retired Indian
army officer put it in 1930, 'in these days one must bow before the domestic
help'—a complete inversion of master–servant relations in the empire,

---

[20] Dane Kennedy, *Islands of White: Settler Society and Culture in Kenya and Southern Rhodesia, 1890–1939* (Durham, NC, 1987), 71, 47.

[21] Huxley, *Man from Nowhere*, 33.

where 'Indian menials' had proved 'maddening but biddable', not to mention cheap.[22]

Taken together, lack of servants and limited finances caused eagerly
anticipated home leaves to fall short of expectations, the former affecting
women more decisively than men. An administrator's wife writing in 1955
provided a female perspective of a characteristic post-war return to Britain
from Africa, when the likelihood was that 'the combined jobs of cook,
houseboy, dhobi [washerman], ayah [nursemaid], and garden boy fall on
our frail shoulders and we begin to lose sight of the nice rest, interspersed
with gaiety, that we had planned'. Moreover, colonial experiences set them
apart from old acquaintances whose views of African life seemed riddled
with misperceptions:

We are delighted to see our old friends again but sad to find how little we have in
common with them. Some are inclined to ask if we have run into their friend
Mary who went to Africa just before the war, to Rhodesia, they think, or perhaps
Nigeria? Others, school-friends who have married money or become big businessmen, intimidate us utterly and we sit in their exclusive clubs listening to
allusive gossip and feeling more up-country with every mouthful. We become
accustomed to references to 'all those great black servants of yours' in tones of
mixed scorn and envy.

Amidst these multiple sources of colonials' resentment when reimmersed in
metropolitan society, relief might happily appear in the form of rediscov-
ered companions from overseas: 'it is with joy that we run into other East
Africans, greeting each other with glad cries and exclamations at unaccus-
tomed smart appearances, after which we much enjoy talking over old days,
completely ignoring the gay whirl seething around us'. Returning to Africa
at leave's end meant a return to pleasurable society and an escape from
housework; 'it will be good to have those rascally "great black servants" to
deal with the dishes', she concluded.[23] An enthusiastic resumption of colonial residence was common after time in Britain, both for adults on leave
and children at school who often chose to go back overseas when they
finished their education. Returns to the empire provided respite from
domestic difficulties and disappointments, but only temporarily. Unlike

---

[22] 'Mauser' (pseud.), *How to Live in England on a Pension: A Guide for Public Servants Abroad
and at Home* (London, 1930), 18, 58, 152.
[23] Ursula Minns, 'Next Leave will be Different', *Corona*, 7/6 (June 1955), 237–9.

white settlers, expatriates who were based in the empire on account of men's careers faced the prospect of a permanent return to a nation from which many felt estranged when, as one writer put it, 'the guillotine of completed service' arrived in the form of retirement or, alternatively, the end of empire.[24] Difficulties readjusting to their homeland then became most acute, taking shape in gender- as well as age-specific ways.

Post-colonial Years: Retirement and Second Careers before and during Decolonization

One of many retirees assessing the transition from working life overseas to pensioner status at home was W. P. A. Robinson, a former army officer who in 1955 published a book advising men in similar circumstances about *How to Live Well on Your Pension*. In outlining 'the dark side' of retirement Robinson counted the decreased income once salaries were replaced by pensions, the rising cost of living in Britain, and the loss of authority that stemmed from professional status as among the hardest changes to accept. Alongside these perils, however, was boredom, epitomized by the lifestyle common in suburbs where 'everyone goes when they retire'. Such places 'have a much better right to be called the "White Man's Grave" than the West Coast of Africa', he asserted. 'Pensioned idleness with nothing to think and talk about except the good old times is as quick a killer of the over-sixties as any tropical fever.' Proceeding to sketch out a typical scene in such a neighbourhood, he continued:

Along the neat stone pavement comes a neat figure, that of a pleasant-looking late-middle-aged man. . . . his eyes are dull and he is dragging along a small fat dog on a short thin lead. When he meets another neatly turned-out figure the dead spit of himself, they pass the time of day, look at their watches, wonder if they ought to, decide they will, amble quickly home and park their little dogs, meet again and depart at a brisker pace for the club. There they linger for an hour over two small pink gins which they can ill afford.

  Colonial Smith recalls to his cronies the halcyon days of '13 at Rumblebelly-pore, while Mr. Jones retaliates with an account of the rubber boom of forty years ago. *And that hour is the highlight of their day.*[25]

---

[24] Alice Perrin, *The Anglo-Indians* (London, 1912), 204–5.
[25] W. P. A. Robinson, *How to Live Well on Your Pension* (London, 1955), 14–15.

Humdrum domesticity with little purposeful activity may have been men's fate after their professional lives were over, but not their wives'. As Robinson noted, 'your wife never retires'; indeed, 'bereft of her native cook' and other household servants, a woman needed to work harder than ever before to run her household.[26]

Robinson's post-war portrayal of colonial retirement added little that was new to a well-established narrative of unsatisfying resettlement experiences when men's overseas careers came to an end. From the Victorian to the interwar era and beyond, writers alluded to the perennial spectre of ennui stalking men once they reached the standard retirement age of 55 that was a deeply entrenched feature of overseas civil and military service. Proposals for ameliorating discontent included suggestions for low-cost new hobbies (ranging from entomology to gardening to becoming a Boy Scout master) for those no longer able to afford shooting and other sports they had enjoyed in the colonies.[27]

Taking refuge in the company of other repatriates also provided welcome diversion for many. Just as men and women on leave enjoyed chance meetings with friends from overseas with whom they shared more in common than old acquaintances at home who lacked interest in or familiarity with their overseas lives, so too did many after retirement. Writing in the 1860s, Waring described their tendency to reside in the same neighbourhoods and form 'colonies' where they could mingle with others of a similar economic status and cultural background.[28] Between the mid-1800s and mid-1900s, Cheltenham Spa, Bedford, seaside resort towns, and areas of London such as Bayswater were well known for attracting Britons who had lived overseas. Various enclave communities of returned colonials—'agglomerations of transplanted empire fragments', as one interwar commentator phrased it—took shape on the basis of offering affordable costs of living, desirable schools for children, or a milder climate, but all provided valued opportunities for perpetuating involvement with kindred colonial spirits.[29] Other

---

[26] Ibid. 72; see also Ella F. M. Leakey, 'On Retiring', *Overseas*, 18/190 (1931), 58–60.

[27] Waring, *Tropical Resident*, 23–39; 'Mauser', *How to Live*, 166–77; J. R. P. Postlethwaite, *I Look Back* (London, 1947), 148–56, 198–200.

[28] Waring, *Tropical Resident*, 59, 62–3.

[29] 'Mauser', *How to Live*, 171. See also 'Bayswater: The "Asia Minor" of Anglo-Indians', *Bayswater Annual* (London, 1885), 5; *Cheltenham: The Garden Town of England* (3rd edn. Cheltenham, 1893), 33; W. J. Moore, *Health Resorts for Tropical Invalids in India, at Home, and Abroad* (London, 1881); Henry Branch, 'The Anglo-Indian's Paradise', in *Cotswold and Vale; or,*

repatriates socialized amongst themselves more sporadically through reunion dinners and membership in overseas-oriented clubs and societies.

Merely reliving the old days overseas, however, tended to be unfulfilling:
some like Robinson even implied that doing so signified a depressing
retirement, at least if it became 'the highlight of their day'. Clinging to their
former identity forged overseas was no substitute for more gainful activity,
and many younger retired men strongly desired a new occupation—partly to
supplement their pensions, and partly to fill their time more purposefully.
Yet finding satisfying remunerative employment was repeatedly said to be
difficult for middle-aged men who had only colonial experiences and skills to
offer, and many struggled to be taken seriously. Writing in 1951, a man who
had worked in the Colonial Agricultural Service in Uganda recounted job
interviews when the transferability of his qualifications was greeted with
scepticism and derision. 'We don't grow coffee and bananas in Clapham
Junction you know!', one interviewer reminded him.[30]

Embarking on a second career acquired a new urgency upon decolonization, for alongside officials who served until the mandatory retirement age
were many younger colleagues made redundant when colonies achieved
independence. Many in their late thirties and forties had no choice but to
carve out a new path, a transition frequently ridden with obstacles. Those
for whom colonial careers had been valued for offering sunshine, sport,
freedom, responsibility at a young age, and the chance to spend much of
their workday outdoors baulked at the thought of leading a predictable
commuter existence in greater London, 'catching the 9.15 from Croydon
with bowler hat and umbrella to spend the rest of the day on an office
stool'.[31] The wife of an officer who had served in Malaya for twenty-five
years described their mutual dread when contemplating his post-colonial
alternatives on the eve of departure:

We vowed that the one thing he should not have to do would be to commute.
I visualized the running for trains in mist and fog, rain and snow, the crushed
strap-hanging in the Underground...A truly ghastly picture had been summoned up...that was half-acknowledged every time he set off gaily in the

Glimpses of Past and Present in Gloucestershire (Cheltenham, 1904), 177; Lawson, *At Home on Furlough*, 203; Bedford Trade Protection Society, *Bedford Town and Bedford Schools* (Bedford, 1913).

[30] A. E. Haarer, 'Preparing for Retirement', *Corona*, 3/3 (1951), 119.
[31] Sir John Rankine, 'Selling the Service to Employers', *Corona*, 14/4 (1962), 145.

mornings, buzzing round the sunlit garden on his Lambretta in his light clothes, waving cheerfully, the embodiment of freedom.[32]

Yet most men could not afford to be overly selective in their search for new employment. Many forced to change careers in mid-life received assistance from a succession of bureaus set up from the late 1940s on by the British government to help relocate men who had served in India, the Sudan, and other colonies. The Overseas Services Resettlement Bureau opened in 1957 to advise Colonial Administrative Service officials making the transition as more colonies ceased to be ruled by Britain. New jobs in business were common destinations, but applicants first needed to combat colonial stereotypes to be offered a post. 'There is a general view current that anyone who has served overseas has lived a life of indolent luxury', the head of the OSRB noted, and prospective British employers failed to realize the de-manding nature and long hours of imperial work.[33] 'Music hall jokes about irascible gentlemen in topees, swigging gin under the waving palms and waited on by a host of servants, were accepted as not too wide of the mark', another commentator added. 'They might be good at dealing with a tribal riot but most unlikely to be of much use in modern industry.'[34] The image of the ex-colonial as having little to offer British modernity proved particu-larly difficult to shed at a time when empire was increasingly becoming a thing of the past—an anachronism and a part of history rather than of acknowledged contemporary relevance.[35] Becoming re-established took time, and many ex-colonial officials accepted positions offering less author-ity and lower salaries than the posts they had been forced to vacate upon decolonization.

Colonial officials' post-independence careers reveal similarities across regionally specific services. Patterns assessed by Anthony Kirk-Greene and other scholars indicate common futures: some gained entry into the Home Civil Service, Foreign Service, or Diplomatic Service, while others who initially had served in India or the Sudan joined the Colonial Administrative Service and continued to circulate throughout the empire until at least the early 1960s. Alongside business careers, public administration and farming

---

[32] Katharine Sims, 'Keeping a Foot in the East', *Corona*, 14/4 (1962), 149.
[33] R. L. Peel, 'O.S.R.B.', *Corona*, 11/4 (1959), 142.
[34] Rankine, 'Selling the Service', 146.
[35] Stephen Howe, 'Internal Decolonization? British Politics since Thatcher as Post-Colonial Trauma', *Twentieth Century British History*, 14/3 (2003), 292.

attracted some ex-officials, while others taught at schools or universities. As widescale decolonization coincided with the expansion of British universities, a noticeable portion of ex-imperial government servants found work in university administration or as lecturers.[36] While in general 'the fact that he is fluent in Ki-Swahili or some other language and has an extensive knowledge of native customs [was] not likely to impress a future employer', some found their niche as language instructors or in academic departments at the School of Oriental and African Studies in London and other institutions.[37]

As transfers to other branches of colonial and diplomatic service suggest, many men actively sought to continue overseas work after their first posts terminated. This applied as much to those who entered non-official positions in commerce and industry as to those re-employed overseas by the state. Returning to the same newly independent nation they had recently left as part of the British high commission or as a representative of a international firm was a recurring feature of post-colonial biographies. Unlike businesses focused on Britain, multinational companies with overseas branches clearly saw men with prior experiences in similar territories as assets due to their familiarity with local languages and customs. Careers that spanned the globe as a result of successive lowerings of the Union Jack were also common, and not just among administrators. One Scottish doctor who started out in the Indian Medical Service subsequently joined the Colonial Service, to be based in Nyasaland and the Bahamas before spending his last working years and retiring in South Africa.[38]

Retiring overseas also appealed to considerable numbers of ex-officials, effectively blurring the line dividing the temporary imperial sojourner from the more permanent settler. This pattern began long before the end of empire in the dominions, and in the interwar years organizations such as

[36] On second careers, see Takehiko Honda, 'Indian Civil Servants, 1892–1937: An Age of Transition', D.Phil. thesis (Oxford, 1996), ch. 5; Oriental and India Office Collections, British Library (OIOC), MSS Eur C536, Ann Ewing, 'Indian Civil Service and Burma Civil Service (Class One) Post-Independence Careers Project: Survey of the Post-Independence Careers of British Members of the ICS and BCS (1), March 1991'; G. W. Bell and A. H. M. Kirk-Greene, 'The Sudan Political Service 1902–1952: A Preliminary Register of Second Careers' (privately published, 1989); Anthony Kirk-Greene, *Britain's Imperial Administrators, 1858–1966* (London, 2000), 260–73; Anthony Kirk-Greene, 'Decolonization: The Ultimate Diaspora', *Journal of Contemporary History*, 36/1 (2001), 133–51; Anthony Kirk-Greene, 'Towards a Retrospective Record: Part I—What Became of Us?', *Overseas Pensioner*, 84 (2002), 30–3.

[37] C. L. Bruton, 'Jobs with Roots', *Corona*, 13/6 (1961), 229; Kirk-Greene, 'Decolonization', 143.

[38] John Goodall, *Goodbye to Empire: A Doctor Remembers* (Edinburgh, 1987).

the Overseas League promoted regions such as Nova Scotia and British Columbia as destinations for Britons who had become accustomed to colonial life.[39] For those anxious about maintaining their standard of living on a pension, both locations were praised for offering lower taxes and costs of living than Britain.[40] While parts of Canada attracted some pensioners, however, those contemplating resettlement there were warned that domestic servants were even harder to come by and less affordable than at home; moreover, the climate acted as another disincentive for those seeking to maintain a lifestyle they had enjoyed in warmer regions.[41] Less affluent imperial Britons seeking to remain overseas after retirement also gravitated towards Australia, a migratory trend that continued well past the peak decolonization years. Taking advantage of Australia's post-war Assisted Passages Scheme that sought to attract those who fit the racial criteria of the White Australia Policy were working-class and other Britons of moderate means—some of whom already had attenuated metropolitan ties after protracted periods overseas.[42]

Kenya and Southern Rhodesia, meanwhile, had attracted middle-class British retirees and their families from India and African colonies since at least the 1920s.[43] Alongside officials who had worked locally and purchased land to live on later were other Britons who opted to relocate to another part of the empire at the end of men's careers instead of going home. Africa's

---

[39] On interwar British emigration to the dominions, see Kent Fedorowich, *Unfit for Heroes: Reconstruction and Soldier Settlement in the Empire between the Wars* (Manchester, 1995); Stephen Constantine (ed.), *Emigrants and Empire: British Settlement in the Dominions between the Wars* (Manchester, 1990).

[40] 'The Over-seas League Migration Committee', *Overseas*, 12/137 (1927), 31–2; Lt.-Col. D. G. Robinson, 'A Suggestion for Would-be Emigrants of the Middle Classes', *Overseas*, 13/153 (1928), 47–8.

[41] 'British Columbia from the Interior, by a Member in B. C.', *Overseas*, 13/144 (1928), 53–4; 'Ruth', 'A Rancher's Wife in British Columbia', *Overseas*, 12/133 (1927), 39–40.

[42] On post-war British migration to Australia, see A. James Hammerton and Alistair Thomson, *Ten Pound Poms: Australia's Invisible Migrants* (Manchester, 2005); James Jupp (ed.), *The Australian People: An Encyclopedia of the Nation, its People, and their Origins* (Cambridge, 2001), 62–5, 314–16. Once the White Australia Policy was relaxed in the mid-1960s, more Anglo-Indians left India for Australia as well. See Alison Blunt, *Domicile and Diaspora: Anglo-Indian Women and the Spatial Politics of Home* (Malden, Mass., 2005), 139–74.

[43] Kennedy, *Islands of White*, 60, 70–2; C. J. Duder, '"Men of the Officer Class": The Participants in the 1919 Soldier Settlement Scheme in Kenya', *African Affairs*, 92/366 (1993), 69–87; 'Another England . . . Southern Rhodesia, the Land in which to Live', advertisement, *Overseas*, 20/235 (Aug. 1935).

attractions included cheap agricultural and domestic labour, and unlike the much-maligned and often non-existent 'modern maid' in Britain, 'the African makes a cheerful and willing servant', as a 1936 report enthused.[44] East and Central Africa continued to attract British retirees even when on the brink of independence and following the violence of the Mau Mau rebellion and other nationalist upheavals.[45] Southern Rhodesia's appeal proved particularly resilient as white minority rule became more deeply ensconced rather than uprooted. Writing in 1960, a man who had retired from Tanganyika recommended Southern Rhodesia to overseas Britons long accustomed to living in 'tropical' territories. Such a colonial official 'may have but a flimsy nostalgic interest in the land of his birth', he ventured, and would be far happier moving to where he and his family could continue to enjoy sundowner parties, familiar topics of conversation, 'warmth and servants', and 'a reasonably adjacent golf course'.[46] Given the settler government's Unilateral Declaration of Independence in 1965, it remained seen as a viable retirement venue well past the end not only of imperial careers, but often of most of the empire itself.[47]

Resettling abroad was not limited to the British empire or Commonwealth, however. Since the nineteenth century, Britons accustomed to overseas life sometimes chose to grow old in Europe, most commonly in expatriate communities on the Mediterranean.[48] Continental retirement destinations continued to beckon many who hesitated before returning to a Britain from which they felt estranged. In the late 1960s, pensioners continued to be told that in places like Portugal they could 'retire to the sun and live the kind of life you used to live in the Colonies. Conditions are good and cost of living reasonable in the Algarve.'[49] One Briton long based

---

[44] OIOC, V/27/820/19, Government of India, *A Report on Southern Rhodesia, Northern Rhodesia, Nyasaland, and Kenya* (Simla, 1936), 3, 11, 121.

[45] On Kenya, see E. B. Hosking, 'The Art of Retiring', *Corona*, 11/11 (1959), 434–6.

[46] C. F. C. V. Cadiz, 'Why Not Rhodesia?', *Corona*, 12/7 (1960), 258–61.

[47] After 1980, white 'Rhodesians' who left Zimbabwe often went to South Africa, yet many relocated once again after the fall of apartheid. See W. G. Eaton, *A Chronicle of Modern Sunlight: The Story of What Happened to the Rhodesians* (Rohnert Park, 1996). Others went to Zambia or Malawi, as Alexandra Fuller describes in *Don't Let's Go to the Dogs Tonight: An African Childhood* (London, 2003).

[48] Leakey, 'On Retiring', 60; C. de Pré Thornton, 'The Advantage of Retiring to the Riviera for Anglo-Indians', *Cooper's Hill Magazine*, 12/5 (1925), 70–2; W. R. McGeagh, 'Retire to France', *Corona*, 11/5 (1959), 185–8.

[49] 'Members' Announcements: Portugal', *Overseas Pensioner*, 13 (1967), 22.

in the Algarve remembered the 1960s as 'a bit like the days of the Raj down there then—servants were a-plenty, booze was cheap and the climate was good'. The Algarve also became home to a number of white settlers departing from Kenya upon its independence under African majority rule; such was the prominence of ex-colonials among the region's retirement population that a book written in 1974 claimed that 'Great Britain may have lost an empire but seems to be gaining a province'.[50]

Foreign options aside, the majority of ex-imperial Britons nonetheless found themselves back home in the wake of empire. Although successive decolonization episodes saw the return of thousands of British sojourners and settlers, Britain did not face *en masse* repatriations on a scale similar to other European nations (such as France experienced when European settlers fled Algeria at the end of the war in the early 1960s, or Portugal with the influx of *retornados* from Angola and Mozambique upon the fall of its empire in the mid-1970s).[51] As suggested above, returns of settlers from British colonies that achieved independence were not a given and occurred more gradually.[52] Within a post-colonial Britain, they engaged in multi-faceted processes of reinvention, both of themselves and of the nation's imperial record. Campaigns for recognition and respect from a society they long accused of lacking adequate appreciation for those who had done the work of empire became all the more important as empire moved from a period of decline and collapse into history.[53]

---

[50] Russell King, Tony Warnes, and Allan Williams, *Sunset Lives: British Retirement Migration to the Mediterranean* (Oxford, 2000), 63–5, 84–6; Charles E. Wuerpel, *The Algarve* (Newton Abbot, 1974), 164.

[51] For a comparative volume on repatriations to France, Portugal, and the Netherlands, see Andrea L. Smith (ed.), *Europe's Invisible Migrants* (Amsterdam, 2003); see also Caroline Elkins and Susan Pedersen (eds.), *Settler Colonialism in the Twentieth Century* (New York, 2005), part iii; Jean-Louis Miège and Colette Dubois (eds.), *L'Europe retrouvée: Les Migrations de la décolonisation* (Paris, 1994); Elizabeth Buettner, *Europe After Empire: Decolonization, Society, and Culture* (forthcoming), ch. 2.

[52] Andrea L. Smith, 'Introduction', in Smith (ed.), *Europe's Invisible Migrants*, 10, 32; Bouda Etemad, 'Europe and Migration after Decolonisation', *Journal of European Economic History*, 27/3 (1998), 457–70.

[53] Recent scholarship has shed new light on the ongoing presence of empire in British culture during, and indeed beyond, decolonization. Within a growing body of work, see esp. Stuart Ward (ed.), *British Culture and the End of Empire* (Manchester, 2001); Wendy Webster; *Englishness and Empire, 1939–1965* (Oxford, 2005); Thompson, *Empire Strikes Back*, ch. 9; Bill Schwarz, '"The Only White Man in There": The Re-Racialisation of England, 1956–1968', *Race and Class*, 38/1 (1996), 65–78; Bill Schwarz, 'Actually Existing Postcolonialism', *Radical Philosophy*, 104

'Setting the Record Straight': Combating Misunderstandings and Making Histories after the End of Empire

In 1966, the Overseas Service Pensioners Association's journal reprinted what it called a 'welcome tribute from the press'. As an example of praise for Britain's imperial endeavours and its representatives who carried them out, the following editorial was singled out as an all-too-rare instance when colonizers' efforts and sacrifices were properly commended within a biased and ignorant metropole:

Tomorrow an event occurs that marks the finish of the old Imperial mission. The Colonial Office vanishes, merged into the department of Commonwealth Relations.

Can you imagine how the passing of the Empire will be gleefully applauded by our so-called progressives, sitting smug and self-righteous in their Hampstead seminars?

They will see 1st August 1966 as the day that closed the history of centuries of exploitation; that ushered in an idyllic new brotherhood of man.

What do THEY know about it?

In the name of the Colonial Office, thousands of dedicated selfless men and women went out to wild, remote lands scattered across Africa, Asia, the Americas, the Indian Ocean, the Pacific.

Where once there was dark superstition and savagery, they shone the light of Christianity. They showed how the sick could be cured, instead of being driven away to die in the jungle. How the land could be made to yield good crops. How beasts could be made to grow from pathetic skeletons into sleek, fat cattle.

Many of the district commissioners and the other Colonial officers spent 30 or 40 years on a steamy island or in an arid shrubland village acting as doctor and priest, friend and marriage counsellor, and even father to their charges.

They were far from well paid. Today some of them are eking out their pensions in humble guest houses in Cheltenham or Bournemouth.

Yet what a rich consolation they have.

(2000), 16–24; Paul Gilroy, *After Empire: Melancholia or Convivial Culture?* (London, 2004); Elizabeth Buettner, '"Setting the Record Straight?": Imperial History in Postcolonial British Public Culture', in Ulrike Lindner, Maren Möhring, Mark Stein, and Silke Stroh (eds.), *Hybrid Cultures—Nervous States: Britain and Germany in a (Post)Colonial World* (Amsterdam and New York, 2010), 89–104.

For they can be certain that they did more for the Colonial peoples in one day than our stay-at-home progressives will accomplish in a lifetime.[54]

Such views both harkened back to familiar defences of the colonizers and incorporated newer forms of vindication at a time when empire was largely dead and widely discredited.[55] In shaping a history of empire and the Britons most directly implicated in its management, ex-colonizers retained some old stories while rewriting others. While narratives of returning home had repeatedly alluded to discontent at the loss of a privileged lifestyle during their time in the empire, post-colonial accounts largely emphasize selflessness, hard work, and sacrifice that brought limited material rewards. Instead, such people were 'far from well paid' while overseas and suffered in old age, 'eking out their pensions'.

Repatriated colonizers exhibited resentment at what they condemned as Britain's betrayal of what they had worked to achieve overseas—often by withdrawing prematurely—as well as its failure to compensate them appropriately for their personal contributions and investments. Having dedicated themselves to setting the colonies on the road to political, economic, and cultural advancement, colonial officials had 'worked themselves out of a job' upon the transfer of power. 'Jobs well done' were rewarded largely with ongoing struggles, first to secure new employment and later to be paid adequate pensions by the British government.[56] Addressing material concerns coexisted with efforts to cultivate appreciation of imperial endeavours. Although some repatriates initially may have downplayed their personal histories overseas in order to ease their resettlement in Britain,[57] others set about overturning the derogatory metropolitan perceptions and

---

[54] 'The End of a Regime', *Overseas Pensioner*, 12 (1966), 17; originally publ. in *Sunday Express* (31 July 1966).

[55] Robert Bickers, *Empire Made Me: An Englishman Adrift in Shanghai* (London, 2003), 336.

[56] As successive issues of *Overseas Pensioner* outline, campaigning for pensions increases in accordance with inflation and for the British government to take over pensions initially meant to be paid by governments of newly independent former territories was an ongoing priority of the Overseas Service Pensioners Association. Protracted negotiations lasted well into, and in some instances beyond, the 1980s. See also Lia Paradis, '"Change of Masters": The Sudan Government British Pensioners' Association and the Negotiation of Post-Colonial Identities', *Journal of Colonialism and Colonial History*, 7/2 (2006).

[57] Bickers, *Empire Made Me*, 337.

conquering the apathy they had long resented with new energy after decolonization. Elspeth Huxley's portrayal of the ex-settler's quest for retribution
in *The Man from Nowhere* implicitly contrasted appropriate with misguided
and futile efforts to win proper recognition. Dick Heron's obsession with
killing the Cabinet Minister he deemed responsible for ruining all he and his
ancestors had worked for as white farmers in Africa ended not with murder
but rather with his own suicide. Instead of becoming acquainted with his
losses, justifiable grievances, or commendable actions, English people he
had met along the way would remember him as merely irrational, violent,
and ultimately self-destructive. He would remain the same man 'from
nowhere', from a place Britons knew too little about, as he had been upon
arrival. Setting a different example by her own actions, Huxley preferred to
focus her efforts on educating Britons about colonials' accomplishments,
investments, and sacrifices—making them 'from somewhere', even if the
colonial world she described had already drawn to a close and her writings
served as a eulogy.

Rather than ineffectually brooding from the sidelines as empire was
condemned or forgotten or despairing of their losses, ex-colonials might
more productively take on roles as interpreters. Having experienced empire
first hand, many like Huxley believed themselves the most appropriate
narrators of empire's true characteristics and achievements—far more
appropriate than the 'stay-at-home progressives' who had never come closer
to empire than the proverbial Hampstead seminar room (or—worse—one
at an American university). That empire had become history made it even
more imperative to rewrite it in a valedictory and celebratory rather than a
critical mode, deploying 'the evidence of experience' as a powerful weapon
in the struggle to vindicate the colonizers and overturn a tarnished reputation.[58] For Huxley, her substantial late- and post-colonial literary output
included her widely read (and later televised) semi-autobiographical work
The Flame Trees of Thika, as well as her account of interwar settler society
Out in the Midday Sun, which helped put Kenya's settlers more clearly on the
map for many Britons. More importantly, her works countered representations of settlers as racist, sexually promiscuous, heavy-drinking 'Happy
Valley' aristocrats by commemorating the 'ordinary' settlers who were

---

[58] Joan Wallach Scott, 'Experience', in Judith Butler and John W. Scott (eds.), *Feminists Theorize the Political* (New York, 1992), 22–40.

committed to the land and whose relationships with Africans were characterized by mutual respect.[59]

Later in life, Huxley believed that 'the colonialist hyena [is] emerging from the shadows into which the comrades drove him in the bad old imperialist days. Now that western imperialism ... has receded into history, the white colonist can be seen not only with his manifest failings, but with virtues it is no longer blasphemous to recognise.'[60] Such an assertion was testament in large part to the revisionist interpretations that she, alongside many other less familiar or unknown individuals, had disseminated both orally and in writing. From the late 1970s on, more and more returned colonials strove to reposition empire as a history of which Britain should be proud rather than ashamed or forgetful. Former participants became key players in the effort to document an affirmative history of overseas Britain, and Britons, for posterity that still continues today.

Shaping the archival record has counted as one of the most important tasks facing ageing ex-colonials in the late twentieth and early twenty-first centuries. Oral history projects, the circulation of questionnaires, and requests for donations of private papers, memoirs, photographs, and film were undertaken at a number of British archives, including the British Library's Oriental and India Office Collections, the Rhodes House Library at Oxford, the Cambridge South Asian Archives, and most recently the British Empire and Commonwealth Museum, which opened in Bristol in 2002. Discussing the development of the Oxford Development Records Project in 1980, members of the Overseas Service Pensioners' Association who had responded to calls for contributions were told that they could 'take a great deal of credit for setting the record straight', having enhanced the 'archive of Britain's colonial achievement'. Echoing Huxley's hopes, their journal argued that 'imperial history is popular again and because of the

---

[59] Elspeth Huxley, *The Flame Trees of Thika* (London, 1959), televised in 1981; Elspeth Huxley, *Out in the Midday Sun* (London, 1985). The 'Happy Valley' set she disparaged was memorably described in James Fox's *White Mischief* (London, 1982), which was subsequently filmed. For a recent biography of Huxley (which veers sharply towards apologist hagiography), see C. S. Nicholls, *Elspeth Huxley: A Biography* (London, 2002). Diverse assessments of Huxley's work include Chinua Achebe, *Home and Exile* (New York, 2000), 60–8; Micere Githae-Mugo, *Visions of Africa* (Nairobi, 1978); Wendy Webster, 'Elspeth Huxley: Gender, Empire, and Narratives of Nation, 1935–64', *Women's History Review*, 8/3 (1999), 527–45; Carolyn Martin Shaw, *Colonial Inscriptions: Race, Sex, and Class in Kenya* (Minneapolis, 1995); Phyllis Lassner, *Colonial Strangers: Women Writing the End of the British Empire* (New Brunswick, NJ, 2004), 118–59.

[60] Cited in Nicholls, *Elspeth Huxley*, 112.

rich variety of evidence historians are coming to a more balanced under-standing and fewer misrepresentations are reaching print'.[61]

Museums, institutes, and archives concerned with imperial history are not viewed disinterestedly by those with personal stake in the narratives of empire that circulate within as well as beyond their walls and are set to outlive those who witnessed empire first-hand. OSPA has watched the emerging collections at the British Empire and Commonwealth Museum with a proprietary eye, asserting that 'at the Bristol museum the current work of building the new library and archive has been made possible by the grant from OSPA. The museum will thus embody a physical memorial to our Service.' Helping document imperial history, in short, was a central plank of 'our commitment to be a guardian of the good name and reputa-tion of [Her Majesty's Overseas Civil Service] and its antecedents, and to spread understanding'.[62]

Those seen to be most in need of such 'understanding' about the 'true' nature of empire and Britons overseas were, revealingly, *not* formerly colon-ized peoples themselves. Regardless of the reality of nationalist opposition and independence struggles, ex-colonizers frequently insist that those once ruled by Britain were, and remain, largely appreciative. Many recalling their time overseas describe returns after decolonization when they were warmly welcomed by Africans or Asians, encounters that provide 'clear refutation of any charge of "colonial oppressors"'. One man remembering a visit back to Africa claimed that 'we certainly got a warmer welcome and greater appre-ciation of what we had done than anything we found on our return to the UK', while another added that 'we were respected a great deal more by "them" than by people in Britain today'.[63]

Whether or not mainstream British society has proven more hostile, nostalgic, indifferent, or forgetful of the nation's imperial past remains a matter of opinion and a subject of lively debate.[64] No consensus prevails on

---

[61] 'University of Oxford Development Records Project', *Overseas Pensioner*, 39 (1980), 10.

[62] 'Forty-Second Annual General Meeting of the Overseas Service Pensioners' Association', *Overseas Pensioner*, 84 (2002), 13. On archival politics, see Antoinette Burton, *Dwelling in the Archive: Women Writing House, Home, and History in Late Colonial India* (New York, 2003), 20–6; Antoinette Burton (ed.), *Archive Stories: Facts, Fictions, and the Writing of History* (Durham, NC, 2005).

[63] Anthony Kirk-Greene, 'Towards a Retrospective Record', *Overseas Pensioner*, 85 (2003), 20.

[64] See the works cited above in n. 53, and more sceptical views expressed by Stephen Howe, including 'When (If Ever) did Empire End? "Internal Decolonisation" in British Culture since the 1950s', in Martin Lynn (ed.), *The British Empire in the 1950s: Retreat or Revival?* (Houndmills, 2006), 214–37; Howe, 'Internal Decolonization?' My own contributions to this discussion

the imperial record or the reputation of the former colonizers, with apologists continuing to clash with critics. But in certain crucial respects, repatriated former empire builders are now more 'at home' within a multicultural Britain than ever before. Although colonizers often returned to a country where they felt misunderstood, unacknowledged, and out of place, their 'insider' status within the British nation was cemented and reconfirmed over time, and in the context of other post-colonial arrivals. Other residents of the overseas Commonwealth, mainly 'black men, black and brown' as Huxley put it, initially were allowed entry into Britain after the Second World War but were greeted with considerable racism—as 'dark strangers'—and, later, with a series of restrictive immigration laws.[65] Between the 1960s and 1980s, British legislation made it increasingly difficult for 'New Commonwealth' immigrants to settle, but significantly persons of British ancestry from the same countries were not targeted for exclusion. British descent, often referred to as 'patriality', became grounds for inclusion within the nation as 'kith and kin', while 'others'—who happened to be of different 'races'—were largely turned away.[66] In an era of protracted and ongoing anxiety about what 'Britishness' should mean and who should count as 'British' after the end of empire, former white colonizers, whether they lived overseas as settlers or expatriates, have been reincorporated within the national community. Their former colonial identities, once so clearly articulated, may have gradually eroded, but they have yet to disappear. While imperial repatriates are now an ageing group whose numbers become smaller with each passing year, their role in determining how empire is remembered and forgotten 'at home' appears certain to outlive them as subsequent generations grapple with their legacy.

---

include Elizabeth Buettner, 'Cemeteries, Public Memory, and Raj Nostalgia in Postcolonial Britain and India', *History and Memory*, 18/1 (2006), 5–42; Buettner, *Empire Families*, 252–70; Buettner, 'Setting the Record Straight?'. Robert Bickers, meanwhile, learnt that many ex-Shanghai policemen largely stopped discussing their experiences due to listeners' indifference; 'families, however sympathetic, have heard all of the Shanghai stories before, and are not much interested in listening again and again. Often the historian's visit turns out to be the first time in years, a decade, that anyone has asked about that life.' *Empire Made Me*, 337.

[65] Chris Waters, '"Dark Strangers" in our Midst: Discourses of Race and Nation in Britain, 1947–63', *Journal of British Studies*, 36 (1997), 207–38; Paul Gilroy, *'There Ain't No Black in the Union Jack': The Cultural Politics of Race and Nation* (Chicago, 1987).

[66] Kathleen Paul, *Whitewashing Britain: Race and Citizenship in the Postwar Era* (Ithaca, NY, 1997), esp. 179–88. Two groups explicitly exempted from restrictive immigration legislation were Kenyan Europeans and Falkland Islanders.

Select Bibliography

ELIZABETH BUETTNER, *Empire Families: Britons and Late Imperial India* (Oxford, 2004).

—— 'Cemeteries, Public Memory, and Raj Nostalgia in Postcolonial Britain and India', *History and Memory*, 18/1 (2006), 5–42.

—— ' "Setting the Record Straight?": Imperial History in Postcolonial British Public Culture', in Ulrike Lindner, Maren Möhring, Mark Stein, and Silke Stroh (eds.), *Hybrid Cultures—Nervous States: Britain and Germany in a (Post)Colonial World* (Amsterdam and New York, 2010).

PAUL GILROY, *After Empire: Melancholia or Convivial Culture?* (London, 2004).

CATHERINE HALL and SONYA O. ROSE (eds.), *At Home with the Empire: Metropolitan Culture and the Imperial World* (Cambridge, 2006).

STEPHEN HOWE, 'Internal Decolonization? British Politics since Thatcher as Post-Colonial Trauma', *Twentieth Century British History*, 14/3 (2003), 286–304.

—— 'When (If Ever) did Empire End?: "Internal Decolonisation" in British Culture since the 1950s', in Martin Lynn (ed.), *The British Empire in the 1950s: Retreat or Revival?* (Houndmills, 2006), 214–37.

DANE KENNEDY, *Islands of White: Settler Society and Culture in Kenya and Southern Rhodesia, 1890–1939* (Durham, NC, 1987).

ANTHONY KIRK-GREENE, 'Decolonization: The Ultimate Diaspora', *Journal of Contemporary History*, 36/1 (2001), 133–51.

BENITA PARRY, *Delusions and Discoveries: India in the British Imagination, 1880–1930* (2nd edn. London, 1998).

KATHLEEN PAUL, *Whitewashing Britain: Race and Citizenship in the Postwar Era* (Ithaca, NY, 1997).

EDWARD SAID, *Culture and Imperialism* (New York, 1993).

BILL SCHWARZ, 'Actually Existing Postcolonialism', *Radical Philosophy*, 104 (2000), 16–24.

ANDREA L. SMITH (ed.), *Europe's Invisible Migrants* (Amsterdam, 2003).

ANN LAURA STOLER, *Carnal Knowledge and Imperial Power: Race and the Intimate in Colonial Rule* (Berkeley, Calif., 2002).

—— and FREDERICK COOPER (eds.), *Tensions of Empire: Colonial Cultures in a Bourgeois World* (Berkeley, Calif., 1997).

ANDREW THOMPSON, *The Empire Strikes Back? The Impact of Imperialism on Britain from the Mid-Nineteenth Century* (Harlow, 2005).

STUART WARD (ed.), *British Culture and the End of Empire* (Manchester, 2001).

WENDY WEBSTER, *Englishness and Empire, 1939–1965* (Oxford, 2005).

ANGELA WOOLLACOTT, *To Try Her Fortune in London: Australian Women, Colonialism, and Modernity* (New York, 2001).

12

Orphans of Empire

John Darwin

Between 1815 and 1914 some twenty million people left the British Isles, and millions more were to follow in the rest of the twentieth century. Indeed, twenty-first-century Britons still display a notable tendency to migrate and to settle, although they are now as likely to go to Andalusia or the Dordogne as to North America or Australasia. But for much of the nineteenth century, the largest part of this migration headed for the United States, with Canada, Australia, and New Zealand trailing (sometimes far) behind. Compared with the tidal flow of migrants to these favoured destinations, the British populations surveyed in this volume may seem like so many drops in the ocean, little wavelets at best that lapped against alien shores until (mostly) pulled off by the long withdrawing roar of decolonization. Small and transient, they are easily dismissed as the detritus of imperialism, the hangers-on and camp-followers of an imperial project that they tried to exploit but could not control. Lacking for the most part the cultural institutions and resources to make their own history—a task feverishly undertaken in the main settlement colonies and in the United States (the 'white man's country' *par excellence*)—they became historiographical orphans with the end of empire. Where they featured at all in the histories of new nations, the treatment was predictably hostile. But for the most part their sentence was oblivion in a historical Siberia.

It is not hard to see why this should have happened. Despite the romantic allure that the emotive word 'settler' enjoyed into the 1950s (before its reputational trajectory turned sharply downwards) the social and cultural reality among transplanted British populations, however exotic the host environment, could be almost heroically drab—a point often made by visitors from 'home'. The more high-spirited the visitor, the more bruising the judgement. Trapped in Aden in the 1850s, Richard Burton dismissed it as a place where 'social intercourse is crushed by "gup", gossip and the scandal of small colonial circles', where 'semi-civilised life abounds in a weary ceremoniousness. It is highly improper to smoke inside your bungalow... [and] you shall be generally shunned if you omit your waistcoat.'[1] Burton's drastic solution was to leave for Somalia. But historians and memoir-writers (not to mention a legion of journalists) have echoed his complaint. Philistine, snobbish, myopic, and racist (the last is an objection that Burton would not have made) have been the usual terms in which settler and expatriate societies have been described not by foreigners but by their own fellow-countrymen.

As the chapters in this book have suggested, in some cases at least this verdict needs shading. But it is not necessary to sympathize with settlers and expatriates to find them interesting or to acknowledge their importance. Wherever they enjoyed any political or commercial influence, their ideas and attitudes, and the internal dynamics of their social systems—however rudimentary they were—shaped the imperial presence. They often determined the basis of the 'collaborative bargain' on which all kinds of empire— formal or informal—almost invariably depended. Secondly, the rise and demise of small settler and expatriate societies has a comparative interest. They highlight the constraints to which such alien bodies were subject except under especially favourable conditions. They expose the frictions and fears that were magnified by a sense of political or cultural vulnerability, but which were close to the surface in much larger settlements whose fate was quite different. They suggest by default some of the reasons why British migrants elsewhere proved much more successful in colonizing their new worlds. Thirdly, although we might be tempted to see the cases examined in this book as forming the outermost margins of a 'British world', they also serve to remind us of the curious shape of the British 'world-system'.[2]

From the 1830s to the 1940s, British power in the world rested upon the maritime, commercial, and industrial strength of the British Isles, and beneficial access to the human and material resources of the settlement colonies and India. We are, said A. J. Balfour, Lord Salisbury's nephew and his successor as premier, 'a great Naval, Indian and Colonial Power'.[3] Of

---

[1] Richard F. Burton, *First Steps in East Africa* ([1856] Everyman edn. London, 1910), 43–4.

[2] John Darwin, *The Empire Project: The Rise and Fall of the British World-System, 1830–1970* (Cambridge, 2009).

[3] N. D'Ombrain, *War Machinery and High Policy: Defence Administration in Peacetime Britain 1902–1914* (Oxford, 1973), 1.

course, as historians have long recognized, there were two other vital components without which this system would have succumbed to attrition much earlier than it did. The first was a business or commercial empire of installations and property, concessions, and investments, much of it lying on or beyond the imperial frontier in Latin America, the Middle East, Southeast Asia, and China. The second was made up of the links in the chain of imperial communications: naval bases and fortresses, strategic zones, and 'spheres of interference' (in Sellars and Yeatman's apposite phrase in *1066 and All That*) that overlooked the sea-lanes (and later the air routes) that held the system together. Both these kinds of empire spawned 'service communities': the settlers and expatriates attracted by the occupational niches they offered—as sailors, mechanics, engineers, hotel-keepers, policemen, clergymen, teachers, doctors, governesses, nurses, and even household servants, as well as the soldiers, officials, and merchants who took centre-stage. It is tempting to see the fate of these service communities and their humbler members, who were least well-protected against the economic competition of locals, as a proxy measure of British imperial power, a sensitive gauge of the advance or retreat of British imperialism. But they are also a witness to an aspect of British expansion that is sometimes forgotten, but whose closest parallel was thrown up by the settlement pattern in the United States. There the forward rush of white occupation often left in its rear what are sometimes described as 'hollow frontiers'— places where the take-off into commercial prosperity was prematurely aborted. These were the districts whose great future was behind them, and whose prospects were blighted early on by bad soil, bad communications, or economic bad luck. On the open frontier of British expansion, there were also many such 'relics'—launched on a flood-tide of economic or political hope but then beached by its ebb. In some cases the ebb began almost at once. With the advantage of hindsight, we might think that the chances of viable, autonomous British settler states on the Canadian model being established in Natal or Southern Rhodesia, let alone Kenya, already looked poor by 1914. To these 'hollow-frontiersmen' it was a source of bitter reproach by the 1950s and 1960s that the imperial firm of which they claimed to be branches showed few signs of regret at closing them down, or even selling them off. They could not have imagined that it would be to defend one of the smallest and weakest of these relic communities that Britain would fight its last great imperial war in 1982.

From one point of view, then, all the cases explored in this book had something in common. Insofar as they wished to retain a 'British' identity, and preserve the expatriate privileges long assured by British power in the world, they were failures. If we dig a little more deeply, the difficulties of anatomizing what might seem at first glance broadly similar societies become increasingly obvious. The first issue to consider is the definitional problem. 'Settler' is an old word, and was used as a synonym for 'colonist' as early as the 1690s. 'Expatriate' in the sense that we use it today is of much more recent coinage. As late as the 1930s, 'expatriate' was still defined (in the *Shorter Oxford Dictionary*) as a verb meaning to banish, or to withdraw one's allegiance. Conventional usage now is to describe as 'settlers' those who migrated with the intention of establishing a permanent overseas home, expecting to live out their full lives there, bring up their children and pass on their property to descendants who would also be permanent residents. A settler was therefore someone who was in process of acquiring—in some part at least—a new identity; someone who deliberately identified his or her fortunes with a new place of residence; and someone who developed a strong sense of ownership not just for his or her property but for the colonized region as a whole. Settlers also expected to take their political rights with them and typically claimed that the conduct of local affairs should be entrusted to those who combined a 'stake' in the country with the civilizational virtues acquired in the homeland. Along with this came a distinctively 'provincial' outlook in which the assertion of 'Britishness' was usually coupled with a critique of the social ethos at 'home' and contempt for the 'spinelessness' of the imperial government. This feeling was (paradoxically) strongest where London's authority was a significant check on settler self-interest—as in Kenya, or later the Rhodesias. Settler self-imagery portrayed settler societies as a healthy recreation of British society at home: replicating its virtues, suppressing its vices, but most of all founding communities that would be as rooted and durable as that in Britain itself.

The 'expat' by contrast seems a mere bird of passage. The expatriate lives overseas for a term. The reason is usually employment. An expatriate might stay in one place for a long time (rather than traversing the globe like a soldier, diplomat, colonial official, or engineer), but the intention is typically to leave when the contract is finished. Indeed, putting down 'roots' may be barred by the rules of the host society, a sense of cultural exclusion tolerable only on a temporary basis, or the practical difficulty of living outside an expatriate 'compound'. The expatriate's children will be educated 'at home', and their careers will begin there. The expatriate may have strong views on local affairs, but he or she will usually enjoy no political rights, except 'corporately' as members of their national or company 'community'. Of course, the expatriate may not actually go home at the end of his service: he may retire elsewhere. But that too will be an 'unsettled' existence: concern for the future of children or grandchildren will play no part in his opinions and attitudes. The expatriate himself is likely to depend not on the success of the local economy (whose commercial backwardness may be an important attraction), but on a pension or remittance paid from elsewhere.

But if we apply this template to the 'overseas Britons' discussed in this book, its shortcomings are obvious. Is it really so easy to distinguish settlers and expatriates? Part of the problem is that both these categories are extremely fluid. People moved into, through, and even between them, perhaps without noticing the transition. A significant proportion of those who migrated (for example, to Canada before 1914) later came home. Some seem to have been 'serial migrants', going out and coming back several times in the course of their working life. An expatriate might turn into a settler; in turn a settler might revert to an expatriate. If we take particular cases, the definition gets harder. Britons and their dependants living in Egypt in official or commercial employment might classify readily as expatriates. But what about the Britons who lived in Argentina? They might send their children 'home' to school if they could afford it. But often the reason (as David Rock points out) was to secure a career in British firms in Argentina, where the pay and prestige would be best. They might pride themselves on being British not Hispanic. But their future was bound up with Argentina's success. The option of going 'home', exercised by some, was always open in theory. But it was viewed as fall-back, if things went wrong, not the natural conclusion of a 'foreign' career.

The British in Shanghai were even more complicated. The wealthier residents, like the *taipans* in the large trading houses, or the managers employed by the large multinationals which moved into China after 1900 (like British American Tobacco), were classic expatriates. But for many of the British population, Shanghai was home (if not 'home'). Their property, prospects, and social position were tied up not so much with the fate of China as with that of their privileged enclave, the 'International Settlement'. In China they were expatriates: in Shanghai they were settlers, self-conscious creators of a new society. They claimed and exercised a degree of self-government and regarded the agents of British diplomacy with all the mistrust (sometimes loathing) that settlers elsewhere reserved for the Colonial Office.

The fourth case raises just as many difficulties. It might have been thought that the British in India were an exemplary case. 'Bound to exile', they were career-long expatriates, periodically released on furlough to marry or recuperate, before eventual return home on comfortable pensions—which members of the Indian Civil Service could draw after twenty years' service. But this picture is too simple for at least two reasons. As David Washbrook reminds us, for all the determination of the East India Company and the post-1858 Raj to exclude 'poor whites', some had settled down before the rule-book was tightened and some arrived later as employees of the railways in their great age of expansion in the late nineteenth century. Often marrying in India, they could bequeath their racial niche on the railway workforce to their children and preserve a privileged status that set them apart from the local population. They might have few political rights and little ambition to control the government, but they were at least half-settler in their ethos and attitudes. We might even be tempted to make a similar claim for the civil servants and soldiers—despite their conventional status. The Indian Civil Service were indeed 'civil servants', but of a peculiar kind. They formed in effect a political oligarchy, until its gradual collapse after 1920. They liked to insist that they alone represented the true interests of India—a very settlerish view—against the short-sighted self-interest of governments at home, and 'native' politicians. Although their power and position were not directly inheritable (and they usually left the country at the end of their service), the extended network of 'Anglo-Indian' families from which the civil servants and officers of the Indian army were substantially recruited created a strong corporate interest, a 'virtual' settler community. When the civil servant or soldier was actually born in India, this quasi-settler mentality could be even stronger: 'Anglo-India' was their country. A contributory factor in the fateful ferocity that Dyer showed at Amritsar might have been this sense of the 'India-born' that the attack on British life and property in the city must be savagely avenged.[4]

---

[4] See Nigel Collet, *The Butcher of Amritsar: General Reginald Dyer* (London, 2006), for a scholarly and perceptive life of General 'Rex' Dyer. Dyer was born in India.

What these cases suggest is that overseas Britons frequently displayed a mixture of 'settler' and 'expatriate' attitudes, and that British communities were often divided between those who were more one than the other. Typically, perhaps, the dividing line might be one of wealth: remaining at least partly an expatriate, rather than becoming a fully fledged settler, was often a question of income. For those who could afford to travel 'home' frequently, to contract a marriage at 'home', to educate their children there, and to hold open the option of where to retire, keeping a foot in two continents, was to have the best of both worlds. Wealthy Canadians, Australians, and 'English' (i.e. English-speaking) South Africans often adopted this practice. Ultimately, however, whether either settler or expatriate attitudes came to predominate in the 'colony' was largely determined by its geopolitical fate.

A striking feature of the groups of overseas Britons discussed in this book is their social diversity. Some were in the vanguard of British commercial enterprise; some formed the rear column in places where imperial influence had begun to retreat before 1914. The wide variation in the pattern of employment as well as social structure reflected the multifarious nature of British expansion in the long nineteenth century. In addition to the main self-governing settlements, that expansion had thrown out four different kinds of 'colony', some of them under full British jurisdiction, some living as 'quasi-protectorates' (as in Egypt or Shanghai), and some who depended on their commercial ties with Britain and the intangible benefits of British prestige. There was, first of all, a clutch of bases and garrisons—what Lord Curzon once called 'the tollgates and barbicans' of empire—mostly to be found in British ruled territories (the extraterritorial base of which the Suez Canal Zone—defined by the Anglo-Egyptian Treaty of 1936—was the grandest example, was mainly a product of decolonization). The military personnel and their dependants, who made up the base population, formed for the most part a self-sufficient community, consciously separated by military discipline and functional transience from local concerns. Yet where the garrison was linked through its military role to the local armed forces—whether a colonial army or an 'independent' formation (like the Egyptian army) with British officers or advisers—or was the main employer or purchaser of labour, goods, and services (as in Singapore or Malta), this formal separation was much less real in practice. Garrisons after all had a dual role. They were part of the imperial 'strategic reserve', available for service wherever British interests needed a military presence. Thus British units in India might be sent to China or (as in 1899) to defend Natal. But they were also the symbol and ultimate source of British power in the country where they were stationed, ready to be used as a threat or in force if the going got rough in colonial politics.

The military 'colony' was thus an adjunct in part to the 'administrative' colony: the officials, advisers, and experts who staffed the colonial governments, or held senior posts under foreign governments whose independence was nominal. As we have seen, the extent to which these imperial 'mamluks' should be seen as the willing tools of their faraway masters in London, without local interests or attachments, varied considerably from place to place and from time to time. Sometimes (as in Kenya) they might feel sympathy with unofficial compatriots who had come to the country as settlers. These ties might be strengthened by sociability or marriage in what were small social worlds. But, of course, the officials were subject to administrative discipline, a Byzantine hierarchy, and the prospect of transfer. Much anecdotal evidence suggests that, in both India and Africa, official life was one of constant upheaval as administrative staff were shuttled from place to place to fill the gaps left by illness, retirement, or leave. The third kind of colony was the bridgehead of trade, whose members supplied the commercial 'steel-frame' for the British connection. Merchants, bank officials, shipping agents, buyers, salesmen, telegraph clerks, journalists, and hotel-keepers all earned their living from the commercial exchange between Britain and those countries where the apparatus and personnel for overseas trade were still underdeveloped. They might overlap with the fourth sort of 'colony': the overseas Britons who managed, or serviced, British-owned property abroad, where local expertise was thought unreliable or lacking. Railway companies, utilities, mines, plantations, and oilfields all had their cadres of managers, engineers, and often artisans. Sometimes they formed part of a larger British community (as in Northern Rhodesia); sometimes they were fenced in to the company compound. Lastly, there were those who had become possessors of the land: as *estancieros* in Argentina; as mixed farmers in the white reserve of the Kenya highlands; as the rulers of the soil and the 'political nation' in Southern Rhodesia or Natal.

All these different kinds of 'colony' had one thing in common. They needed more or less constant reinforcement from 'home': supplies of men (and women) and infusions of capital. They needed the assurance that their status, claims, rights, and privileges would be defended if necessary by the exertion of British power. For those whose living was drawn from trade or the profits of property, this meant protection from the risks of expropriation and, above all, the continued enforcement of the 'open economy', including free trade and the free repatriation of profits and interest. It was not just the overseas Britons living outside the empire for whom this was important. In Singapore, Hong Kong, and even Ceylon (where Colombo became one of the world's leading ports), British mercantile interests were bound up with the huge expansion of trade in the late nineteenth century. In the last decades before 1914 (but not much earlier), it might have been easy to think that these conditions were permanent: that the 'semi-globalized' world would always favour free movement and reward the skills of the migrant and expatriate. Even so, few of the communities surveyed in this volume could have doubted their vulnerability to external shocks. The Baring 'crash' of 1890, the South African War of 1899–1902, the Boxer uprising in 1900, the *swadeshi* campaign in Bengal, and the great naval 'scare' of 1908–9, suggested how quickly their fortunes could change. After 1918, this anxiety became chronic. With the shrinkage of trade, more assertive nationalisms, and the shortage of capital (partly a result of Britain's war debts at home and abroad), the geopolitical and 'geo-economic' setting became more and more hostile. It was hardly surprising that fears of decline or collapse sharpened political feeling—against the City and (for those who demanded diplomatic or military support) against the imperial government. This sense of danger, or even betrayal, also threw into sharp relief the question of how far these overseas Britons were really communities in anything more than the most limited sense.

As the case studies presented here show, the variation was wide. It might even be argued that in the Indian case there was no real British community at all, merely a number of parallel bureaucracies chiefly united (except in moments of crisis) by mutual antagonism. Before and after 1858, those who governed the Raj were just as determined to exclude the political influence of unofficial rich whites as the physical presence of their poorer compatriots. Disparaged as 'box-wallahs' engaged in trade, the mercantile British enjoyed a status below that of the civil service or the army—a distinction reinforced by the rigidly hierarchical style of colonial society in India with its apex at the Viceroy's or provincial governor's court. The large British garrison, of some 70,000 men after 1860, was secluded in 'cantonments', the military stations found on the edge of larger Indian towns. Railway employees lived in 'railway colonies', and had their own clubs. Even among those on the official payroll, service distinctions were all-important. In the table of ranks, the Indian Civil Service men (the covenanted 'civilians') took precedence. The coveted letters 'ICS' after his name gave the civilian a status like that of a viscount or marquess in society at home. The Public Works staff were at the bottom of the pile. When the governor came and the photographs were taken, they stood at the back, furthest from favour. What mattered most, in normal times, was career advancement in a particular service: the ethos and outlook was bureaucratic, relieved at times by the collegiality of shared recreation. In fact, outside Calcutta, there were very few places where there were more than a handful of British who were not employed by government in one of the services.

Similar fissures along the fault-lines of class, status, pay, job security, and prospects existed in all the British populations surveyed in this volume. They were not easily bridged, especially where the status-line coincided with the distinction between those who looked forward to a comfortable retirement at 'at home' and those whose circumstances required that, willingly or otherwise, they 'stay on'. But there were other dividing-lines as well. As Tim Harper points out, the ethos of the British in 'upcountry' peninsular Malaya was bound to be different from that of the more cosmopolitan residents of Singapore, one of the world's great trading cities and already, before 1914, a meeting place for a spectrum of peoples and cultures. In Northern Rhodesia, the white working class of miners and railwaymen had little in common—save the colour of their skins—with the farmers who had been the protectorate's first settled community. In Shanghai, the whites employed by the municipality or by foreign-owned business in the International Settlement as artisans, clerks, policemen, or petty officials lived in a world that was far less secure, economically and physically, than that of the managerial cadres of Jardine Matheson or Swire or the Hong Kong and Shanghai Bank or of the British officials recruited from home into the Chinese maritime customs service.[5]

Of course, these differences might have been even more visible had it not been for the growing tendency in the later nineteenth century to define Britishness more restrictively in racial and ethnic terms. In most of the settler and expatriate groups surveyed in this book, social closure along racial lines had a double effect. It excluded 'Anglicized' members of the local indigenous elite from entry and reinforced the sense that the settler and

---

[5] Life among the poorer whites in Shanghai is convincingly recreated in Robert Bickers, *Empire Made Me: An Englishman Adrift in Shanghai* (London, 2003).

expatriate presence was an embattled bridgehead, whose vitality depended upon its lifeline to Britain. Why this should have happened has been much debated. In larger settler societies, demographic mass may have been the key factor: the racial exclusion (of non-whites) became the corollary of social cohesion (among whites). But for most of the groups in this book, the reasons may have been different. A number of changes may have encouraged the sharpening of racial boundaries. The greater frequency and regularity of long-distance sea travel (especially eastwards of Suez after c.1870) increased the number of visitors, reduced the costs of furlough at home, and swelled the population of British-born women. The cultural effect was to focus attention upon local habits and customs that seemed more likely to weaken a sense of British identity than to enhance British prestige. It was one thing to live far more grandly than at home, attended by scores of servants, and enjoying a deference scarcely to be hoped for by a duke in England. But it was quite another to speak with an 'accent', to eschew 'manly' diversions, to eat a vegetable diet, or incur social obligations (for example, through a local marriage or concubinage) that conflicted with those recognized in British society. If the definition of 'Britishness' was to be able to fit without difficulty into society at home, and if the claim to be 'British' (with its protections and privileges) was to be plausibly maintained, the solution seemed obvious: a pattern of physical, social, and cultural segregation whose detailed application would vary with place.

Within the ethnically British populations, there were some institutions that transcended the social fissures and fractures. In the Indian *mofussil* it was conventionally the 'Club'. The club assumed a rough equality of ('gentlemanly') social status, but it also seems likely that its internal economy was a faithful reflection of the official hierarchy, with the collector of the district as the *de facto* president. Whether the social activity of the club did more to bring the British residents together through sport, the card table, or seasonal jollity than it did to remind them of their different stations in life we can only speculate. Social reminiscence of the Raj has been dominated by the rosier recollections of civil servants and soldiers, the most privileged members of the ruling race. Where there were the resources to support them, the churches claimed a central role in constructing a 'community'. The clergymen's task was to uphold the moral order of 'home' on the imperial (or quasi-imperial) frontier, making pragmatic allowance for local conditions. It would be interesting to know much more than we do of the way that they did so in small settler and expatriate populations. Where these were of more than minimal size, more than one denomination would usually be present, a situation that made for a certain competitiveness and perhaps a hardening of sectarian (and class) boundaries. In some places, at least, the clergy were a militant voice, resisting accommodation with local society and variously asserting the claims of Christianity, Protestantism, or their own denomination against religious rivals and foes. In South Africa, the Anglican clergy took a prominent part in defending the imperial connection against the 'Christian National' onslaught of Calvinist Afrikanerdom and its *predikants*. In Argentina and elsewhere in Latin America, Protestant churches were a visible symbol of expatriate solidarity in overwhelmingly Catholic societies. The Anglican cathedral in Cairo, completed in 1938, was a remarkable affirmation of British and Anglican influence despite the formal recension of British power in the country under the 1936 Treaty.

The clergy were also active in education, sometimes taking the lead in the founding of schools. The elite schools established in Southern Rhodesia, Natal, and elsewhere in 'English' South Africa reflected this clerical influence—Anglican, Methodist, or Catholic. But this kind of education was not available to the settler or expatriate population at large: it was much too expensive. In Southern Africa, certainly, it was designed on the model of the public schools in Britain and consciously intended to train a leadership class committed to maintaining the imperial connection.[6] Schools of this sort were often staffed by expatriates, young British graduates deliberately recruited to maintain the school's 'tone'. Whether this served to strengthen a sense of British community, or raised the barriers of class that were so familiar at home, is unclear. Where the expatriate population had no need of schools because their children were sent home, or lacked the means for a private education, the 'British' hospital (as in Buenos Aires) might serve as the institutional focus of expatriate loyalty. Charitable activity, flag days, and committee meetings brought expatriates together amid vivid reminders of their mutual dependence. But of all the institutions that helped to create and preserve a sense of a distinctive identity, and some sense of community, perhaps none was so powerful as the newspaper.

'When men are no longer united among themselves by firm and lasting ties,' wrote Tocqueville, 'it is impossible to obtain the cooperation of any

---

[6] For some discussion of this, and the contribution of the Rhodes Trust, see John Darwin, 'The Rhodes Trust in the Age of Empire', in Anthony Kenny (ed.), *The History of the Rhodes Trust* (Oxford, 2001), 463–517.

great number of them unless you can persuade every man ... that his private interest obliges him voluntarily to unite his exertions to the exertions of all the others. This can be habitually and conveniently effected only by means of a newspaper'.[7] Among settlers and expatriates, arriving singly or in small family groups, dispersed in pockets or living amongst a large host population, the greatest barrier to a sense of collective identity was isolation and the ignorance that came with it. Bound to the routines of their work—manual, commercial, or administrative—often in a harsh or demanding environment, with limited time or means to travel, and with family connections (and the correspondence that went with it) that tied them more closely to 'home' than to their compatriots 'on the spot', knowledge of their local 'world' could be very exiguous. The more bookish might read, but often what existed in print about their place of exile was an official compilation or a gazetteer. For some expatriates at least, reading was favoured as a way of escape from the tedium of exile, not as a means to embrace it more deeply. Where expatriates were separated from an alien host population by the barriers of language, religion, and culture, as in India or China, there was often at best only a muted desire to learn more about this non-British universe. The time and effort required, and the convenience of the stereotypes that covered most of the likely encounters (usually in the workplace), discouraged the attempt. Indeed, it was likely that overzealous activity to become better-informed would attract the opprobrium of fellow expatriates, or their suspicion that this veiled other less respectable interests. In the expatriate world, like an officers' mess, reading and thinking—necessarily solitary activities—were often regarded as signs of mental unbalance, private shortcomings, and general 'unsoundness'.

This void in the sources of information and opinion above the level of gossip was filled by the newspaper. Newspapers sprang up among settler and expatriate populations for a number of reasons. They provided commercial information, reprinted news from 'home', and advertised local events. They could serve as the vehicle for the ambitions of their politician-proprietors and editors like Sir Edgar Walton's *Eastern Province Herald* (in Port Elizabeth), Charles Crewe's *East London Daily Despatch*, or Leopold Moore's *Livingstone Mail*. But even where they did not serve explicitly as partisan mouthpieces, they were intensely political. They supplied the expatriate

---

[7] A. de Tocqueville, *Democracy in America* (Everyman edn. London, 1994), part 2, p. 111.

with what he or she would otherwise have lacked, a sense of their place in an alien world. Their reporting of news of the most humdrum occurrences was a constant reminder that expatriates were different. They often enjoyed an effective monopoly over the supply of local news, with the editor acting as the 'stringer' or local correspondent for the papers published 'at home'—a common practice in India—so that the expatriate reading the 'news' from 'home' found his local prejudices authoritatively confirmed. They purveyed the assumption that their expatriate readers shared the same views and emotions. And as local businesses, they were likely to take a less detached and roseate view of expatriate prospects than that propounded by transient officials or flannelling diplomats. Kipling, after all, cut his imperialist teeth as a sub-editor on the *Civil and Military Gazette* in Lahore.[8] In this limited sense, it might even be argued that, as readers of a newspaper claiming to serve their peculiar interests, expatriates became an 'imagined community', collectively reassured, alarmed, or outraged by what they read in 'their' newspaper. But it has to be said that we know much less than we should about such expatriate journals, or even the newspapers that served settler societies.

Yet even a newspaper was a poor substitute for the sense of distinctive identity created by the possession of political and legal rights and the institutions that went with them. If Shanghailanders or Southern Rhodesians displayed an entrenched local patriotism, it may have derived in large part from the enjoyment of self-rule—restricted of course in the case of Shanghai to the municipal business of the International Settlement. Representative government, however Lilliputian the scale, reduced the sense of dependence upon others and the need to defer to indigenous notables or to the British officials appointed to supervise them. It encouraged a rhetoric of self-reliance. More to the point, it gave expatriates and settlers a degree of control over public resources. These could be mobilized to create civil employment, and a thus strong vested interest in the expatriate regime. They could be applied to education if the demand arose. They could be used to fashion a distinctive public memory by the commemoration of dates, the celebration of heroes or the erection of monuments. It is tempting to argue that political rights came first, and 'community' followed on, not the other way round. But in most of the cases examined in this book, political rights

---

[8] There is a good description of his duties in Andrew Rutherford (ed.), *Early Verse by Rudyard Kipling 1879–1889* (Oxford, 1986), 13–18.

or extraterritorial privilege (of the kinds from which British expatriates in China, Egypt, Iran, Thailand, and elsewhere had long benefited), even where they existed, were not enough to preserve the settler or expatriate groups from absorption, expulsion, dissolution, or the amputation of their status. Directly (in the case of the Shanghailanders) or indirectly (for Kenyan whites, Southern Rhodesians, and Natalians), self-identification as a distinct British society and its physical reality, required the preservation of a colonial world order, and Britain's willingness to act as its main guarantor.

It was inevitable then that the decline of British power, both economic and political, after the Second World War, coming on top of the contraction of British trade and investment in the 1930s (as in the Argentine case) should have put both expatriate groups and small settler societies under great strain. Britain had no means of preventing the communist victory in China in 1949, which led not just to the end of treaty-port life (which would have happened any way under a Nationalist government) but to the wholesale expulsion of British expatriates. The sale in 1948 of the British-owned railways in Argentina to buy a year's worth of meat marked the virtual end of the pre-war Anglo-Argentine relationship and of a distinct British community in the country. The crisis with Iran in 1951, when the British lacked the will to compromise or the means to coerce, ended with the abandonment of the great refinery enclave at Abadan. Britain's withdrawal from the Canal Zone in 1956 (after years of acrimonious negotiation), capped by the abortive reoccupation in October the same year, liquidated what remained of the British unofficial presence in Egypt. Independence in Sub-Saharan Africa, beginning with the Gold Coast (Ghana) in 1957, brought a steady (rather than immediate) shrinkage of British officialdom. But fears about physical security, the loss of employment privileges, and financial anxiety (over the repatriation of capital) led to the shrivelling of white artisan and settler-farmer numbers in Northern Rhodesia (Zambia) and Kenya. South Africa's exit from the Commonwealth (a consequence of political change in British colonial Africa) did not mean the end of English-speaking South Africa, but it erased the lingering sense of political attachment to Britain among the South African 'English'. Even where significant numbers of British stayed on, the drastic contraction of trade that set in (for example, in Britain's economic relations with India) made even the mercantile presence a reminder of past glories not a springboard for a new post-colonial commerce.

Yet of course many British did stay on, sometimes because they had no other choice, or were reluctant to face the impoverished existence that awaited at home without pension, employment, or family support. Some were able to move sideways: much of what remained of British enterprise in China relocated to Hong Kong after 1950. 'When I was in Kenyah', could often be heard on the stoeps of Durban residential hotels. Some were absorbed into the host society where the cultural barriers were low—as in Argentina. An embattled few rejected the inevitability of decolonization and struggled on for a decade: ironically it was their almost complete freedom from any British control that made it possible for Southern Rhodesia's whites to revolt against the Africanization of Africa. Those that returned to Britain in the 1950s and 1960s faced some of the same strangeness that had always afflicted expatriate returnees, whether they were retired planters, soldiers, or Indian Civil Servants. Climate, diet, a cramped urban life, and the bored indifference of home-grown Britons to accounts of life overseas could make a painful transition and diminish the sense of self-importance and worth—although it has to be said that not all returnees cherished sweet memories of their expatriate life. For some, the best view of India 'was over the stern of the ship'. In the 1950s and 1960s this strangeness was compounded by the rapidity of change in British views of empire—and of settlers. The values shared in the imperial age between Britons at home and Britons abroad either disappeared altogether or could no longer be expressed, at least not in public.

Today we live more than ever in a world of expatriates. Britain itself is now a prime destination for both migrant settlers (who intend to remain) and expatriates (who plan to go home). British people still settle in large numbers not only in the old destinations of British migration (Canada, Australia, the United States, New Zealand) but also in new ones like France and Spain. The emergence or revival of open-market economies in many parts of the world has created new opportunities for expatriate Britons with a wide variety of manual, technical, or commercial skills. In some cases, their lives are as segregated from those of the native inhabitants as they would have been in the age of empire. Yet the settler and expatriate experience chronicled in this volume was fundamentally different in a number of ways. No small settler minority today could cherish the hope (however deluded) of becoming another Canada or Australia—a fully self-governing 'British' country—the aspiration of white settler communities in the Rhodesias and (more briefly) Kenya. The territorial enclaves and legally privileged status that sheltered many British expatriates in the imperial age are a thing of the past: perhaps the special regime in post-British Hong Kong is the nearest approximation to a treaty port still to be found. However much it might be affirmed in private, the ostentatious celebration of British cultural primacy no longer forms part of the public ritual of expatriate communities, or not when they are sober. Enforced separation from the host society is more likely to be felt as a tiresome inconvenience than as a necessary mark of respect. Nor of course can overseas Britons share the assurance of their Victorian or Edwardian counterparts that Britain was the world's most advanced material civilization and the head and centre of the global economy. However patriotic their feelings, they are unlikely to see their foreign sojourn as an imperial duty or regard themselves as the far-flung citizens of a world-wide empire. For the settlers and expatriates whose lives we have followed in this book were not simply migrants or overseas workers on contract—even if part of their worlds could be described in this way. In their different ways (and much variation) they were the vanguard and camp-followers of the British 'world-system'—that cumbrous amalgam of empires formal and informal. When it died they were orphaned.

INDEX

Lightning Source UK Ltd.
Milton Keynes UK
UKOW04f0159170414

230127UK00001B/1/P